ID0932480

THE PUNISHER'S BRAIN

Why do we punish, and why do we forgive? Are these entirely learned behaviors, or is there something deeper going on? This book argues that there is indeed something deeper going on, and that our essential response to the killers, rapists, thieves, and liars among us has been programmed into our brains by evolution. Using evidence and arguments from neuroscience and evolutionary psychology, Morris B. Hoffman traces the development of our punishing brains throughout human history.

Humans, he argues, evolved to cooperate with one another, albeit grudgingly, in order to ensure our survival. That grudging cooperation focused on two areas that were essential for our survival as a social species: not stealing each other's property or well-being and not breaking promises. Punishment made stealing and breaching sufficiently expensive, and therefore deterred enough of it, to enable our intensely social species to survive and flourish. We blame and punish based on our assessment of two factors: the wrongdoer's intent and the harm caused. But punishing wrongdoers was also costly to the group, because it risked retaliation and the loss of group members if the wrongdoers left the group. We therefore also evolved a deep reticence to punish and a corresponding urge to forgive, also based on intent and harm. Our ancestral groups delegated the responsibility and authority for punishing and forgiving to one group member – the judge – or a subset of the group – the jury. Over time, these urges to blame, punish, forgive, and delegate became codified into our present legal systems. After tracing the trajectory of this development, Hoffman shows how these urges inform our most deeply held legal principles and how they might animate some legal reforms.

Morris B. Hoffman is a trial judge for the Second Judicial District (Denver), State of Colorado. He is a member of the John D. and Catherine T. MacArthur Foundation's Research Network on Law and Neuroscience and is a Research Fellow at the Gruter Institute for Law and Behavioral Research. He is an adjunct professor of law at the University of Colorado and the University of Denver, where he teaches courses on jury history and selection, law and neuroscience, and law and the biology of human nature. His law articles have appeared in many journals, including the law reviews of the University of Chicago, New York University, the University of Pennsylvania, Duke, George Mason, Northwestern, Stanford, and Vanderbilt. He has written op-eds on legal topics for several national newspapers, including the *New York Times* and the *Wall Street Journal*. His scientific publications include papers in *The Royal Society's Philosophical Transactions B* and *Social, Cognitive, and Affective Neuroscience*. Judge Hoffman received his J.D. from the University of Colorado School of Law.

Cambridge Studies in Economics, Choice, and Society

Founding Editors
Timur Kuran, *Duke University*
Peter J. Boettke, *George Mason University*

This interdisciplinary series promotes original theoretical and empirical research as well as integrative syntheses involving links between individual choice, institutions, and social outcomes. Contributions are welcome from across the social sciences, particularly in the areas where economic analysis is joined with other disciplines, such as comparative political economy, new institutional economics, and behavioral economics.

Books in the series:
Terry L. Anderson and Gary D. Libecap, *Environmental Markets: A Property Rights Approach* 2014
Morris B. Hoffman, *The Punisher's Brain: The Evolution of Judge and Jury* 2014
Peter T. Leeson, *Anarchy Unbound: Why Self-Governance Works Better Than You Think* 2014
Benjamin Powell, *Out of Poverty: Sweatshops in the Global Economy* 2014

The Punisher's Brain

THE EVOLUTION OF JUDGE AND JURY

Morris B. Hoffman

CAMBRIDGE
UNIVERSITY PRESS

CAMBRIDGE
UNIVERSITY PRESS

32 Avenue of the Americas, New York, NY 10013-2473, USA

Cambridge University Press is part of the University of Cambridge.

It furthers the University's mission by disseminating knowledge in the pursuit of education, learning, and research at the highest international levels of excellence.

www.cambridge.org
Information on this title: www.cambridge.org/9781107038066

First published 2014

Printed in the United States of America

A catalog record for this publication is available from the British Library.

Library of Congress Cataloging in Publication Data
Hoffman, Morris B., 1952–
The punisher's brain : the evolution of judge and jury / Morris B. Hoffman.
    pages cm – (Cambridge studies in economics, choice, and society)
Includes bibliographical references and index.
ISBN 978-1-107-03806-6 (hardback)
1. Punishment – Social aspects.   2. Human evolution.   3. Social evolution.   I. Title.
GT6710.H64   2014
303.3′6–dc23   2013037018

ISBN 978-1-107-03806-6 Hardback

Cambridge University Press has no responsibility for the persistence or accuracy of URLs for external or third-party Internet Web sites referred to in this publication and does not guarantee that any content on such Web sites is, or will remain, accurate or appropriate.

CONTENTS

ACKNOWLEDGMENTS

Before I thank the many people who have contributed to this book, a few apologies and explanations are in order.

Although I spend my days punishing people, I am no expert in the science of punishment. Amateurism is, unfortunately, part of this interdisciplinary territory. Whether you prefer a scientist stomping around in law or a lawyer in the china shop of science may be a matter of taste and perspective. I just hope the chasm I leave between the law and the other disciplines I invade is not so great that I cannot be saved by helping hands from the other side.

Some of my descriptions of natural selection and neuroscience may sound naive or even flat out wrong to science-savvy readers. No doubt there are many examples of both naiveté and error. But other times missing the mark has been quite intentional, when I've decided to sacrifice scientific precision on the altar of readability. Examples include phrases that seem to suggest evolution is goal-oriented, including the very first sentence in the Introduction ("Evolution built us to punish cheaters"). I know that natural selection proceeds by chance, driven by random mutations and the ineluctable fact that genes will tend to be selected for whenever they give their carriers a fitness advantage in a particular environment.

A special apology goes to my biologist friend Tim Goldsmith, who schooled me early on in our joint writing efforts never to use the words "urges" or "instincts" to describe behavioral predispositions. But until Tim or someone else comes up with words substantially less clunky than "behavioral predispositions," "urges" and "instincts" will just have to do.

I have sacrificed some of the legal discussions in the text on the same altar of readability, including summarizing some difficult criminal law concepts like attempt, insanity, and the four modern theories of punishment. Special apologies in this regard go to my friends Gideon Yaffe, who has written what I think is the definitive book on attempt, and Stephen Morse, a pre-eminent criminal law theorist with whom I have written about the insanity defense. Throughout the book, whether short-shrifting science or law, I hope readers find that the notes, and especially the sources mentioned in the notes, will be an adequate safety net.

Now for the thanks. I owe my interest in law and biology to the late Margaret Gruter, whose foresight and inspiration continue to animate this discipline, and to her granddaughter Monika Gruter Cheney, who has carried on Margaret's work as executive director of the Gruter Institute for Law and Behavioral Research with fierce dedication and panache. Monika has been assisted by the irrepressible Oliver Good- enough, an extraordinary law and biology scholar. My introduction to the Gruter Institute I owe to Steven Pinker and especially to Al Alschuler, a powerfully creative legal scholar and a hopeless Chicago Cubs fan, who somehow managed to get me invited to my first Gruter conference in 2000.

My introduction to law and neuroscience came mostly from my colleagues at the John D. and Catherine T. MacArthur Foundation's Research Network on Law and Neuroscience and its antecedents, and especially Owen Jones, who directs the Network. It was Owen who suggested the title of this book, a vast improvement on the terrible working title I was using. Other MacArthur colleagues whose help and friendships have been invaluable include Richard Bonnie, B. J. Casey, Andre Davis, Robert Desimone, David Faigman, Martha Farah, Willie Fletcher, Mike Gazzaniga, Scott Grafton, Hank Greely, Josh Greene, Peter Imrey, Yasmin Hurd, Doug Husak, Stephen Hyman, Julie Iles, Kent Kiehl, Gerard Lynch, René Marois, Read Montague, Stephen Morse, Michael Moore, Bill Newsome, Liz Phelps, Marc Raichle, Jed Rakoff, Jenn Richeson, Adina Roskies, Michael Saks, Jeff Schall, Fred Schauer, Buffy Scott, Francis Shen, Walter Sinnott-Armstrong, Larry Steinberg, Kim Taylor-Thompson, Anthony Wagner, Amy Wax, Susan Wolfe and Gideon Yaffe. I have also been inspired by three gifted neuroeconomists I first met at the Gruter Institute: Paul Glimcher, Kevin McCabe, and Paul Zak. It was at the Gruter Institute that I also first met Paul Robinson, whose work on the concordance of relative blameworthiness has left its mark on much of this book. I also want to thank my very first science paper coauthor, Frank Krueger, for having sufficient confidence in me to allow me to collaborate on such interesting neuroscience experiments; I look forward to many more.

Friends who were kind enough to read drafts of the manuscript include Owen Jones, John Kane, Bill Pizzi, Stephanie Shafer, Francis Shen, Edie Sonn, and Paul Zak. Their comments were invaluable, and made this a far better book. The anonymous reviewers were also extraordinarily helpful. I thank my former editors David Pervin at the University of Chicago Press and Scott Parris, now at Oxford University Press, for encouraging me to begin, and my wonderful editors at Cambridge University Press, Karen Maloney and Kristin Purdy, who so skillfully helped me finish. Special thanks to my copyeditor Heidi Sias for her hard work, and to Shashank Shankar for capably seeing the book through production.

On a more personal note, I want to thank my late father, who taught me how to be a good husband and parent, and Charles D. Pierce, who gave me the privilege to clerk for him so long ago, and who taught me how to be a good judge.

Most importantly, this book would not be this book, and I would not be me, but for the love and support of my beautiful and talented wife Kate, on whom I endlessly inflicted requests to read and reread parts of the manuscript, and commandeered our kitchen table to boot. Writing this, my first book, often had the feel of lugging around a giant unruly child, years beyond when it should be walking on its own. I loved it and hated it, and always felt its relentless tug, reminding me I had to pay attention to it. As with everything else, Kate gave me the energy to carry on.

Denver, Colorado
2014

INTRODUCTION

Evolution built us to punish cheaters. Without that punishment instinct, we would never have been able to live in small groups, and would never have realized all the significant benefits that small-group living conferred, including mutual defense, cooperative hunting, property, divisions of labor, and economies of scale. In fact, to a large extent our notions of right and wrong, of empathy and compassion, of fairness and justice, all come from the tensions of group living, and thus indirectly owe their very existence to punishment.[1] It may sound strange that one key to civilization is our willingness to punish each other, but every parent knows it's true.

Every parent also feels the irresistible pull not to punish too much, and in fact maybe not to punish at all – to forgive – and this, too, is a remnant of evolution. Our punishment instinct is not so much a sword ready to fall as it is a finely tuned balance, sometimes susceptible to the gentlest of breezes.

But there's at least one substantial weight on this otherwise delicate balance: the idea that we generally do not punish accidents. Cheaters cheat intentionally, and the intentional wrongdoers, not the careless ones, get most of our punishment attention. We all blame the contract killer more than the inattentive driver who kills a pedestrian. We therefore care as much or more about the wrongdoer's state of mind – evil or just careless? – than we do about the actual harm his wrong has caused.

Several years ago I presided over a first-degree murder trial in which a young Czech émigré was charged with stabbing his Brazilian au pair girlfriend.[2] The crime took place in the au pair's bedroom, in the basement of her employer-family's house. The young man stabbed her seventy-four times. He confessed to the murder but denied it was

1

premeditated. Despite his denial, the premeditation evidence was pretty strong. He not only entered the bedroom through a window, armed with a knife and carrying some duct tape, but he also admitted to police that a few days before the killing he tried to dig a small grave in a remote field but gave up because the ground was frozen.

On the other hand, he testified that he regularly went through the window for late-night visits with her, and that he went there that night not to kill her but only to see if she would change her mind about breaking up. He claimed he had the knife and duct tape because he was moving. As for the grave, he testified that he started to dig the hole in the field to "bury her memory," and that all he intended to bury there were a few items of personal property that reminded him of her. When he went to see her that final time, and she told him she was set on leaving him, he "snapped."

But he didn't say the word "snapped." What he said was, "A darkness came across my eyes." He even said it a second time in cross-examination. It seemed oddly and rather beautifully phrased, and vaguely familiar. Neither of the lawyers asked him about it. Long after the jury convicted him of first-degree murder and I sentenced him to the mandatory life in prison without the possibility of parole, it hit me. "Darkness covered his eyes," and variations of that phrase, are used over and over by Homer to describe many of the battle deaths in The Iliad.[3]

Was this a bad literary joke played by a deranged killer, a coincidence fueled by awkwardness in a second language, an unconscious conflation from a literature class, or some deeply insightful way of expressing this terrible act? Was he describing his own loss of consciousness, a blackout of memory, a kind of disassociation of his moral bearings, or the unbearable blackness of his actions? I have no idea.

But I do know that the task facing the jury in that case – to decide not so much what happened, because that was clear, but rather what was in the defendant's mind at the time of the killing – was the same daunting task that often faces judges and juries in virtually all legal systems. This is one of the Big Secrets of the criminal law. Whether a defendant actually committed the charged act is seldom the subject of serious dispute, even in those few criminal cases (roughly 5 percent in the United States) that go to trial.[4] Sure, there are some crimes, and even some categories of crimes – like sex assault with no forensic evidence – that are whodunits or whether-anyone-dunits. But much more commonly there is no doubt at all that the defendant killed the victim or robbed the liquor store or stole the car; the only issue for the jury to decide is what in the world was going through the defendant's mind at the time of the crime.

These judgments about whether a criminal defendant acted intentionally, unintentionally, or with some state of mind somewhere in between can have enormous consequences. A young mother leaves her infant in the bathtub to go downstairs to charge her cell phone, and the baby drowns. If a jury determines the mother was just a clueless nitwit, in my state she is guilty of a crime called negligent child abuse resulting in death and could be punished anywhere from getting released on probation to spending sixteen years in prison. But if the jury finds she "knew" she should not leave but did so anyway, this crime is tantamount to first-degree murder and carries a mandatory sentence of life in prison without the possibility of parole.

Even in civil cases, jurors must sometimes make difficult judgments about people's states of mind. In a negligence case, they may have to decide whether the defendant was simply unaware of the risky nature of his conduct, which is the essence of ordinary negligence, or whether there was something more, some kind of gross negligence that might justify some punitive damages beyond mere compensation of the victim. Even in cases of ordinary negligence, where the defendant's state of mind is not usually in play, the jury's judgment is a *community* judgment, not so much about what happened as whether the community should tolerate what happened. Some accidents are the product of such carelessness that they need to be punished – if not with incarceration then with the hammer of damages. I presided over a medical malpractice case several years ago that put these community judgment aspects of negligence in particularly sharp relief.

The plaintiff was a woman with advanced lung cancer. She claimed that several years earlier the defendant-radiologist misread her chest X-ray, and that in the intervening years what would have been a highly curable case had developed into a hopeless one.[5] Of course both sides called experts who testified that a reasonable radiologist would, or would not, have diagnosed lung cancer based on the X-ray, or at least would, or would not, have called for further tests, and the jury, as usual, was forced to pick between the two expert narratives. So far, this case was no different from any failure-to-diagnose case.

But by the time this case reached my jury, Colorado had joined the states implementing several kinds of jury reforms, and one of those reforms was to allow jurors to submit written questions to witnesses, including expert witnesses. One of my jurors submitted this question to the plaintiff's expert: "What percentage of radiologists would have diagnosed cancer based on this X-ray, or at least called for more tests?"

Strangely, this is not a question permitted by the law in most states. Experts may opine about the standard of care to which a fictitious "reasonable" professional must adhere, but the law generally prohibits witnesses from putting any kind of statistical gloss on that fiction by telling jurors their view about whether this standard of care would be followed by 10 percent, 51 percent, or 99 percent of professionals. But there were no controlling cases in my state. So in a fit of either insight or confusion, but in either event fueled in part by the fact that this question was being asked by one of our jurors and not by a lawyer, I decided to allow the question. The plaintiff's expert responded by testifying that 95 percent of radiologists would have tested further. The jury returned a very large verdict for the plaintiff.

In post-trial motions the defendant's lawyers argued that I had erred in permitting the statistical question, and after mulling it over I decided they were right, and that my error likely infected, indeed perhaps even drove, the verdict. I granted the defendant's motion for a new trial, but the case settled before any retrial.

This rule that expert witnesses cannot describe the standard of care in terms of adherence probabilities seems crazy. How can a "standard" be standard unless at least a majority of practitioners adhere to it? Conversely, how can it not be the standard if 99 percent of practitioners adhere to it? There are many justifications for this rule, but the central one is that negligence – even negligence by a professional in a specialized area as far from ordinary experience as radiology – is the kind of community judgment we want ordinary citizen-jurors to be able to make, not the professionals themselves by plebiscite.[6]

Even in civil cases as seemingly cut-and-dried as contract cases, these kinds of squishy community judgments, often dependent on guesses about what was in the contracting parties' minds, are not uncommon. Whether there was a contract at all depends on a determination of whether the parties had a "meeting of the minds." If they did form a contract by having a meeting of their minds, whether one party breached that contract can also depend on an assessment of mental states. For example, a buyer's obligation to pay for a shipment of rotten avocados may well depend on whether the shipper used his best efforts to deliver them before they spoiled. "Best efforts" is hardly a straightforward test, and might not only require an inquiry into what the shipper did and did not do to contribute to the delay but also what was in the shipper's mind as he made these contributing decisions. Modern law now implies in all contracts the duty of the contracting parties to act in good faith.[7] Trying to weasel through loopholes in contracts – once the proud domain of all commercial lawyers – is now largely blocked by this troublesome good-faith requirement. Today, two shippers whose delayed delivery is the product of identical acts may well suffer very different legal fates if one shipper's acts were motivated by bad faith and the other's were not.

These are just a few examples of the profoundly democratizing and morality-setting roles of jurors. They not only get to decide whether a defendant committed the acts he's charged with committing; they often get to draw the community's lines in deciding whether those acts are wrong enough to be punished.[8] And in deciding the "wrongness" of the acts, jurors often must make judgments about the wrongdoer's intentions.

This emphasis on the state of mind of the wrongdoer is hardly unique to the law. Imagine coming home and finding your teenage son holding a hammer, standing in front of your brand new, but now completely smashed, big-screen high-definition television set. When you ask him what happened, you would probably not be satisfied if all he told you was "I hit the TV with the hammer." The "Why," the "Was it an accident and if not what the hell were you thinking?" is as big a part of the What Happened as anything else. It is, in fact, the *moral* part of the inquiry, the part that will determine whether your son gets a hug, a month-long grounding and a bill for a replacement TV, or a class in home repairs.

And it has always been so, with virtually every aspect of human interaction. We are social animals highly attuned to the behaviors of others, constantly monitoring, evaluating, and predicting those behaviors. We instantly recognize behaviors that don't make sense, that by their very irrationality and unpredictability threaten us or our families. And we are drawn irresistibly to imagine the minds behind those behaviors.

When the behaviors of others get more and more irrational and unpredictable, and more distant from the ordinary experiences of inquiring parents or jurors – like stabbing your ex-girlfriend seventy-four times – it becomes more and more difficult for the judges to put their minds into the minds of the judged. At some point we all come to a big fork in the road of responsibility. Some say, "That was so crazy he must be insane," or, less technically, he "snapped." That is, his mind is, or at least was at the moment of the crime, so unlike ours that we cannot apply the ordinary human presumptions of intentionality to him, and thus cannot justly hold him as responsible as we would a less mentally disabled person.

But some take the other fork. "He wasn't crazy, he was evil." He didn't "snap," he was just a possessive, jealous lout who was so self-centered that when the victim told him he couldn't have her he made sure no one else ever would. All of us have faced rejection, but only evil people kill a helpless girl whose only wrong was to say she wanted out.

This apparent divide between crazy and evil faces every one of us in one form or another in some context or another. Legal academics have debated it for as long as there have been legal academics. Citizens ponder it each time they read about a young mother drowning her children or the latest shoot-up by a disgruntled employee or student. Judges and jurors deal with it in almost every serious criminal case, even when insanity is not formally an issue, the "crazy" narrative presented by the defense and the "evil" narrative by the prosecution.

Of course, the task of navigating these two narratives is made doubly difficult by the fact that the one person most likely to know for sure What Happened, in the interior sense of those words, is the accused himself, and he usually has a huge incentive to lie about his state of mind. "Jason was tossing the hammer to me and it slipped."

"I was burying her memories, not her." I suspect that when you read my condensed version of the Czech defendant's testimony, your immediate reaction was that he was lying. There are good evolutionary reasons for this strong presumption that all people know what they are doing, and for the corollary that people who claim harmful acts were accidental, or the product of diseased minds, are lying.

But in the right kind of case this strong presumption bumps up against an almost equally strong presumption that accidents should not be punished the same as intentional wrongs. We know from our own lives that accidents sometimes happen, even accidents that don't look like accidents from the outside. We also know, or think we know, that with sufficient pressure, ordinary humans like us might lose control and "snap." And yet most of us have never stabbed someone seventy-four times, or even come close to doing so, or had the legal incentive to lie about such "snapping." Whether that's because we have not suffered the same pressures as our young Czech killer, or because his brain was less able to withstand those pressures (either because he was crazy, or evil, or for some other arguably more informative reasons), are questions humans have been asking ourselves for as long as we have roamed the planet.

This book is about the evolutionary roots of this interior struggle in which we all engage when we judge the behaviors of others (and, of course, simultaneously judge ourselves by comparison). Evolution's last laugh, when it came to the human animal, was that it built our brains with two deeply conflicting predispositions. We are predisposed to cooperate with each other, because living in groups gave us a substantial long-term survival advantage. But we are also born cheaters, because cheating in the right circumstances gave us a short-term survival advantage. As these two conflicting tendencies tugged for our souls, we simultaneously evolved punishment behaviors – a way to dampen cheating by increasing its short-term costs to the cheater. But our punishment instincts are infected with the same conflict – our brains have been built to punish cheaters, but that punishment urge is intrinsically restrained, in no small part because we all know that we, too, are born cheaters.

What modern judges and juries do is essentially what our ancestors have been doing for 100,000 years when they had to decide what to do with misbehaving individuals.[9] As clans banded with other clans to form larger groups, and groups of groups formed tribes and ultimately settled into villages and towns, these punishment decisions became more and more formalized and institutionalized. They also changed to reflect the specific challenges of each society and culture. But at their heart is the same ancient three-pronged punishment strategy natural selection has bequeathed us, and which will be the central topics of this book:

1. We punish ourselves with conscience and guilt.
2. We punish our tormentors with retaliation and revenge.
3. As a group we punish the wrongdoers we are able to detect with retribution.

Conscience helps us avoid the temptation to cheat in the first place, and guilt makes us feel bad after we've cheated, so that next time maybe we'll be less likely to cheat. When conscience and guilt are not enough to deter us, the risk that our victims will retaliate may be. And when neither conscience nor fear of retaliation is enough, the fear of detection and punishment by the group adds a third level of deterrence.

But this last level of punishment, this socialization of punishment, carried its own special evolutionary problems. With everyone primed to punish everyone else for every transgression, our groups would have dissolved into a kind of punishment free-for-all. Several things prevented that. First, our urge to punish came with some built-in thresholds; our brains are not in fact primed to punish every single kind of social transgression no matter how minor. We don't bother with small slights, or even with large ones when we are sure they were accidents. We also sometimes forgive. Finally, our urge to punish third-party wrongdoers comes with a simultaneous urge that someone else inflict the punishment.

In our early groups, dominant members likely took charge of most third-party punishment, as they took charge of many group-wide decisions. As societies became more and more complex, and divisions of labor started to take root, dominant members delegated third-party punishment to other members (judges), as they delegated many of their ancient tasks. For certain kinds of particularly risky punishments (for example, when the wrongdoer was powerful or came from a powerful family), it made sense for the leader to delegate punishment not to a single member but to a small group of punishers (the jury). Thus began judge and jury, as communal representatives of group blame.

The decision of whether, and in what circumstances, a group of humans should punish one of its misbehaving members may not sound important enough for natural selection to have cared about. But 100,000 years ago these punishment decisions were not just important; they were existential. Our most significant predator was ourselves. Homicide was as big a survival concern as food and shelter. Quite apart from the risks of being killed by each other, our lives were hard, our life spans were short, and we were often on the brink of death. Even one cheater could be the difference between a successful hunt and an unsuccessful one, between a strong and prosperous group and an unraveled one, between life and death.

But punishing cheaters could also be disastrous. The two most serious kinds of punishment were execution and banishment. Because banishment was in effect an almost certain death sentence, both of these punishments risked deadly resistance not just by the wrongdoer himself but also by his relatives and friends. Even without any resistance, execution and banishment reduced by at least one the number of members who could hunt, guard, cook, and do all the other work of the group. And if a banished wrongdoer's entire family decided to leave with him, the group could be devastated.

Punishments short of execution or banishment might also be resisted. When we lived on the edge of survival, being forced to pay any kind of punishment price was often a serious matter. For many of us today, missing a meal might improve our health. Missing one 100,000 years ago might have tipped us into unrecoverable illness. So deciding who should be punished, how they should be punished, and for what infractions, was an incredibly important problem for our ancestors – important enough for evolution to have some say in a solution.

Natural selection has painted our natures both in broad themes and in subtle details. In many ways, this book is about bringing these two images together, through the lens of punishment. The big issues of guilt, innocence, responsibility, blameworthiness, apology, atonement, and forgiveness impact the dirty little daily processes the law uses to make very practical decisions about how to punish. Law is applied human nature, and understanding that nature – not just the nature of the people being judged but also the nature of the people doing the judging – is critical to understanding the foundations of law. Understanding those legal foundations may in turn allow us to gauge the distance between them and some of the legal outbuildings our cultures have erected. I will spend time in later chapters discussing some legal dissonances – legal doctrines that seem to be in conflict with our evolved moral intuitions and punishment instincts – and whether those doctrines should be reformed. I will also explore the extent to which an evolutionarily informed view of blame and punishment might help improve our legal processes, and might even help make sense of our famously disparate and seemingly irreconcilable theories of punishment.

In the end, though, my efforts will not be focused on legal reform or on improving legal processes or theory. My goal is less lofty, more personal. My hope is that by the end of this book readers will be able to feel the connections between the twelve people who decided that my young Czech defendant must spend the rest of his life in prison and our ancestors 100,000 years ago who made similar life-and-death decisions.

After introductions to the problem of social cooperation and defection in Chapter 1 and to the evolution of detection and blame in Chapter 2, the next three chapters examine the three layers of punishment. Chapter 3 addresses first-party punishment (conscience and guilt), Chapter 4 second-party punishment (retaliation and revenge), and Chapter 5 third-party punishment (retribution). Chapter 6 deals with forgiveness – evolution's yin to punishment's yang – and the related topics of apology, atonement and repatriation. Chapter 7 considers the delegation of third-party punishment to a single member (judge) and to multiple members (jury) and surveys the history of the Western jury. Chapter 8 analyzes the general problem of legal dissonances – rules that conflict with our evolved blaming and punishing instincts – and suggests a five-step framework to decide when a legal rule should give way to a conflicting evolved instinct. Chapter 9 addresses some tensions between how our brains process information and how our legal procedures expect judges and jurors to process information. Chapter 10 uses the five-step approach introduced in Chapter 8 to make some suggestions for a handful of substantive legal reforms. Chapter 11 explores how an evolutionarily informed view might help make sense of our disparate theories of punishment.

When we look at judges and juries through the lens of natural selection, we see us judging us, and these mirrored looks can teach us important things about human nature. Recognizing the connections between modern punishers and our punishing ancestors will increase our appreciation of the central role blame, forgiveness, and punishment have played, and continue to play, in the human story.

Notes to Introduction

1. Exactly how punishment might have evolved to enable our social living remains a hot topic among evolutionary theorists. Scholars across many disciplines, from evolutionary biology and psychology to economics and even neuroscience, seem to be converging on the idea that we needed punishment to help bind us into our extraordinarily intense social groups. In evolutionary theory and anthropology, see R. Boyd et al., *The evolution of altruistic punishment*, PROC. NAT. ACAD. SCI., **100**, 3531–3535 (2003). In economics and evolutionary psychology, see E. Fehr & U. Fischbacher, *Social norms and human cooperation*, TRENDS COGN. SCI. **8**, 185–190 (Apr, 2004). In neuroscience, see J. Bucholtz & R. Marois, *The roots of modern justice: cognitive and neural foundations of social norms and their enforcement*, NATURE NEUROSCIENCE, **15(5)**, 655–661 (2012). Robert Frank's book, PASSIONS WITHIN REASON: THE STRATEGIC ROLE OF EMOTIONS (Norton 1988), is an interdisciplinary tour de force surveying the evolution of right and wrong in human societies and the instantiation of those behaviors in our brains through emotional and cognitive processes. Matt Ridely's book, THE ORIGINS OF VIRTUE: HUMAN INSTINCTS AND THE EVOLUTION OF COOPERATION (Penguin 1998), is an equally engaging treatment.
2. People v. Novotny, Denver District Court, Case No. 06CR10572.
3. For example, Homer describes the very first battle death of a Trojan soldier, killed by a Greek named Antilochus after a truce erupts into war, this way:

   > Antilochus thrust first, speared the horsehair helmet ridge, and the bronze spearpoint lodged in the man's forehead, smashing through his skull and the dark came whirling down across his eyes.

Homer, *The Iliad*, Book 4:530 at p. 160 (tr. R. Fagles, Penguin 1990). Many more follow with the same kind of description, by my count at least a dozen.

4. The average federal criminal plea bargaining rate is 96%, the average state rate 95%. BUREAU OF JUSTICE STATISTICS, U.S. DEP'T OF JUSTICE, SOURCE BOOK OF CRIMINAL JUSTICE STATISTICS, at tables 5.46.2004 and 5.24.2007, available at www.albany.edu/sourcebook.

5. Eby v. Fortner, Denver District Court Case No. 00CV3366.

6. See, e.g., Davis v. Portlines Transportes Internacional, 16 F.3d 532, 545 (3rd Cir. 1994). Other explanations include that these adherence probabilities are inherently difficult to measure, and that in any event the constantly changing nature of science-based professions, especially medicine, makes adherence probabilities the wrong inquiry. On this last point, the Mississippi Supreme Court put it this way:

> [P]hysicians incur civil liability only when the quality of care they render falls below objectively ascertained minimally acceptable levels. Use of such concepts as "average" are misleading and should be avoided, particularly in jury instructions, for such notions understood arithmetically suggest that the lower 50 percent of our physicians regularly engage in malpractice.

Hall v. Hilbun, 466 So.2d 856, 871 (Miss. 1985). I would add that the converse is just as true: it is equally inappropriate to suggest that the upper 50% of practitioners necessarily enjoy some immunity from charges of negligence. The test is what reasonable physicians would do. Practitioners are constantly trying to catch up to an ever-moving line of minimal competence and will always have disagreements about where exactly that line is at any particular moment in time. Juries, not doctors, get to decide where that line is in any particular case.

7. RESTATEMENT (SECOND) OF CONTRACTS § 205 (1981).

8. In most jurisdictions, judges, not jurors, decide punishment. But as we will see in Chapter 7, jurors have always indirectly decided punishment, and still do, by making judgments about the levels of crime they find the defendant committed, levels that often depend on the jury's judgments about the defendant's state of mind at the time he committed the criminal acts.

9. Throughout this book, I will use the convention of dating human emergence to 100,000 years ago. But our genetic emergence was much earlier, at least 200,000 years ago. One of the most important unanswered questions of anthropology is the apparent fact that human culture as we know it – the use of things like drawn images, ornamentation, burial, and carvings – seems not to have emerged as a coherent behavioral package until around 50,000 years ago, about the time of the second large human migration out of Africa. What were we doing for the 150,000 years before that, and what happened to turn on the cultural light, is the subject of great debate. We know very little

about this behavioral dark age, or even whether it was as dark as it seems. It may be an artifact of the incompleteness of the fossil record, or it may be real but not as long as 150,000 years. In any event, when we now talk about the "emergence" of humans, it is important to recognize there is significant ambiguity in the word. I will split the genetic and cultural difference and talk about us emerging about 100,000 years ago.

1 THE MOST ORIGINAL OF ORIGINAL SINS

Now the serpent was more subtle than any beast of the field which the Lord God hath made....

Genesis 3:1

THE SOCIAL PROBLEM: CHEAT OR COOPERATE?

If only Adam and Eve had not eaten that tempting fruit, then God would have let them live in the Garden of Eden in eternal peace and happiness. Whether the fruit was knowledge, sexual desire, consciousness or, in one even more basic account, our need to steal protein from other living things, it was irresistible.[1] Eve, and then Adam, ate it, God evicted the pair from paradise, and the rest was sin-laden history.

The choice that Adam and Eve faced – whether to cooperate with God or cheat – is a choice humans have faced since our emergence, not as a choice between cheating and cooperating with God but as a choice between cheating and cooperating with each other. We evolved in small groups of mostly related individuals, which gave us enormous survival advantages, and therefore enormous incentives to cooperate with one another. As a result, we have deep emotional ties to our groups, and a powerful hunger for social belonging. But because natural selection was operating at the individual level, it also gave us a paradoxical incentive to cheat. After all, if we could cheat and not get caught, we could still enjoy all the advantages of social living and yet get a leg up on everyone else. This deeply embedded tension between cooperation and cheating, between community and individuality, between selflessness and selfishness, is what I will call The Social Problem.[2] It has been the central challenge of our species since our emergence.

The Social Problem leads to another problem – what to do with the cheaters we catch. God banished Adam and Eve, and banishment from the group is in many ways the most serious punishment any group can impose on a cheater. Banishment wrenches the wrongdoer from all his physical and emotional ties to his community, in a way that no other punishment does, perhaps even execution. But of course not every cheater deserves the ultimate or even penultimate punishment. Just as we have been struggling forever with the individual problem of whether to cooperate or cheat, so too have our groups and societies been struggling forever with the institutional problem of whether, and how, to punish cheaters.

The Social Problem is hardly unique to the human species. Every social animal faces it, since by definition living in social groups means giving up some measure of selfishness in exchange for some measure of cooperation. The lines that nature has drawn between individuality and community are dizzying in their variety.

At one end of the spectrum are the social insects, which mindlessly cooperate for the common good with virtually no cheating, because they are all genetic twins. What is good for all is good for each. Or, to put it in more proper evolutionary and entomological terms, the only way an individual sterile worker bee's genes get passed down to future generations is through the queen, so doing everything possible to protect the queen *is* the way worker bees are "selfish." This kind of extreme socialization, called "eusociality" by biologists, is most common in insect species, but it is not unique to them. There are even some mammals – two species of mole rat, to be precise – that are eusocial. The females are all sterile, except for the queen, and the queen rat alone produces the next generation.[3]

At the other end of the spectrum are the solitary animals – such as some species of sharks – who have little or no social connections at all and who, but for mating and in some cases spending a short time with their mothers after birth, treat other members of their species pretty much like any other source of food or danger.[4] The list of solitary animals is quite long, and includes many mammals as diverse as cougars, giant anteaters, grizzly bears, and even a few primates.

But most primates are social to varying degrees, and their sociality is complicated and sometimes magnified by complex brains that can change their cheat/cooperate decisions as changing circumstances might warrant. And there's the rub for humans. Not only are our brains the most complex in the animal kingdom, powerful enough even to turn an eye inward to contemplate things such as free will, but we are also more intensely social than any genetically heterogeneous (that is, non-eusocial) species. These two facts are not unrelated. We needed massively networked brains just to be able to keep track of each other. And we needed to keep track of each other in order to survive the drastic environmental changes that were happening all around us.

The warm, wet, and rich Southern African jungles in which our predecessor primates lived were giving way to colder, drier, open savannahs. This not only drove us upright, so we could survey long distance threats and opportunities, it also put a premium on guile and cooperation. We are intensely social because being intensely social gave us significant survival advantages in areas such as mutual defense and hunting. None of this would have been possible if we had the selfish brains of sharks.

But our powerful social brains, built for cooperation, were also that much better at cheating. We could imagine being punished for cheating, but we could also imagine a thousand ways to get away with cheating. All of this has left us with a terrible, and terribly significant, neural paradox. Our cooperation is of a limited, grudging sort. We are constantly probing for chances to cheat, and just as constantly on the lookout for cheaters. Our brains have sophisticated and sensitive systems for detecting opportunities to cheat – so that we can decide whether other members will catch us if we steal that food the group worked so hard to gather, and, if so, whether and how they will punish us. We have equally sophisticated and sensitive systems to detect signals of cooperation and cheating in others, so that we can decide whether to trust or be wary of that other fellow. We are born cooperators and born cheaters, both versions living simultaneously inside our brains. We are born punishers and born forgivers, again torn between conflicting instincts.

We also evolved language, which was an important glue of our intense sociality. The gift of gab bound us together in a way analogous to how identical genes bind social insects. Our brains could not only imagine the future, we could convey that imagination to each other through language. We could talk to each other about cheating and about punishing cheating. We could standardize all this talk into rules. Suddenly, social cooperation was not just a matter of trial and error – seeing what you could and could not get away with, as a young pre-verbal child does with a parent. Rules could now be conveyed *ex ante*, as the legal philosophers put it, meaning everyone in a group could know ahead of time exactly where the group drew the line between acceptable and unacceptable behavior.

The rules not only memorialized a compact for behavior, they also memorialized a compact to punish. No longer could a strong member prey indiscriminately on a weak one with the confidence that the only punishment risked was some tepid resistance by the victim. Now every member was enforcing the rules. Punishment itself had been socialized.

But of course language also allowed us to become better rule-avoiders, for now we could conspire with each other, using words, to beat the rules. Social conspiracies have a long evolutionary pedigree. Chimpanzees, in particular, have a well-documented proclivity to form and break alliances as the circumstances demand, and they do this even without the gift of an explicit language.[5] By comparison, our giant social brains, armed with language, give us conspiracy capabilities that make chimp alliances seem amateur. We are constantly tussling with each other in a strategic social dance, hiding our intentions and seeking to unmask the intentions of others. Those strangers coming over the hill may be a trading party or a war party, and our brains are armed with a package of strategies to help us decide which.

OUR NATURES LOST AND REDISCOVERED

We have, of course, known about our moral schizophrenia forever. It's what gives the human story its richness, and has been told and retold countless times. It is no exaggeration to say that our version of The Social Problem is what makes literature literature and art art, because in the end it is what makes humans human. Whether it is Homer's *Odyssey*, a painting by Caravaggio, or a symphony by Beethoven, all great art traces humanity's journey of self-discovery, and ends on the shores of these unavoidable dilemmas about group and individual, right and wrong, punishment and forgiveness.

And yet one half of this moral schizophrenia seemed to have gone lost for the past several hundred years. Fueled by classical economists such as Adam Smith and political philosophers such as Thomas Hobbes, and burst into conflagration by a misunderstanding of Darwin, this new vision of human nature saw humans only as relentlessly selfish creatures. If you were Hobbes, governments had to be strong to prevent the worst excesses of unbounded cheating.[6] For the classical economists, markets worked only because people could always be counted on to do the abjectly selfish thing. Adam Smith's unseen hand was in fact the assumption that every human acted like a solitary shark. *Homo economicus* was the tongue-in-cheek description of our new self-discovery.[7]

In fact, for the past 100 years or so the social sciences in general, especially anthropology, have denied the existence of *any* human nature. Culture, in this view, is what drives human behavior, and culture is unique and unpredictable. For a century, an abiding faith in this kind of cultural relativism drove two generations of anthropologists to focus on the *differences* between human cultures, largely ignoring any behaviors shared across cultures. Our brains were blank slates, waiting to be filled by experience.

But we were wrong – both about how culture drives all our behaviors and about how humans are essentially selfish. With no small amount of irony, it was the economists, along with some psychologists, who helped us see that we were wrong.

One experiment was particularly effective in exploding the myth of *Homo economicus*. Called the One-Shot Ultimatum Game, it is a real experiment that has now been played by researchers millions of times.[8] Here's how it works. There are two players, A and B. The investigator gives Player A some amount of money, let's say ten dollars, and instructs both players on the following rules of the game. Player A must offer Player B some portion of the ten dollars, anything from one dollar to ten dollars, at Player A's complete discretion. Then, after Player A makes the offer to Player B, Player B gets to decide whether to accept the offered amount or not. If he accepts the offer, then the money is divided as Player A has proposed, and the game is over. But if Player B rejects the offer, then neither player gets any money, and the game is over.

Notice that if humans are truly one-dimensional short-term self-interest machines, if we really are *Homo economicus*, then Player A should always offer the minimum of one dollar, not just because he is a selfish brute but also because – and here's the profound elegance of the game – he assumes Player B is also a selfish brute who will always prefer even just one dollar to nothing.

This idea of picking the strategy that is most immune to the other actors' decisions was first formally described by the mathematician John Nash, of *A Beautiful Mind* fame, and won him the Nobel Prize in Economics in 1994.[9] Nash proved that in every sufficiently complex game there is at least one such strategy, now called a "Nash equilibrium."[10] Offering one dollar is Player A's Nash equilibrium in the One-Shot Ultimatum Game.

But when the One-Shot Ultimatum Game is actually played with real people, they do not play at the Nash equilibrium, or even close to it. As you might imagine, if Player A offers just one dollar, Player B is almost always insulted by the low offer and will punish Player A by rejecting it, even though by doing so Player B ends up also punishing himself by being one dollar worse off.[11] Player A can anticipate this rejection, which drives his offer up above one dollar.

Researchers all over the world have conducted the One-Shot Ultimatum Game. In industrial societies, Player A offers an average of a little less than four dollars, with a surprisingly small amount of variance from that average, and Player B overwhelmingly accepts at that level. These results not only hold cross-culturally, they are also largely independent of the relative amount of the stakes.[12] They even hold in preindustrial societies, although in those societies Player A plays slightly closer to the purely selfish level, offering on average a little less than three dollars.[13]

To classical economists, these numbers are staggeringly "unselfish." But they are not as unselfish as they could be. You might think, because Player A can anticipate that Player B is willing to cut off his nose to spite his face if the offer is too low, that Player A will judge that Player B will insist on a "fair" division of half and half, and thus make his

offer at or close to five dollars. But Player A does not do that. He may
offer three dollars or four dollars but he does not move all the way up
to five dollars, because he knows he doesn't have to. He knows Player
B will most likely be insulted by a one-dollar offer, but most likely will
not be insulted by a three-dollar or four-dollar offer.[14] Why doesn't
Player B insist on a "fair" division of 50–50, and why doesn't Player A
expect Player B to so insist?

One explanation is that both players recognize that Player A feels a
kind of ownership interest in the whole ten dollars because he was given
the ten dollars to begin the game. This is a form of what economists
call the "endowment effect," which we will see more of later in this
chapter, and it operates even when the players flip a coin to decide
who gets to be Player A and who gets to be Player B. Possession, it
turns out, may be nine-tenths of the law, but it is about six-tenths in
the ultimatum game.

In any event, these are astonishing results, from both players' perspectives. Despite some cultural variations in the average offer and
in the average offer that is accepted, no human Player A from any
society or demographic routinely offers just one dollar, even though
that is the most selfishly "rational" offer, and no human Player B routinely insists on five dollars, even though that is the "fairest" offer.[15]
We simply are not the relentless self-interest machines of classical economic theory, nor the selfless do-gooders of the Romantics. Moreover, we know that the other player isn't either of these things, and he
knows that we aren't. Remarkably, all of this reverberating knowledge
about our natures effortlessly passes between Players A and B in those
two instants when Player A decides on his offer and Player B decides
whether to accept or reject.

Another influential game that helped us rediscover the guardedly
cooperative half of our natures is called The Prisoner's Dilemma.[16]
Imagine you and a confederate rob a bank, and are picked up for
questioning. The police interrogate you separately, and you've not had
time to agree on your stories. If you admit the crime, you will receive
a short jail sentence, whether your confederate confesses or not. If
you both hold firm and deny any involvement, you will both walk free
because there is insufficient evidence. But if you hold firm and your
partner confesses, then he will get the short jail sentence and you will

be sent to prison for a very long time. That is, the best result is that you both hold firm and deny your involvement, the next best result is that you confess, but the very worst result is that you hold firm when he confesses.

The beauty, and power, of The Prisoner's Dilemma is that it shows that our decisions about whether to defect in a social context are bound up with, and indeed largely defined by, our best guesses about what the other social members will do, and about how they in turn will guess about what we will do. If I am sure my partner will hold firm, then I should hold firm. The same goes for him. That is, being "selfish" in a social context might, in the right circumstances, mean being cooperative. But if either of us is unsure whether the other will hold firm, then, depending on the magnitude of that uncertainty, the next best decision would be to confess. Confessing is the Nash equilibrium of The Prisoner's Dilemma. It is not always the best play, but it is the safest play if we have no confidence in what our confederate will do.

These kinds of strategic decisions about whether to cheat or cooperate faced our ancestors over and over, and shaped the way our brains were built to handle the original sin of social defection. Even Jean-Jacques Rousseau, the quintessential Romantic, recognized that these tensions between cooperating and defecting were palpable whenever our ancestors engaged in important tasks, such as group hunting. He articulated one of the first versions of the so-called stag hunt game, although without any of the sophisticated mathematical or social psychological overlays that the game has since commanded.[17]

In Rousseau's version, he assumes a stag, say, is a prize catch, big enough and tasty enough for our ancestors to have devoted the considerable resources of a group hunt to try to catch it. But it is also an elusive prey, and it will take the cooperation of many hunters to catch it. During the hunt, Rousseau imagines that one of our ancestral hunters stumbles on a hare that he can easily capture and eat himself, but that by dropping out of the hunt even for a few moments the stag will be lost to the group.

Like the ordinary prisoner's dilemma, the decision whether to defect (abandon the hunt to catch the hare) is informed not just by the relative risks and payoffs of the decision itself, but also by a hunter's strategic guesses about the decisions of the other hunters. After all, even if a loyal hunter decides to cooperate and stay with the hunt, he will still lose the stag if even one of his colleagues decides to grab the hare, and for his loyalty he won't even get to share in the hare. This is a critical point: even a single defector ends up being much better off than all the other cooperators, although admittedly not as well off as if everyone cooperated. That means that without some assurance that *no one* will cheat, everyone will be sorely tempted to cheat. And of course knowing that everyone else faces the same temptation means that we'd probably all be fools not to grab the hare and abandon the group's efforts at the stag. In such an environment, how could we have ever had a successful hunt?[18]

And yet we know that our ancestors somehow managed to be able to cooperate enough to render living in small groups advantageous, because in fact we evolved in small groups. For small group living to have been a net survival advantage we somehow had to suppress our individual desires to cheat. We did that by evolving punishment. If the putative defector faced severe punishment for grabbing the hare and abandoning the hunt for the stag, suddenly the hare doesn't look so good. Punishment deterred enough cheating so that living in groups was possible. Having brains that punished allowed us to have brains that cooperated. To see more clearly why we needed punishment to survive, let's consider another famous model of The Social Problem, called The Public Goods Game.

The Public Goods Game is an important kind of generalization of the stag hunt and other social cooperation games, with an overlay of The Prisoner's Dilemma. There can be as many players as the experimenters want, but for simplicity let's say we have four. Each player is given some stake, let's say ten dollars. He or she must then decide how much of the ten dollars to contribute to the public good. Whatever is contributed to the public good is then doubled and, here's the catch, divided equally between all four players without regard to who made the contributions. So the Nash equilibrium is zero – a player who contributes nothing keeps the original ten dollars and even has an upside of sharing in the other players' public generosity.

If each player had sufficient assurance that the other players would cooperate, the best result for each would be to contribute all ten dollars, have the forty dollars doubled to eighty dollars, then share that total in equal payments of twenty dollars. Members of a perfectly cooperative group thus end up doubling their money. But a player could do even better if he were the only one to defect, keeping his ten dollars and refusing to make any public contribution. The other three each contribute their ten dollars, the thirty dollars is doubled to sixty dollars, and the sixty dollars shared in equal fourths of fifteen dollars. Our sole defector ends up with twenty-five dollars – the original ten dollars he kept plus his fifteen dollars share of the public goods – five dollars more than he could have gotten if everyone cooperated and ten dollars more than the three suckers who did cooperate. The rub, of course, is that all the players know they can do better by defecting, but only if there is a limited number of defectors. In our example, if even just two players decide to defect, they cannot do better than if they had all cooperated.[19]

When real people play The Public Goods Game, they play it like the other social games – not at the Nash equilibrium but also not with unbounded cooperative optimism. They play instead with a skeptical presumption that everyone else will cooperate, contributing a large chunk of the ten dollars but keeping some back as a hedge against defection. When the game is played over and over, as opposed to single-shot exchanges, cooperation tends to begat cooperation, but defectors are also quickly identified. With no punishment options, the public goods game quickly degenerates into selfish anarchy, with all players eventually driven to the Nash equilibrium by the fear that if they are the only one to cooperate they will do worse than all the defectors.

The Public Goods Game suggests that some kind of punishment was necessary for the long-term value of cooperation to have exceeded the short-term value of cheating. Whatever its form, we needed some deterrence to reduce the payoff from cheating. How much deterrence, and what kinds, no doubt depended on the details of the particular social challenge we faced. Hunting a valuable but elusive stag may have required more cooperation, but offered more benefits, than, say, gathering berries. Cheating in these various endeavors therefore required varying degrees of deterring punishments.

In almost all models of human social interaction, the difference between cooperating and cheating is often a matter of whether the other fellow can be trusted. Economies of any complexity depended, and still depend, on individuals' willingness to trust one another. If I lend you my spear in exchange for your promise to let me share in the kill, I am trusting that you will follow through and keep your promise. Many well-known economic games examine the phenomenon of trust.

One of the simplest and most well-known starts out like an ultimatum game – the researcher gives ten dollars to Player A and asks him to decide how much to give Player B. But the researcher then tells both players he will triple whatever amount A gives B, and that B will then get to decide how much of the tripled amount to give back to A. The "selfish" play for A – the Nash equilibrium – is still to give B just one dollar, keeping nine dollars. He may be giving up the prospect of sharing in the tripling, but he is also avoiding having B defect and keep the entire tripled amount. On the other hand, the most trusting, the most "pro-social," play for A is to give B all ten dollars, with the hope that once it is tripled to thirty dollars B will return a fair amount (say, fifteen dollars). But in fact, Player A on average behaves somewhere in between these two extremes – exhibiting some trust that Player B will return some of the tripled amounts, but, as we saw with The Public Goods Game, holding some back as a hedge against B's defection.[20]

Notice that from B's perspective the issue is not whether to trust A but whether to act in a way that justifies A's trust. Player B's most "selfish" and "rational" play – his Nash equilibrium – is to keep all the money and not share any with A, because in this version the game ends when B defects, and A cannot retaliate. But B does not act in this selfishly rational way. He typically divides the tripled amount, and in general the closer A was to showing complete trust in B the more likely it is that B will reciprocate by dividing the tripled amount equally. With some differences across cultures, up to 66 percent of Players B reciprocate Player A's trust to some extent, with the other 34 percent regularly playing selfishly and keeping all the tripled money no matter how trusting Player A has been.[21]

It is not entirely clear what prevents up to 66 percent of Players B from acting like the other 34 percent and keeping the entire tripled amount. After all, the game ends with Player B's decision, and there is no downside to him if he keeps everything. Yet two out of three Players B reciprocate A's trust. Why? The most accepted explanation is that our brains are built to play these games as if they were repeat games, because of course living in a social group is one giant repeat game. In the artificial game, Player B knows in some rational part of his brain that he will never see Player A again, and that his best play is to defect and keep all the tripled funds. But his brain is a gnarl of embedded rules that are highly sensitive to the behaviors of others, and, especially when A exhibits unwarranted trust in him by giving him all ten dollars, B is driven by that gnarl of social rules to reciprocate that trust. This is a kind of guilt, an emotion that compels us to live up to the expectations of others even if, and especially if, they are in no position to punish us. It is part of the guilt and conscience I call "first-party punishment."

Player A of course anticipates this kind of "irrational" trust. If he didn't think there was a significant chance that B would return some part of the tripled amount, A would play at his Nash equilibrium and give B just one dollar.

That all of these guardedly cooperative and trusting behaviors are in fact driven by our social natures has been elegantly shown in experiments in which humans play these same games against computers or, more deviously, are *told* they are playing against computers when they are really playing against other humans. Armed with information that the opponent is not human, players revert to the predictions of classical economics and play selfishly, at or near the Nash equilibrium.[22] Conversely, the extent to which human players are allowed to communicate or even just see each other before the game begins, as opposed to playing anonymously, strongly predicts their degree of cooperative departure from the Nash equilibrium.[23]

Language immeasurably strengthened the cooperative bonds of humans, but it also gave us an entirely new way to cheat – by lying. Now, we could steal then lie about it afterwards. Our lies could even happen before our bad actions: we could, for example, make promises we had no intention of keeping, or send others on wild goose chases so we could pilfer their property. So powerful was this new tool of language, and so critical to our social networks, that it could even be its own defection: we could kill rivals by using words to send them into danger, without lifting a finger. Not surprisingly, it seems we lie pretty much the same way we cheat; that is, we are presumptive but guarded truth tellers.[24]

The proposition that our guarded tendency to cooperate is an evolved predisposition finds some support in the mixed evidence of cooperation in other species. Some of our nearest evolutionary relatives are also guarded cooperators, although others are much more classically selfish. The amount of cooperation a species exhibits does not appear to have anything to do with how evolutionarily close it is to humans. Chimpanzees, who along with bonobos are our closest living primate relatives, are the very epitome of asocial selfishness when they are faced with versions of these games. They play at or very near the Nash equilibrium, and are rarely cooperative even in repeat games.[25] Bonobos seem to be a bit more cooperative, at least in some circumstances.[26] And yet capuchin monkeys – who are our much more distant relatives – engage in widespread cooperation and reciprocal sharing when they are faced in experiments with the problem of retrieving food that can only be retrieved cooperatively.[27] Capuchins are also exquisitely sensitive to unfairness in experiments involving unequal rewards for performing the same task.[28]

That the degree of social cooperation exhibited in a species does not vary exactly according to that species' evolutionary age is a perfect example of the phenomenon that natural selection is haphazardly practical, and not at all ideological. Social cooperation is not an abstract good. When it gave a particular species in a particular environment a fitness advantage, as with capuchins, then it was selected for; when, as with chimpanzees, it offered no selective advantage then it was not selected for.

A word of caution. These generalizations – chimpanzees are selfish and capuchins are cooperative – are just that, generalizations, and quite gross ones at that. Chimpanzees are indeed less cooperative than capuchins in many circumstances, but in fact all nonhuman primates, and indeed all social animals, regularly exhibit some cooperative behavior. That is, after all, the very definition of being a social species. As Frans de Waal has so aptly noted, in-captivity experiments purporting to test complicated notions such as cooperation, or even general intelligence, are often handicapped by a kind of anthropocentrism that can produce inaccurate caricatures. Chimpanzees in captivity may be rational maximizers in experiments using a sliding apparatus that allows them to share food, but in the wild, like all great apes, they engage in a myriad of cooperative behaviors, including coming to the defense of others being attacked by leopards or consoling distressed companions with tender embraces.[29]

The biochemistry of cooperation also suggests some deep and old evolutionary core. Oxytocin, an important mammalian hormone that gets released in females in large amounts during labor and breastfeeding, plays a significant role in the mediation of cooperative human behaviors in both sexes. The level of naturally occurring oxytocin in human subjects, male and female, is a strong predictor of how cooperatively they will play these economic trust games. And when subjects have their oxytocin levels artificially increased they play the games more cooperatively than the control group.[30] Not only does oxytocin increase trusting behavior, but trusting behavior releases oxytocin. Any kind of gentle touching – massage, stroking, grooming – causes oxytocin to be dumped into the brain and bloodstream. Even a remote and symbolic act of economic trust – say, in a trust game – releases oxytocin, both in the person doing the trusting and the person being trusted.[31]

Oxytocin seems, literally, to be the soup in which our social natures, and the trust that is required for social living, are bathed. But it is not an ordinary kind of soup. It works to increase trust only in the presence of social cues. When human subjects play asocial versions of these games – that is, when they are given cues suggesting they are not playing against other humans – artificially increased levels of oxytocin actually drive us to become *more* selfish rather than less.[32] Maybe this is because in these asocial contexts the only message we are getting from the oxytocin is an ancient cue that we are pregnant, nursing, or otherwise in charge of a baby, and need to act to maximize our resources to take care of that baby.

The role of oxytocin in mediating cooperation also goes a long way toward explaining an important observation from primatology – that as primate groups get larger and larger, they spend more time per member grooming each other. The grooming releases oxytocin, which increases cooperation to the levels needed to overcome artificially high group numbers. When our groups are too big, we don't see each other often enough to feel comfortable trusting one another, but as soon as we fondle each other's scalps looking for fleas, or stick out our hands and shake them, or slap each other on the back, oxytocin gets pumped into our brains and bloodstreams and partially recreates the feelings we would have had if we were members of a smaller, more intimate, group.

The hormone testosterone, also present in mammals in both sexes, seems to have the opposite effect. That's not surprising, given that one of the things testosterone does is block the effects of oxytocin. In the ultimatum game, high-testosterone Players B reject low offers much more frequently than do low-testosterone Players B. It also seems that high-testosterone Players A offer less than low-testosterone Players A.[33] As with oxytocin, the trust/testosterone pathway seems to be a two-way street. Being mistrusted releases testosterone precursors.[34]

The role of oxytocin in social cooperation, and its older role in mother-child bonding, is a beautiful example of the way in which natural selection can take existing material and mold it to new conditions. Even asocial mammals already had a system to encourage bonding between mother and child, and when new environmental challenges forced some mammals into cooperative groups, evolution recruited those existing cooperation channels to bind unrelated adults. When humans added language to strengthen our cooperative bonds even further, we became the most intensely social of all genetically heterogeneous animals.

These ruminations about cooperating, cheating, and punishing are not just guesses about how our brains might have worked 100,000 years ago. We still have those brains today, because natural selection typically acts so excruciatingly slowly. Our modern brains are a kind of behavioral fossil record in which we can see the strategic leftovers of our emergent struggles. Indeed, a large part of the modern human dilemma comes from the fact that our brains were built to operate in an environment that largely no longer exists. The miracle of culture has changed our world so rapidly and so profoundly that our poor Pleistocene brains, built to solve yesterday's problems, can sometimes hardly recognize today's. But some problems are forever. We will always be torn between cooperating and cheating, there will always be cheaters among us, and we will therefore always be faced with the problem of what to do with cheaters. The powerful predispositions we evolved to deal with The Social Problem remain salient because The Social Problem remains salient.

These behavioral observations about our natures as reluctant cooperators faced one giant theoretical hurdle: how could evolution ever select for a behavioral trait that by its very nature reduced the short-term advantages to the individual? This is a more generalized version of what biologists called the "altruism problem." There are many species of animals that engage in a wide variety of altruistic and cooperative behaviors, including sacrificing their own lives for the benefit of kin. If natural selection proceeds blindly, guided only by the calculus of individual self-interest, how could such altruistic and cooperative behaviors ever have evolved, when such tendencies make an individual less fit rather than more fit?

There were three big conceptual breakthroughs that helped solve this problem. The first two came from the British evolutionary theorist W. D. Hamilton. He had the insight that what natural selection really cares about are genes, not individuals.[35] Hamilton also recognized that if genes are the real units of natural selection, then in making the calculation of whether a behavior helps or hurts that gene we must consider not just the individual's gene, but copies of that same gene carried by others. That is, it may be perfectly adaptive for a parent to sacrifice itself for many offspring, even though by doing so the gene in the parent is lost, if enough copies of that gene are saved in the offspring. This proposition became known as "kin selection" and Hamilton also quantified it. The amount of altruism and its targets should be predicted by the degree of relatedness between the sacrificing and benefitted individuals. In his famous rendition, a parent should sacrifice itself for three or more children but not for two or less, because on average a child carries one-half of the parent's genes.

The third contribution to solving the problem of altruism and cooperation came from the American evolutionary theorist Robert Trivers, who showed that in the right social milieu these altruistic and cooperative behaviors could be adaptive even if they were aimed at non-kin, and indeed even at other species.[36] These insights cleared the theoretical path to the notion that socially cooperative behaviors not only could have evolved in our species, but that they almost certainly did in fact evolve.

Anthropology has also belatedly played its part in this rediscovery of human nature. Sparked by a series of books questioning the evidence on which Margaret Mead and other cultural relativists had grounded their views,[37] these new anthropologists began looking at common behaviors shared by all human societies, rather than focusing on their differences. They have found a breathtaking number of human universals, including, most significantly for our purposes, living in groups larger than the immediate family, notions of individual responsibility, rules against murder, rape, and other kinds of violence, rules against breaking promises, and rules about punishing rule-breakers.[38]

Of course, the interplay between culture and biology is complicated, in exactly the same way that the relationship between nurture and nature is complicated, or the relationship between the inherited predispositions in our brains and the brain's ability to soak up new information from the environment to overcome those predispositions. Not only that, but these complications played out over a history in which, in general, the small groups in which we evolved our social tendencies grew larger and larger. Brains built to address the challenges of living in small groups of mostly related individuals now had to face the very different challenges of larger bands and tribes. Culture – with its ability to convey rules quickly across generations – played an important role in meeting this new challenge of size.

CULTURE: OUR SMALL GROUPS BECOME LARGE

Language not only raised our social stakes, binding us more tightly and tempting us more deeply, it also bloomed into culture, and culture has spun its infinite variations onto this basic dilemma of cooperating and cheating. Every human every day in every society has been and always will be faced with the question of whether to cheat or cooperate. How we answer that question in any particular circumstance depends in large part on cultural norms. A Waukegan realtor might return a lost wallet; a Bantu tribesman might not return a lost knife. Every society has likewise faced the same punishment dilemma, with infinite cultural variations. Even in England, and even as late as the eighteenth century, death was the punishment for many crimes that today are not even considered felonies. The central problem of punishment may have been the same for 100,000 years, but it seems we've tried to solve it in 100,000 different ways.

In fact, these economic games and experiments also showed how complex the interplay can be between culture and human nature. Not only are members of preindustrial societies a tad closer to pure selfishness than members of postindustrial societies, but the extent to which they depart from pure selfishness seems to depend on a variety of cultural factors, including the degree to which their societies are economically integrated (markets needing a certain level of trust in order to work) and even the degree to which a given society participates in religions that contain fairness-based codes.[39]

Our modern culture may make us more cooperative in some dimensions, but it makes us less so in others. The modern myth of rugged individualism pervades Western culture, but is often quite a puzzle to primitive man. The anthropologist Ronald Cohen tells a story about the Kanuri of Northern Nigeria, with whom he had spent a year in the field. One day he went off by himself to the edge of the tribal lands to reflect about his project. He was sitting on the edge of a log for only about twenty minutes when a young boy from the village appeared and sat down at the other end. Cohen asked the boy why he had come. The boy said, "The Chief sent me." Cohen asked why, and the boy replied, "He said you were alone and therefore must be ill."[40]

On the other hand, the bucolic picture of small groups of humans presumptively getting along and cooperating, and punishing occasional cheats, ignores one giant and significant evolutionary fact: our brains were built to presumptively cooperate only with members of the our own group. Out-group members triggered exactly opposite presumptions. Strangers walking over the hill were presumed not to be trusted or trusting. We were not primed to cooperate with those strangers or they with us. When it came to dealing with outsiders, our social brains switched largely over to shark brains.[41]

The story of civilization is in many ways the story of how our small groups got bigger and bigger, and the problems our shark brains caused during those periods of expansion. Language, law, religion, and many other kinds of social institutions helped keep our shark brains in check, and helped our social brains add new members to our definition of who was in the group. Still, in-out rifts have always run deep, and have been difficult to overcome. Especially when there are physical markers of being a member of this group or that – racial or ethnic differences, for example – these rifts have driven much of our sorry history of violence. But within our small emergent groups we remained highly cooperative.

Indeed, human-on-human violence, with a few exceptions, has been in steady decline as our groups have gotten bigger and the number of outsiders correspondingly smaller. Forensic archeologists estimate that before agriculture, when we were still living in relatively small nomadic tribes and regularly clashing with other tribes, 15 percent of us died violent deaths (homicide, suicide, and accidents). That compares to a 3 percent violent death rate in the earliest states, after agriculture settled us down in one place and those places began to aggregate with other places into states.[42] These rates of violence are almost incomprehensible when we compare them to modern rates. In Western Europe today, approximately 1 person in 100,000 (0.001 percent) dies a violent death; in the United States that number is approximately 6 in 100,000 (0.006 percent).[43] Even in the modern world's most dangerous places and times the rates of violent death are miniscule compared to our emergent and ancient rates. To use just three examples, violent death rates in the U.S. Civil War, in Afghanistan in 1979, and even in the Soviet purges of the late 1930s, reached "only" into the 400 per 100,000 level (0.4 percent). This is one-tenth the violent death rate in our earliest states, and one-fiftieth of our emergent rate.[44]

In fact, the myth of *Homo economicus* is in large measure an artifact of looking at human nature *across* groups rather than within them. It was an easy mistake to make. As our groups got bigger and bigger, and our brains lagged behind in recognizing those larger groupings, we killed and raped and enslaved "each other" with great aplomb. But we were not typically accosting our own clan or tribe members; we were accosting outsiders whom the march of civilization labeled insiders, but whom our brains still counted as outsiders.

THE CULTURE AND EVOLUTION OF LAW

So we really have two deep neural paradoxes, and two versions of The Social Problem. We want to cooperate with other group members, but we occasionally also want to cheat them. We want to fight with outsiders, but we also occasionally want to cooperate with them. As our groups got bigger and bigger, these two visions of our natures came together like two images in a pair of binoculars. The rule of law was one of the ways that helped us integrate these two images. Laws automatically redefined the expanding social whole, and entitled, at least in theory, all members of the new groupings to the protections of the old ones. Protestants may not really treat Catholics the same as they treat each other, but when they are all Irishmen then Irish law expects them to, and punishes them when they don't. The ideal of community in groups too big to be real communities helped our shark brains switch back to more and more inclusive social brains.

No matter how The Social Problem is solved in a particular society – the cultural details of where the balance between selfishness and selflessness might generally be struck – the important point is to recognize that the problem is universal. In every human culture, humans must sometimes decide when to act in ways that may be beneficial to themselves but harmful to the group, because in every culture humans remain social animals, torn constantly between the short-term benefits of defection and the long-term benefits of cooperation, between the exhilarations of individuality and the comforts of community. In all cultures we are likewise torn between our feelings that outsiders are outsiders, and our cultural norms that demand we treat them as insiders.

It is no coincidence that our prisons mirror our dual natures, and take from us what we most deeply need and want. We want to be free, free even of the small group and its cloying rules that interfere with our short-term fitness, free to break the rules ourselves and even to leave the group.[45] Yet we also want to be part of the group, to relish in the long-term fitness advantages it confers. Prisons are designed precisely to deprive the worst wrongdoers among us of the very two things that we most cherish: freedom and society. And we are often able to do that only by labeling our worst offenders as moral outsiders, monsters.

Law is not just one of the ways we have tried to solve The Social Problem by imposing a level of group-enforced deterrence, it is one of the few remaining modern reminders of our deeply embedded evolutionary schizophrenia over cooperating and cheating, over right and wrong. Law is about right and wrong, or at least about what we humans in any particular culture and setting *think* is right and wrong, or at the very least what we *say* to each other about what we think is right and wrong. It is also about what we do, once we settle on right and wrong, to the wrongdoers among us.

Law is *about* right and wrong, but the overlap between morality and law is not complete, either in terms of content or enforcement. English common law famously distinguished between acts that were *mala in se* (inherent wrongs) and those that were merely *mala prohibitas* (prohibited wrongs). Of course, many acts are both morally wrong and illegal, like most homicides. But many other acts have been made illegal, especially by a robust regulatory state, that have no intrinsic moral bite, such as selling pots and pans door-to-door without a required license. Conversely, some acts that are widely viewed as wrong may not be unlawful, such as adultery, at least in many Western cultures. Finally, some acts may be morally acceptable, indeed morally required, even if they are unlawful (Jean Valjean in *Les Miserables* stealing that loaf of bread to feed his sister's starving family).

For most of human history even *mala in se* were typically dealt with by way of private revenge. With just a few exceptions for things such as treason and regicide, most ancient and even medieval states simply did not get involved in the punishment of crimes, even *mala in se* like homicide. These were left to the victims and their family, clan, or tribe. Our small groups may have been accumulating into larger and larger political units, but we left the evolutionarily significant job of punishing miscreants to our smaller, more natural groups. In fact, one way to think about the development of the state is that over time it has taken on, among many other things, the punishment obligations of smaller antecedent groupings. As those groupings became larger and larger, the state not only began to enforce rules of behavior that had been the exclusive province of smaller groups, it also began to create more and more *mala prohibita* as the state-as-family needed more rules to sustain it in an increasingly complex world.

In the end, though, big chunks of law, across all cultures, are about what our original small groups considered to be norms of cooperation, and how they thought we should punish various kinds of defections from those norms. Admittedly, there are three big problems with these kinds of narratives about the evolution of morality, and its instantiation into law.

First, we know virtually nothing about how our ancestral groups were really organized or how they really solved The Social Problem. This is a weakness common to the whole discipline known as evolutionary psychology. We can posit all the hypotheticals we want, and we can use evolutionary theory to try to reason backward in time to claim our current brains are based on past environments, but in the end we know very little about those past environments, especially when it comes to behaviors as complex as cooperating, cheating, and punishing. This critique is often called the "just-so" problem. Not knowing how our ancestors really behaved, it is easy to assume in hindsight a behavior that just-so happens to make evolutionary sense.[46]

However, one potentially important clue to how our ancestral groups may have solved The Social Problem is how existing primitive societies are solving it. There is little doubt that for most of our evolutionary history we lived in small nomadic forager bands, of which there still remain a few, mostly in Africa and Australia.[47] The consensus among anthropologists and evolutionary theorists is that these extant societies are the best evidence of what our ancestral groups might have been like.[48] There are many significant differences between these extant societies, but in general they are organized into small residential groups that anthropologists call "bands." These bands typically consist of about thirty mostly-related individuals. The bands break up into smaller parties to forage and hunt. Food is liberally shared, and centrally stored. About half of all food is gathered, the other half hunted or fished.[49] Most of these societies recognize individual ownership of small amounts of personal property – clothing, tools, cooking utensils – but because of their nomadic lifestyle few recognize real property.[50] They robustly trade with other bands, and even other tribes. They show a high degree of cooperation within the band, although they also occasionally defect in the usual ways, including theft, assault, and homicide.[51] These core defections are all recognized as defections, and the most serious of them can result in third-party punishment.

So although the historical record is hazy at best, it is not complete guesswork. We can use evidence from existing primitive societies to make some reasonable inferences about how our ancestors lived 100,000 years ago.

A second problem with the idea that we evolved a presumptively cooperative ethos is the so-called first mover problem. It is difficult for some evolutionary theorists to imagine how those first cooperative genes could ever have given their owners a net survival advantage, in a world full of defecting *Homo economici*. This is the prisoner's dilemma writ large. Without some assurance that the other guy will cooperate, the rational play is always to defect. How did enough cooperators accumulate into a group large enough to achieve a fitness advantage big enough to overcome their inherent one-on-one disadvantage when dealing with a bunch of other cheaters?

It turns out that cooperators who were sufficiently *related* to each other could in fact achieve sufficient net advantages. As we have already seen, when we cooperate with relatives, we not only benefit our long-term survival but also the long-term survival of the genes we share with those relatives. We are thus much more likely to trust other group members if they are related to us. Just like in The Prisoner's Dilemma game, that trust gave us the ability to achieve a great advantage by cooperating. And in fact, our earliest groups, like current nomadic foragers, were likely composed of largely related individuals.

The third criticism of the notion of an evolved morality is that even if cooperative behaviors gained some selective traction in groups of mostly related individuals, it is hard to see how they sustained themselves. Our small groups gave us a net survival advantage – that is, the *average* benefits of cooperation exceeded the *average* costs of defection. But these are only averages. In any given situation, an individual member might calculate that he would be better off defecting. "I will steal that food because I have more children than anyone else, and we are hungry. It seems to me that the remote group advantages I enjoy, say, from mutual defense, hardly matter at this moment, when my children and I may all die from hunger." Or, less sympathetically, "I will steal that food because I see that everyone is gone and they will never discover it is me." Because such situations undoubtedly occurred to many of our ancestors at some time, how did natural selection solve the problem of groups unraveling over time because individual members' cost/benefits necessarily drifted outside the averages?

The answer is that it was just too costly to have brains completely blank on the cheat/cooperate issue, and armed to decide everything on a situation-by-situation basis. That's because even in an environment as complex as our ancestors' group living, there were just a handful of really important and common challenges in which the cheat/cooperate decision had to be made. The solution, then, was to have brains armed with a few predispositions to solve the most common problems. Such brains could solve those common problems at little or no computational cost, enjoying a significant fitness advantage over agnostic brains waiting to calculate every possible social dilemma.

Among the biggest sources of social tension were disputes over materiél – food, shelter, clothing, tools, weapons, mates – the very stuff of fitness. This is what the law of course calls property.[52]

THE PROBLEM OF PROPERTY[53]

We needed many kinds of things to survive in our new harsh environment, including shelter from the openness of the savannahs, clothing to protect our hairless bodies from cooling temperatures, and weapons to hunt and to ward off out-groups. Living in groups necessarily created deep and fundamental tensions about the use of those things. Who had the right to use them, and on what conditions? Every parent knows that there's nothing more likely to cause an eruption between children than fights over toys. Imagine if we needed the toys for our survival.

Territoriality – the possession of one kind of property, namely space (what lawyers call real property), coupled with the willingness to defend that space against competitors – is one way to solve the problem of property. Many animal species, though an overall minority, are territorial. Creatures as diverse as birds, lizards, elephant seals, cats, dogs, gibbons, and even a handful of insect species, mark and defend territories. Territories often, though not always, contain nests or dens and sufficient surrounding resources to enable survival. Thus, the exclusive possession of real property is almost always also bound up with the possession of personal property, the stuff of survival. In fact, even species that exhibit remote territoriality – areas they will defend that are distant from nesting sites – do so to protect some kind of remote resource, whether certain feeding territories (as in the case of some types of birds) or special mating areas (some types of antelopes).

Possession of real and personal property, both in law and nature, generally requires two elements: physical control of the property and the expression of a willingness to defend it. In nature, the expression of an intention to defend property typically involves signals to potential squatters or thieves that the possessor is willing to fight to retain control over the property. But if a resource is equally valuable to the possessor as it is to a challenger, then the challenger should be just as willing to fight for it as the current owner. In fact, not having the property might well give the challenger more incentive to take it, all other things being equal. You can imagine what kind of chaos would result from such a generalized willingness to fight over property, especially in social species that depend on certain levels of cooperation.

Nature's solution was to invest the brains of first possessors with an overvaluation of their possessed property, giving them more incentive to keep it than challengers have to take it. This is what biologists, and property professors, call the first-in-time rule. Both with territoriality and the possession of things, it is quite common for the first possessor to be able to defeat a challenger who is significantly stronger, so common in fact that the challenger will often recognize the asymmetric incentives and back down. This happens not just with mammals, which might be able to communicate their incentives to one another with gestures, but even with some insects. Some species of butterflies, for example, exhibit the first-in-time rule when they compete for sunny spots.[54]

The first-in-time rule is an elegant solution to the problem of property. If the individual who first acquired the property values it more than all other strategic actors (whether other group members in the case of social animals or competitors in the case of nonsocial animals), and assuming the costs of fighting over the property are sufficiently high, then those other actors will be unwilling to pay the fight costs required to wrestle that property from the possessor. With no external "rulemaking" whatsoever, and therefore just as effective in birds and butterflies as in humans, the first-in-time rule greatly reduces fights over property.

As with most evolved behavioral traits, however, the first-in-time rule is not absolute, and its adaptive value required flexibility. It is a strategic predisposition only, which must be able to give way when tactical circumstances demand it. So, for example, the magnitude of the first-in-time advantage must not be so large that property never changes hands. A given property in a given circumstance may be so much more valuable to a challenger than it is to the original owner that it would make no sense for the original owner to fight to keep it. The magnitude of the first-in-time advantage thus can vary over time and circumstance. For example, the willingness to fight to keep property generally increases the longer the possessor is in possession of it.[55]

The first-in-time rule is a general version of the endowment effect mentioned earlier in this chapter in connection with the ultimatum game. Humans, and in fact several species of nonhuman primates, value property possessed more than identical property not yet possessed but easily available, in the case of humans, in markets. The moment property is acquired, it suddenly becomes more valuable to the owner than the owner was willing to pay for it just moments before. The endowment effect causes theoretical economists all sorts of fits because it clogs up the mathematics of market exchange. But it is a beautiful thing to evolutionary biologists, because it is yet another example of how natural selection can sometimes recruit an existing trait and put it to new uses. The first-in-time rule, followed by butterflies and birds, gets recruited by higher order social animals to serve as a kind of check on relying too much on market-based promises of future performance by fellow group members. The very same internal sense of inflated value that reduced fights over property in nonsocial species can now do double duty in social species. It not only cuts down on fights over property, it protects members from over-relying on the promises of others, whether within or between groups.[56]

That extra function became especially valuable to humans because of the institution of the promise. The human animal needed forward-looking property strategies because we can imagine the future and communicate with each other about it. It was not enough for us to be equipped with the endowment effect; we needed strategies for acquiring and then distributing property within the group. A central tool in dealing with this distributive problem was the promise.

THE PROMISING ANIMAL: HOMO EXCHANGIUS

It may not be too much of a stretch to say that the single most significant human invention of all time was the promise. It freed us from on-the-barrelhead barter economies, allowing us to exchange goods and services today for goods and services tomorrow. It eventually allowed us to exchange promises for promises, to develop currency as a conduit of those mutual promises, and ultimately to engage in the divisions of labor that led, even early on and at least compared to our primate cousins, to the creation of enormous wealth and a resultant freedom from want. We really shouldn't even call the promise an "invention." It seems as deeply embedded in our humanity as any other trait. Language itself, that defining of all human characteristics, may have evolved principally to allow us to convey promises to one another – anything from "you cover the left flank on this hunt and I'll cover the right," to "we, who have more food than we need but not enough skins, will exchange with your group who has too many skins and not enough food."[57]

Promising is so much a part of us it is sometimes hard to notice. I often ask my law and biology students to try to use a single word to describe humans, and they've come up with many over the years, including "conscious," "talkers," "imaginers," and "worriers." But the one word I think is best, and one no student ever suggests is: "traders." We are, and always have been, incessant traders. Watch any children play with toys, and you will see endless trading. They don't have to be taught how to do it or see others do it; they *know* how to do it. *Homo economicus* is really *Homo exchangius*.

Promising is a sentient, language-based version of what biologists call reciprocity, and although there is only weak evidence of market-type promises in existing nonhuman primates, there is no doubt that trading, and the promises it required, was one of the glues that kept our groups together. Trading also propelled us, or at least assisted us, to overcome our fears of out-groups.

When we search for a common challenge from our emergence, a challenge so frequently faced that natural selection would likely have armed our brains with some presumptive solutions, promises have to be near the top of the list. Every promise creates its own kind of Promisor's Dilemma. I am incurring a cost today in the hopes of a future benefit, and that hope is grounded in nothing more than the word of a fellow human. How can I be sure he will not defect? If I am insecure about his performance, that insecurity will reduce the price I am willing to pay for the promise, which will only further reduce his likelihood of performing.

We can escape this Promisor's Dilemma the same way we were able to escape the destabilizing problem of fighting over property – with solutions that give us an instinct that avoids, or at least greatly dampens, the problem. Having brains that instinctively value possessed property more than non-possessed property helped us overcome the problem of property, and having brains that instinctively believe promises should be kept helped us with the Promisor's Dilemma.

TWO SOLUTIONS TO THE SOCIAL PROBLEM

So I propose that these are the two core rules of right and wrong bequeathed to us by natural selection and driven by the common problems of property and promise:

Rule 1: Transfers of property must be voluntary.
Rule 2: Promises must be kept.

Our brains were *built* to respect others' property, to expect them to respect ours, to keep our promises, and to expect others to keep theirs.

As with all instincts, culture shaped these two solutions to The Social Problem, molding them over time to fit new conditions. Who "owns" what property, even what property is "ownable," are details that are very much culturally dependent. One of the epic struggles in the early Church was over the question of the nature of property, both real and personal, and eventually whether the Church itself could

own property. More generally, the ownability of real property seems
to depend in many societies on the extent to which agriculture, or
the presence of other kinds of sustainable resources, has tied them
to place. As we have seen, our nomadic forager ancestors most likely
had no concept of real property; when resources ran out they just
moved on.

The contours of an enforceable promise have likewise been shaped
significantly by culture. Some promises enforceable in one culture are
unenforceable in others, usually because of differing views about the
legality of the act being promised. The promise to do an illegal act
is not only typically unenforceable, the promise itself is often illegal.
Solicitation to commit murder is one example. Even where the object
of the promise is legal, there can be tremendous cultural differences
in the extent to which promises are deemed worthy of enforcement.
For example, the promises of rulers to marry their offspring to one
another was not only widespread throughout most of human history,
it was an important tool of political alliance. The remnants of that
practice survived in the common law "heart balm" action, a suit under
which broken promises to marry (in modern times, only between the
marrying couple, not their parents) entitled the jilted party to damages.
Both in England and almost all U.S. states, however, anti-heart balm
statutes have now abolished the common law right to sue for a broken
promise to marry.[58]

The remedies for a broken promise can also vary significantly across
time and societies. Ancient law enforced promises the way our small
groups likely did – by forcing the wavering promisor to perform on pain
of serious sanction (often death). Under Roman law, for example, if
someone breached a contract to pay money, the creditor had the right
to chain the debtor and drag him around the market on three successive
days. If the debt remained unpaid, the creditor had the right to cut the
debtor up into tiny pieces.[59] In other contexts, the group or ruling
authority might simply confiscate the object of the promise from the
breaching party and turn it over to the party who suffered the breach.
If John entered into a contract to sell Mary a goat, and Mary paid
John the purchase price but John then simply refused to part with the
goat, the ancient remedy was to have the group confiscate the goat and
turn it over to Mary. Today, by contrast, there are only a few special

categories of promise – for example, promises to sell real estate – that are deemed special enough to justify actions for specific performance. All other breaches of contract are remedied by substitute performance in the form of money damages.[60]

Despite these cultural differences surrounding remedy, the law of contract remains at its core the law of the moral imperative of the promise. Promises have always carried with them a moral component, even though modern law has come to recognize the utility of substitute performance.[61] It is *wrong* to break a promise to sell you widgets, even if I later compensate you completely by giving you the money you would have been able to make from reselling them. Our brains have been built to disapprove of one who breaks a promise, whether or not one later makes the other party whole.[62]

The same is true of the rule against taking property. Theft is not simply the law's artificial prediction that a thief will be punished if he is caught. It is a reflection of our deepest instincts that tell us stealing is wrong. And if we stretch the idea of property a little bit – to include one's own life and health – then Rule 1 covers virtually all of the criminal law and the law of torts as well. When you physically injure me you have "taken" my well-being without my consent, whether by intentionally shooting me or by negligently crashing into me.

Our evolved rules against stealing and breaching seem to be encoded in specific areas of our brains. Human subjects show a characteristic activation pattern on functional Magnetic Resonance Imaging (fMRI) when they engage in the endowment effect. The neurological signatures are so robust that in a 2008 experiment researchers were able to predict quite successfully, by *first* looking at fMRI results, which human subjects would be most likely to exhibit strong endowment preferences.[63] By valuing our own property more than others do, we are in some primitive way recognizing that it is wrong for others to take that property. There is an even richer literature exploring the neural correlates of keeping promises and breaking them, showing significant brain differences between the two.[64]

So we need to adjust our model of human nature from *Homo economicus*, selfish man, and *Homo exchangius*, trading man, to *Homo juris*, rule-following man. The two rules our brains have been built to presumptively follow are: don't steal and don't breach. Laws based on these two rules, and civilization itself for that matter, are not cultural Johnny-come-latelys to the human story. We have been mostly following these two rules and occasionally breaking them forever, because our brains were built by evolution to do so.

But there is a third rule. And that's because, like our instinct to cooperate in general, our instincts not to steal and not to break promises are not overwhelming; they are weak enough that humans regularly violate them, as part of our overall tendency to defect occasionally. Neither of these first two rules could have done much evolutionary work if we did not also have rules for their enforcement.[65] So:

Rule 3: Serious violations of Rules 1 and 2 must be punished.

It is, of course, on this third rule that much of this book will be focused.

Before we turn to the specifics of Rule 3, including what natural selection might have had to say about how "serious" a violation had to be to justify punishment, and what kinds of punishment, we turn in the next chapter to the twin problems of how we discovered cheaters and what our brains made us feel about them when we discovered them.

Notes to Chapter 1

1. Joseph Wood Krutch, in his 1956 book THE GREAT CHAIN OF LIFE (U. Iowa Press 1956), devoted an entire chapter to this idea that the deepest of original sins is the animal need to steal protein from other living things:

   [A]ll animals must eat something which is or was alive. It may be either a plant or another animal but only plant or animal matter contains protein and without it they cannot live. No animal, therefore, can be innocent as a plant may be. The latter can turn mere inorganic chemicals into living tissue; the animals cannot. All of them must live off something else. And that, perhaps is the deepest meaning of Original Sin.

   Id. at 41.

2. The Social Problem goes by many different names, and comes in many different flavors, often depending on the particular discipline describing it. Economists and political scientists typically call it the "commitment" or "collective action" problem, whereas biologists and anthropologists usually call it the "trust," "reciprocity," or "altruism" problem. In his wonderful book, PASSIONS WITHIN REASON: THE STRATEGIC ROLE OF EMOTIONS (Norton 1988), Robert Frank describes the commitment problem

this way: in order to solve many of the problems that faced us during our emergence, we had to "commit ourselves to behave in ways that may later prove to be contrary to our interests." That is, we had to be willing to keep our promises even when, and especially when, doing so was no longer advantageous.

3. The two species of eusocial mole rats are the naked mole rat (*Hetercephalus glaber*) and the Damaraland mole rat (*Fukomys damarensis*). They both live in underground burrows, which they dig with external teeth. The naked mole rat lives in parts of East Africa, primarily near the Somali edge of the horn. The Damaraland mole rat lives in Damaraland – a tiny corner of the southwest African nation of Namibia. These two species of mole rat are the only known examples of eusocial mammals.

4. There are more than 400 species of shark, and, contrary to popular belief, most are not solitary. Many species are quite adept at many different kinds of social tasks, including group hunting. Even the traditionally solitary species, like the great white, have been known to cooperate with each other occasionally. See J. Mourier et al., *Evidence of social communities in a spacially structured network of a free-ranging shark species*, ANIMAL BEHAV., **83(2)**, 389–401 (2012).

5. FRANS DE WAAL, CHIMPANZEE POLITICS: POWER AND SEX AMONG APES (Johns Hopkins 2007).

6. If you were Herbert Spencer, the fellow who popularized "Social Darwinism," governments needn't worry too much because "survival of the fittest" ensured that the best people would also be the most successful.

7. There seems to be some controversy about whether the term *Homo economicus* was coined in the 1960s by the science historian Thomas Kuhn, or in the 1920s by game theorist John von Neumann.

8. The German economist Werner Güth is generally credited with the first articulation of the ultimatum game, in the early 1980s.

9. Figuring out Player A's Nash equilibrium in the One-Shot Ultimatum Game is easy because Player B's most selfish strategy is always to take whatever money Player A offers. With other more complex games, like The Prisoner's Dilemma and The Public Goods games we will discuss later, determining the Nash equilibrium can be more complicated as the number of choices the opposing player has increases. This is why the most common lay description of the Nash equilibrium is that it's the play that best immunizes a player from the other player's strategic choices; that is, the play that maximizes my return when I am forced to consider *all* of the opposing player's strategic responses.

10. John Nash, *Equilibrium points in n-person games*, PROC. OF THE NAT. ACAD. OF SCIENCES USA, **36**, 48–49 (1950).

11. The economists typically call this "costly punishment," and the biologists call it "strong reciprocity" or "altruistic punishment."

12. E. Fehr & S. Gächter, *Fairness and retaliation: the economics of reciprocity*, J. ECON. PERSP., **14**, 159–181 (2000).

13. J. Henrich et al., *In search of* homo economicus: *behavioral experiments in fifteen small-scale societies*, AM. ECON. REV., **91(2)**, 73–78 (2001). Henrich has found just one society – the Machiguenga in the Peruvian Amazon – in which Player A regularly makes, and Player B regularly accepts, very low offers.

14. These explanations are not surmise. There is a wealth of empirical literature demonstrating that when Players B reject low offers they report subjectively that they did so because they are "insulted" or "angered" by Player A's offer. M. Pillutla & J. Murnighan, *Unfairness, anger and spite: rejection of ultimatum offers*, ORG. BEHAV. HUM. DEC. PROC., **68**, 208–224 (1996). Their emotional reactions to low offers even show up objectively in the form of increased sweating. M. van't Wout et al., *Affective state and decision-making in the ultimatum game*, EXP. BRAIN RES., **169(4)**, 564–568 (2006). These emotional responses to being insulted by low offers in the ultimatum game appear to be driven by the same subcortical "fight-or-flight" network, centered in the amygdala, that comes on line when we sense we are being placed in physical danger. K. Gospic et al., *Limbic justice – amygdala involvement in immediate rejection in the ultimatum game*, PLOS BIO., **9(5)**, May 3, 2011.

15. This is true as long as they are not psychopaths. As we will see in Chapter 3, psychopaths lack the moral intuitions that the rest of us have, including Player A's ability to predict that Player B might reject an offer if it is too low, and Player B's reciprocal ability to predict Player A will not offer five dollars. As a result, psychopathic Players A play close to the Nash equilibrium of one dollar, and psychopathic Players B tend to reject offers if they are not at least five dollars. M. Koenigs et al., *Economic decision-making in psychopathy: a comparison with ventromedial prefrontal lesion patients*, NEUROPSYCHOLOGIA, **48(7)**, 2198–2204 (2010).

16. Two Princeton game theorists, Melvin Dresher and Merrill Flood, are generally credited with inventing The Prisoner's Dilemma in the 1950s, although a third, Albert Tucker, formalized it and gave it its name. It soon made its way from math to psychology, and then to evolutionary theory.

17. For an extensive discussion of the stag hunt and its decidedly non-Romantic implications for the evolution of cooperation, see BRIAN SKYRMS, THE STAG HUNT AND THE EVOLUTION OF THE SOCIAL STRUCTURE (Cambridge 2004).

18. The stag hunt game also suggests that it would have been critical for our ancestors to appreciate that different types of cooperating tasks require different numbers of cooperators, and therefore might require the delegation of different tasks to different members – paying attention not just to members' different skills but also to the sheer number of members participating in the task. We needed enough to get the job done, but not so many to needlessly

increase the chances of a defection. Punishment may have been just such a task. We will discuss the delegation of punishment in Chapter 7. The stag hunt also suggests that theorizing about how humans cannot work together in groups of more than X – with X some approximation of the size of our emergent groups (the so-called Dunbar number postulated by anthropologist Robin Dunbar and popularized by Malcolm Gladwell's book BLINK: THE POWER OF THINKING WITHOUT THINKING [Back Bay Books, 2007]) – is probably oversimplified.

19. The number of defectors needed to make defection an ineffective strategy is n/m, where n is the number of players and m is the public goods multiplier. In our example, n was 4 and m was 2, so the break point at which defection would have been useless is 2, meaning that if two players defect, they are no better off than if everyone cooperated. In our example, two defectors keep their ten dollars, and get only another ten dollars each from the public distribution (given that only two players cooperated and contributed a total of twenty dollars, which was then doubled to forty dollars and shared by all four). The total twenty dollars they get from defecting is the same as the twenty dollars they would have gotten if everyone cooperated. But if three defect, the defectors do worse (fifteen dollars) than if they had all cooperated (twenty dollars), although not as badly as the sole cooperator (five dollars). And of course if all four defect they just keep their original ten dollars and there are no public goods to divide.

20. J. Bergm et al., *Trust, reciprocity, and social history*, GAMES & ECON. BEHAV., **10(1)**, 122–142 (1995).

21. E. Fehr & S. Gächter, note 12 supra.

22. M. van't Wout et al., supra note 14.

23. I. Bohnet & B. Frey, *The sounds of silence in prisoner's dilemma and dictator games*, J. ECON. BEHAV. & ORG., **38(1)**, 43–57 (1999).

24. J. Greene & J. Paxton, *Patterns of neural activity associated with honest and dishonest moral decisions*, PROC. NAT. ACAD. SCIENCES, **106(30)**, 12506–12511 (July 2009). Research into lying has traditionally been hampered by the problem that in most experiments subjects are directed to lie by the experimenters, and these kinds of "lies with permission" may be very different, both behaviorally and neurally, than the lies we tell for our own purposes. Greene and Paxton solved this problem in a clever way, by designing an experiment where subjects' uninvited departures from what was supposed to be a random task was a measure of their lying. Behaviorally, Greene and Paxton showed that roughly one-third of their subjects always told the truth, one-third occasionally lied, and one-third regularly lied. Neurally, they showed that the honest brains recruited relatively little by way of traditional control areas of the brain (the frontal cortex). Telling the truth seemed to come quite naturally to them without having to think much about it. The dishonest brains struggled mightily against the impulse to tell the

truth – their frontal control areas eventually winning the utilitarian battle. It seems we really are born truth tellers and born cooperators, but not infallibly so, and there is of course a wide distribution across populations about the degree of that infallibility, no doubt driven by complex cultural and environmental factors.

25. K. Jensen et al., *Chimpanzees are rational maximizers in an ultimatum game*, SCIENCE, **318**, 107–109 (October 2007).

26. B. Hare et al., *Tolerance allows bonobos to outperform chimpanzees on a cooperative task*, CURRENT BIO., **17(7)**, 619–623 (April 2007).

27. F. de Waal, *Food transfers through mesh in brown capuchins*, J. COMP. PSYCHOL., **111**(4), 370–378 (1997).

28. S. Brosnan & F. de Waal, *Monkeys reject unequal pay*, NATURE, **425**, 297–299 (July 2003).

29. Frans de Waal, *The Brains of the Animal Kingdom*, WALL STREET JOURNAL, March 23, 2013, at C1–C2.

30. M. Kosfeld et al., *Oxytocin increases trust in humans*, NATURE, **435**, 673–676 (June 2005).

31. For a comprehensive and readable discussion of the role of oxytocin in human evolution and behavior, written by a leading oxytocin researcher, see P. ZAK, THE MORAL MOLECULE (Dutton 2012).

32. C. Declerk et al., *Oxytocin and cooperation under conditions of uncertainty: the modulating role of incentives and social information*, HORMONES & BEHAV., **57(3)**, 368–374 (2010).

33. T. Burnham, *High testosterone men reject low ultimatum game offers*, PROC. ROYAL SOC., **274**, 2327–2330 (2007).

34. P. Zak, *The neurobiology of trust*, SCIENTIFIC AMERICAN (June 2008).

35. W. D. Hamilton, *The genetical evolution of social behavior*, J. THEOR. BIOL., 7, 1–52 (1964). This means that traits, both behavioral and physical, could be selected for even if they made individuals less fit, as long as they made the individuals' genes for the trait – shared by relatives – more fit. For a wonderful biography of Hamilton, see ULLICA SEGERSTRALE, NATURE'S ORACLE: THE LIFE AND WORK OF W. D. HAMILTON (Oxford 2013).

36. R. L. Trivers, *The evolution of reciprocal altruism*, Q. REV. BIOL. **46**, 35–57 (1971).

37. The most important of these books was Derek Freeman's, in which he showed that Mead was wrong in her central observation that adolescence in Samoa was uniquely free of stress. It turns out that Samoan teens are just as angst-filled about their transition into adulthood as teenagers around the world. DEREK FREEMAN, MARGARET MEAD AND SAMOA: THE MAKING AND UNMAKING OF A MYTH (Penguin 1986). See also EKKEHART MALOTKI, HOPI TIME: A LINGUISTIC ANALYSIS IN THE HOPI LANGUAGE (de Gruyter 1983); MELFORD SPIRO, OEDIPUS IN THE TROBRIANDS (Trans. Publ. 1991).

38. Donald Brown's tour de force on human universals identifies some four hundred candidates. DONALD E. BROWN, HUMAN UNIVERSALS (McGraw-Hill 1991).

39. J. Henrich et al., *Markets, religion, community size and the evolution of fairness and punishment*, SCIENCE, **327**, 1480–1484 (March 2010).

40. Lionel Tiger, *Credit Where Credit Isn't New*, FORBES, March 19, 2009.

41. The in-group/out-group difference is a human universal. Brown, supra note 38, at 138. All theorists, however, do not accept its evolutionary origins. Some believe that the benefits of our small groups were so great, and our interactions with other groups so rare, that our cooperative instincts were not limited to in-group members. See, e.g., A. Delton et al., *Evolution of direct reciprocity under uncertainty can explain human generosity in one-shot encounters*, PROC. NAT. ACAD. SCI., **108(32)**, 13335–13340 (2011). Even if this were originally true, as our groups got bigger and bigger, and started bumping into other expanding groups, it quickly became a good idea to view those other groups with a special level of skepticism. Whether that skepticism is primarily evolutionary or primarily cultural may be an interesting question in theory, but the bottom line is that for much of our existence we have profoundly mistrusted out-groups, and of course continue to do so.

42. STEVEN PINKER, THE BETTER ANGELS OF OUR NATURES: WHY VIOLENCE HAS DECLINED (Viking 2011).

43. The Violent Death Project, www.violentdeathproject.com.

44. Id. Of course, this difference derives in large part from the "accidental death" category, which in turn consists in part of accidental deaths caused by non-human agents. Still, there is no question that human violence in all its forms is substantially less today – several orders of magnitude less – than it was when our brains were being built by evolution.

45. The law and economics scholar Paul Rubin has written an intriguing book arguing that the universal human yearning for freedom is a vestige of our evolved proclivity to leave an over-dominated group. PAUL H. RUBIN, DARWINIAN POLITICS: THE EVOLUTIONARY ORIGINS OF FREEDOM (Rutgers 2002).

46. For a general critique of evolutionary psychology, see J. Panskeep & J. Panskeep, *The seven sins of evolutionary psychology*, EVOL. & COGN., **6(2)**, 108–131 (2000). For a response to the Panskeep critique, see I. Pitchford, *A defence of evolutionary psychology*, EVOL. & COGN., **7(1)**, 39–45 (2001). For a more specific criticism of the use of evolutionary psychology to analyze blame and punishment, see D. Braman et al., *Some Realism about Punishment Naturalism*, 77 U. CHI. L. REV. 1531 (2010). For a response to the Braman paper, see P. Robinson et al., *Realism, Punishment & Reform*, 77 U. CHI. L. REV. 1611 (2010).

47. Classifying existing primitive societies as being sufficiently primitive to be evolutionarily instructive can be somewhat arbitrary. Two economists from

George Mason have attempted to standardize this task. Using a data set called the Standard Cross-Cultural Codes, they argue that eighteen existing primitive societies qualify, including the Mbuti, who live in the forests of the Democratic Republic of the Congo, and whose punishment practices we will touch on in Chapter 5. D. Youngberg & R. Hanson, *Forager Facts* (2010), unpublished paper available at http://hanson.gmu.edu/forager.pdf.

48. F. Marlowe, *Hunter-gatherers and human evolution*, Evol. Anthro., **14**(2), 54–67 (2005). On the other hand, some anthropologists have argued that the very fact that these primitive societies have persisted into our time suggests they might be very different from our ancestral groups. R. B. Lee & I. DeVore, *Problems in the Study of Hunters and Gatherers*, in Man the Hunter 5–12 (R. B. Lee and I. DeVore, eds., Aldine 1968).

49. For a comprehensive survey of the practices of these extant primitive forager societies, see F. Marlowe, id.

50. That is, our ancestral lands were likely not privately owned. The group communally "owned" its lands to the extent it was willing to stay on them to the exclusion of other groups. But those ancestral groups were nomadic, so they typically did not stay on lands to the exclusion of others. Even after agriculture tied us to place, the history of private land ownership is mixed and complicated. Different societies managed to cobble together different combinations of public and private land ownership in endless varieties. See, e.g., Eric T. Frayfogle, *Ethics, communities and private land*, **23** Ecology L. Q. 631, 632–638 (1996). This mixed history of private *land* ownership is to be contrasted with the universal and unbroken history of the private ownership of personal property – things such as clothing, tools, and cooking utensils. Brown, supra note 38, at 139–140; S. Bowles & J.-K. Choi, *The First Property Rights Revolution*, paper presented at Workshop on the Co-evolution of Behaviors and Institutions, Santa Fe Institute, January 10–12, 2003, available at http://international.ucla.edu/crns/files.bowles_choi.pdf.

51. In their survey, Youngberg and Hanson found that homicide and trespass rates in nomadic forager societies were consistently lower than modern rates (trespass lower no doubt because of restricted notions of real property), but that assault and theft rates varied from much higher to much lower than modern rates, depending on the particular nomadic forager society. Note 47 supra.

52. Property is not the only fundamental distributive problem faced by groups. Another one is sex. Dominance hierarchies did much to solve both problems. And of course in many societies, though not all, the two problems were solved simultaneously by having mates treated like property.

53. Much of the discussion in this section is based on the work of my friend and Gruter Institute colleague, Jeffrey Stake, who has written extensively and insightfully on the evolutionary roots of property, and their connections to common law property doctrines. See, for example, his essay *The Property*

Instinct, in LAW AND THE BRAIN **185** (S. Zeki & O. Goodenough, eds., Oxford 2004).

54. N. B. Davies, *Territorial defence in the speckled wood butterfly* (Pararge ageria): *the resident always wins*, ANIMAL BEHAV., **26(1)**, 138–147 (1978).

55. The sheer amount of time of possession is not the only factor; possession during some periods can be more important than during others. For example, to a robin a single day of possessing a territory during the critically important spring mating time is the equivalent of ten days of possessing the same territory during the winter. J. Tobias, *Asymmetric territorial contests in the European robin: the role of settlement costs*, ANIMAL BEHAV., **54**(1), 9–21 (1997).

56. For a comprehensive discussion of the endowment effect and its evolutionary roots, see S. Brosnan & O. Jones, *Law, Biology and Property: A New Theory of the Endowment Effect*, **49** WM. & MARY L. REV. 1935 (2008).

57. So dearly do we hold this notion of the sanctity of promise that it plays a central part in all our great religions. In most ancient religions, gods were all powerful dictators who caused everything to happen for no more reason than that they wanted it to happen. The gods of the Egyptians, Babylonians, and Assyrians, for example, though they had some jurisdictional limitations, were the capricious repositories of everything over which we humans had no control. Some years they made the Nile flood, some years they didn't. You'd better do what they say. You'd better make sacrifices to them. But then the God of the Old Testament came along, and something happened quite unique in the history of religion, indeed, in the history of human thought. God the Dictator became God the Promisor. He was all-powerful, but with one giant exception. God himself somehow became bound to keep his own promises, the most important ones called "covenants." "Testament" and "covenant" both mean "promise" in Greek, and indeed the Old Testament is a collection of stories about the promises between the Jews and God, the Jews' various breaches of those promises, the punishment God inflicts for those breaches, and God's serial reformation of the contracts after each of the breaches. This was a very different kind of God than the God of Gilgamesh or the Pharaohs, who just toyed around with us. This new God had a conscience, and he knew it was wrong to break his own promises (and of course for the Jews to break theirs). Christianity completed this humanization of God. The God of the New Testament is not only a famously kinder, gentler, and more feminine God, he does something very human – he dies. He dies so that we might complete a second kind of covenant: renew your faith in God, and he will give you the biggest prize of all. Not land or high fertility rates or prowess in battle, but eternal life. Islam, the last of the Abrahamic religions, is also replete with the centrality of promise. In fact, the Qur'an says that when a Muslim makes a promise, Allah is not only a witness to the promise but also

a guarantor of it. Every promise, at least between Muslims, is enforceable by the power of Allah.

58. Promises *in* marriage, just like promises *to* marry, were sometimes enforceable and sometimes not, depending on the society and the era. The common law recognized that a married person (traditionally, only the husband) could sue a third party for adultery ("criminal conversation"), and if the adulterer won the wife away from her husband then the jilted husband could sue the adulterer for what the law called "alienation of affection." Here again, these causes of action have been abolished in most common law jurisdictions.

59. C. P. THORPE & J. C. L. BAILEY, COMMERCIAL CONTRACTS 158 (Kogan Page 1999).

60. In general, damages for breach of contract are compensatory, and designed to place the wronged party in the economic position, if not in the actual position, he would have been in had the breaching party not breached. RESTATEMENT (SECOND) OF CONTRACTS § 3474 (1981). A second kind of substitute remedy is disgorgement, under which the wronged party is awarded not the monetary value of what he would have received under the contract, but rather the monetary benefit the breaching party enjoyed from breaching. Disgorgement is typically limited to so-called opportunistic breach, or what economists would call efficient breach, where the breaching party intentionally breached because the contract became economically disadvantageous. See RESTATEMENT (THIRD) OF RESTITUTION § 39 (2010). If, by contrast, a party to a contract enters into it without any present intention of performing it, his breach might be considered fraud, entitling the wronged party to compensatory and punitive damages. RESTATEMENT (FIRST) OF CONTRACTS § 473 (1932); RESTATEMENT (SECOND) OF TORTS § 530 (1965).

61. Many legal scholars have recognized this point. See, e.g., CHARLES FRIED, CONTRACT AS PROMISE (Harvard 1981). By contrast, more economically-minded scholars have attempted to remove moral imperatives from the law of contracts. Oliver Wendell Holmes, Jr., once famously pleaded that we should try to remove all moral language from the law, so that, in the case of contracts, "the duty to keep a contract at common law means a prediction that you must pay damages if you do not keep it – and nothing else." Oliver Wendell Holmes, Jr., *The Path of the Law*, 10 HARV. L. REV. **457**, 462 (1897).

62. This question can become a bit complicated if the contract itself addresses remedies for breach, as modern contracts almost always do. In a sense, one is *performing* a contract, not breaching it, if one pays the very damages contemplated by the promise. See Steven Shavell, *Is Breaching a Contract Immoral?*, HARV. L. & ECON. DISCUSSION PAPER NO. 531 (2005), available at http://papers.ssrn.com/sol3/papers.cfm?abstract_id=868592&rec=1&srcabs=899774##.

63. B. Knutson et al., *Neural antecedents of the endowment effect*, NEURON, **58(5)**, 814–822 (2008).

64. E.g., J. Rilling et al., *A neural basis for social cooperation*, NEURON, **35(2)**, 395–405 (2002); F. Krueger et al., *Neural correlates of trust*, PROC. NAT. ACAD. SCI., **104(50)**, 20084–20089 (2007).

65. Although we will see in Chapter 3 that these embedded rules gain some salience by the sheer force of our own consciences, what I call "first-party punishment." Adherence to them was also helped by the fear of retaliation, what I call in Chapter 4 "second-party punishment."

2 DETECTING AND BLAMING

Draw the curtain, the fraud is over.

François Rabelais

DETECTING CHEATERS

At the end of the movie *Casablanca*, Rick (Humphrey Bogart) shoots a German major who is trying to prevent Ilsa (Ingrid Bergman) and her husband from fleeing. The local police arrive, led by Rick's friend Louie (Claude Rains). Louie knows Rick was the shooter, but rather than arrest him Louie famously tells his officers to "round up the usual suspects."

It seems obvious that we cannot effectively punish cheating without knowing who to punish. If deterrence had mattered less to the social stability of our emergent groups, we probably could have gotten away with a symbolic kind of halfhearted punishment, with "rounding up the usual suspects." On the other hand, if deterrence had mattered more we might have gotten away with punishing everybody or a subset of everybody, without caring much about individual guilt. Roman legions suffered a practice called decimation, under which every tenth soldier in a disobedient or cowardly legion was killed regardless of the extent of his individual participation in the disobedience or cowardice.[1]

But the groups in which our ancestors evolved were not like either of these two extremes. Cheating was a major threat to group stability, so punishment had to be real, not symbolic. But over-punishment was also a major threat, because our groups were only loosely and precariously bound, at least compared to Roman legions. Too much punishment was as destabilizing as too little. For real punishment to work in these kinds of groups, for it to heal the wounds of defection instead of reopening them, it had to be reliably aimed at individual cheaters. Punishing the innocent in our emergent groups not only did not deter the guilty, it encouraged cheating. If I am going to be punished whether or not I am guilty of cheating, then I might as well cheat.

To one extent or another, our legal systems have always been concerned with the problem of reliably detecting the guilty, and thus with minimizing the risk of punishing the innocent. Guilt-detection took many forms across systems and over time, including, as we will see in later chapters, theological methods that sound awfully unreliable to our modern ears. Whatever their particulars, these systems were all designed to achieve some acceptable level of reliable guilt-detection, precisely because our brains were built at a time when individual blame and punishment was substantially more adaptive than either symbolic punishment or group punishment.

But these cultural systems for guilt-detection are probably quite recent by evolutionary standards. Detecting cheaters was not much of a problem 100,000 years ago because the defections that mattered most were really big defections, and our groups were small. Consider a shockingly common kind of big defection – murder. Some anthropologists have estimated that homicide was responsible for as many as one in five human deaths when we were emerging as a species, an astonishing number considering the harshness of the conditions and our resulting short life spans.[2] With survival so precarious, it is hard to imagine that there were enough of us left to murder, especially at a 20 percent clip. But murder could be a brilliant survival strategy. In many circumstances, there was no more adaptive a human behavior than killing one's sexual rivals and stealing their mates.[3] And that's often just *within* groups. Our territorial clashes with other groups were unrestrained by any cooperative instincts, and in fact were greatly enhanced by our ability to cooperate with each other to wage war against outsiders.

The special kind of violence aimed at rivals is not unique to humans. Males of several different species of mammals, including lions, cougars, cheetahs, wolves, and hyenas, kill the offspring of rival males. These killings not only remove a future rival, they often put the mother of the dead cub into estrus, and the killers impregnate them. Similar infanticide-then-sex behaviors have been documented in mountain gorillas and several species of monkeys.[4] Territorially-driven adult male-on-male rival killings are also well-documented in chimpanzees.[5]

When humans lived in relatively small groups of mostly related members, these kinds of spectacular defections typically became known the moment they happened. Aunt Jane would notice right away if someone killed her brother and his children and then moved in with her sister-in-law. Not only did we live with many other members, those other members were built by natural selection to be on the lookout for all kinds of cheaters, let alone killers. Less spectacular defections – the faking of an injury to avoid the hunt, the stealing of a small bit of food – were still likely witnessed by group members with a direct stake in the costs of the wrong. The intensity of our social living meant that almost all behaviors, both prosocial and antisocial, were there for all to see.

Even when the cheating was secret, our small groups probably didn't have to spend lots of energy on detection. Many of these secret wrongs, by their very nature, were likely to cause small harms – harms that, even if detected, were likely to be too small to punish. And most importantly, even when a secret wrong caused great harm, everyone knew everyone else in the small group, and detection was often simply a matter of talking to each other. We do this all the time in our modern small groups. Imagine you come home from work, find your expensive vase broken, and hear your children blaming each other. You don't need complicated truth-finding institutions or forensic experts to reliably get to the bottom of things. You *know* your children, and it is pretty easy to figure out what happened. This is probably how our small groups handled most secret wrongdoing.

In fact, our brains are at their detective best when reasoning about social violations versus other kinds of violations. In a series of experiments done in the 1980s, researchers discovered that even though the forms of the logical problems were identical, subjects were substantially better at logical reasoning when the problem was presented as a social problem rather than as an abstract problem.[6] We are especially good at detecting social defection.

So our brains evolved without the need to devote much special attention to the problem of detecting wrongdoers. In our small close-knit groups, most important wrongs were obvious, most secret wrongs did not cause enough harm to justify punishment, and even the occasional secret wrong with high harm was not hard to figure out, especially with our socially well-tuned brains. In fact, as we have already seen, the whole notion of a "crime" being committed against anything larger than a family unit is, with a few exceptions, entirely a modern invention. For most of human history the reach of the criminal law was generally no longer than the reach of the authority of the family, and as a result there was very little need for investigation or other truth-finding mechanisms.

But now change our vase example to your child and a *neighbor's* child blaming each other for breaking the vase. Now your feelings about the situation are completely different, and much more complicated. You worry very much about whether it was your child or the neighbor's, and you don't quite know how to decide. You worry about how certain you need to be, and what exactly you will tell the neighbors if you decide it was their child who broke the vase. When the "group" is not a neighborhood but a whole town, now detection becomes a significant problem. Lost in the anonymity of many strangers, wrongdoers not only have more opportunities to do wrongs that likely will be difficult to trace back to them, but they and their victims are also more likely to be strangers, and more skeptical of one another.

Institutions for detection have always lagged far behind institutions for punishment, reinforcing the idea that our punishment instincts were forged at a time when we largely punished only the crimes we witnessed.[7] Institutions for detection are a relatively recent invention. In England, police forces were unknown until the first appearance of constables in London in the mid-1500s. Even then, their function was largely a peacekeeping one, not an investigatory one. In fact, although constables in this period could in theory arrest people pursuant to a written warrant, the written warrant was almost unheard of, mostly because so few people, even officials, could write. The great bulk of arrests took place only in two circumstances: when the constable witnessed the crime himself; or when others did and the constable witnessed their "hue and cry."[8] It was not until the 1700s that constables began to change from peacekeepers to investigative agents.

When we survey the history of the jury in Chapter 7, we will see many examples of a similar tension between the jury as a new-fangled truth-finding body and the jury as an ancient blaming and punishing body. In fact, many jury historians believe that the first function of the jury was simply to decide which of the guilt-assuming punishments a defendant must endure. As our groups got bigger and bigger, as the opportunities for undetected crime grew and as we simultaneously lost confidence in our informal ability to separate the guilty from the innocent, the jury – already in place as a blaming and punishing institution – became over time the truth-finding institution we think of today. And yet its original blaming and punishing purposes remain paramount. Even modern juries and judges seldom perform any serious sort of truth-finding function. Their role continues to be focused on what it has been for 100,000 years: to blame then punish.

BLAMING CHEATERS

Sentencing proceedings have all the trappings of a morality play, with blame playing the starring role. It is, after all, at the imposition of the sentence where the community, through its representative the judge, finally gets to shake its collective finger at the criminal.[9] Real blame, as opposed to representational blame, happens in our brains much sooner: the moment we are convinced another person has committed a wrong. Everything else – handwringing about whether the defendant was too crazy, drunk, or young to be held criminally responsible, and, if he is responsible, what kind of punishment we should impose – are inquiries that come much later. This is because our brains evolved in an environment in which it was important to make very quick blaming decisions. We "blink" to our blaming judgments, to use Malcolm Gladwell's phrase, and in fact blame is not really even a "judgment" at all.[10]

Picture yourself standing in line at the grocery store, when you see the man ahead of you take a stick of gum from the shelf and put it in his pocket. You immediately feel outraged and angry. You may well take several moments to reflect about what to *do* about the situation, and your choices may be difficult ones. But these difficult decisions are all post-blame decisions. Blame is that powerful, and in fact largely uncontrollable, voice you hear yelling, "Hey, *I* have to follow the rules, why doesn't *he*?"

It may sound like the blame reaction is nothing more complex than being angry at a cheater. But it turns out it is much more nuanced than that. Not only do we blink our way to blame, but those immediate blaming judgments are highly graded to the kinds of wrongs we see. You will feel much stronger waves of blame if that person in front of you stabs the clerk than if he just pockets some gum. Of course, culture plays a big role in the amount of blame we feel. Perhaps a South Sea Islander blames the theft of a boat more than a Manhattan teacher blames the theft of a subway pass. Even as between Manhattan teachers, they will bring the sum of their different life experiences to bear when they engage in this act of blaming. Because blame seems so complicated, it has long been commonly held that the blame reaction, even within a single culture, is a highly individualized response. The legal version of this commonly held belief is the conventional wisdom that ten judges will impose ten different sentences in identical cases because they feel ten different levels of blame.

But it turns out that blame is not nearly as individualized, or complicated, as this conventional wisdom assumes. A few years ago Paul Robinson, a criminologist at Penn, John Darley, a Princeton legal philosopher, and Rob Kurzban, a Penn psychologist, decided to test this assumption that blame is rife with cultural, temporal, and individual overlays, and indeed that the act of blaming may itself be entirely a learned behavior. Robinson and his colleagues wrote twenty-four short crime scenarios, and asked subjects, in both live and online versions of the experiment, to rank the crimes from least to most "blameworthy."[11] They gave the subjects no definition of "blameworthy." Each of the twenty-four scenarios involved what the experimenters labeled "core" crimes – crimes involving taking property or inflicting physical injury. That is, in our parlance, crimes that violated our Rule 1 – don't steal (with "steal" taking on its more generalized connotation of also not taking someone's health).

The ranking task was on its face quite difficult. This was not a matter of asking whether armed robbery or shoplifting was more blameworthy. The twenty-four narratives not only spanned a wide range of harm, they also required subjects to make a host of seemingly complex and nuanced judgments about crimes that appeared very similar. In in-person versions of the experiment participants were often seen changing their minds about their ordering. I took a sample of the web-based version, and found myself switching my initial ordering several times.[12] A few examples of the actual scenarios Robinson and his colleagues used should give the flavor of how difficult and subtle these judgments seemed. Here are three so-called adjacent scenarios at the high harm end ("adjacent" means Robinson and his colleagues predicted these would be ranked next to each other on the continuum of blame):

1. John works out a plan to kill his 60-year-old invalid mother for the inheritance. He drags her to her bed, puts her in, and lights her oxygen mask with a cigarette, hoping to make it look like an accident. The elderly woman screams as her clothes catch fire and she burns to death. John just watches her burn.

2. John kidnaps an 8-year-old girl for ransom, rapes her, then records the child's screams as he burns her with a cigarette lighter, sending the recording to her parents to induce them to pay his ransom demand. Even though they pay as directed, John strangles the child to death to avoid leaving a witness.

3. A woman at work reveals John's misdeeds to his employer, thereby getting him fired. John devises a plan to get even with her. The next week he forces the woman into his car at knife point and drives her to a secluded area where he shoots her to death.

Before I reveal Robinson's results, take a few seconds to think about which of these scenarios you would rank as least, next and most "blameworthy." I can tell you now that as long as you do this honestly, I should be able to predict your rankings, no matter who you are or where you come from. And like all of Robinson's subjects, you don't need a definition of "blameworthiness"; you were born to make quite subtle blame distinctions.

Here are three additional adjacent scenarios at the low harm end. Try to rank these as well, again, from least to most blameworthy:

1. The owner has posted rules at his all-you-can-eat buffet that expressly prohibit taking food away; patrons can only take what they eat at the buffet. The owner has set the price of the buffet accordingly. John purchases dinner at the buffet, but when he leaves he takes with him two whole pies to give to a friend.

2. John is a cab driver who picks up a high school student. Because the customer seems confused about the money transaction, John decides he can trick her and gives her $20 less change than he knows she is owed.
3. John notices in a small family-owned music store a T-shirt with the logo of his favorite band. While the store clerk is preoccupied with inventory, John places the $15 T-shirt in his coat and walks out, with no intention of paying for it.

All the adjacent narratives along the continuum of twenty-four narratives involved seemingly close calls just like these. And yet subjects showed a breathtaking degree of agreement, across all measured demographic differences. Virtually every participant ranked the twenty-four narratives in exactly the same way, and where there were differences they were almost always just one ranking off between adjacent narratives.

The pair-wise agreement – whether any given scenario was ranked more or less blameworthy than any other given scenario – was in excess of 90 percent. A more sophisticated measure of whether lists agree, called Kendall's W, was even more impressive. Kendall's W ("K"), also sometimes called the coefficient of concordance, is a statistical measure of the agreement between different rankers in ranking lists of items, which takes into consideration not only differences in rankings but the degree of those differences. When K = 1.00, all rankings of all rankers are exactly the same. When K = 0.5, the rankings can be said to be in moderate agreement. When K = 0 there is no agreement beyond that which would be expected if the rankings of each ranker were random. The in-person results from the Robinson et al. study had an average K of 0.95. The web-based results had an average K of 0.88.[13]

It is hard to overstate the magnitude of this agreement Robinson offers a couple comparisons for some perspective. In a study asking subjects to rank Israel, Canada, and New York according to the risk of suffering a terrorist attack there, the outcome, which researchers described as representing a "general agreement," had a K = 0.52. When men are asked to rate women's attractiveness, they show even better agreement, with K = 0.54. The only tasks that even remotely approach the levels of agreement in the Robinson blameworthiness studies are tasks that can only be described as rote or self-evident. For example, unimpaired subjects score a $K = 0.95$ when asked to rank objects by brightness, and $K = 0.97$ when ranking faces by how much pain they are feeling.[14]

These blaming results cut across gender, age, race, income, education, political party, marital status, number of children, religion, and religious activity. So it easy for me now to reveal that you most likely ordered the co-employee ambush killing as the least blameworthy of the three high harm scenarios, burning up mom as next and the child kidnap-torture-murder as the most blameworthy. You probably ranked the low end harms beginning with stealing the pies as the least blameworthy, stealing the T-shirt next, and the crooked cabbie as the most blameworthy.[15]

In a second part of the experiment, Robinson and his colleagues constructed twelve additional scenarios, which they guessed would not recruit any deeply shared blaming intuitions. These so-called noncore crimes involved things such as drug use, drunk driving with no harm to others, prostitution, and bestiality. And, in fact, the results were substantially less robust, with pair-wise agreement of only around 50 percent and the average $K = 0.55$.[16] This lack of agreement for noncore crimes, unlike the agreement for core crimes, seems quite dependent on several demographic measures.[17]

Core crimes touch on the things that all humans care about for our survival – being free from having our property stolen and our persons violated. Brains built to blame these kinds of wrongs in a predictable fashion would be brains that would have helped us glue our groups together with just the right amount of deterrence.[18]

So if we all share refined instincts about relative blame, why are judges' sentences still so variable between what appear to be similarly situated defendants? Indeed, Congress believed that federal sentences were so wildly variable that it created the Federal Sentencing Commission in 1984, which in turn created the federal sentencing guidelines, in an effort to rein in that variability. Robinson and his colleagues explain this variance by what they call the "problem of endpoint." They posit that the real culprit in the varying sentences judges mete out is not the differing blaming intuitions of the judges, but rather the fact that those judges simply have different internal scales on which they lay their presumably quite uniform judgments about relative blameworthiness. That is, when Judge A gives a bank robber sixty months in prison and Judge B gives an identical bank robber six months in prison, that's not because Judge A thinks bank robbery is ten times worse than Judge B does. On the contrary, like all of Robinson's subjects, Judges A and B would rank bank robbery scenarios pretty much the same as everyone else in the pantheon of blameworthiness relative to other crimes. It's just that Judge A uses a different, harsher, yardstick on which to place those ranked crimes. His endpoint for the most blameworthy crime may be life in prison or the death penalty, and Judge B's may be twenty years in prison. The same is true for the start point – a very minor crime may trigger a two-month sentence in Judge A's court and probation in Judge B's court.[19]

OK, so humans have a deeply embedded instinct to blame cheaters, and that instinct is remarkably refined and consistent across different kinds of crimes. But what drives that instinct? That is, what factors make almost all of us blame the child kidnapper-torturer-murderer a little bit more than we blame the man who lit his mother on fire? The answer is that the amount we blame (at least for core wrongs that violate Rule 1) seems to be the product of only two variables: the intent of the wrongdoer and the amount of harm he caused, with intent, perhaps surprisingly, being the more important of the two.

Robinson's experiments were all about how blame is driven by our perceptions of harm, given that his hypothetical John was acting intentionally in all the scenarios. But it turns out that how we judge the intentions of wrongdoers is much more important to our sense of blame than the amount of harm they cause. This hierarchy between intent and harm makes some evolutionary sense, given that blame is the first step toward punishment, and punishment was a serious and costly matter to our ancestors. If we gauged our blame only to the amount of harm, we would be grossly over-blaming (and therefore grossly over-punishing) by natural selection's cost-benefit metric.

To see why, imagine an ancestor who blamed (and punished) based only on harm. Let's call him Rex. If you punch Rex, Rex punches back. If you bump Rex, Rex bumps you. So far, this is a kind of reflexive retaliation, or second-party punishment. But because Rex is also a social creature, he will also feel a similar reflexive urge to punish others when he sees them commit wrongs against third parties. This is retribution, or third-party punishment. As both a second- and third-party punisher, Rex is strictly an eye-for-an-eye guy.

But accidents happen, and when they do Rex and Rex's group pay the same big costs punishing accidents as they do punishing intentional wrongs, even though they get a much more modest deterrent benefit with the accidents. Punishing accidents may make some people more careful (and may also deter the faking of accidents), but some accidents happen even when people are as careful as they can be. Punishing in these circumstances is all cost and no benefit. In fact, punishing accidents can be a counter-deterrent. We are exquisitely sensitive to being treated fairly, and punishing the undeterrable just to deter others doesn't quite seem fair. As C. S. Lewis put it:

> What can be more immoral than to inflict suffering on me for the sake of deterring others if I do not deserve it? And what can be more outrageous than to catch me and submit me to a disagreeable process of moral improvement without my consent, unless (once more) I deserve it?[20]

Punishing accidents is a bit like punishing innocent Roman legionnaires by decimation – it doesn't deter them (because there was nothing to deter), and it doesn't really deter anyone else, except from faking accidents.[21]

So now imagine a more sophisticated ancestor – let's call him Nigel. In the first place, Nigel doesn't even pay blaming attention to extremely low-level harms. He'll notice being bumped a bit in a crowd, but his blaming instincts don't even get triggered by such small slights. More importantly, for harms above this de minimis threshold, Nigel blames first based on his assessment of the intent of the harmer rather than on the amount of the harm. He is socially attuned enough to be able to detect whether a group member harmed him or another group member on purpose or accidentally. If Nigel determines it was an unavoidable accident, he does not blame at all, even if the harm is high. If he determines it was intentional, his full blame instincts kick in, graded to harm.

Our brains are Nigel brains because Nigel brains had a significant evolutionary advantage over Rex brains. Ancestors who blamed (and risked having to punish) every slight no matter whether intentional or accidental would have been spectacularly unsuccessful in our delicately balanced social groups. They would have incurred the high costs of punishing every harm without deriving any significant deterrent benefits for accidental harms. Their groups would have unraveled from over-punishment, and they would not have survived. Brains that could instead blame (and punish) only when the benefits of such acts would likely outweigh their costs, and by a large amount, would have been much more successful.

In a perfect world, if our Nigel brains had unlimited time and energy, we could in theory have calculated each blaming decision by weighing the costs of punishment against its deterrent benefits. But our emergent world was not perfect. We had neither unlimited time nor unlimited energy to make these deterrent calculations. And the deterrent calculations are in any event impossibly complicated. The costs of punishment, as we have already seen, were dear to our ancestors, and depended on things like the risk of violence by a resisting wrongdoer and his family, not to mention the more mundane but still deadly risk of having him and his family bolt the group entirely. These are hard risks to measure, and require strategic guesses about how much punishment a wrongdoer and his family will accept before resisting, how vigorously they will resist, and how their resistance will impact the group.

The benefits side of the calculation is even more daunting. There are two kinds of deterrence – what criminologists call "special deterrence" and "general deterrence." Special deterrence is the deterrence of the wrongdoer himself. General deterrence is the deterrence of everybody else watching us punish the wrongdoer. On the special deterrence side, our calculating brain would have to determine the chances that, without blaming and punishing this particular wrongdoer, he will defect again in the future, and the costs of that future defection. It would also have to calculate the amount that these risks, and costs, decrease if we impose a particular amount of punishment. These same impossible guesses, in spades, are required of the general deterrence component. No one can reliably calculate, before the fact, how many armed robberies will not be committed in my community because I sentenced one armed robber today to seventeen years in prison instead of fifteen years.

Blame, with its two components intent and harm, is a remarkably good proxy for these impossible deterrence calculations. A wrongdoer who is willing to cause harm to satisfy his own personal desires is very likely to be willing to cause similar levels of harm in the future, for no other reason than we can be sure he will have future desires. The same is true for general deterrence. We can be sure that all of our group members will have future desires, and it is therefore important to deter them from future harms by blaming (then punishing) intentional wrongdoers.

As between intentional wrongdoers, it then makes sense to blame those who caused high harms more than those who caused small (or no) harms, because harm is a pretty straightforward measure of the costs of the crime and therefore of the benefits component of both special and general deterrence.

On the other hand, if our wrongdoer was not satisfying his desires – if he was just careless – then our blame instinct should get ratcheted way down, precisely because the deterrent effects will be so much less. Punishing accidents may still have some deterrent benefit – it will tend to make both the negligent actor and all of us in the group more careful in the future. But in both cases blaming those kinds of acts will give us much less deterrent bang for the buck than blaming intentional wrongs, simply because real deterrence happens when we consider choices, not when we ignore risks. Rational criminals considering robbing a bank will have to take into account the risks of detection and the costs of punishment; teenagers blowing through a stop sign aren't considering anything.

Our brains, and our legal systems, work just this way. First, we do not pay any blaming attention at all to most small harms. For harms that do grab our blaming attention, we use the wrongdoer's intention as our most important measure of blame. Then, as between wrongs inflicted with the same level of intention, we break the tie with the amount of harm. We do this quite automatically, and without making any conscious evaluation of intent and harm.

To see how deeply engrained these notions are in all our brains, consider this famous hypothetical from behavioral psychology. Grace and her friend work at a chemical factory, and are having lunch in the break room. The friend asks Grace to retrieve some sugar from the counter.

From this stem set of facts we construct four different variations covering each of the four possibilities generated by intent and harm:

1. Intent/Harm. In this version, Grace decides to murder her friend, and intentionally gives the friend poison instead of sugar. The friend dies.
2. Intent/No harm. Grace decides to murder her friend, and gives her what Grace thinks is poison. It turns out to be sugar and the friend is not injured.
3. No intent/Harm. Grace does not realize the substance she gives her friend is poison rather than sugar, and the friend dies.
4. No intent/no harm. Grace intends to give her friend sugar, and in fact does so. The friend is not injured.

Humans across virtually all cultures and demographics blame these four scenarios exactly in the order they are listed here: intentional harm is the most blameworthy; bad intentions with no harm is next; no bad intentions with harm is next; and no bad intentions and no harm is the least blameworthy, and in fact not blameworthy at all.[22] The law also reflects these blaming instincts exactly. The first scenario is murder, the second attempted murder, and the third probably at most civil negligence (if Grace should have been more careful). Here's a matrix summarizing the typical interaction between intent and harm, together with the labels the law puts on the interactions (in parentheses):

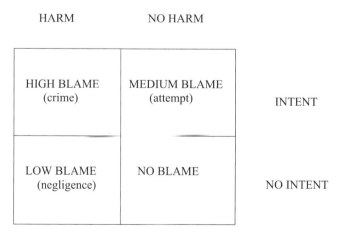

Figure 2.1. Blame matrix.

Our adult brains work just like this matrix. They have dedicated circuits devoted to the assessment of intentionality and harm, and to the calculation of blame based on those two assessments, using intent as the main driver and harm only as a tiebreaker. Part of those blaming circuits lie in a region called the temporoparietal junction, or TPJ. It is an area of the cortex roughly even with the top of the ears. See Figure 2.1. It seems that the right TPJ (rTPJ) performs a central role in integrating intent with harm. This was proved in 2010 in a spectacular experiment by an MIT neuroscientist Rebecca Saxe and her colleagues.[23]

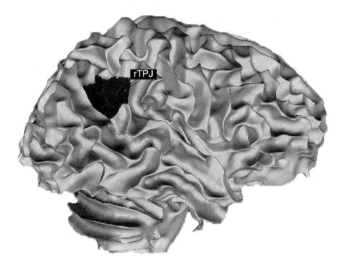

Figure 2.2. The right TPJ. Courtesy of Matthew Ginther.

Saxe ran the Grace poison/sugar experiment with two groups of subjects. One was the control group, and of course they ordered the four hypotheticals just like all psychiatrically unimpaired adults do – blaming the intentional killing most, the attempted killing next, and the accidental killing least. But then Saxe and her colleagues put a second group of subjects in a device called a transcranial magnetic stimulator, which creates a powerful magnetic field that can be aimed rather precisely to temporarily deactivate the electrical signals in parts of the brain. Saxe and her colleagues aimed the machine to deactivate the right TPJs in this second group of subjects' brains. When those subjects were then asked to assess blame in the four Grace hypotheticals, they blamed based on harm, using intention to break the ties, completely flipping around the ordinary intent/harm hierarchy. They blamed the intentional killing most, the accidental killing next, and the attempted killing least. They did all of this while they were completely conscious, and completely unaware of how the disruption of their blame circuits were so profoundly affecting their moral judgments.

The Saxe experiment shows the rTPJ is necessary to the integration of intent and harm, but not necessary to the evaluation of either. Subjects with their rTPJs deactivated could still assess harm accurately, and indeed blamed based primarily on that assessment. They could also assess intent accurately, since they used intent to break the tie when the harm was identical. And they could still put the two together, but just not in the way unimpaired brains put them together. All of this suggests that the brain may have three quite distinct circuits – one for assessing intention, one for assessing harm, and a third to integrate the two assessments into a level of blame.

By the way, young children also blame based primarily on harm, with intention only as a tiebreaker. That's probably because it takes some development time for their blaming circuits, including their TPJs, to come fully on line. But with fully-developed blame circuits, psychiatrically unimpaired humans blame first on the basis of their assessment of intention and use harm only as a tiebreaker. So here's what we might call the adult Blaming Tree:

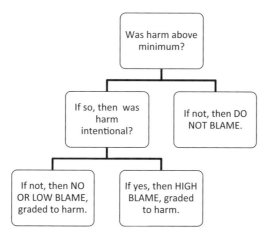

Figure 2.3. Blaming tree.

Each step in the brain's blaming tree can of course be deeply influenced by culture and context, including the very first step – the level of threshold harm. Japanese subway riders may tolerate a push to the point that they don't even notice it; Afghan feudal lords may consider that same level of push a mortal threat. Another important complication is that both intent and harm have gradations, in kind as well as degree.

Gradations of Harm

Harm can of course range over magnitude. Killing victims harms them more than just breaking their arms. But harm can also range over type. For example, all things being equal, we seem to blame harms to kin more than harms to non-kin, and harms to the very young and very old more than harms to everyone else. Thus, the worst harm of all along these dimensions is when a wrongdoer harms his own children. This kind of sensitivity to intra-family harm made sense. Harm to one's children does great evolutionary damage because it reduces the chances that the parent's genes will make it into future generations.[24] Thus, in Robinson's experiment (where, remember, intent was held constant because all the wrongs were intentional), we blame the fellow who burns up his mother a little bit more than the coworker killer, most likely because of the kin/non-kin difference. And youth seems to trump kin when we are talking about injuring unrelated young victims versus related old ones. Thus, we blame the child kidnapper-torturer-murderer a little bit more than the mother-murderer. We might also blame him a little more because he not only violated Rule 1, he also violated Rule 2 by breaking his promise to return the child after the ransom was paid.

Vulnerability in general, quite apart from age but sometimes touching on it, also seems to grab our blame attention. Harm to particularly vulnerable victims, or even just to victims who are relatively vulnerable compared to the wrongdoer, triggers higher blame. This is also a part of why we blame the mother-murderer more than the co-employee-murderer. It also explains why, in Robinson's low harm examples, we blame the taxi driver more than the other two wrongdoers. The taxi driver is taking advantage of a particularly vulnerable high schooler whose skill at making change is not what it should be. Taxi drivers by the very nature of their business are almost always dealing with the vulnerable – people who do not know their way around a strange city and who must therefore depend on the driver's honesty.

We also seem more sensitive to face-to-face harm than to remote harm. This, too, is a likely remnant from our evolutionary past. It was difficult to inflict great harm at any great distance 100,000 years ago. A thrown rock or spear could kill, but we couldn't drop bombs from 30,000 feet.[25] It was the very close harms about which we had to worry most, and to which our blaming instincts are therefore specially attuned.

Similarly, we generally blame physical harm more than either property harms or purely emotional harms. In the Pleistocene, physical harms could kill us immediately. Stealing could be serious, but it was still at least one step removed from dying. And we'd be long dead from either of those harms before the ravages of purely emotional injuries would really start to affect our survival. This hierarchy of physical/property/emotional is deeply reflected in the law. Crimes of violence are usually more serious than property crimes. Most serious crimes of violence require "serious bodily injury," and the law has generally required some aspect of physical harm for "serious bodily injury." Purely emotional harms, with no physical intrusion at all – things such as defamation and the infliction of emotional distress by outrageous conduct – are usually not even criminal, and are instead typically consigned to civil remedies.[26] There are a handful of exceptions, such as rape and the crime of menacing (using a deadly weapon to cause fear of imminent bodily injury), but by and large the criminal law has traditionally required actual physical harm for its most serious crimes.[27]

The intentional prolonging of pain – torture – also seems to fire up our blaming instincts, and might even by itself explain why Robinson's child kidnap narrative was blamed most. Indeed, in states that have the death penalty, torture is often an express aggravating factor. All psychiatrically intact humans hate pain; that's exactly what pain is – a feeling our brains intensely dislike. So it is hardly surprising that we would be specially attuned to wrongs involving great pain spread over long periods of time.

Assessing harm may be even more complicated than integrating all these factors about the impacts to the victim. Recent neuroimaging experiments have suggested that when we assess harm in a third-party punishment context we also use networks attuned to the benefits enjoyed by the wrongdoer.[28] In other words, the measure of harm we use to blame may be a kind of "net harm," taking into consideration the benefits to the wrongdoer. Although surprising as a matter of traditional legal analysis,[29] this treatment of harm is entirely consistent with our brains being designed to solve The Social Problem. We are all potential cheaters, and even when we engage in third-party blame we consider, in effect, whether we might also have cheated in these circumstances if the benefits were big enough.

Our brain takes all these factors into account in assessing harm, and then seems to integrate them into a single harm value. These harm values are sensitive, specific, and remarkably consistent across individuals. That's why, when the wrongdoer's intention is held constant, we get the spectacular results of the Robinson studies, with blame meticulously and predictably graded to the amount of harm, as driven by all these subtle considerations.

Gradations of Intent

Our brains were also built to recognize different varieties of intent. We've already discussed two of the most important kinds – intentional wrongs and accidents – and the deep evolutionary engines driving that difference. Every ancient civilization that has left a record on the issue – including the Babylonians, Jews, Egyptians, Greeks, and Romans – has recognized that blameworthy wrongs must usually have some component related to the wrongdoer's state of mind, in order to distinguish them from pure accidents.[30] Thus, blameworthy wrongs have almost always consisted of a harmful act plus a bad intention. The act alone, without some level of intention, is generally not a crime. This central notion of what constitutes a crime is remarkably old. The English precept from which the law gets its phrase *mens rea*, which means "guilty mind," comes from the twelfth century, but the principle is much older than that.[31]

All unimpaired humans recognize, and are extraordinarily good at recognizing, the difference between intentional wrongs and accidents. From almost the moment we are born, human infants (and, indeed, many other newborn animals) are visually sensitive not to color or shape but to motion, and not to just any kind of motion but to unexpected motion. From about the age of three and a half months in humans, our brains pay special attention to objects that are behaving as if a force other than ordinary gravity is being applied to them. In the most famous of these experiments on human infants and force-driven motion, conducted by David Premack and his colleagues in the 1980s, human infants paid no attention or looked away quickly from movies showing various geometric shapes behaving inertially or ballistically (that is, without any force being applied to them other than gravity). But as soon as a shape accelerated in a direction other than down, or changed directions, or otherwise behaved as if some unseen force other than ordinary gravity were moving it about, the infants paid a great deal of attention.[32]

Brains tuned to forces would have been good brains to have. Forces are what kill us, whether they are tree limbs driven by tornadoes or spears flung through the air by our enemies. Force-driven movement is also a reliable predictor of the presence of other life-forms, which might not only be threats but could also be food or mates. Force-driven motion also suggests at least the possibility of an *intention* behind the force, and in this very rudimentary way even infants can distinguish accidents from non-accidents, by distinguishing movements with forces behind them from movements with just gravity behind them.

Human infants from the same tender ages can even infer the nature of the intentions behind the forces. In another series of experiments, Premack and his colleagues showed human infants four different kinds of abstract animations involving two moving disks. In one case, one disk gently touched the other ("touching"). In the contrasting case ("hitting"), it sharply struck the other and the other recoiled. In the "helping" case, one disk seems to assist the other in escaping from an enclosure; and in the contrasting "hurtful" case, one disk seems to be preventing the other from escaping. Not only can human infants distinguish touching from hitting, and helping from hurting, they react positively to the touching and helping movies (by looking longer at them), and negatively to the hitting and hurting movies (by turning away from them).[33] It is a short distance from that kind of ability to the deep ability all of us have to distinguish intentional and accidental wrongs.

Our brains are so well-tuned to the difference between accidents and intentional harms that we detect that difference in a fraction of a second. Within 60 milliseconds (six-hundredths of a second) after seeing intentional harms, our TPJs send detectable signals they do not send when the stimulus is an accidental harm. Within 180 milliseconds after the intentional harm, those signals reach the amygdala and ventromedial prefrontal cortex. We are then primed to blame, in about a tenth of a second after we witness intentional harm, which is probably even before we are conscious of the intentional harm.[34]

But our brains are even better than that. We can also distinguish between two kinds of accidents, avoidable and unavoidable, and even between two kinds of intentions, the kind where the wrongdoer desires the harm that he causes and the kind where the wrongdoer is willing to harm even though that might not be his primary desire.

At the accident end, we are pretty good at distinguishing those kinds of accidents that seem caused by the fates from those caused by human inattention. No one gets blamed (anymore) for tornadoes, but everyone blames a driver who runs a red light while fumbling with his cell phone. We probably emerged with, and still have, a powerful urge to blame mysterious harms on each other. Brains that assumed that the giant rock rolling down the mountain at us was pushed by someone trying to kill us, or by angry gods, would probably have been good brains to have, provided our suspicions had the effect of making us more alert as opposed to running off on endless and baseless vendettas. In our worst collective moments, we have acted on those evolved suspicions of human cause. Last year's crop failures were caused by witches. My poverty is being caused by immigrants.

But as more and more of nature's secrets have yielded to our scientific inquiries, fewer and fewer harms seem mysterious to us, and this evolutionary prejudice seems to be waning. There are still pockets of it, though. I suspect the most extreme climate change activists need to worry about whether their strong views are being affected by this evolutionary assumption that all poorly understood harms are caused by humans. Medical malpractice defense lawyers worry constantly about whether jurors have an embedded urge to punish someone, anyone, for bad outcomes, regardless of whether those outcomes were the product of professional negligence.

Despite these pockets of irrationality, we are pretty good overall at distinguishing blameworthy accidents from blameless ones. All of us can understand that accidents can be caused by different degrees of inattention. A perfectly careful neurosurgeon may still nick a tiny nerve; the resulting harm may simply be an unpredictable and unavoidable risk of some kinds of brain or spinal surgery. By contrast, a thoracic surgeon may nick a big nerve not because it's unavoidable but because he just wasn't paying attention to it. The law objectifies this inquiry into carelessness by having jurors ask themselves what a hypothetical reasonable surgeon would have done. If a reasonable neurosurgeon could well have nicked the nerve despite being as careful as he should be, then our neurosurgeon is not negligent. If a reasonable thoracic surgeon would not have nicked the nerve had he been as careful as he should be, then our thoracic surgeon is negligent.

In general, modern law does not criminalize negligence. Even the inattentive thoracic surgeon is at most facing a civil claim for money damages. Still, the tort system is a kind of punishment system – we blame the wrongdoer, and then we punish him by forcing him to pay money damages for his harm (and also by forcing him to go through the torture that is civil litigation). Jurors can punish grossly negligent actions even more, by awarding punitive damages above and beyond what it takes to compensate the victim.

But there is another kind of carelessness that we recognize is much worse than ordinary negligence, and bad enough that our systems criminalize it in certain limited contexts. Negligence, by definition, means the wrongdoer was unaware he was taking untoward risks. But what of the person who *knows* there is a great risk of harm but decides to act anyway? The law has called this state of mind many different things, most recently "reckless."[35] By whatever name, the idea is pretty simple. Someone who consciously disregards a substantial risk of harm is acting worse than someone who takes the same risk but simply does not perceive the risk. A surgeon may be negligent when he cuts a nerve not realizing it is there; he is reckless if he realizes it might very well be there but because he has a looming tee time he consciously disregards the risk in order to finish up quickly.

This kind of reckless behavior starts to cross over from the land of inattention to the land of desire-based harms, from accident to intention. Of course the surgeon did not desire the harm but he was consciously willing to risk it. Because of that, reckless behaviors are sometimes criminalized, especially when the harm is great. Almost every state criminalizes reckless homicide. When you consciously disregard a substantial risk that your actions may cause someone to die, and he does die, you have in most jurisdictions committed the crime of manslaughter. It is much less serious than a purposeful murder, but much more serious than mere negligence.[36]

Legal systems throughout history have recognized this difference between clueless carelessness and conscious carelessness, and it seems almost as deeply rooted as the difference between accidents and non-accidents. One of the earliest Anglo-Saxon descriptions of the distinction was contained in the *Laws of Alfred*, written in the 800s, and was lifted almost verbatim from the Book of Exodus:

> If an ox gore a man or a woman, so that they die, let it be stoned, and let not its flesh be eaten. The lord shall not be liable, if the ox were wont to push with its horns for two or three days before, and the lord knew it not; *but if he knew it, and he would not shut it in, and it then shall have slain a man or a woman, let it be stoned; and let the lord be slain.*[37]

Just as we distinguish between two kinds of accidents (negligent and reckless), we also distinguish between two kinds of intentional wrongs. The most blameworthy kind of wrong, and in many ways the simplest to describe and understand, is when the wrongdoer specifically intends the harmful results that his actions cause. This most culpable state of mind has also been called by various names, including the confusing catchall "intentional."[38] To avoid that confusion, the modern convention is to call this kind of intentional act "purposeful."[39] If I step up to you, announce that I have always hated you and that you don't deserve to live, then pull a gun, shoot you in the head and kill you, I have committed a purposeful homicide, which in most states is called first degree murder and justifies the most severe of all punishment (death or life in prison in most states).[40]

But there is another kind of intentionality that we blame less than purposefulness. Modern law calls it "knowing," and moral philosophers sometimes describe it as the "side-effect problem" or the "problem of double effects."[41] Consider two different groups of men flying bombers in a war. One group bombs cities in order to destabilize and demoralize the population, à la London or Dresden. They have purposefully killed, because, though they had a more generalized purpose of sowing terror, the way they chose to achieve that purpose was to kill. The killing *is* the terror. Contrast that with a group bombing a factory. Their purpose is to knock out the factory, and although they know that people will almost certainly be killed, such killing is not in the stream of their desires. They would be perfectly happy to knock out the factories with no loss of life. The latter group of pilots are said to have killed "knowingly," and in general modern law punishes knowing wrongs less harshly than purposeful ones.[42]

This blaming distinction between purposeful wrongs and knowing wrongs has a long philosophical history, but a much shorter legal one. Thomas Aquinas is generally credited with its first formal exposition, and moral philosophers have been arguing about it ever since.[43] The general philosophical consensus is that, all other things being equal, a desired wrong is more morally blameworthy than a harm that is a mere side effect of some other desire. But the law has been much slower to recognize this difference.

Legal systems have always recognized that what a wrongdoer "knows" about a circumstance surrounding a crime might be important. For example, if it is a crime to have sex with a girl under a certain age, then in most systems and in most definitions of such a crime the prosecution must prove that the defendant did in fact know that the girl was underage. Legal scholars call this kind of "knowing" as being knowledge of a "circumstance element," and it has been around forever.[44] But the kind of knowledge giving rise to the side-effects problem – knowledge that one's actions will almost certainly cause harm without any particular desire to cause that harm – is quite a modern legal distinction. It does not appear to have been recognized in any ancient legal system, nor by the triumvirate of legal traditions – Roman, German, then English – that made modern Western law. In fact, the first formal suggestion that "knowingly" might describe a level of culpability somewhere below purposeful but above recklessness seems have appeared in an American legal treatise on Indian law, of all things, published in the 1940s.[45]

In any event, knowingly is now rather fixed as a one of the four horsemen of culpability, in no small part because of its acceptance into the Model Penal Code. So our intentionality component of blame – which, remember, is the most important of the two components – is now typically categorized into these four varieties of states-of-mind, from most blameworthy to least: purposeful, knowing, reckless, and negligent, with negligence, though blamed civilly, seldom justifying criminal sanctions.

Although this is now the relatively settled state of the law of intentionality, at least in the United States and other common law countries, it is not at all clear that humans actually blame the way the law assumes. We know that when we hold intentionality constant we do in fact blame according to harm, and indeed that our brains have harm-dedicated circuits capable of making very fine distinctions. But what about the converse? When we hold harm constant, do humans in fact blame purposeful wrongs more than knowing ones, knowing ones more than reckless ones, and reckless ones more than negligent ones? Are our brains, which we know can distinguish accidents from non-accidents, even capable of these finer gradations of intent?

Surprisingly, there has been very little behavioral research on these questions, and almost no neuroscience. It appears, on the basis of some very recent studies, that people are in fact able to distinguish most of these intent categories, and that we do in fact blame in just the hierarchy that the law predicts.[46] The neuroscience of that hierarchy is still largely unknown.[47]

BLAME AND PUNISHMENT

Natural selection built our brains with refined blaming instincts for one immediate reason: so that those instincts could be deployed efficiently to optimize deterrence, usually by punishing the person we blame. But of course blame is not always a prelude to traditional punishment. In highly social creatures, to whom reputation is everything, expressions of blame can themselves be the punishment.

Think of the popular practice of local police forces publishing the names of prostitutes' customers. This kind of blame-as-punishment can be highly effective in the right circumstances, and it is also cheap, avoiding most of the palpable costs of more physical forms of punishment. The expressions of blame might be broadcast widely, as with the prostitutes' customers, but even one-on-one expressions of blame can be devastating in the right setting. When you harshly scold your dog for some misbehavior, its ears pull back, its tail hangs low between its legs, and it cowers in submission, all without any physical contact at all.[48] Parents can seldom punish children any more effectively than saying those words every child, and every adult for that matter, so dreads to hear: "I am very disappointed in you."

Another alternative to punishment is simply to decide not to punish. After all, our Rule 3 is to punish only *serious* violations of Rules 1 or 2. Just as there are some wrongs that cause so little harm that our blame instinct never gets ignited, so too are there wrongs and wrongdoers that we blame but nevertheless decide not to punish. This is one kind of forgiveness.

But when the harm is big enough to blame, and the circumstances do not warrant forgiveness, what exactly happens to turn the abstract feeling of blame into the concrete desire to punish? We might ask an even more fundamental question: whether the feeling of blame really is different in kind than the urge to punish. Maybe punishment is simply uninterrupted blame. That certainly seems to be the case with second-party punishment, when we are blaming people for the wrongs they commit directly against us. But it does not seem to be true for third-party punishment.

Go back to that supermarket line where you saw the fellow in front of you steal a pack of gum. Feelings of blame wash over you in a fraction of a second, quite automatically and largely uncontrollably. But the decision about whether to take punishing action against the thief, and indeed even whether to turn him in, feels like something very different, and much more complicated, than that initial rush of blame.[49] Compare that to the situation where instead of stealing a pack of gum from the store you catch the wrongdoer trying to pickpocket *your* wallet. Now, unlike in the third-party situation, your blame and punishment instincts feel like one coherent retaliatory reaction. In fact, both behavioral studies and brain scanning studies have detected this difference between blame and punishment depending on whether they are directed at a third party or one's own wrongdoer.

When we are reacting to wrongs committed against us, for example in trust games when our trust is not requited, blame almost always turns into punishment, and the emotional circuits that get engaged first typically swamp the cognitive ones that seem to want to take a second look at the costs and benefits of actually engaging in punishment.[50] We blame then we almost always punish our own tormentors. But when our blame gets triggered by wrongs to other people, the initial emotional gain is not nearly as strong, and our cost/benefit analysis often tells us to turn the other cheek. When the muscle-bound bully kicks sand in our face, we are powerfully driven to retaliate even though doing so makes no objective sense. When the bully kicks sand in someone else's face, we feel blame well up inside us, but seldom so fast or so strong that we are not able to calculate the irrationality of physically confronting him.

There are three keys to understanding this difference between how we blame then rather reactively punish our own tormentors, and how we blame then more coolly decide whether to punish the tormentors of others. First, and not at all surprisingly, the neural systems we use to measure harm are much more intensely activated when we suffer the harm ourselves than when we see others suffer.[51] Because blame is a product of intent and harm, we simply blame people who harm us more than we blame people who harm others, the amount of that harm and the level of intent otherwise being equal. Just go back to that line at the supermarket, and imagine how very different you would feel if the stranger ahead of you slapped you for no reason, compared to how you would feel if he slapped someone else for no reason.

Second, it may very well be that the "intent is more important than harm" rule that we discussed generally in the context of blame, is a rule that applies only in the third-party situation. Remember that the Robinson experiments, and even the Grace poisoning experiments, were all about third-party wrongs. Subjects were asked to blame John and Grace on the basis of actions that hurt others. But when we blame those who injure us, it appears we blame based almost exclusively on our assessment of harm, which is already inflated, rather than on our assessment of whether the person harming us intended to do so.[52] This too makes a lot of survival sense. Injuries to our own persons were considerably more threatening, at least in the short run, than injuries to other group members. Brains that did everything they could to deter such injuries by making it clear there would be automatic retaliation would have had a significant advantage over brains that calmly and coolly blamed and punished those harms as if they had been committed against others. This doesn't mean our second-party blame automatically turns into retaliation when we are confronted with clear proof there was no intent, but it does mean we have very strong presumptions to blame then punish those who hurt us.

Finally, whether in the second- or third-party context, we punish based on harm. Harm almost exclusively in the second-party situation and harm as a tiebreaker in the third-party situation, when intent is equal. This further magnifies into punishment our already magnified blame instincts when we are the ones harmed. It makes good evolutionary sense that our brains would base third-party punishment on harm rather than on intent. The benefits of third-party punishment are remote, but the costs are palpable. It is one thing to feel a general outrage at bullies and quite another to risk one's own health to punish them when we aren't their victim.

All of this means that in the case of second-party wrongs, our sense of harm not only starts out inflated compared to third-party wrongs, but then that inflated sense of harm directly drives our punishment decisions. The harm signals we get are so strong, at least when we suffer great harm, that they typically swamp any cognitive aspects of the punishment decision. As a result, our second-party punishment instinct often takes on the feeling of reactive retaliation. We *feel* our way to both blame and punishment.

But the third-party situation is very different. We blame on the basis of intent. The harm we then use as a tiebreaker is ratcheted way down in the third-party context. When we get to the punishment decision, the amount of that punishment is therefore likewise ratcheted way down, so far down that we are able to bring cognitive circuits to bear on the question of whether we should actually punish at all. When it comes to punishing third parties, we *feel* blame, but we *think* about punishment. On the other hand, we can't think *too much* about punishing third-party wrongdoers. Ancestors paralyzed with worry about a wrongdoer's state of mind might never have overcome the already daunting costs of third-party punishment.

It seems natural selection solved this problem by cleverly divvying up the processes of third-party blame and third-party punishment, and then driving each process by different neural engines that hardly talk to each other. One process (blame) screens primarily for intent. Blame is sometimes difficult to determine, because of that thorny problem of intent – what was in the wrongdoer's mind? – but we don't have to worry too much about that because, after all, we are just blaming, not actually punishing. The other process (punishment) kicks in only after getting a simple go-ahead from blame, but it screens only for harm, a fairly routine screen that is routine enough that we can get over our misgivings about imposing punishment. It is as if we have two uncommunicative parents hidden inside our judging brains, a blaming mother who makes the tough decisions about whether and how much to blame, and a punishing father who makes the easy decisions about how much to punish.[53]

So here's our third-party punishment tree, beginning where our blaming tree left off:[54]

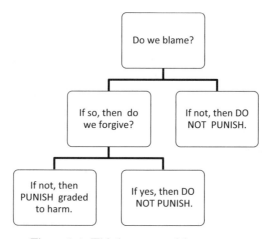

Figure 2.4. Third-party punishment tree.

The disconnect between third-party blame and third-party punishment occasionally makes for spectacular dissonances. One is what moral philosophers call the "problem of moral luck." Moral luck is what happens when wrongdoers who commit identical acts with identical intentions cause vastly different harms, just as a matter of chance. When the intentions are equally bad, and one bad intention causes great harm but the identically bad intention causes little or no harm, we are in the category of attempt. As we've seen, the law punishes Grace severely for her attempted poisoning of her friend, although not as severely as when she actually manages to poison her friend. That's the law of attempt, and although legal philosophers struggle mightily over attempt, it is only a weak version of moral luck.

A much stronger, and troubling, version happens at the opposite end of the intention scale, where neither wrongdoer intends to do wrong (say, both are just negligent), but where one does great harm and the other just lucks out into doing no harm at all. The classic modern example is drunk driving. Two drivers with identical cars and identical driving records have identical amounts to drink. On their way home, driving at identical speeds, one of them runs up over a sidewalk and hits a fire hydrant, and the other runs up over an identical sidewalk and kills a child. Our laws have universally punished the killer more harshly than the hydrant damager, and yet most of us have an uneasy feeling about the morality of such disparate treatment. Both did the same wrong act with the same state of mind, but one just happened to be lucky in avoiding any great harm.[55]

Much of the tension we feel about moral luck likely comes from the different circuits we use to blame and to punish, and the different inputs to those circuits, at least when it comes to third parties. One part (the blaming part, based on intent) wants to treat these two drunk drivers the same, because they did the same act and had the same (lack of) intent. Because one of them caused such great harm, we feel pulled to punish both of them severely. But another part of our brains (the punishment part, based on harm) sees the two cases as completely different, because the harms were completely different. We feel a tension because these two circuits are not integrated to produce a single result.

As we have already seen, young children (and adults with their rTPJs disabled) blame based primarily on harm. They therefore never feel any tension in moral luck situations because for them their harm-driven blame moves right into harm-driven punishment. They punish third parties just like they punish people who harm them – with retaliatory brains gauged to the level of harm. They are exquisitely able to distinguish degrees and kinds of harm, presumably because their harm-based punishment circuits come on line earlier in development than the TPJs they need to integrate intent with harm.

The difference between the act of blaming third parties and the act of punishing them also plays an important political role, as we will discuss in Chapter 8, in driving the one-way American sentencing ratchet of ever-increasing penalties.

Our blame and punishment instincts, calibrated differently depending on whether we were the victim of a wrong or only a witness to it, helped glue our small groups together by deterring wrongdoers. But even without these external threats, human brains were built to follow Rules 1 and 2 – don't steal and don't break promises – by a kind of internal blame and punishment system we call conscience and guilt. We turn to that internal system in the next chapter.

Notes to Chapter 2

1. The blood feud – requiring the killing of a member of the killer's family – is another kind of practice where guilt is borne more widely than by the individual wrongdoer. It is common among many existing primitive societies.

2. These rates are based in part on the relatively scant fossil record, showing a substantial number of violent deaths, but even more on the rates observed in existing primitive societies. Joshua Duntley & David Buss, *The Plausibility of Adaptations for Homicide*, in THE INNATE MIND: STRUCTURES AND CONTENT 291 (P. Carruthers et al., eds., Oxford 2005). For example, among the Dugum Dani in the central highlands of New Guinea, one in three adult deaths is the result of murder; among the Yanomamö in the Amazon rainforest, one in ten. Even the allegedly peaceful !Kung San of Botswana have a homicide rate four times that of the United States. Id. at 301.

3. Id. at 291. The classic evolutionary treatment of infanticide is the 1984 collection INFANTICIDE: COMPARATIVE AND EVOLUTIONARY PERSPECTIVES

(G. Hausfater & S. Hrdy, eds., Aldine 2008). The classic evolutionary treatment of homicide more generally is M. WILSON & M. DALY, HOMICIDE (Aldine 1988).

4. Duntley & Buss, supra note 2, at 300.

5. M. Wilson & R. Wrangham, *Intergroup relations in chimpanzees*, ANN. REV. ANTHRPOL., **32**, 363–392 (2003).

6. A well-known test called the Wason Selection Task requires subjects to reason about inferences. When the test is presented abstractly (with propositions P, not P, Q and not Q, and the inference P→Q), subjects perform quite poorly. Researchers noticed that these results were not just a problem with the symbolic nature of the presentation; when they replaced the propositions and inferences with words, they got results that varied wildly depending on context. Leda Cosmides and John Tooby discovered that the contexts that worked best were social contexts. When P and Q are socially relevant statements, such as "You are drinking alcohol" and "You are over 18," and when the inference P→Q is something like "If you are drinking alcohol then you must be over 18," then subjects' performances skyrocket. L. Cosmides, *The logic of social exchange: has natural selection shaped how humans reason? Studies with the Wason Selection Test*, COGNITION, **31(3)**, 187–276 (1988).

7. Such a model would also help support the idea, discussed in Chapters 4 and 5, that evolution developed third-party punishment by recruiting second-party punishment: *seeing* a wrong committed against another would have triggered some form of retaliatory response, even though the witness was not the victim.

8. The earliest English references to the power of arrest make no mention of arrest warrants.

9. In all but five American states, judges, not juries, impose noncapital sentences. In all death penalty states, the jury decides life or death.

10. MALCOLM GLADWELL, BLINK: THE POWER OF THINKING WITHOUT THINKING (Little, Brown 2005).

11. Paul Robinson & John Darley, *Intuitions of Justice: Implications for Criminal Law and Justice Policy*, **81** S. CAL. L. REV. 1 (2007); Paul Robinson. & Rob Kurzban, *Concordance and Conflict in Intuitions of Justice*, **91** MINN. L. REV. 1829 (2007). My discussion of these experiments is taken largely from a previously published essay, Morris B. Hoffman, *Evolutionary Jurisprudence: The End of the Naturalistic Fallacy and the Beginning of Real Reform?*, in 13 CURRENT LEGAL ISSUES: LAW AND NEUROSCIENCE 483 (ed. M. Freeman, Oxford 2010).

12. On the other hand, what people seem to do is make pair-wise comparisons, so what appears to be "switching" may really just be inserting new narratives into the previous ordering.

13. These results were also statistically significant. For the statistically inclined, the p-values in each experiment – a measure of the probability that the data was random – were less than 0.0001. The in-person study used 64 subjects; the online one 246.

14. Each of these comparative studies is discussed and referenced by Robinson and his colleagues in their Minnesota paper, supra note 11.

15. The three high harm scenarios were Robinson scenarios 23, 24, and 22 and the low harm scenarios were numbers 5, 7, and 6. Appendix A, P. Robinson & R. Kurzban, note 11 supra.

16. Here, the results were also not as statistically significant, with p < 0.001.

17. Robinson and his colleagues did not analyze the demographic data on the non-core aspects of the experiment, but Kurzban and others have shown that attitudes about one of the non-core crimes – drug use – is correlated to political ideology and religious practice, but even more highly correlated with, and in fact predicted by, attitudes about sex. R. Kurzban, A. Weeks, & J. Weeden, *Sex, drugs and moral goals: reproductive strategies and views about recreational drugs*, PROC. R. SOC. B, **277**, 3501–3508 (2010).

18. For a comprehensive evolutionary treatment of Robinson's results, see Paul Robinson, et al., *The Origins of Shared Intuitions of Justice*, **60** VAND. L. REV. 1633 (2007).

19. There is also no reason to assume the two scales are necessarily linearly related to each other. That is, Judge A's 22nd scenario may be twice as serious in his mind as the 21st scenario, and Judge B's only 10% more serious. But Robinson's insight is that when all is said and done, these scales will be the same in terms of *relative* blameworthiness.

20. C. S. LEWIS, THE PROBLEM OF PAIN 91–92 (HarperCollins 1940).

21. The undeterrable include not only those who cause accidents, even though they are as careful as they should be, but also people who cannot control their actions. Blaming harms caused by sleepwalking or spasms or other uncon trollable actions is just as evolutionarily senseless as blaming unavoidable accidents – we get only marginal benefits (in deterring the faking of being uncontrollable) but at all the ordinary high costs of punishment. This is why virtually all legal systems punish only voluntary actions. Likewise, virtually all systems recognize the futility of punishing people whose minds are so diseased that they could not appreciate the wrongfulness of their actions. I discuss these justification and excuse defenses in Chapter 6, as a specialized kind of forgiveness.

22. There are some primitive societies that blame and punish some kinds of accidents – usually involving great harms – the same as if the harm was intended. And of course modern criminal systems, especially in the West, have defined more and more so-called strict liability crimes. Drunk driving is the most common.

23. L. Young et al., *Disruption of the right temporoparietal junction with transcranial magnetic stimulation reduces the role of beliefs in moral judgment*, PROC. NAT. ACAD. SCIENCES, **107(15)**, 6753–6758 (2010).

24. This is the harm version of what biologists call kin selection, the theory, as discussed in Chapter 1, that explains in part why animals behave altruistically.

25. We will also see when we discuss the Trolley Problem in Chapter 3 that we blame (ourselves) for hand-to-hand wrongs more severely than we blame (ourselves) for remote wrongs, even when those wrongs cause objectively identical harms.

26. In fact, until recently the negligent infliction of purely emotional distress could not even be remedied in the civil courts of most jurisdictions. The common law imposed the requirement that the emotional harm be accompanied by some physical impact. Thus, screaming outrages into someone's face was not actionable unless, say, some spittle managed to find its way onto the victim. This so-called impact rule has been relaxed in the past fifty years, and now in a majority of states the victim of negligent emotional harm need only be in the zone of danger of some physical contact, not actually suffer any physical contact. RESTATEMENT (SECOND) OF TORTS § 436 (1965). Still, the remedy is civil, not criminal. Almost all jurisdictions have nevertheless begun to recognize that purely emotional harms might be the basis for criminal liability – stalking and harassment are two common examples.

27. To the extent neuroscience is closing the mind/body gap, this predisposition to blame physical harms more than emotional ones is coming under some legal attack. *See* Francis X. Shen, *Mind, Body, and the Criminal Law*, **97** MINN. L. REV. 2036 (2013).

28. In an experiment Frank Krueger and I have finished but not yet written up, we gave Robinson's blame task to subjects in the scanner. We discovered not only that subjects use more medial aspects of the prefrontal cortex to assess harm, in contrast to the more lateral aspects used to assess intention, but that our harm assessment seems to be an integration of three psychological factors: expected harm based on the seriousness of the norm violation, actual harm to the victim, and, surprisingly, the benefit to the wrongdoer. Evaluating the expected harm is associated with increased activations in the dorsomedial prefrontal cortex (dmPFC), the actual harm with the posterior cingulate (PC), and the benefit to the wrongdoer with the ventromedial prefrontal cortex (vmPFC). Connectivity studies suggest that the ventromedial prefrontal cortex then integrates these three harm inputs into a kind of net harm signal then reported to other regions (including the TPJ) for integration with the intent signals into a blame decision.

29. As we will see in Chapter 5, the law separates the responsibility inquiry – did defendant cause harm with some sufficiently blameworthy state of mind – from some aspects of justification, which is a legal defense. Thus, for example, the prosecution proves the criminal case against Jean Valjean by proving he

stole the food and that he intended to do so. It is a matter of defense for him to then convince the jury (or at least raise the prospect) that his crime was justified because his sister's family was starving, a justification defense the law calls "choice of evils." The neuroimaging results discussed in note 28 suggest that the inquiry may not always be as linear and segmented as the law assumes, and that in our brains the harm inquiry is sometimes a net harm inquiry bound up from the very beginning with aspects of justification.

30. In fact, our notions of intentionality are a human universal. DONALD E. BROWN, HUMAN UNIVERSALS 135 (Temple 1991). That is not to say that the ancients had no strict liability laws; they certainly did, including the Roman law that slave-owners were strictly liable for the harms caused by their slaves. 2 FREDERICK POLLACK & FREDRIC MAITLAND, THE HISTORY OF THE ENGLISH LAW 470–473 (2nd ed. 1968). The ancient Norse had an even broader notion of strict liability in their doctrine of deodand – the strange idea that when property injured people the property itself was blamed and destroyed. In Chapter 10 we will examine the equally strange modern notion that a corporation can be held criminally responsible.

31. The complete mens rea precept is *"Actus non facit reum nisi rea sit,"* which means "An act is not guilty unless the mind is guilty." It dates from the time of Henry I in the early 1100s, but has antecedents that go back at least to Augustine. Francis Bowes Sayre, *Mens Rea,* 45 HARV. L. REV. 974, 983 & n. 30 (1932).

32. David Premack, *The infant's theory of self-propelled objects,* COGNITION, **36(1)**, 1–16 (1990).

33. D. Premack & A. Premack, *Intention as psychological cause,* in CAUSAL COGNITION: A MULTIDISCIPLINARY DEBATE 185 (D. Sperber et al., eds., Oxford 1995).

34. J. Decety & S. Cacioppo, *The speed of morality: a high-density electrical neuroimaging study,* J. NEUROPHYSIOL., **108(11)**, 3068–3073 (2012).

35. Rough synonyms have included gross negligence, vincible ignorance, and willful blindness. The Model Penal Code – a 1962 attempt by legal scholars to standardize several criminal law notions, including notions of culpability – settled on the term "reckless" and defined it this way:

> A person acts recklessly [with respect to a result] when he consciously disregards a substantial and unjustifiable risk that [his conduct will cause the result].

MPC § 2.02.

36. There is often a good deal of overlap between the kind of gross negligence that could justify punitive damages in a civil case and the kind of recklessness that might be criminal. That's because many states define gross negligence in terms that sound very much like recklessness – typically, in ways that require a showing that the defendant "willfully and wantonly" ignored the risk of

harm. But not every harmful act done with a willful disregard of the risk of harm is criminal. The criminal law is able to cabin its reach into gross negligence by how it defines the act portion of the crime. Running a red light while texting may be gross negligence justifying punitive damages in a civil case, but in most states it is still not yet criminal (unless someone dies). Driving drunk, by contrast, is in most states gross negligence for civil purposes and in all states a crime (no matter whether there is any harm at all).

37. ANCIENT LAWS AND INSTITUTES OF ENGLAND 22 (B. Thorpe, ed., 1840) (emphasis added).

38. "Specific intent" is another common way the law has described this most culpable mental state.

39. The Model Penal Code uses the term "purposeful," and defines it this way:

> A person acts purposefully [with respect to a result] if it is his conscious object . . . to cause such a result.

MPC § 2.02.

40. Unless I can convince the judge or jury that I should not be blamed because I am insane. Insanity, as a special kind of forgiveness, is discussed in Chapter 6. In most Anglo-American jurisdictions, first-degree murder also requires proof that the murder was committed "after deliberation."

41. The Model Penal Code defines "knowing" this way:

> A person acts knowingly [with respect to a result] if he is aware that it is practically certain that his conduct will cause such a result.

MPC § 2.02.

42. Of course, the war circumstance itself may justify the killings under common law, and render them beyond the reach of the criminal law.

43. Aquinas used self-defense to analyze the problem of side effects. Thomas Aquinas, *Summa Theologica* (II–II, Qu. 64, Art.7). To most modern legal thinkers, this was probably not the best way to frame the issue, because the death of the aggressor may be the only way to achieve the primary purpose of self-defense. In that case, the killing is arguably within the primary stream of the desire for self-defense. Modern law frames self-defense as an issue of justification, not an issue of unintended side effects.

44. Paul H. Robinson, *A Brief History of Distinctions in Criminal Culpability*, **31** HASTINGS L.J. 815, 846 (1980).

45. Id. at 846. American law arguably went off the rails when it imported wholesale the idea of "knowing" from the circumstances arena into the results arena. Rails or not, "knowing" in the results context seems to be unique to American law. In England, for example, there remain only two grades of homicide – a purposeful killing (murder) and a reckless killing (manslaughter), with no equivalent of the American knowing killing (second degree

murder). There have been efforts to insert a level of knowing homicide into English law, to date unsuccessful.

46. Francis X. Shen et al, *Sorting Guilty Minds*, **86** N.Y.U. L. REV. 1306 (2011). As discussed in more detail in Chapter 10, this experiment showed that except at the knowing/reckless boundary, subjects were quite good at distinguishing all the intent gradations, even without the aid of any definitions (jury instructions), and did in fact blame consistent with the law's hierarchy of purposeful most, knowing/reckless next, and negligent least. But subjects had great difficulty differentiating knowing from reckless actions, even with definitions.

47. It is becoming clear that when we assess the intentions of other people we engage circuitry that is part of the so-called theory of mind network, which in turn is part of a broader social cognition network encompassing the medial and lateral prefrontal cortices as well as the temporal pole (TP) and TPJ. See, e.g., R. Saxe et al., *Understanding other minds: linking developmental psychology and functional neuroimaging*, ANN. REV. PSYCHOL., 55, 87–124 (2004); F. Krueger et al., *The medial prefrontal cortex mediates social event knowledge*, TRENDS IN COGN. SCI., **13(3)**, 103–109 (2009); C. Forbes & J. Grafman, *The role of the human prefrontal cortex in social cognition and moral judgment*, ANN. REV. NEUROSCI., 33, 299–324 (2010).

48. In the case of dogs, this could well be a conditioned behavior – the expressions of disappointment triggering a reaction anticipating physical punishment because in the past those expressions of disappointment were in fact followed by physical punishment. But even without any conditioning at all, dogs are highly sensitive to the disapproving tone of the human voice, probably because we share a long evolutionary history.

49. This decision about whether to take punishing action yourself or turn wrongdoers over to the group is a version of the delegation phenomenon discussed at length in Chapter 7.

50. Generally, witnessed social wrongs trigger increased activations in the victim's amygdala, which is the brain's alarm center, and which then seems to drive the actual punishment decision in the dorsolateral prefrontal cortex and the anterior cingulate. See T. Baumgartner et al, *The neural circuitry of a broken promise*, NEURON, **64(5)**, 756–770 (2009).

51. Those harm-measuring systems are located mainly in the amygdala, ventromedial prefrontal cortex, and posterior cingulate. See note 28. One neural explanation for this difference between personal harm and perceived harm to others is that the latter are messages carried mainly by mirror neurons, and fewer mirror neurons fire when a harm to others is perceived than when a harm is directly experienced.

52. I am hedging this proposition a bit because there is very little behavioral data about second-party blame. The economic games have certainly studied retaliation, and have clearly shown that the amount of retaliation is generally

proportional to the amount of harm, but as far as I know they have all looked at intentional harms, and therefore are unhelpful in teasing out the relative influences of harm and intent in the second-party context.

53. The punishing father must also make the nontrivial decision of whether to forgive, as discussed in Chapter 6.

54. As we will see in Chapter 6, the forgiveness module of this tree is quite an oversimplification. There are many kinds of forgiveness, and not all of them even reduce let alone eliminate punishment.

55. I thank Fiery Cushman for this drunk-driving example of moral luck. F. Cushman & L. Young, *The Psychology of Dilemmas and the Philosophy of Morality*, **12** ETHICAL THEORY & MORAL PRAC. 9 (2009).

3 FIRST-PARTY PUNISHMENT: CONSCIENCE AND GUILT

> The first and greatest punishment of the sinner is the conscience of sin.
>
> Seneca

THE MORAL ANIMAL

Konrad Lorenz, the famous Austrian zoologist, and someone who knew a thing or two about the dangers of anthropomorphism, once wrote about an incident that happened to his old French bulldog, Bully. When Lorenz came home one day with a new dog, Bully was racked with jealousy. The two dogs got into a bitter fight in Lorenz's bedroom, and as Lorenz was trying to separate them Bully bit Lorenz's finger. Lorenz, the trained observationalist, reports on Bully's behavior after the bite:

> [H]e broke down completely and although I did not admonish him and indeed stroked and coaxed him, he lay on the carpet as though paralysed. A little bundle of unhappiness, unable to get up. He shivered as in a fever and every few seconds a great tremor ran through his body. . . . [F]rom time to time a deep sigh escaped his tortured breast, and large tears overflowed his eyes. As he was literally unable to rise, I had to carry him down on to the road several times a day; he then walked back himself . . . but he could only crawl upstairs with an effort. . . . It was several days before he could eat and even then he could only be cajoled into taking food from my hands. For several weeks he approached me in an attitude of humble supplication, in sad contrast to the normal behavior of the self-willed and anything but servile dog. His bad conscience affected me the more in that my own was anything but clear towards him.

My acquisition of the new dog now seemed an almost unforgivable act.[1]

Whether or not Bully felt true guilt we will never know. He probably lacked the brainpower – including the ability to sense the passage of time and to compare the past to an imagined future – that allows the kind of guilt we humans experience. Most nonhuman animals are prisoners of the present, unable to compare what they did to what they should have done because they are largely only aware of what they are doing. But Lorenz felt the guilt *for* Bully, and of course his own guilt for bringing in the new dog. Just from reading this excerpt I suspect most readers felt a kind of remote guilt over the sad and helpless reactions of a French bulldog more than a half-century dead. That's a fairly remarkable reaction, and it shows how finely tuned our brains are to guilt, even a dog's probably imaginary guilt.

Guilt is central to many religions. In the Abrahamic traditions, guilt works at the day-to-day level of following God's expectations. When we worry that God may not approve of the actions we are contemplating or have already taken, we are feeling a kind of ex ante theological guilt, whose whole purpose is to help us not disappoint God and thus act rightly. Guilt seems to play a more spotty role in non-Western religions. When asked once whether there was guilt in Buddhism, the Dalai Lama responded "There is no guilt in Buddhism." The questioner pressed him. "Suppose a son disappoints his parents deeply by failing to live up to their expectations?" The Dalai Lama smiled and said, "It happens."[2] Polytheistic religions such as Hinduism, focused neither on day-to-day rules of living nor on the contractual relationships between a single God and his flock, also seem to show less theological interest in conscience and guilt. Confucianism, on the other hand, is awash in different kinds of guilt. Absorbed with the relationships between individuals and their families and communities, Confucianism recognizes at least three different species of guilt – one from feelings of failed responsibility (as teachers to their students), one from social defection (breaking a moral code), and another for legal defection (breaking the law).[3]

We will see in Chapter 6 that apology and atonement are important evolutionary signals for forgiveness, and that forgiveness was an important way to keep the damper on over-punishment. But before a wrongdoer can apologize or atone, he needs to appreciate the wrongness of his actions. This is one aspect of what guilt is – our brain's recognition that we have cheated, that we now may be facing the wrath of the group, and that we may want to consider signaling behaviors like apology and atonement to blunt that wrath.

Guilt in its traditional meaning is retrospective. It's how our brains make us feel after we've cheated. But imagine how much more successful an intensely social species would have been if it had brains that could warn it ahead of time not to defect when the benefits of the defection would likely be outweighed by its costs. We call this kind of prospective guilt "conscience." Conscience is a kind of first solution to The Social Problem. Brains with built-in systems that make their owners feel bad when they cheat, and even when they contemplate cheating, are brains that will not cheat as often as brains without conscience.[4] Groups of such brains would have been less likely to unravel from the lure of social defection, even without any external systems of blame and punishment.

Conscience saves our brains from the high costs of trying to calculate whether we should cheat, analogous to how blame saves us the high costs of calculating whether punishing others will deter. When we see others cheat, we blame them. When we are deciding whether we should cheat, we blame ourselves in a way that quite automatically and unconsciously reproduces our best guess about how others will blame us if we go through with it. Conscience is a kind of coming attraction that gives us a peek at how others will feel about us if we cheat.

We blame ourselves for our own contemplated wrongs using the same two deterrence proxies we use when we blame others for their completed wrongs – intent and harm. But of course because we are talking about the feelings our brains generate when we think about committing *future* wrongs, we are, by definition, talking about future *intentional* wrongs. We don't mull over whether to be negligent. That leaves us with harm as the central measure of conscience. Unless you are a psychopath, the negative feelings you get from contemplating killing a neighbor are substantially greater than the negative feelings that come from contemplating illegal parking.

Of course, there will be times when the benefits of a defection do not, in hindsight, justify its costs. A brain that could learn from its mistaken defections would have a real leg up with The Social Problem. But how will it know if it was wrong? Again, it cannot calculate the actual costs and benefits, although doing so in hindsight might be a little easier than doing so prospectively. Guilt is retroactive blame that complements conscience's prospective blame. Guilt totes up the negative and positive feelings from having already cheated, although it has a few additional valuable inputs that the prospective systems lacks, including how other group members actually reacted to the defection and whether the anticipated feelings really came to pass. So guilt's function is not just to remind us that we may want to ask for forgiveness; it also teaches us when, in emotional hindsight, defecting was not the right choice.

There is great overlap between these two systems of guilt and conscience, especially with brains as sophisticated, and socially focused, as ours. We can feel a kind of guilt just by imagining we have already cheated. Likewise, we can look back at some of our decisions, and imagine that our consciences might have driven us to cooperate when in fact we cheated, and vice versa. Both of these kinds of emotional exercises will help us fine-tune our decision-making the next time we need to decide whether to cooperate or defect.

Conscience and guilt *feel* internal to us; they don't feel like shortcuts to some utilitarian decision about whether to cooperate or cheat depending on whether we'll be caught and punished. But of course that's the whole point of evolved behavioral predispositions. When we feel the gnaw of conscience as we contemplate cheating, it feels like we are facing a categorical wrong. In fact, if we worry about getting caught and punished it doesn't feel like true conscience. Despite that categorical feeling, our brains are also quite good at distinguishing different levels of wrongs, gauged, as we have seen, to harm. Just as we blame and punish the murderer more than the illegal parker, we pre-blame ourselves more for contemplating murder than for contemplating illegal parking. The *amount* of the negative feelings our conscience gives us predicts the likelihood that we will cheat. As a result, most of us are more tempted to park illegally than to kill, and indeed most of us *do* park illegally more often than we kill.

In fact, for most serious defections our strong feelings of conscience are usually so strong that they are not even accessible to our conscious minds because there is simply nothing to balance. No need to "decide" anything. Robbing banks is just plain wrong, and so most of us never seriously consider it. The same general categorical feeling comes after we cheat. The bite of true guilt comes without any conscious worry about getting caught and punished. In fact, we may feel even more guilty if we think we've gotten away with it. These automatic feelings are precisely what instincts are – emotional shortcuts to impossible calculations, in this case about whether we should cooperate or cheat.

We therefore seldom "decide" whether to cheat or cooperate in the sense that we consciously tally up the bad feelings conscience gives us versus the good feelings we get when imagining the object of our defection. But when we are faced with extreme circumstances – say, our sister's children are starving and stealing a loaf of bread is the only way to save them – now conscience rears its explicit head and we start the struggle of balancing the pull of conscience against our particular circumstances of great need.

Forward-looking conscience and backward-looking guilt are elegant ways of maximizing the chances that we will make the correct decision about whether to cooperate or defect in a rapidly changing world where these decisions need to be grounded in abstractions, not hardwired to narrow circumstances. In other words, conscience and guilt help us follow Rule 1 (don't steal) and Rule 2 (don't breach), and therefore helped our groups stabilize. Brains tuned properly to the feelings that come from cooperating and defecting, and with an overriding desire to feel good about themselves, will be brains that in large part will automatically navigate The Social Problem without any external systems for punishment. We are able to avoid really serious group-unraveling harms all on our own, and yet continue to be tempted to cheat on the little things that might help us greatly with little social harm. This is just the kind of flexible and adaptive brain that negotiated The Social Problem to its best advantage.

There are a few other ways of looking at the adaptive value of conscience and guilt. Herant Katchadourian suggests that guilt might have evolved as a kind of cheat detector that enables victims of cheating to differentiate between sincere apology and faked apology.[5] Guilt in this view is not so much aimed at the wrongdoer's own reevaluation of his defection as at other group members, as a signal of genuine contrition and a request for forgiveness. In this account, guilt is a kind of atonement. "I've done you wrong, and I am so sorry about it that I am now going to cause myself to suffer by feeling guilty."

Robert Frank's treatment of guilt is similar. He sees it, and other emotions, as playing a critical evolutionary role in solving The Social Problem, not just by deterring our own defections in the first instance but also by inspiring confidence in other group members that we can be trusted again despite our past defections.[6]

At its most basic level guilt may be a kind of "reparative altruism," as Katchoudourian has put it.[7] Feelings of guilt can help drive a cheater back into the fold of a skeptical group. Guilt helps the cheater want to return to the group, and it simultaneously gives the group confidence that his desire to return is genuine.

Conscience and guilt can go terribly wrong at the edges, like any behavioral predisposition. Brains that lack the overriding desire to feel good won't respond correctly to the emotional cues of conscience and guilt. Many classical neuroses may be grounded in the sufferer's deep-seated desire to feel bad rather than feel good. Conscience and guilt systems that mismeasure harm will also produce bad social decisions. Someone who gets only a small negative feeling from a big contemplated harm might have antisocial personality disorder. People without any conscience or guilt at all are psychopaths, whom we will discuss in the next section.

Too much conscience and guilt, on the other hand, can lead to their own problems. An overabundance of them may be the root of obsessive-compulsive disorders (OCD). Long before psychiatry recognized OCD, medieval Church thinkers noticed behaviors they called "scrupulosity." People suffering from scrupulosity see sin where there is none (in themselves and others), feel guilt from events in which they had no role, and tend to go to serial confessions seeking absolution.[8]

Of course, conscience and guilt are no longer primarily, or even mostly, dedicated to solving The Social Problem. They have gotten heavily recruited by culture. The inner voices a Madison Avenue copywriter hears day-to-day are undoubtedly very different from the inner voices of a Kamchatka fisherman. The specific social rules individual societies create to meet their particular challenges get poured by conscience and guilt into the same self-help systems as do Rules 1 and 2, by learning. Just think of the conversations we have with our growing children. Sure, don't steal and don't break promises are staples of our daily moral teachings, but they are a tiny part of the overall social arsenal we as adults try to provide to our children. In modern technological cultures, we spend enormous time teaching our children things such as not putting fingers in electrical outlets, looking both ways before crossing the street, and eating with utensils.

These learned rules, whatever their cultural differences, get inculcated into the conscience and guilt systems every bit as much as deeper, evolved, moral intuitions. As a result, we engage these same anticipatory feelings of conscience and retrospective feelings of guilt whenever we contemplate breaking and then break a rule, whether the rule is evolved or learned. And of course because brains are all about soaking up experience, even within the same society and therefore within the same systems of culturally dependent rules, as individuals have different experiences those experiences will feed back into their conscience and guilt systems. What a fifteen-year-old boy needs to do to survive on the streets of Baltimore will influence what his conscience tells him to do and what his guilt tells him he should have done.

That conscience and guilt are highly dependent on culture is apparent just from looking at the etymology of the words. The Hebrew equivalent of the word "guilt" does not appear at all in the Old Testament.[9] Likewise, ancient Greek had no word for "guilt" in the sense of feeling bad about one's social defections; the closest thing was *hamartia*, which means "missing the mark," that is, making a mistake. The ascendance of Christianity did much for our modern conceptualizations of guilt. It took the Latin word for guilt or fault (*culpa*) and merged it with the Old German word for debt (*schuld*). The idea of debt – keeping track of reciprocity's running scores – is a key to our notions of guilt; indeed, in modern German *schuld* means both debt and guilt.

The linguistic richness of our descriptions of some of guilt's "neighbors," as Katchadourian describes them, also tells us much about the innumerable cultural influences on these notions, and their great sensitivity to those influences. Guilt is a kind of self-directed disgust, and in fact both kinds of emotions are associated with increased activations of a part of the brain called the insula, which is important for disgust.[10] The insula-based emotion of disgust was probably critical to keeping our half-starved ancestors from eating poisonous foods. Our own experiences can of course retune brain circuitry, including the insula, from its original evolutionary purposes to warn us of more modern challenges. Think of the last time you got sick eating something, perhaps that bit of whipped cream that went bad. Probably just reading these words fired up the insula a little and gave you a bit of queasiness, even though rotten whipped cream was hardly the insula's original evolutionary target.[11]

But guilt and disgust are not synonyms. We can be disgusted by a myriad of outside things, such as a piece of rotten food. Guilt, by contrast, is exclusively interior. "Embarrassment" gets to the interior nature of the feeling of guilt, but real embarrassment requires an audience. Real guilt, though of social origins, requires only a social defection, not an audience; indeed, it is intensely personal, and suffered most purely alone. Besides, the things we are "embarrassed" about are generally less serious than the things we feel guilty about. Our word "shame" may get a little closer to guilt, but it carries connotations of concealment.[12] Shame also seems to involve something more personally disappointing than does guilt. There is an aspect of guilt that is less self-loathing, more matter-of-fact. Perhaps we somehow recognize, down deep, that even when we feel guilty about defecting we have all been driven by natural selection to defect sometimes.

Despite the language variations, across societies with wildly different religious beliefs, wildly different norms, and wildly different survival challenges, our brains are still built to be highly attuned to conscience and guilt, because we are all still social animals who must solve that particular society's version of The Social Problem. Hindus may not focus on conscience and guilt in their formal adherence to rules of cultic purity. But they *feel* the bites of conscience and guilt just as much as any other human. Gandhi was racked with guilt for much of his adult life, arising from the fact that he was having sex with his wife at the moment his father died.[13] City street gangsters may have no compunction about stealing or killing outsiders, but all gangs have powerful social rules that govern behaviors inside the gang – the very

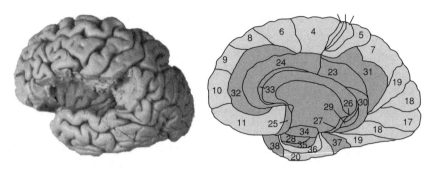

Figure 3.1. The brain's paralimbic region (right, gray) includes much of the insula (left). Drawing of paralimbic region from N. Anderson & K. Kiehl, *The psychopath magnetized: insights from brain imaging*, TRENDS COGN. SCIENCE, **16**(1), 62–60, Fig. 1A (2011). Drawing of insula from T. Tsukiura, *Neural mechanisms underlying the effects of face-based affective signals on memory for faces: a tentative model*, FRONT. INTEGR. NEUROSCI., Fig. 3 (July 24, 2012) (on-line).

same kinds of rules our ancestors needed to live in their small groups. It is simply a matter of defining the relevant group. No matter the culture, religion, or survival pressures, and no matter how antisocial a group's behaviors toward other groups appear to be, within a relevant group we will find the same kinds of conscience and guilt.

Our powerful feelings of conscience and guilt have specific neural correlates. In the very first neuroimaging study of guilt, done in 2000, researchers asked subjects in a PET (Positron Emission Tomography) scanner to recall personal events that generated the most guilt they had ever felt. As a control condition the experimenters asked the same subjects to recall past events with no emotional content. Recalling guilt-producing events triggered increased activations in the anterior, or front, portions of the paralimbic region of the brain.[14] The paralimbic region generally covers the lower part of the cortex adjacent to and including portions of the basal ganglia and limbic structures. It forms a kind of girdle surrounding the middle and lower portions of the brain's two hemispheres. See Figure 3.1. It contains many important structures, including the insula, our old friend in charge of disgust – not surprising, given that guilt has a filament of self-disgust. Many of these paralimbic structures are involved with the tasks of moral reasoning, affective memory (memory of emotional events), and inhibition, exactly the kinds of things one might expect to be involved in conscience and guilt. To be restrained by conscience, or reminded post hoc by guilt, requires us to be able to generalize the bad feelings associated with cheating (moral reasoning), to remember those bad feelings from past decisions to cheat (affective memory), and then to be able to refrain from cheating again until we determine whether those bad feelings outweigh the temptation to cheat again (inhibition).

Some recent imaging work suggests there might even be two different kinds of conscience and guilt – a generalized attitude about right and wrong (the researchers call this "deontological guilt") versus feelings of conscience and guilt directed toward a particular social setting (they call this "altruistic guilt"). Although both kinds of guilt are associated with anterior paralimbic regions, they appear to involve different circuits in those regions. Researchers have suggested that this separation may explain why some people (largely, psychopaths) can recognize right and wrong in the abstract but have great difficulty applying these general principles to specific social settings.[15]

This distinction between feelings of abstract guilt and social guilt may also help to explain the evolution of third-party punishment and its delegation from dominant members to others. People with a strong internal feeling that it is wrong, say, to whip other people will be difficult to convince to act as punishers of wrongdoers who deserve whipping. But compartmentalized brains that are able to turn off their ordinary rules of conscience when inflicting punishment could have had an easier time of it.

Joshua Greene and his colleagues used a well-known dilemma from moral philosophy – the Trolley Problem – to try to disentangle the neural correlates of conscience.[16] Subjects are presented with the following hypothetical. A runaway trolley will kill five workmen unless you pull the switch to divert it off its main line onto a spur. But there is one workman on the spur, and if you divert the trolley to the spur he will be killed. Do you kill one to save five?

It turns out the Trolley Problem has been played experimentally thousands of times, and roughly 80 percent of people say they would pull the switch (let's call these folks "utilitarians"), with only 20 percent refusing to do so ("deontologists"). This 80–20 split is fairly constant over all kinds of demographics, including age, gender, race, and ethnicity, and even seems to hold cross-culturally.[17]

But moral philosophers noticed that if you tweak the problem just a little bit, these results can change dramatically. In one version – called the bridge variation – subjects are asked to place themselves on a bridge spanning the track down which the runaway trolley is hurtling. In this variation, there are still five workmen who will die if the subject does not intervene, but the only way to intervene is to throw a very large man (or woman) off the bridge to stop the trolley. The utilitarian calculus in the bridge variation is exactly the same as it is in the original: do I kill one to save five?

But the very personal act of throwing the victim off the bridge changes people's moral decisions dramatically. Now the deontologists predominate over the utilitarians: an average of only 25 percent of subjects say they would push the victim off the bridge to save the five; 75 percent let the five die. If we reach moral decisions through pure reason, then why do most of us kill one person to save five in one scenario but not the other?

Greene and his colleagues tried to unpack this problem by scanning the brains of subjects as they made Trolley Problem decisions, to see what kinds of brain systems seemed to be associated with which kinds of decisions. They showed that these moral decisions are in fact not the exclusive products of cognitive versus emotional systems, but rather represent a highly context-dependent interplay between emotion and reason. In both variations, emotional systems are automatically engaged first, telling us that killing is wrong, but in the original version those emotional systems eventually get overridden in most people by the cognitive calculation that it is better to save five people by killing one than letting five die to save one. It seems that in the initial version whether you are a utilitarian or a deontologist is determined largely by the strength of the initial emotional signal. The 20 percent who do not throw the switch have a stronger initial emotional surge not to kill than those who do, so strong that that surge is not overridden by later cognitive calculations about the utility of killing.

In the bridge variation, by contrast, the emotional surge associated with throwing the victim off the bridge is on average much stronger than the emotional surge of pulling the switch, and therefore much less likely to be overridden by the utilitarian calculation. This bigger emotional surge likely has something to do with the fact that our brains rate personal harms more blameworthy than impersonal ones. Because, as we've seen, the strength of our conscience is largely a function of the harm we imagine, the surge of conscience we get from thinking about pushing another human off a bridge is considerably stronger than the surge we feel contemplating pulling a switch. As a result, our cognitive systems are much less able to override the emotional gain in the bridge variation. For most of us, pushing another human to his death is so conscience-ridden that we refuse to do so even to save five other lives.

This account shows the complexity of the relationship between what was traditionally thought to be "emotional" and "cognitive" aspects of decision-making.[18] We may think we are "deciding," but our decisions are a complicated gnarl of emotion and cognition. We may report to ourselves that we balanced two options – killing one person versus killing five – but the balance we strike may have been predetermined by the strength of emotions we quite unconsciously and uncontrollably assigned to the options before we did any balancing at all.

These results also show there is great variation even between healthy individuals when it comes to moral decision-making. The 20 percent who do not throw the switch in the original version are not diseased overscrupulous outliers. Their brains just soaked up a lifetime of experience in ways that are different from the other 80 percent. Likewise, the 25 percent who elect to push the person off the bridge are hardly psychopaths. The brain's plasticity makes all of these phenomena – the initial surge of conscience, whether and how much we judge personal harm as being more blameworthy than remote harm, and how in the end we make the utilitarian judgment of five lives versus one – highly individualized.

For our purposes the important point about this research is that it shows, regardless of the outcomes, that our brains have embedded prosocial moral preferences that can be overcome only with some effort. None of us decides to kill, in either version, without being able to overcome our serious pangs of conscience against killing. This research also shows that on average those pangs against inflicting harm on others to achieve some higher purpose are much weaker when we are being asked to inflict the harm remotely than when we are being asked to harm someone directly. This goes a long way to explain why the delegation of third-party punishment was so important.

Our embedded moral intuitions, reinforced by conscience and guilt, may also be responsible for a big problem faced by military planners. In 1947, in what has become a rather controversial book, a military historian and brigadier general named S. L. A. Marshall reported on his post-combat interviews with U.S. Army riflemen who had seen action in World War II. Based on those interviews, Marshall concluded that only 15 percent to 20 percent of American soldiers fired at what Marshall called "exposed" enemy – that is, enemy soldiers who could easily be killed with little risk to the American rifleman. This contrasted to group-fired weapons such as machine guns, which were almost always fired. Rifle firing rates also increased dramatically in any kind of group setting – where, for example, an officer had ordered a platoon to begin firing. But left alone, and faced with a chance to kill an exposed enemy, the great majority of soldiers did not fire.[19]

In response to Marshall's findings, military trainers around the world changed their entire approach to combat training – for example, moving from inanimate targets to lifelike ones – all in an attempt to condition soldiers around their supposed reluctance to kill. Modern military combat training remains to this day premised on the notion that intense training needs to overcome powerful urges not to kill. Firing rate numbers in modern engagements – as high as 90 percent – have been touted as proof of the effectiveness of modern training in response to our innate reluctance to kill.

Marshall's results have been roundly criticized on methodological grounds, especially in a 1988 article by Roger Spiller.[20] Spiller and others have shown that it was very unlikely Marshall could have conducted as many interviews as he claimed, that even the claimed number changed drastically over time, that personnel who accompanied Marshall on these post-combat interviews do not recall him asking any questions about firing rates, and that Marshall's field notes contain no firing rate information.[21] Spiller concluded that Marshall, a former newspaperman, simply made this data up from whole cloth.

Several military historians have tried to resolve this controversy by looking at more reliable firing data from other wars, including the Napoleonic Wars and the American Civil War, by looking at weapons recovered from the field. For example, in one study of the more than 27,000 muskets recovered from the battlefield at Gettysburg, historians found that 24,000 were loaded and ready to fire. No surprises there – it just meant that infantrymen were reloading quickly, which in fact was quite possible with the particular rifles that made up the vast majority of the arsenal. With such fast reloading, chances were high that a soldier's rifle was loaded the moment he was killed. But of those 24,000 loaded rifles, 12,000 had been improperly loaded twice – with one charge and ball being ramroded right over another. More amazing still, 6,000 of those 12,000 contained more than three rounds loaded on top of one another. Ten rounds were not uncommon, and one rifle had twenty-three! What was happening, and happening quite regularly, was that soldiers were pretending to fire their rifles, reloading and pretending to fire them again, and repeating that process until they themselves were killed.[22]

Pretending to fire was not the only way soldiers in combat avoided killing. Data from many different nineteenth- and early twentieth-century conflicts, comparing rounds fired to hits, strongly suggest that soldiers quite frequently fired over each others' heads. For example, in the 1870 battle of Wissembourg during the Franco-Prussian War, French defenders fired 48,000 rounds against Germans advancing toward them on an unprotected open field, but struck just 404 of them, a hit ratio of 1:119. Although poor marksmanship explains some of this performance, there is little question but that a good portion of French soldiers were intentionally missing.[23]

The Federal Bureau of Investigation (FBI) has also begun to study historical firing rates, focusing on law enforcement officers in shooting situations. The FBI, and virtually every other American law enforcement agency, state and local, began to modify their training procedures to desensitize officers to killing, though in the police context the challenge between distinguishing the good guys from the bad guys, and the circumstances justifying deadly force, is typically much harder than in a traditional standing army combat situation.

Virtually all these studies confirmed Marshall's results, although generally not quite as spectacularly. It seems soldiers and law enforcement personnel do in fact exhibit some fairly strong reluctance to use deadly force. Yet the debates about General Marshall's findings continue to rage, not so much over the firing rate data themselves as over the conclusions we are to draw from them.

Are humans born killers or born pacifists? The answer, of course, is neither. And in fact this simply isn't the right question. The right question, as economist Alexander Field so cogently put it, "is not so much why humans kill each other, but why this isn't more frequent, and whether the explanation for this is to be found entirely in the realm of culture."[24] The answer to that question, as we have seen, is that we evolved moral intuitions and consciences because they helped us live in intensely social groups, all of which gave us palpable but still quite rebuttable prosocial predispositions. But as we've also seen, our predispositions were reversed when it came to dealing with outsiders. I suspect that modern military training has been effective in increasing firing rates not so much by overcoming any general reluctance to kill but rather by conditioning soldiers to view the enemy as outsiders.

EMPATHY

A big reason we are not constantly hurting each other is that we are able to imagine the pain that we would suffer if we were hurt. Empathy is the main emotional current on which conscience and guilt ride. As Shakespeare so beautifully put it, "O, I have suffered / With those that I saw suffer."[25]

There has been endless speculation about exactly what empathy is, how it works and how it animates our moral judgment. The Scottish philosopher David Hume first articulated the idea that the roots of morality may lie in the process of socializing our own desires. Like all sufficiently complex animals, we unfailingly avoid pain and seek pleasure, at least if we are psychiatrically intact. If we could somehow redirect those selfish drives to other people we would begin to treat others as we wished to be treated. The golden rule evolved in us because it gave those of us with this ability to empathize the tremendous fitness advantages of being able to live in groups.

Until recently, empathy has been a neurological mystery. It has not been clear how our brains are able to accomplish this astonishing feat of refraining from causing pain to others by imagining their pain as ours. But clues are starting to accumulate. We know, for example, that portions of our ordinary emotional systems that are activated by our own experiences are also activated when we see or hear or read about other people's emotional experiences. So, for example, the insula is activated when we experience disgust as well as when we observe others being disgusted.[26] The same is true of the amygdala and fear, and of the anterior cingulate and pain.[27]

But we also know that additional neural networks are needed for empathy.[28] These seem to be responsible for the process called "mentalizing" – imagining how other people's brains might be reacting to certain stimuli – or what is sometimes also called "theory of mind." These additional theory-of-mind areas show increased activation when subjects have empathetic experiences in the scanner. More spectacularly, when these areas have been damaged by trauma, or deactivated by transcranial magnetic stimulation, subjects are less likely to be empathetic.[29] To feel for others, we need not only to be able to feel for ourselves but also to be able to imagine that others will feel the way we do.

We have empathy not just when we see others suffer physical pain, but also when we see them suffer emotional pain. In creatures as intensely social as humans, one of the most significant forms of emotional pain is being excluded from the group. We are exquisitely attuned not just to being excluded ourselves but also, through empathy, to the exclusions of others. Adolescents, for whom the forming of new groups outside the family is so important, are particularly empathetic to behaviors of exclusion. In an imaging experiment published in 2010, researchers at the University of California Los Angeles and the University of Oregon put adolescents in scanners and told them to watch screens showing three of their peers playing a video ball-toss game. But their peers were not really playing the game; it was being played by a computer controlled by the experimenters. In the first round, the control round, all three of the "peers" participated equally in the games. But in the next round the computer manipulated the games so it appeared two of the three peers were tossing the ball only to each other, excluding the third. The adolescent subjects witnessing this excluding behavior showed strong reactions in the cortical areas associated with theory-of-mind. These strong reactions corresponded to the subjects' verbal reports after the experiment, expressing their degree of discomfort at the fact that two of the fictional players had excluded the third.[30]

The most stunning development in empathy research was the discovery of a specialized kind of neuron, dubbed the "mirror neuron," through which it appears we actually feel others' pain. The discovery of mirror neurons was not just an important neurological discovery in its own right, it was one of those serendipitous stories science loves to tell.

In the early 1990s, the Italian neuroscientist Giacomo Rizzolatti and his colleagues were measuring single motor neurons in macaques as the macaques reached for offered fruit, using electrodes surgically inserted into the motor cortices of the macaques. This was a very common technique to map the neural pathways of a given motor action or a sensory response. When the macaques reached for the fruit, if the electrode was in contact with a neuron in the motor chain driving that action of reaching, then the electrode would activate as the single neuron activated. Using single neuron electrodes in this way enabled researchers to map motor pathways with great precision.

During a lunch break one day, Rizzolatti and his colleagues noticed that the electrodes in their macaques were still firing even though none of the macaques was reaching for anything. First they thought there was an equipment malfunction, but they soon realized that the electrodes were firing because the monkeys were watching the researchers reach for food during lunch. The very same neuron that was involved in the motor action of reaching was activated whether the macaque was in fact reaching or just watching someone else reach.[31] Mirror neurons have now been confirmed to exist in a host of nonhuman primates, and in 2010 were confirmed in humans.[32]

The discovery of mirror neurons suggests that the roots of empathy go all the way down to the neuronal level. If some of the same neurons I use when I punch are activated when I see punching, perhaps it is through those mirror neurons that this mysterious emotional transfer we call empathy actually gets made.

It turns out that only a fraction of neurons in a motor circuit also fire when that motor action is observed, with the size of that fraction varying greatly by brain region and motor activity. That's a good thing, otherwise we might not be able to tell the difference between us being hurt and someone else being hurt. This may also explain why, as discussed in Chapter 2, our blaming instincts are more inflamed when a wrongdoer injures us (*all* of our pain neurons for that stimulus are firing) than when he injures someone else (only a fraction of our pain neurons are firing as mirrors).

Regardless of its mechanism, empathy was an enormously valuable trait for sentient creatures living in small groups. It was a wonderfully efficient, elegant, and quite automatic way to "enforce" Rules 1 and 2. We follow these rules against stealing and breaching not just because we have been taught to follow them, but because we actually hurt when we hurt others, and healthy brains want to avoid hurting. Moreover, because we can imagine the future, we can imagine hurting when we hurt others, thus our conscience suppresses the temptation to engage in hurtful defections. Because we can also remember the past, we hurt when we remember hurting others, thus our guilt reinforces future cooperation. Empathy even drives us to become third-party blamers, because we hurt whenever we see others hurt, whether by our own hand or the hands of others.

There is little doubt that before we could have evolved conscience and guilt we needed empathetic systems to generate the feelings on which conscience and guilt depend. One stark way to see how central empathy is to our ability to navigate The Social Problem is to look at psychopaths, who lack empathy.

PSYCHOPATHS[33]

Kent Kiehl, a neuroscientist who studies imprisoned psychopaths, told this story to Herant Katchadourian, who included it in his book on guilt. One of Kiehl's subjects had a fight with his mother as soon as he was released from prison. When she tried to call the police, he was furious. As he put it to Kiehl, "Man, do you believe the balls on that chick?" So he strangled her with a telephone cord, and threw her down the basement stairs. But because he wasn't quite sure she was dead, he got a kitchen knife and stabbed her repeatedly. "[H]er body made these weird noises, I guess it was the gas escaping, but I wasn't sure, so I grabbed a big propane canister and bashed her brains in." He then went out and partied for three days before disposing of his mother's body.[34]

The idea that some people can commit such horrible wrongs without what appears to be an ounce of conscience or guilt has puzzled and fascinated all of us forever. Psychopaths seem to have been a part of the human story from the very beginning. They have confounded everyone, including their own victims, medical professionals, moral and legal philosophers, and corrections officials.

Psychopaths are grossly overrepresented in prisons. It is estimated that just 1 percent of adult males are psychopaths, but they make up 20–25 percent of prison populations. There is no single factor that is more highly correlated to being in prison than psychopathy – not race, poverty, substance abuse, child abuse, or even early head trauma. Psychopaths also recidivate at rates substantially higher than non-psychopaths. In one of the most comprehensive and longest of longitudinal studies, researchers found that 90 percent of violent psychopaths were back in prison after twenty years (often more than once), compared to 40 percent of non-psychopaths.[35] Yet psychopathy remains a controversial diagnosis, and appears in the current DSM (Diagnostic and Statistical Manual of Mental Disorders, the bible of psychiatric diagnosis) only as the watered-down over- and under-inclusive diagnosis of "antisocial personality disorder."

Despite their utter lack of conscience, guilt, and empathy, psychopaths manage to hide in our midst. At any one time, for every psychopath in prison roughly two and a half are not in prison. Most of them, even the ones in prison, are not the obvious monsters of Hollywood caricature. They can be, and in fact often are, engaging and likeable. Some are successful businessmen, politicians, scientists, doctors, and even psychiatrists. These are the "snakes in suits," a phrase coined by Robert Hare, the father of the modern clinical instrument used to diagnose psychopathy.[36] And in fact the psychopath's ability to trick the rest of us, at least in the short run, is one of psychopathy's most enduring paradoxes. Hervey Cleckley, one the American pioneers of the clinical study of psychopathy, called it the "mask of sanity."

Kent Kiehl told me the following story, about a very different one of his prison psychopaths, who was every bit as much of a psychopath as the one who strangled and stabbed his mother. This fellow, let's call him Andy, was in prison for a nonviolent offense. He carried a car repair manual around with him at all times. He told anyone who would listen that he was studying to be a car mechanic, and that when he was released from prison he was going to enroll in a mechanics school in the interior of British Columbia. As chance would have it, Kiehl was driving up to the prison on the very day Andy was released on parole. Andy was waiting for the bus, and as usual he had the car repair manual under his arm. Two buses pulled up at the same time, one to the interior and one to Vancouver. Kiehl watched as Andy casually tossed the manual in a trash can and jumped on the bus to Vancouver. Two weeks later Kiehl was doing his rounds in the prison, and there was Andy. Kiehl asked him how he managed to get sent back to prison so soon, and Andy told him the story. He went to Vancouver, robbed several banks on the very day of his release, rented a penthouse apartment, cavorted with prostitutes, and even bought front row tickets to some Vancouver Canuck hockey games. "Best two weeks of my life," reported Andy. Kiehl asked him why he decided not to go to mechanics school, and Andy, looking perplexed and a bit comical, replied, "What fun would that be?" It was all a scam, and Andy had fooled everyone, including parole officials and Kiehl himself.

Andy was not an aberration. Psychopaths are able to fool prison psychiatrists and psychologists just as easily as they fool the rest of us, if not easier. A 2009 study examined the files of 310 male offenders serving at least two years in a Canadian prison between 1995 and 1997. Ninety were determined, retrospectively, to be psychopaths. Researchers found that the psychopaths were roughly 2.5 times more likely to be conditionally released than the non-psychopaths. Psychopathy was only a slightly less effective predictor of the early release of sex offenders, psychopathic sex offenders being released 2.43 times more frequently than non-psychopathic sex offenders.

In fact, some mental health treatments traditionally offered in prisons – such as group therapy – seem to make psychopaths even more dangerous. In a famous 1991 study of incarcerated psychopaths about to be released from a therapeutic community, those who received group therapy actually had a *higher* violent recidivism rate than those who were not treated at all.[37] One explanation is that being exposed to the frailties of normal people in group therapeutic settings gives psychopaths a stock of information that makes them better at manipulating normal people. Before these kinds of group therapies, the typical psychopath had no idea that one could, for example, manipulate people by threatening their loved ones, because psychopaths themselves cannot imagine caring so much for another person. As one psychopath put it, "These programs are like a finishing school. They teach you how to put the squeeze on people."[38] Group therapy is also, of course, an endless source of excuses – my parents didn't love me, I was abused, my wife left me, I am numb and empty inside, I am useless – none of which the psychopath actually feels but all of which he can use to his tactical advantage at the right moments, especially when trying to manipulate mental health and corrections professionals.

OK, so psychopaths are impulsive and manipulative, make bad moral choices, and commit more crimes and then recidivate at higher rates. But what is "psychopathy" exactly, other than a post hoc description of incorrigible criminality? Many skeptics, both within and outside of psychiatry, have been reluctant to recognize diagnoses based on social and especially forensic failures, and even more reluctant to put a quasi-scientific label on behaviors that have such a palpable ring of moral judgmentalism. "Psychopaths are evil" simply does not seem to be a reliable clinical description, and sounds more like a society lumping its wrongdoers together and then giving up on them in a pseudo-scientific way.[39]

It turns out, however, that psychopathy is a real mental condition with identifiable and characteristic behavioral patterns that can be reliably diagnosed clinically. It has such robustly characteristic neural signatures that it may soon be diagnosable by brain scan alone.

Behaviorally, it has long been known that psychopaths can reason in all dimensions other than moral ones, and that this incapacity seems to stem from a combination of impulsiveness, an inability to recognize and remember emotionally-laden facts, and a difficulty with moral reasoning. Psychopaths, compared to non-psychopaths, exhibit a marked lack of inhibition in classic psychological tests designed to study inhibition.[40] They likewise have significant problems with affective memory – being able, as non-psychopaths are able, to remember emotionally-laden words better than emotionally-neutral words.[41]

The behavioral data on moral reasoning is a little more ambiguous. In the classic experiment to test moral reasoning, subjects are shown a

Factor 1 – Interpersonal/Affective	Factor 2 – Behavioral/Impulsive
Glibness/superficial charm	Need for stimulation/proneness to boredom
Grandiose sense of self-worth	Parasitic lifestyle
Pathological lying	Poor behavioral control
Conning/manipulative	Promiscuous sexual behavior
Lack of remorse or guilt	Lack of realistic long-term goals
Shallow affect	Impulsivity
Callous/lack of empathy	Irresponsibility
Lack of realistic long-term plans	Juvenile delinquency
Failure to accept consequences of actions	Early behavioral problems
Irresponsibility	Revocation of conditional release

Figure 3.2. Hare Psychopathy Check List – Revised (PCL-R). From R. D. Hare, MANUAL FOR THE REVISED PSYCHOPATHY CHECKLIST 38 (2nd ed., Multi-Health System).

series of pictures and asked to rate them for moral violation, 1 being no moral violation and the highest of the scale (typically 5) being severe moral violation. Some pictures have obvious moral content (Ku Klux Klan cross burning), others are ambiguous (a car on fire), and still others have no moral content at all (picture of the moon). Most of these studies show there are no statistically significant differences between the ability of psychopaths and non-psychopaths to recognize the moral content of these pictures, but that psychopaths take a bit longer to decide. These reaction time differences have led some researchers to suspect that psychopaths may be using different circuitry than non-psychopaths to reach their moral conclusions.

Clinically, Robert Hare and his colleagues have developed a series of clinical instruments to diagnose psychopathy. They developed a general instrument called the PCL-R (psychopathy checklist revised), a youth version called the PCL-YV, and a screening version called the PCL-SV. In all the instruments, Hare's insight was to combine emotional or affective factors (grouped together as "Factors 1") and behavioral or impulsive factors ("Factors 2"), and to apply a scale to them that rigorously measures their contribution to the overall diagnosis. The twenty factors from the PCL-R are shown in Figure 3.2. The Hare instrument requires the clinician to give a score on each of these criteria of 0 (item does not fit), 1 (item fits somewhat), or 2 (item definitely fits). The minimum score is therefore zero and the maximum forty. Hare himself rather arbitrarily defined psychopathy as a score of thirty or more. Typical group studies break down the Hare scores into the low (20 and below), moderate (21–29), and high (30 and above) ranges. The ratings are done by trained clinicians doing an extensive interview of the subject, typically lasting more than four hours, as well as a comprehensive review of the subject's criminal history. With properly trained clinicians, the Hare instruments have proved to be reasonably reliable in diagnosing psychopathy, both within and between clinicians.

In fact, with no small amount of controversy, Hare's instruments are starting to find their way into the batteries of psychological testing commonly done by probation departments, prison officials, and parole boards. The probation department in my court gives a Hare instrument to every sex offender about to be sentenced, and reports the results to us before we impose the sentence. Like all clinical instruments, we need to be careful that these Hare tests are being implemented correctly. I have concerns, for example, that the folks doing them for me and my colleagues report that it takes them about an hour per defendant. Kent Kiehl, who trained under Robert Hare, tells me his graduate students spend four to eight hours per prisoner administering these tests.

Even if they are reliable, critics of the use of clinical instruments to measure psychopathy complain that once a prisoner is labeled as a "psychopath" that one label might unfairly dominate the correctional picture.[42] These are complicated issues. On the one hand, given the woeful recidivism data associated with psychopathy, it seems to me that prison officials would be foolish not to consider a prisoner's psychopathy score in making various correctional decisions, especially including the release decision. That's particularly true since parole boards across the country are already using considerably less reliable risk assessment instruments to predict future recidivism.

But I share the critics' worry that the psychopathy score might become a shortcut to fuller, better informed, decisions. After all, most psychopaths are not in prison, and a good chunk of them are fully able to navigate the outside world without getting snared by the criminal law.

What distinguishes psychopaths who commit crimes from psychopaths who don't is pretty much shrouded in the same mystery as what distinguishes non-psychopaths who commit crimes from non-psychopaths who don't. The same is true when it comes to predicting which prisoners, psychopaths and non-psychopaths alike, will recidivate.

Sure, being a psychopath dramatically increases the risk of recidivism, but these are group risks. People we incarcerate are entitled to be treated as individuals, especially when it comes to release decisions. The psychopath who scores a forty on the PCL-R (the highest score) is substantially more likely to recidivate than the non-psychopath who scores a five, all other things being equal. But all other things are never equal, and the forty-point psychopath has the right to a process that will accommodate the possibility that he has changed and his five-point colleague has not. The rub, of course, is that these decisions about future behavior are not just impossibly difficult to make, they are shrouded in political pressures. The jury is probably still out on whether the Hare tool will become a useful part of the correctional toolbox or a lazy bureaucratic rubber stamp.

The most exciting developments in psychopathy research have been in neuroscience. Kent Kiehl and his colleagues gave the Hare instrument to incarcerated subjects then put them in the scanner and blindly gave them all the classic behavioral tests for impulse control, affective memory, and moral reasoning.[43] Psychopaths showed markedly lowered activations in all the key paralimbic regions associated with these tasks. The results were so robust that they are close to diagnostic.[44] Of course, if psychopathy gets easier to diagnose, the diagnosis gets easier to misuse.

One of the most interesting aspects of Kiehl's experiments comes from the moral reasoning tests, where psychopaths do as well as non-psychopaths behaviorally. Kiehl's experiments showed that psychopaths have increased activations in various frontal areas of the brain, compared to non-psychopaths, when doing these moral reasoning tasks. This goes a long way toward confirming the guess that psychopaths can mimic some moral intuitions with enough cognitive attention. Psychopaths can reason that other people might consider it wrong to take a wallet someone has just dropped, but they don't *feel* that wrongness inside of them like the rest of us do. They do not hear the warning bells of conscience before they act, or feel the bite of guilt afterwards. As Kiehl has put it, psychopaths can read the lyrics of morality's song, but they don't hear the music.

Psychopaths are a kind of half-informed *Homo economicus*. They almost always play at the Nash equilibrium, defecting when they think it is in their best short-run interest to do so. They are able to consider the long run, but only in a detached, cognitive way, and those detached calculations are seldom strong enough to overcome the emotionally-laden lure of the short run. Psychopaths are living proof that having an explicit social knowledge of right and wrong, and of the threat of punishment, is simply not enough. To truly appreciate the benefits of the long run, social animals must have brains with implicit moral knowledge, driven, at least in the case of the human animal, by conscience, guilt, and empathy.

Notes to Chapter 3

1. KONRAD LORENZ, MAN MEETS DOG 186–187 (M. Wilson, tr., London 1954).
2. HERANT KATCHADOURIAN, GUILT: THE BITE OF CONSCIENCE 237 (Stanford 2010).
3. Herant Katchadourian devotes an entire chapter of his book on guilt to guilt in Hinduism, Buddhism, and Confucianism. Id. at Chapter 9, 227–255.
4. Provided, of course, that the brains are also equipped with the rule that they don't want to feel bad and also provided they are sufficiently complex to be able to imagine the bad feeling they will get from a future defection.
5. Katchadourian, supra note 2, at 179–181.
6. ROBERT FRANK, PASSIONS WITHIN REASON: THE STRATEGIC ROLES OF EMOTIONS (Norton 1988).
7. Katchadourian, supra note 2, at 180.
8. JOSEPH W. CIARROCHI, THE DOUBTING DISEASE: HELP FOR SCRUPULOSITY AND RELIGIOUS COMPULSIONS (Paulist Press 1995).
9. Katchadourian, supra note 2, at 21.
10. A. J. Calder et al., *Neuropsychology of fear and loathing*, NATURE REV. NEUROSCI., **2**, 352–363 (May 2001).
11. This example of retuning the insula is courtesy of Abigail Baird, a neuroscientist at Vassar and a former MacArthur colleague, whom I once heard use it in a lecture.

12. Darwin himself observed that shame involves "a keen sense of conceal-ment. We turn away the whole body, and most especially the face, which we endeavor in some manner to hide." Charles Darwin, THE EXPRESSIONS OF THE EMOTIONS IN MAN AND ANIMALS 319–320 (London 1872; Harper 1998). There have been some interesting empirical efforts to tease out the differences between guilt, embarrassment, and shame. See, e.g., J. P. Tagnet et al., *Are shame, guilt and embarrassment distinct emotions?*, J. PERSONALITY, **70(6)**, 1256–1269 (1996); P. Luyten et al., *Does the test of self-conscious affect (TOSCA) measure maladaptive aspects of guilt and adaptive aspects of shame? an empirical investigation*, PERSONALITY & INDIV. DIFF., **33(8)**, 1373–1387 (2002); B. Fedewa et al., *Positive and negative perfectionism and the shame/guilt distinction: adaptive and maladaptive characteristics*, PERSONALITY & INDIV. DIFF., **38(7)**, 1609–1619 (2005).

13. MOHANDAS K. GANDHI, 39 THE COLLECTED WORKS 29–30 (1929, Ahmadabad 1970). His Herculean guilt may also have been driven by latent bisexuality. JOSEPH LELYVELD, GREAT SOUL: MAHATMA GANDHI AND HIS STRUGGLE WITH INDIA (Knopf 2011).

14. L. M. Shin et al., *Activation of anterior paralimbic structures during guilt-related script-driven imagery*, BIOL. PSYCHIATRY, **48(1)**, 43–50 (2000).

15. B. Basile et al., *Deontological and altruistic guilt: evidence for distinct neurobio-logical substrates*, HUM. BRAIN MAPPING, **32(2)**, 229–239 (2011).

16. J. Greene et al., *An fMRI Investigation of Emotional engagement in moral judg-ment*, SCIENCE, **293**, 2105–2108 (September 2001).

17. P. O'Neill & L. Petrinovich, *A preliminary cross-cultural study of moral intu-itions*, EVOL. & HUM. BEHAV., **19(6)**, 349–367 (1998).

18. Some critics have suggested that Greene is actually perpetuating the false Cartesian dichotomy of "emotional" and "cognitive" systems. J. Mikhail, *Emotion, neuroscience and law: a comment on darwin and greene*, EMOTION REV., **3(3)**, 293–295 (2011). For a fabulous survey of the history of the thinking on emotion and reason, and the impact neuroscience is having on this dichotomy, see PAUL GLIMCHER, NEUROECONOMICS: DECISION MAK-ING AND THE BRAIN (Academic 2008). For a somewhat more popular but equally engaging treatment, see ANTONIO DAMASIO, DESCARTES' ERROR: EMOTION, REASON AND THE HUMAN BRAIN (Harper 1995).

19. S. L. A. MARSHALL, MEN AGAINST FIRE (William Morrow 1947; U. Okla-homa Press 2000).

20. Roger J. Spiller, *S. L. A. Marshall and the Rate of Fire*, 133 ROYAL UNITED SERV. J. **63** (1988).

21. See, e.g., John Whiteclay Chambers III, *SLA Marshall's Men Against Fire: New Evidence Regarding Fire Ratios*, 23 U.S. WAR COLLEGE Q. PARAMETERS **113** (2003).

22. FRANCIS A. LORD, CIVIL WAR COLLECTOR'S ENCYCLOPEDIA (Stackpole 1976).

23. RICHARD HOLMES, ACTS OF WAR: BEHAVIOR OF MEN IN BATTLE 168 (Free Press 1986). Holmes also claims that there is similar data from the American Indian Wars. In the Battle of Rosebud Creek in 1876, for example, he reports that General George Crook's men fired 25,000 rounds against the Sioux and Cheyenne, yet casualties (on both sides) never rose above the double-digit level. These dreadful hit ratios cannot be explained simply by rifle inaccuracy, because by the time of these wars in the late 1800s bore technology had dramatically improved the rifle's accuracy. See generally Alexander J. Field, *Behavioral Economics: Lessons from the Military* (April 2009), unpublished manuscript available at http://papers.ssrn.com/sol3/papers.cfm?abstract_id=1382422.

24. Id. at 3–4.

25. William Shakespeare, *The Tempest*, Act I, scene ii, lines 4–5. This line is spoken by Miranda, as she is telling her father that she has just witnessed a ship's crew drown in the storm that opens the play.

26. B. Wicker et al., *Both of us disgusted in* my *insula: the common neural bases of feeling and seeing disgust*, NEURON, **40(3)**, 655–664 (2003).

27. P. Whalen et al., *A functional MRI study of human amygdala responses to facial expressions of fear versus anger*, EMOTION, **1(1)**, 70–83 (2001); T. Singer et al., *Empathy for pain involves the affective but not sensory components of pain*, SCIENCE, **303**, 1157–1162 (February 2004).

28. T. Singer, *The neuronal basis and ontogeny of empathy and mind reading: review of literature and implications for future research*, NEUROSCI. & BIOBEHAV. REV., **30**, 855–863 (2006). Not surprisingly, these are the very same theory-of-mind areas we saw associated with blame, and that we will also see associated with third-party punishment, as punishers assess the intentions of wrongdoers.

29. J. Moll et al., *The neural correlates of moral sensitivity: a functional magnetic resonance imaging investigation of basic and moral emotions*, J. NEUROSCI., **22(7)**, 2730–2736 (2002).

30. C. Masten et al., *Witnessing peer rejection during early adolescence: neural correlates of empathy for experiences of social exclusion*, SOC. NEUROSCI., **5(5–6)**, 496–507 (2010).

31. G. di Pellegrino et al., *Understanding motor events: a neurophysiological study*, EXP. BRAIN RES., **91(1)**, 176–180 (1992).

32. R. Mukamel et al., *Single-neuron responses in humans during execution and observation of actions*, CURRENT BIOLOGY, **20(8)**, 750–756 (2010).

33. This section is taken in large part from Kent A. Kiehl & Morris B. Hoffman, *Criminal Psychopaths: History, Neuroscience and Economics*, **51** JURIMETRICS 355 (2011).

34. Katchadourian, supra note 2, at 130–131.

35. M. Rice & G. Harris, *Cross-validation and extension of the violent risk-appraisal guide for child molesters and rapists*, J. L. & HUMAN BEHAV., **21(2)**, 231–241 (1997).

36. ROBERT D. HARE, SNAKES IN SUITS: WHEN PSYCHOPATHS GO TO WORK (2006).

37. G. T. Harris et al., *Psychopathy and violent recidivism*, L. & HUM. BEHAV., **15(6)**, 625–637 (1991).

38. ROBERT D. HARE, WITHOUT CONSCIENCE: THE DISTURBING WORLD OF THE PSYCHOPATHS AMONG US 199 (Guilford 1999).

39. For a discussion of the history of psychiatry's struggle with recognizing psychopathy, and its relationship with antisocial personality disorder, see Kiehl & Hoffman, supra note 33, at 361–368.

40. See, e.g., J. Newman et al., *Passive avoidance in syndromes of disinhibition: psychopathy and extroversion*, J. PERS. & SOC. PSYCHOL., **48(5)**, 1316–1327 (1985). The classic inhibition test is the so-called go/no-go test, in which subjects are instructed to push a button when they see a certain object on the screen, but not to push the button when they are shown a slightly different object. Refraining from pushing the button when the "no-go" object is shown is a challenge, especially when the objects are flashed on the screen rapidly. Psychopaths are substantially less able to restrain themselves in the "no-go" condition than non-psychopaths.

41. See, e.g., S. Williamson et al., *Abnormal processing of affective words by psychopaths*, PSYCHOPHYSIOLOGY, **28(3)**, 260–273 (1991). When subjects are shown a large list of words and then asked later whether a certain word was or was not in the list, normal subjects remember emotionally-laden words – like "blood" or "kill" – much more often than they remember emotionally-neutral words – like "table" or "windy." Psychopaths exhibit no difference in their ability to remember these words. The word "blood" no more reaches them emotionally than the word "table."

42. Hare himself has expressed reservations about the inappropriate use of his clinical instruments by correctional officials. See the story on National Public Radio broadcast May, 26, 2011, available at http://www.npr.org/2011/05/26/136619689/can-a-test-really-tell-whos-a-psychopath.

43. See, e.g., K, Kiehl, *Without morals: the cognitive neuroscience of psychopathy*, in 3 MORAL PSYCHOLOGY: THE NEUROSCIENCE OF MORALITY: EMOTION, BRAIN DISORDERS, AND DEVELOPMENT (W. Sinnott-Armstrong, ed., Bradford Books 2007); C. Harenski et al., *Neuroimaging, genetics, and psychopathy: implications for the legal system*, in RESPONSIBILITY AND PSYCHOPATHY. INTERFACING LAW, PSYCHIATRY AND PHILOSOPHY (L. Malatesti & J. McMillan, eds., Oxford 2008); K. Kiehl et al., *Brain potentials implicate temporal lobe abnormalities in criminal psychopaths*, J. ABNORMAL PSYCH., **115(3)**, 443–453 (2006); K. Kiehl, *A cognitive neuroscience perspective on psychopathy: evidence for paralimbic system dysfunction*, PSYCH. RES **142(2–3)**, 107–128 (2006).

44. These paralimbic differences are not the only emerging neurological indications of psychopathy. It also appears psychopaths in a resting state (that is, not being directed to perform any tasks in the scanner) exhibit

markedly reduced connectivity into and out of the vmPFC – the area we saw, in Chapter 2 at note 28, may be critical to assessing harm and to integrating harm and intent into blame. J. Motzkin et al., *Reduced prefrontal connectivity in psychopathy*, J. NEUROSCI., **31(48)**, 17348–17357 (2011).

4   SECOND-PARTY PUNISHMENT: RETALIATION AND REVENGE

From panic, pride and terror, revenge that knows no rein.

Rudyard Kipling

THE AVENGING ANIMAL

History is full of retaliation and revenge because people are full of retaliation and revenge. When the invading Romans made the mistake of flogging the Celts' king's widow, Boudicca, and raping her daughters, she raised an army that wreaked havoc from one end of Britain to the other. It took three legions to restore order, and by that time Boudicca had burned three Roman settlements, including London. Her army was finally defeated in the West Midlands. As she and her daughters rode around on her chariot to rally her doomed troops for the final lost battle, Tacitus reports that she told them:

> I am not fighting for my kingdom and wealth. I am fighting as an ordinary person for my lost freedom, my bruised body and my outraged daughters.... The gods will grant us the vengeance we deserve.[1]

God's vengeance is retaliatory precisely because when we sin we sin against God's direct commands. Punishments by deities are not restrained third-party punishments meted out against remote wrongdoers. They are in divine and terrifyingly unrestrained retaliation for cheating the gods directly. Adam and Eve were banished from Eden because God was retaliating against them for breaking his rules. Constructs of Hell are likewise a type of heavenly revenge. The fear of heavenly revenge is meant to deter us from earthly wrongs. One of the profoundly civilizing effects of all religions is to turn social codes – which inherently may have insufficient bite – into divine commands with infinite bite.

Mankind's greatest tour guide to divine retaliation, Dante's *Inferno*, was itself largely a product of revenge. Dante wrote much of it, and his larger *Divine Comedy*, as a kind of revenge fantasy against Pope Boniface VIII and his allies, who drove Dante from his beloved Florence, tried and convicted him in absentia on trumped-up charges of extortion, confiscated all of his property, and sentenced him to permanent exile on pain of death by burning. Dante never returned to Florence. In the twenty years that remained of his life, he wandered from kingdom to kingdom, city to city, exacting his revenge through his writings. In the *Inferno*, Dante's St. Peter denounces the papacy as having made the earth a sewer of blood, and announces that God's papal throne on earth is vacant. Dante got a lot more personal with Boniface directly, whom he condemns to the eternal hellish torment of having his face buried in rock and his feet exposed and on fire.

Dante's genius included a deep reverence for The Social Problem and the moral ambiguity nature built into the human brain. In Canto XVII, a terrifying creature called Geryon carries Dante and his traveling companion down into the eighth circle, which is reserved for those who commit fraud. Geryon has the face of an honest human but a body that's a combination of bear, snake, and scorpion. He is the embodiment of the duplicity that is fraud. And the fact that fraud in Dante's world is serious enough for one of the lowest levels of Hell (eight out of the nine circles, eclipsed only by the circle devoted to treachery) speaks volumes about the revenge-based emotions we all feel when our trust is violated by cheaters.[2]

We are all attuned to, if not obsessed with, retaliation and revenge. We have been taking action to right the wrongs committed against us, real and imagined, since our emergence. From the Torah's and the Qur'an's commands to take an eye for an eye, to a website called revengeguy.com, dedicated to giving advice to revenge seekers, we seem triggered to lash out against those who injure us.[3] Our literature is full of stories of revenge, from Seneca's Roman tragedies and the revenge dramas of the Elizabethans, to Mel Gibson's 1991 movie *Payback*. It seems as if every important human myth has an aspect of revenge to it. The story of Hephaestus' revenge against his mother, Hera, is both a typical revenge myth and typically full of that famous Greek ambiguity and nuance.

Hephaestus, the Greek god of fire and metallurgy (Vulcan in the Roman nomenclature), was the son of Zeus and Hera, but he was born lame, the only Greek deity with any significant physical imperfection. When Hera saw the baby's deformed leg, she threw him off Mount Olympus and into the sea. But he was rescued and raised by two sea nymphs. When Hephaestus came of age, and discovered the truth about his mother's rejection of him, he hatched a plan for revenge. He built a beautiful but magically deadly golden throne, and sent it to Hera on Olympus. When she sat on it, chains hidden inside the throne suddenly appeared and bound her to it. She cried for help, but none of the gods, not even her husband Zeus, could break the magic chains. The gods appealed to Hephaestus, who replied, "I have no mother." So they enticed Dionysus, the god of wine, to make Hephaestus drunk and bring him up to Olympus. The drunken son freed his mother's chains, and the gods rewarded him with Aphrodite as his wife.

But the gods' "reward" of Aphrodite was yet another clever Greek revenge tragedy in waiting, and perhaps was itself Hera's re-retaliation. Just like her mother-in-law, Aphrodite was repulsed by Hephaestus' physical deformity, and immediately began an affair with the god of war, Ares. When Hephaestus caught them in flagrante, he ensnared them in a set of his patented unbreakable chains, and dragged the two of them to Olympus, hopeful that the other gods would inflict some third-party punishment on them. But when the other gods saw the two naked lovers bound in chains, they just laughed. Poseidon convinced Hephaestus to release them, in exchange for Ares' promise to pay an adulterer's fine.[4]

Revenge permeates the Old Testament, and the Hebrew God is the most reliable of all the revenge-seekers.[5] Revenge also plays a role in Islam, although it seems largely to be theologically directed, that is, revenge for wrongs against Allah. In one of the hadiths, or commentaries on the Qur'an, the commentator reports that Muhammad never took revenge for wrongs done to him, but only when "Allah's limits were exceeded, in which case he would take revenge in Allah's sake."[6]

But another hadith reports a rather quirky example of Muhammad's temper and willingness to retaliate. One day he was home ill, but for some reason or another he commanded his family and servants not to give him any medicine. They did so anyway, and when he improved and discovered their violation, he scolded them, and announced, "There is none of you but will be forced to drink medicine, and I will watch you."[7]

Retaliation and revenge are not just mythical and literary universals. They populate our myths and literatures because they populate our brains. Like all our instincts, the instincts to retaliate and to seek revenge are shaped by the particular cultures in which they reside. But there are some striking commonalities.

The blood revenge for homicide – the practice by which family members of a homicide victim kill the killer or one of his family members – is common in modern primitive societies, from the Inuits and plains Indians in North America to the aboriginal tribes in Australia.[8] An astonishing 95 percent of all the cultures that have been examined, past and present, show some evidence of blood revenge.[9] As late as the 1960s, 44 percent of all extant societies on the planet practiced, and recognized, some form of blood revenge.[10]

The practice is not only widespread across cultures, it permeates some of them. In one study, the Murngin in Australia engaged in seventy-two battles between tribesmen in the first twenty years of the twentieth century, and of these seventy-two battles fifty were undertaken as blood revenge.[11]

And yet the rule of law has managed to replace the blood revenge in virtually all modern Western societies. We may all feel the burning desire to exact vengeance, but most of us never act on those desires because in most of our cultures the state has come to monopolize punishment. Still, even the rule of law must accommodate the fact that we all are driven by feelings of vengeance. As the psychologist Michael McCullough has put it, "The search for the society that knows nothing of vengeance is only marginally more likely to be successful than the search for the society of three-armed people."[12]

We all know this to be true without doing any cross-cultural studies at all. Imagine you are standing at a bus stop (or cattle crossing or town square) minding your own business when someone you do not know comes up to you and pushes you in the chest, knocking you down. Your amygdala explodes with activity, directing the immediate release of adrenalin into your bloodstream as you stand, clench your fists, and prepare for fight or flight. Depending on innumerable environmental and cultural circumstances – such as whether the aggressor is armed, is bigger than you, is accompanied by friends, the state of your health, whether you are a Quaker, whether you once retaliated and got severely injured – you may be able to resist the urge to retaliate. But no matter how old you are, what culture you are in, or what experiences you have had, every automatic system in your body will prepare you to retaliate. And even if you turn the other cheek, or turn and run, chances are you will spend the next hours, and maybe days and months, plotting real and imagined revenge. Even if you try to forget about the slight and eschew revenge, you will probably spend some time feeling terrible about your ineffectualness. This is true whether you are an accountant in Minneapolis or a nomadic forager in the Kalahari.

As with our instinct to cooperate, the universality of retaliation and revenge has also been demonstrated empirically. In experiment after experiment, human players across all demographics exhibit a healthy willingness, indeed an eagerness, to retaliate against other players who do them wrong, even if that retaliation comes at a cost. One embedded aspect of the traditional ultimatum game is already a test of Player B's willingness to retaliate against Player A for an unfair division, at a cost to Player B. Recall that Player A is given ten dollars and directed to propose a division with Player B – from one dollar to ten dollars. Player B then gets to accept the proposal or reject it, but if he rejects it then neither player gets any money. Whenever Player B rejects what he considers an unfair offer he is retaliating against Player A by causing Player A to not receive any money, and that retaliation comes at a cost to Player B because he is willing to take nothing in exchange for causing Player A to get nothing. As we've seen, humans from all societies, primitive and non-primitive alike, are willing to punish stingy offers in this costly manner.

As we have also seen, one of the most common defections in higher social species is a violation of trust, and we regularly retaliate against such violations. Trust games with a retaliation component have shown the universal human willingness to retaliate against unrequited trust, even when, again, the retaliation comes at a cost. So, for example, experimenters have built a retaliation move into the standard trust game. That game, remember, involves two players A and B and starts out like an ultimatum game. The experimenter gives ten dollars to A, and directs him to share with B. But the experimenter also informs both players that whatever A gives to B will be tripled, and that B can then decide how much if anything to give back to A. The most selfish play for A is to give only one dollar, but he can do better than that by giving all ten dollars to B, having it tripled to thirty dollars, then trusting B to give back a "fair" amount, say fifteen dollars. Like the traditional ultimatum game, this version of the trust game has a built-in retaliation component: if Player A is too stingy on his first move, then Player B will retaliate by being stingy in the extent to which he shares the tripled amount. Just like in the ultimatum game, we all quite regularly exhibit retaliating behaviors when faced with a stingy Player A. But this kind of retaliation comes at no cost to Player B, because he gets to keep the tripled amount.

So experimenters have designed different versions of the trust game that impose a cost on retaliation. In one version, Player A gets the last move by being able to punish a non-reciprocating Player B, for example, by getting to determine how much of Player B's retained funds should be forfeited back to the experimenter. Not surprisingly, if Player A can punish Player B at no cost then he is quite willing to do so, in our example by causing a non-trusting Player B to forfeit all of the tripled amount. But even if the retaliation is costly to Player A – let's say he must forfeit one dollar for every dollar he decides to forfeit from Player B – he still regularly punishes Player B for unrequited trust. In fact, in one version of the game, where both players are staked with some money before the game starts, Player A will even go out of pocket to punish a treacherous Player B. There is a rich literature demonstrating that this kind of costly retaliation is common across all societies, both industrial and preindustrial, although the amount of costly punishment individuals are willing to impose can vary greatly both across and within cultures.[13]

Retaliation and revenge are not just common human behaviors, they have cellular roots that go back to the first forms of life. The immunological response – which was once thought to be restricted to complex creatures but is now known to be present in a primitive form in animals as simple as flatworms – is the most widespread of all systems of retaliation. We don't think of white blood cells attacking viruses as "retaliation," probably because that term connotes more complex, extra-organism behaviors. But surely those white blood cells are retaliating against the invading virus every bit as much as a male grackle is retaliating against an invading competitor. In fact, one of early life's most difficult problems was how to achieve multi-cellularity in a world of single-cell organisms where the "I/them" response was built into single cells, and the boundary between the selfish gene and the rest of the world lay at the cell wall of each single-celled organism. The earliest forms of cooperation were those that somehow allowed single-celled creatures to give up their deeply engrained immunological response and to bind with other single-celled creatures to form a bigger self.

But no matter how big our selves got, we retained powerfully embedded notions of our own boundaries, and many multi-celled animals retained vigorous systems for fighting off outsiders. Certain kinds of algae fire projectiles at would-be microscopic predators at speeds as fast as a bullet from a low powered rifle.[14] With no brain, no spinal cord, and no neurons, these simple life forms still manage to distinguish themselves from others and then kill those trying to feed on them. Higher-order kinds of retaliation and preemptive strikes are also common across animal species, from fish to birds to mammals. Male guppies exposed to environments in which there are many predator fish "inspecting" which guppy to swallow, retaliate against the inspecting predator by attacking them. Even though they have no hope of winning a fight, their retaliatory behavior seems to ward off the much larger predators.[15] Queen mole rats will retaliate against lazy worker rats that fail to do the queens' bidding, despite the fact that the retaliation itself slows down the work. So will queen wasps.[16]

Retaliatory behaviors that have a component of delay I will call "revenge," but I don't mean for that word to carry with it any anthropomorphic connotations. The "vengeful" vampire bat is engaged in time-delayed retaliation. It does not "hate" its fellow bat or plan sweet revenge. For humans, with language and consciousness, the distinction between retaliation and revenge may seem more significant than a mere passage of time. We can imagine retaliating, and the imagining itself imposes a delay, maybe forever. The delay may even make the revenge more satisfying, thus the saying "revenge is a dish best served cold." Revenge may also connote a more sophisticated, cognitive, kind of planning, and retaliation a more automatic, emotional, reaction. But as forms of second-party punishment, I will generally use the terms retaliation and revenge interchangeably, with the only difference a matter of timing.

In social species, one of the most common kinds of retaliation is a simple refusal to reciprocate. If you have not cooperated with me, I will not cooperate with you. It may have been weeks ago that you refused to cooperate with me, but I keep score, even if I am a vampire bat, and when I later become positioned to cooperate with you I may refuse to do so because of your earlier refusal. Animals also engage in more active kinds of retaliation and revenge – in which they are willing to pay the costs of actively punishing a wrongdoer when that wrongdoer commits a wrong against the punisher. Biologists call this "costly punishment," or sometimes "altruistic punishment." Even our simple alga is capable of this kind of costly punishment, given that it costs lots of energy for it to fire its projectile.

In its most basic sense, retaliation – whether passive or active, free or costly – is the yang of cooperation's yin. We punish one another whenever we do not cooperate, if our decision not to cooperate is in response to a defection. If that prior defection was aimed at us, then our refusal to cooperate is a form of second-party punishment.[17]

Retaliation in whatever the form, even though it imposes some cost on the person doing the retaliating, was a net evolutionary benefit in our emergent groups. Yes, it costs me to poke out the eye of my aggressor, but he's already poked out my eye, and reacting quickly and decisively will send him and his friends and relatives a strong message, not at all unlike the guppy's message, that the next time they decide to pick on someone they'd be better off choosing someone else (unless they determine that my one-eyed-ness now makes me an even easier target). The threat of retaliation added an additional level of deterrence beyond the restraining voice of conscience.

Retaliation and revenge probably evolved because conscience and guilt were just not enough to keep defections down to tolerable frequencies. With only our own consciences to guide us, we would have defected far too often, our social networks would have unraveled, and with them the evolutionary benefits of group living. Retaliation was a second line of defense against the temptation to violate Rules 1 and 2. If my conscience was not enough to prevent me from robbing that fellow group member, maybe the certain knowledge that he would violently resist would be enough to give me second thoughts. Groups containing brains built with consciences *and* instincts to retaliate would have had fewer defections, and would therefore have been more likely to stay together, than groups containing brains built just with consciences.[18]

This does not mean retaliation evolved after conscience and guilt. On the contrary, as we have already seen, forms of retaliation are quite old and can be seen in species as primitive as algae. Conscience was a much later evolutionary invention, and may, as we've discussed, be unique to humans. Once we arrived on the scene, with our devilishly complicated brains and our deep ambivalence about cooperating, we were able to recruit those older forms of retaliation to help keep our groups stable.

Even if it were theoretically possible to have groups bound tightly enough only by conscience and guilt, those bonds would quickly have been broken by defectors without conscience and guilt – psychopaths. If just one psychopath were born into a group of non-psychopaths, the psychopath would probably have had a significant adaptive advantage over everyone else. His defections would go unpunished if retaliation were not a part of anyone else's social toolbox, and his selfishness would inure entirely to his own advantage. To the extent psychopathy is genetic, and there is some evidence it is, he would produce more psychopaths who would likewise have a significant survival advantage over members dragged down by conscience and guilt. At some point, the psychopaths and non-psychopaths might reach some equilibrium in distribution, but that equilibrium point might well not be conducive to continued group living. A group needs a critical mass of cooperators to remain a group.

Besides, even if the number of psychopaths stabilized at a low enough number to allow our groups to continue, other non-psychopath members of the group are watching. Without the behavior of retaliation, these normal group members would see a whole class of other members who regularly defect without suffering any consequences. Soon, everyone would be defecting and our groups would unravel.

But even psychopaths will think twice about defecting if they know their victims will retaliate.

There is an important connection between conscience and revenge, between first-party punishment and second-party punishment. We are restrained by our consciences not just from cheating, but also from overreacting to those who cheat us. If killing feels wrong, then killing in retaliation also feels wrong, though admittedly a bit less wrong. Like any kind of aggression, retaliation can be costly. The wrongdoer and his family might re-retaliate. With retaliatory instincts on a hair trigger, every defection would have risked sending us into a spiral of destabilizing cyclical revenge. So it was important that our retaliation instincts, like our consciences, be nuanced. Our retaliatory instincts needed to be strong enough to overcome our instinct not to harm one another, but not so strong as to risk the anarchy of endless vendettas. Conscience and guilt therefore restrained us even from retaliating. Just as our first-party punishment instincts make us presumptive but skeptical cooperators, our first- and second-party punishment instincts make us presumptive but careful retaliators.

We have already seen that retaliatory behaviors are common across many animal species, social and nonsocial, primitive and complex, from algae to mole rats. Our closest primate cousins also engage in second-party punishment as a regular part of their social diet, both in the wild and in captivity. Chimpanzees, for example, will attack members of their coalition if those members refuse to participate in coalition-benefitting activities, such as food gathering.[19] In experimental conditions, chimpanzees consistently exhibit a willingness to retaliate – for example, by collapsing the tables of fellow chimps that steal their food, making it harder for the thieves to enjoy the fruits of their crime.[20]

There is also an emerging neuroscience of second-party punishment. Because these behaviors are so closely related to trust, we should not be surprised that oxytocin, which we've seen regulates trust in a reciprocal fashion with testosterone, also seems to be involved in our urge to retaliate. The complementary relationship between oxy-tocin, cooperation, and forgiveness, on the one hand, and testos-terone, defection, and retaliation, on the other hand, is complex and not entirely understood. But most important for our purposes, the relationship is not entirely symmetric. Increased testosterone, as you might guess, decreases cooperation and increases the willingness to retaliate.[21] Because testosterone blocks the effects of oxytocin, one might imagine that increased oxytocin would do just the opposite – increase cooperation and decrease the willingness to retaliate. Increased oxytocin does in fact increase cooperation, as we have seen, but it does not appear to decrease our urge to retaliate. In the ultimatum game, for example, increased testosterone makes Player A more stingy and Player B more willing to punish a stingy offer. Increased oxytocin makes Player A less stingy, but it seems to have no impact on Player B's willingness to punish stingy offers.[22]

One explanation for this asymmetry is that once an in-group mem-ber defects, the oxytocin in our retaliating brains seems to treat him as an outsider, at least for some time. After all, a defecting insider can pose an even more immediate threat to the group than outsiders. Despite oxytocin's generalized function of increasing trust, it seems that evolution developed mechanisms to deactivate that function when we are faced with palpable threats. As we have already speculated, the message we may be getting from oxytocin in these threat situations may be something like, "You and your baby are being threatened, so go ahead and retaliate."

When human subjects play trust and retaliation games inside brain scanners, their retaliatory behaviors activate quite specific areas of the brain. First, there is increased activity in two structures involved in the emotional response to being wronged. The amygdala – which we've already discussed and is well-known to be involved in reward and punishment – is part of this emotional signaling circuitry.[23] So is the insula, which should be no surprise because, as we've seen, the insula is associated with the emotion of disgust, and dis-gust at the initial defection is a big part of the emotional engine of retaliation.[24] Figure 4.1 depicts the amygdala, in the lower left labeled "A," and the insula, as the partially obscured grey quadrangle in the center.

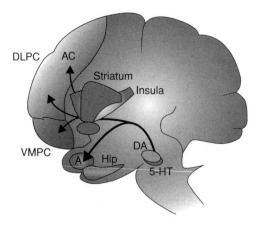

Figure 4.1. The risk/reward circuit. From A. Bechara, *Decision making, impulse control and loss of willpower to resist drugs: a neurocognitive perspective*, NATURE NEUROSCI., 8, 1458–1463, Fig. 1 (2005).

After getting these initial inputs from the amygdala and insula, a brain contemplating retaliation next shows increased activations in three particular cortical areas – the ventromedial prefrontal cortex (VMPC in Figure 4.1), the cingulate (part of which is labeled AC), and the dorsolateral prefrontal cortex (DLPC). These frontal areas seem to be involved in the decision about whether to override the initial urge to retaliate.[25] These are the same three areas we've seen are associated with blame and punishment generally.[26]

These five areas – amygdala, insula, vmPFC, cingulate, and dlPFC – are all part of a larger neural network involved in assessing risks and rewards. That's not surprising, since punching someone in retaliation for being punched is taking a big risk that the whole exchange will explode into serious violence, and therefore requires some sophisticated social judgment.[27]

Imaging studies have also confirmed that when we retaliate it is because the emotional signals generated from the amygdala, insula, and deeper parts of the cortex swamp the signals we get from the so-called control areas of the frontal cortex. As we've already seen, we blame third-party wrongdoers by assessing their intent, and the amount of harm they inflict matters only as a tiebreaker. The assessment of intent is in turn a complicated matter, performed primarily in prefrontal areas of the cortex (including vmPFC and dlPFC). But when we blame people who injure us, we blame based only on harm. Our assessment of harm in turn is almost entirely limbic (amygdala), and therefore largely visceral and immediate. When we retaliate, our brains seem literally to skip the blame part and move right to the brink of punishment. When you knock me down and my fight or flight instincts are rocketing their way from my limbic system into my muscles, those instincts are driven by the amount of harm I have just endured. At the beginning at least, they don't care one whit whether the push was intentional or accidental. I am about to become a one-man judge, jury, and executioner. All sorts of other considerations come on line later to determine what I will actually do, but at the moment I blame you for your wrong and am about to retaliate, I don't care whether your harm was intentional or accidental, I care only how much harm you have inflicted on me.

SELF-DEFENSE AND ITS COUSINS

The law recognizes this urge to retaliate, and from all accounts it always has. One of the purest forms of this recognition is in the law of self-defense. Despite a cacophony of variations at the margins, the right to use force to protect one's self from the aggressions of others has been recognized in every society that has left a record on the matter.[28]

In his work entitled *Laws*, Plato argued there was a right to kill in self-defense, and he characterized it as a moral justification for murder, not just a pardonable excuse.[29] That is, self-defense was automatically justifying; defendants did not have to rely on the largesse of the ruler to pardon them. These were not mere philosophical ramblings; they found their way into the written laws of Athens, and from there into many other ancient legal systems.[30]

In Jewish law, self-defense was not only a justification for homicide, it was a positive duty. A Jew had the obligation to confront a thief, threaten him with death if he persisted, and then carry that threat out if the thief did not stand down.[31] Chinese legislation from as early as the Zhou dynasty in the third century BC enshrined the right of self-defense.[32] The Romans recognized the right of self-defense in their Twelve Tables, bronze tablets displayed in the Forum for a thousand years, and Justinian codified the right in his Corpus Juris.[33] Muslim legal theorists described self-defense as a "natural right" seven

hundred years before the Enlightenment.[34] Self-defense was even part
of the Church's canon law, was refined by Thomas Aquinas and others, became a part of the melding of western and Islamic law into the
Spanish legal tradition, and survived the Reformation. And of course
self-defense was a staple of English common law.[35] It is recognized in
every American state, and has even found its way into the contemporary pronouncements of the European Human Rights Commission.[36]
The right to defend one's self from the aggressions of others is an
unbroken thread connecting every human society with every other.

The ubiquity of self-defense in the human story is not limited to
the legal dimension. Martial arts are a perfect example of the extrale-
gal institutionalization of self-defense. They first appeared in ancient
Indian literature and then were exported as part of the spread of Buddhism, first to sixth-century China, then to Okinawa, then Japan, then
the rest of the world.[37] Systems of individual self-defense were common in societies where the state could not protect the average person
from the violence of others, especially where political instability made
such violence commonplace. Buddha himself, albeit before his enlightenment, killed a man he caught trying to sabotage a boat ferrying 500
merchants. The Hindu principle of *ahimsa*, or nonviolence, recognizes
exceptions for war, capital punishment, and self-defense.

The notion of self-defense has always been bound up with two
ideas: 1) all individuals have the essential right to be free from the
violence of others (our Rule 1 in its broadest sense); and 2) when
such violence is threatened, force to prevent it, in some cases even
lethal force, is justifiable because all reasonable people would inflict
such force to prevent injury to themselves. Self-defense recognizes our
universal urge to protect ourselves, a kind of pre-injury retaliation.

One variety of self-defense is the defense of others. All of the author-
ities discussed in the previous paragraph recognized that "self" defense
necessarily included the defense of family. Indeed, as we have seen, the
blood revenge dealt with retaliating for the homicide of a family member. The family unit was always recognized as part of one's "self" for
purposes of the urge to protect and retaliate, and the legal justification to do so. This makes perfect sense from an evolutionary point
of view. We are protecting our genes not our "selves," although I am
unaware that the self-defense laws of any society have ever made the

kinds of fine relatedness distinctions suggested by the theory of kin selection. The English common law, for example, made the defense of others available in the defense of family regardless of either the degree of relatedness or the type – whether by blood or marriage. It also recognized the right of an employer to defend an employee, and vice versa, perhaps reflecting the centrality of commerce in English culture.[38]

The defense of others has, in very general terms, expanded from family to clan to town to city-state to nation and, at least in modern systems, to all of humanity, as the reach of the law itself has marched beyond the confines of family and largely eliminated the in-group out-group distinctions under which we evolved. Today, in all legal systems the defense of others is largely identical in definition and application to self-defense, and in fact both defenses are sometimes defined as a single defense, phrased as the right to defend one's self or others.[39] Many jurisdictions have also retained the common law alter ego rule, which makes the defense of others justified only if the person being defended would have been justified in using self-defense.[40]

There are many other legal doctrines besides self-defense that reflect the idea that reasonable people will retaliate and therefore must be forgiven by the law, in whole or in part, when they do. One such doctrine is provocation, sometimes also called "sudden heat of passion." Even if one is not in immediate danger, and thus cannot take advantage of the complete defense of self-defense, the provocation doctrine recognizes that a mind inflamed with retaliatory passion may be less blameworthy than one free from such flames. At common law, the provocation defense had three substantive elements: 1) the defendant must have acted in the heat of passion; 2) the passion must have been the result of adequate provocation (that is, provocation that would cause a reasonable person to act as the defendant acted); and 3) the defendant must not have had a reasonable opportunity to cool off. If a defendant could prove these three elements, intentional homicide was reduced to voluntary manslaughter.[41]

There were only a few types of provocations recognized at common law, and they covered just the kinds of things one might expect would drive ordinary people to the brink of homicide. Observing a spouse committing adultery was the quintessential provoking circumstance, although it was undoubtedly less frequent in actual practice than being the victim of an aggravated assault, another of the recognized provocations. The adultery version required the actual *observation* of the infidelity – hearing about it was not enough to qualify (and in any event, the defense would probably be unavailable in such circumstances because of the cooling off element). Early common law versions famously permitted the provocation defense to be asserted by cuckolded husbands, but not by cuckolded wives. Apparently, male infidelity was to be expected, and could not, as a matter of law, inflame the passions of any reasonable wife.[42] A provoking assault had to be with a weapon – that's what the common law means by an "aggravated" assault. Physical violence without weapons, like male infidelity, was apparently frequent enough in England when the common law was developing in the thirteenth and fourteenth centuries that a simple assault, with fists and kicking, was just not expected to inflame the passions enough to justify a retaliating homicide. That was true even though such an assault was of course *more* likely to pose a risk of death then than it is today, with modern medicine and emergency rooms preventing many simple assaults from turning into homicides.[43]

Like self-defense, provocation seems to have roots that reach back to emerging societies. And in some sense provocation really is just a special kind of expanded self-defense, pushing its application later in time to a point after the wrong has been committed, and beyond circumstances in which the defendant or others are necessarily in physical danger, recognizing that more than just physical insults can trigger our retaliatory urges. In exchange for expanding the reach of this special kind of post hoc self-defense, the common law reduced its effect. It was not a complete defense, as self-defense was; instead, it generally reduced the grade of the charged crime.

Provocation is now largely a matter of statute, and virtually every modern provocation statute preserves the common law elements and mitigating effects, but without limiting those elements to particular categories of provocation. Like the common law, these provocation statutes limit the defense's application to the most serious of offenses – murder and in some cases serious assaults. In my jurisdiction, which is quite typical, provocation will reduce a second-degree murder, punishable by a mandatory prison sentence of between sixteen and forty-eight years, to manslaughter, for which a defendant could theoretically get probation.

These kinds of doctrines reflect the law's acknowledgment, from a third-party point of view, of our common second-party urges. Whether we are judges, juries, parents, or teachers, we all forgive the infliction of harm in self-defense, and partially forgive it when it is provoked. In fact, these two kinds of urges – self-defense and provocation – are likely two sides of the same evolutionary coin, at least in a species as complex as ours, where we can *imagine* harm we did not witness. Through the magic of imagination, we can recruit provocative urges that in less intelligent animals well up only in self-defense or defense of others contexts. I don't need to *see* my wife beaten by an intruder to have my urge for revenge well up once I learn about the beating. This ability probably played a crucial role in the evolution of third-party punishment in humans, and may well explain why, as we will see in the next chapter, third-party punishment is spotty at best in our nearest primate relatives.

But our feelings of revenge when we are not the targets of the wrongdoing can also present some problems in our institutions of third-party punishment, where we expect jurors, and especially judges, to be more dispassionate third-party punishers.

ANGRY SENTENCING JUDGES: ARE WE JUDGING OR RETALIATING?

Several years ago I read about a high profile criminal case in which the sentencing judge made the following statements: "Defendant asks for mercy. We are not in the mercy business; we are in the justice business." As I was thinking of the many ways these comments seemed so off the mark, I realized that my objections to them could be summed up this way: this trial judge has confused second-party punishment with third-party punishment, revenge with retribution. Our revenge instincts, as we have seen, are visceral and largely automatic, are graded to harm and are fairly insensitive to the wrongdoer's state of the mind. The emotional gain of these feelings is difficult to overcome. For most of us, especially when we have suffered great harm and are responding with an urge to retaliate immediately, the urge wins out.

But when we punish others in the name of the group, the evolutionary and neurological dynamics are very different. When we punish in the name of the group, we use blame circuits tuned to intent, and then punishment circuits tuned to harm, and these two circuits seem carefully insulated from each other. When we punish third parties, we have a neurological ability, and therefore a deeper obligation, to think about the costs of punishment and whether those costs outweigh the deterrent effects. We have an obligation to do justice. We must be restrained, proportionate, and prudent. We must show mercy where in our judgment mercy is warranted.[44]

The rule of law itself is in its most basic sense a recognition of the inadequacies of our embedded and almost irresistible urge to retaliate, and an attempt to overcome those urges. One of the main reasons all private disputes cannot be efficiently or justly resolved by the two disputants is that the disputants' emotions are often enflamed by the urge to retaliate. Third-party punishment replaces that powerful urge with a duller version. Frans de Waal put it this way:

> Systems of justice . . . can be regarded as the successful transformation of a deep-seated urge for revenge – euphemized as retribution – which keeps the urge within acceptable boundaries.[45]

Don't misunderstand. Humans did not invent the institution of third-party punishment because we saw the inadequacies of first- and second-party punishment. As we will see in the next chapter, third-party punishment is every bit as embedded in our evolved natures as second-party punishment. It evolved in tandem with first- and second-party punishment because only all three could solve The Social Problem in a species as clever and devious as ours. Third-party punishment allows us to make punishment judgments that are more dispassionate than if we had victims doing the punishment. The retaliatory urges in third parties will, by the very fact that they are third parties to the crime, be muted.

When judges, like the one in this high profile case, become second-party punishers by taking on the attributes of the injured victim, when they suggest that mercy is not itself inseparably bound up with justice, then we might as well have victims impose sentences. We don't do that because we recognize that their judgments typically are infected with second-party feelings of retaliation and revenge. A former prosecutor in the economic crimes unit of our District Attorney's office once told me that his victims all want the same thing: all their money back and the execution of the defendant. We don't let victims impose such sentences, and we should not impose them by channeling victims' second-party outrage. Mercy and forgiveness are real evolutionary considerations that our brains are built to consider when we punish, because over-punishment was as deadly to our groups as under-punishment. By muting the strength of our retaliatory urges when we act as third-party punishers, natural selection allowed our feelings of restraint – of our own conscience and guilt in punishing and our urge to forgive – to play a more important role when we punish strangers than when we retaliate against our own wrongdoers.

Of course, judges and jurors are human, and are therefore inherently empathetic, unless they are psychopaths. Judges and jurors will feel second-party urges whenever the facts of a crime are brought to light in the courtroom. The more lurid and time-consuming those facts, the greater the risks of second-party urges. Evidence of that comes from the data on the so-called trial penalty. It is well-known that, all other things being equal, a defendant who pleads guilty to a crime gets punished less severely than a similarly-situated defendant who exercises his constitutional right to a trial and then gets convicted.[46] Many commentators have wrung their hands over this difference, some suggesting that judges are punishing defendants who exercise their constitutional right to trial. But there is an explanation that is much less nefarious, and in many ways much more difficult to manage.

When cases go to trial, judges are exposed day after day to the emotional details of the crime, given to us by the very people who suffered and/or witnessed it. By their very nature trials engage our second-party urges to retaliate much more than when the details of the crime are conveyed in the dry words of a written complaint and a guilty plea process that lasts a few minutes. That difference is particularly big if judges allow a defendant to waive the factual basis during a plea – that is, if they allow the defendant merely to say the word "guilty" without specifically admitting what he did.

I am not at all sure how we can solve this problem. Surely we should not categorically sentence defendants who plead guilty more severely, or those who go to trial less severely, in an attempt to pre-adjust for the trial penalty. The English have a much more restricted kind of plea bargaining, generally limited to set discounts for specific crimes, and as a result the "trial penalty" does not seem to loom so large. But it is hard to see how such a system could work in the United States, where plea bargaining is widespread and largely open-ended. Perhaps we could devote more time to sentencing proceedings on guilty pleas, in an effort to increase the emotional gain in those proceedings. We could, as I do, also refuse to accept waivers of the factual basis, and refuse to take plea bargains that contain a specified sentence.

These solutions might eliminate the trial penalty, but some might also exacerbate the problem. More details about the crime, whenever and however those details are disclosed, might increase the chances of third-party judges becoming second-party punishers. Maybe just being aware of the problem will help us apply some level of cool reason to our job as third-party punishers, and avoid the powerful second-party urges that come with trials.

What's an appropriate "cool" sentence and an inappropriate "hot" one is of course not an easy question to answer. I once sentenced a sixty-one-year-old sex offender to thirty-six years in prison, and the moment I left the bench I could feel myself seething with anger. After I calmed down I told my law clerk to set the case for reconsideration because I was positive my emotions had blurred my judgment.[47] In my jurisdiction, trial judges don't set cases for sentencing reconsideration very often, not only because there is value in the certainty of a sentence but also because we know the very act of setting a case for a reconsideration hearing will have emotional impacts on both sides. The victims will be re-traumatized not just by having to go through the process again, but also by worrying that the sentence will be reduced (we cannot *increase* a sentence on reconsideration). Defendants will get their hopes up.

Despite these organic reservations, I was sure that once I calmed down I'd realize that the thirty-six-year sentence in this case was too much. But at the reconsideration hearing, after hearing all the arguments again, I decided that thirty-six years was appropriate. I learned a valuable lesson – being emotional at a sentencing hearing does not necessarily mean the emotion has inappropriately infected the sentence. And in fact, the real infecting emotion was my reaction to the emotion, by immediately telling my law clerk to set it for reconsideration. Now I try hard, after an emotional sentencing hearing, not just to calm down from the sentence, but also to calm down from any emotional rebound from the sentence. I try not to reach any decision on whether to set it for reconsideration until at least several days pass.

Our second-party urges drive all judges to say and do dumb things at sentencing. I once described a white collar thief as a "sociopath in a three-piece suit," and, as some of my prosecutors still delight in reminding me, a drug dealer as a "gangster doofus," to name just a few examples. I thought these turns of phrase were clever at the time, and so did the newspapers. But in retrospect, I see that I let my second-party anger get out of control. These defendants deserved the sentences I gave them, but they did not deserve my parting shots.

From talking to many judges over the years, I've come to learn what all criminal lawyers already know: there is a wide variety of judicial sentencing styles. In my jurisdiction, which has no sentencing guidelines and therefore generally requires no specific findings during sentencing, some of my colleagues say almost nothing other than the words required to impose the sentence. Others are inveterate moral lecturers. I probably fall somewhere in the middle, despite consciously trying to say as little as possible. In the end, at least for me, it is impossible not to say a few words about *why* I am imposing the sentence I am imposing. Sentencing is, after all, a moral act of community opprobrium, even though talking too much about that opprobrium risks igniting second-party flames.

The best confessional I've ever heard about the excesses of moralizing during sentencing comes from my friend and federal judge John Kane. He was sentencing a young woman embezzler on her first offense. She was a bank teller from Nebraska, who moved to Denver, got into financial straits, and caused the bank records falsely to state that the bank had received some payments on her auto loan. This was before the federal sentencing guidelines, and as most judges would do in such a case, John decided to give the woman probation. But as is also the temptation for many trial judges, he decided to put the fear of God into her while announcing the sentence:

> Look around you. Do you see what shame you have brought on your family and yourself? People trusted you and you have thrown that trust away. Now you will have to earn that which before was freely given to you. I never want to see you in this courtroom again, and if you do come back it will be just a short stop on your way to prison. I'm placing you on probation for three years and ordering you to pay full restitution to the bank before you are discharged. Do you understand?

He reports that the defendant let out a bleat "like a wounded rabbit," and that her parents thanked him profusely as they left the courtroom. Then:

> As I declared a recess I looked down on the well of the court and saw a small puddle. The young woman had urinated on the floor. I left the courtroom and returned to my chambers. I slammed the door behind me. I looked at the black robe I was wearing. I had disgraced it.[48]

When we impose third-party punishment, we speak with the authority of the whole group, and because of that we must try to transcend the emotions of retaliation and revenge. The theater of the courtroom is all about that transcendence, both in the eyes of the public and in our own minds. The trappings of judges – the high bench, the robes, the salutations – are important reminders to everyone that when we sentence we are not acting as outraged agents of the victim, or for that matter as loving and forgiving parents of the wrongdoer, but as a kind of oracle, empowered rather magically to punish in the name of the whole. The figurative mask we wear in court is a mask of communal authority. It hides our individuality and transforms us from homeowners with chores to do and bills to pay into priests of the common good. As Lord Justice Alan Moses said in his wonderful 2006 lecture, "It is the mask which creates a belief, which creates authority."[49]

But the mask is more than that. We oracles must not only convince the public of our magical powers to transcend various group memberships, but we must convince ourselves. Perhaps a more pertinent observation about the importance of the mask comes from Oscar Wilde: "Man is least himself when he talks in his own person. Give him a mask and he will tell you the truth."[50] Let's turn in the next chapter to the truth of third-party punishment.

Notes to Chapter 4

1. TACITUS, THE ANNALS OF IMPERIAL ROME 328–331 (Penguin 1996). The story of Boudicca comes to us indirectly, through the Roman historians, and it is often difficult to separate facts from fiction. Tacitus suspiciously reports that in the final battle virtually every member of Boudicca's army was killed – 80,000 of them – with the Romans suffering only 400 casualties. Boudicca's fate is not clear. Some report she was killed with her army, others that she survived the battle and killed herself at home. She has become a revered folk symbol of pre-Norman courage and fidelity. Queen Victoria dedicated a statue to her in 1905 on the Thames embankment near the Houses of Parliament, where it still stands.

2. These writings were not just Dante's revenge fantasies. They had practical political impact by contributing to Boniface losing his moral and then political authority. Bonaface's opponents eventually liberated Florence, pardoned Dante and all other exiles, and invited them to return. The price of that return, however, was public penance, which Dante refused to perform. He died in exile in Ravenna, where his tomb contains this epitaph: "Florence, mother of little love." Florence eventually came to regret its treatment of its most important poet, and began demanding his remains from Ravenna. It even built a tomb for them in 1829. In a final act of revenge, Ravenna has refused to release the body, and Dante's Florentine tomb remains empty to this day.

3. When I first visited the site, a revenge-seeker wrote for advice about how to get back at his late father's gold-digging widow. Revenge Guy treaded into difficult legal waters, advising the revenge-lorn writer to sue the widow to contest the will.

4. Like many Greek myths, the story of Hephaestus comes to us largely from the Homeric Hymns, an anonymous collection of thirty-three stories written down as early as the seventh century BC, and erroneously attributed to Homer. See generally THOMAS W. ALLEN ET AL., THE HOMERIC HYMNS (Oxford 1936).

5. The most famous revenge story in the Old Testament is probably the story of Mordecai and Esther, which comprises the *Book of Esther* and is the

basis for the Jewish holiday Purim. Some scholars have argued that Dante's revenge story in Canto XVII was deeply influenced by the tale of Mordecai and Esther. Jo Ann Cavallo, *Canto XVII: On Revenge*, in LECTURA DANTIS, PURGATORIO, A CANTO-BY-CANTO COMMENTARY 178 (A. Mandelbaum et al., eds., 2008).

6. Al-Mughira, Vol. 8, Book 82, No. 829. Another hadith reports that when a follower tells Muhammad that he would kill any man he finds in bed with his wife, the prophet chastises him for a lack of self-respect: "Do you wonder at [the man's] lack of ghira [self-respect]? Verily, I have more sense of ghira than [the man], and Allah has more sense of ghira than I." 'Aisha, Vol. 8, Book 42, No. 836.

7. Ad-Diyat no. 6897.

8. Although blood revenge has some third-party connotations, it is one kind of transitional second-party punishment, where a family unit retaliates against harm inflicted on any of its members. We will look at the transition from second-party punishment to third-party punishment in Chapter 5.

9. MARTIN DALY & MARGO WILSON, HOMICIDE 221–223 (de Gruyter 1988).

10. K. Otterbein & C. Otterbein, *An eye for an eye, a tooth for a tooth: a cross-cultural study of feuding*, AM. ANTHRO., **67(6)**, 1470–1482 (1965).

11. W. J. WARNER, A BLACK CIVILISATION (Harper 1937).

12. MICHAEL E. MCCULLOUGH, BEYOND REVENGE: THE EVOLUTION OF THE FORGIVENESS INSTINCT 78 (Jossey-Bass 2008).

13. J. Henrich et al., *Costly punishment across human societies*, SCIENCE, **312**, 1767–1770 (June 2006).

14. R. Gordon, *A retaliatory role for algal projectiles*, J. THEOR. B., **126(4)**, 419–436 (1987).

15. J. Godin & S. Davis, *Who dares, benefits· predator approach behaviour in the guppy* (Poecilia retuclata) *Deters Predator Pursuit*, PROC. R. SOC. LOND. B, **259**, 193–200 (1995).

16. See generally, T. Clutton-Brock & G. Parker, *Punishment in animal societies*, NATURE, **373**, 209–216 (January 1995). This may sound more like third-party punishment given that the queen has not herself been directly injured, but remember that mole rats and wasps are eusocial, and that any injury to the group is therefore a direct injury to the reproductive fitness of the queen.

17. The *Elder Edda*, a thirteenth-century collection of Norse epic poems, put this relationship between cooperation and retaliation elegantly:

> To his friend a man a friend shall prove
> And gifts with gifts requite
> But men shall mocking with mockery answer
> And fraud with falsehood meet.

Hovamol at l. 42, in HENRY ADAMS BELLOWS, THE POETIC EDDA 37 (Am.-Scand. Foundation 1923).

18. See, e.g., R. Boyd et al., *The evolution of altruistic punishment*, PROC. NAT. ACAD. SCIENCES, **100(6)**, 3531–3535 (2003); E. Fehr & S. Gächter, *Cooperation and punishment in public goods experiments*, AM. ECON. REV., **90**(4), 980–994 (2000).

19. FRANCE DE WAAL, CHIMPANZEE POLITICS: POWER AND SEX AMONG APES (JHU 1982). Again, this may sound like third-party punishment, but the punishing chimp has actually been injured himself by the coalition member's refusal to cooperate, so it may be an example of the kind of transitional second-party punishment we will discuss in Chapter 5.

20. K. Jensen et al., *Chimpanzees Are vengeful but not spiteful*, PROC. NAT. ACAD. SCIENCES, **104(32)**, 13046–13050 (2007). Interestingly, though, chimpanzees will not retaliate against other chimps in this experimental design when a human experimenter steals the food and gives it to the other chimp. That is, chimpanzees seem to be able to recognize the difference between a wrongdoer and an innocent beneficiary of another's wrong.

21. See, e.g., P. Mehta et al., *Neural mechanisms of the testosterone-aggression relation: the role of the orbitofrontal cortex*, J. COGN. NEUROSCI., **22**, 2357–2368 (2010).

22. One explanation is that the testosterone is doing something other than blocking the effects of oxytocin. And, indeed, testosterone has diffuse and complicated effects, including its association with status and general aggression in protecting that status. It may, quite apart from blocking oxytocin, make us generally more aggressive toward and intolerant of defectors, increasing our willingness to punish them regardless of our oxytocin levels. Another, perhaps overlapping, explanation might be that because oxytocin's effects are highly dependent on social context, once a group member defects, even an oxytocin-laden fellow member is willing to punish the defector. Indeed, as mentioned in the last chapter, oxytocin's prosocial effects are limited to in-group members, and it has no effect on out-group cooperation, and in fact may even *increase* the willingness to punish an outsider. C. De Drue et al., *The neuropeptide oxytocin regulates parochial altruism in intergroup conflict among humans*, SCIENCE, **328**, 1408–1411 (June 2010).

23. A. Bechara et al., *The role of the amygdala in decision-making*, ANN. N.Y. ACAD. SCI., **985**, 356–369 (2003).

24. P. R. Montague, *To detect and correct: norm violations and their enforcement*, NEURON, **56**(1), 14–18 (2007).

25. A. Sanfey, *The neural basis of economic decision-making in the ultimatum game*, SCIENCE, **300**, 1755–1758 (June 2003).

26. Chapter 3, Note 28.

27. This risk-reward network is sometimes called the "corticostriadal loop," because it involves bundles of neurons connecting lower areas of the

striatum – a structure in the basal ganglia critical to the production of the neurotransmitter dopamine – with higher structures in the frontal cortex. It appears that these dopamine-driven circuits may be the key to how we assess risks and benefits, and how we turn those assessments into decisions. Interestingly, these same areas are involved in the choices made by rhesus monkeys when playing various economic games, further demonstrating that the risk/reward function, and the retaliation portion of that function, is a deep part of primate social strategy. D. Lee et al., *Reinforcement learning and decision making in monkeys during a competitive game*, COGN. BRAIN RES., **22(1)**, 45–58 (2004). Neuroscience is also beginning to build models of addiction based on the idea that addiction is bound up with defects in the way in which these risk/reward circuits release dopamine in response to both our anticipation of certain behaviors and the actual feelings we get from those behaviors. See generally DAVID LINDEN, THE COMPASS OF PLEASURE: HOW OUR BRAINS MAKE FATTY FOODS, ORGASM, EXERCISE, MARIJUANA, GENEROSITY, VODKA, LEARNING AND GAMBLING FEEL SO GOOD (Viking 2011).

28. The variations include many interesting and beguiling issues: 1) what kinds of crimes should be subject to the defense of self-defense?; 2) whether someone who is not the initial aggressor has a duty to attempt to retreat before using force to defend (the so-called retreat to the wall doctrine); 3) whether the belief one is in danger must be objectively reasonable, and, if not, whether an unreasonable but genuine belief one is in danger should reduce the charges even though it is not a complete defense; 4) whether a pregnant woman can use "self" defense to defend her fetus; and 5) the extent to which the defense applies to modern circumstances of battered women and children.

29. PLATO, 9 LAWS 216 (Benjamin Jowett trans.), available at http://www.gutenberg.org/dirs/ctext99/plaws11.txt (emphasis added):

> If a brother kill a brother in self-defence during a civil broil, or a citizen a citizen, or a slave a slave, or a stranger a stranger, let them be free from blame, as he is who slays an enemy in battle. But if a slave kill a freeman, let him be as a parricide. A man is justified in taking the life of a burglar, of a footpad, of a violator of women or youth; and he may take the life of another with impunity in defence of father, mother, brother, wife, or other relations.

30. One of those statutes provided: "If any man while violently and illegally seizing another shall be slain straightaway in self-defence, there shall be no penalty for his death." J. H. Vince, *Introduction to "Against Aristocrates"* in 3 DEMOSTHENES, ORATIONS 212–213 (1935) (originally delivered in 352 BC).

31. The Book of Exodus contains what was probably the first "make my day" law: "If a thief be found breaking up [in], and be smitten that he die, there shall

no blood be shed for him." Exodus 22:2. Talmudic commentators expanded this passage and made the right of self-defense a duty:

> What is reason for the law of breaking in? Because it is certain that no man is inactive where his property is concerned; therefore this one [the thief] must have reasoned, "If I go there, he [the owner] will oppose me and prevent me; but if he does, I will kill him." Hence the Torah decreed "If he come to slay thee, forestall by slaying him."

HEBREW-ENGLISH EDITION OF THE BABYLONIAN TALMUD: Sanhedrin, folio 72a. (I. Epstein ed., 1994). This last sentence is sometimes translated "If someone comes to kill you, rise up and kill him first," and under this command a Jew has a positive duty, not just a right, to do so. In fact, the duty to prevent homicide was extended in the Talmud to mere bystanders.

32.   Whenever one kills those who attack the districts and towns and drag away persons from their families it will not be considered an offence.

M. J. Meier, *Self-Defense*, in THOUGHTS AND LAW IN QIN AND HAN CHINA: STUDIES DEDICATED TO ANTHONY HULSEWÉ ON THE OCCASION OF HIS EIGHTIETH BIRTHDAY 226 (W. Idema & E. Zürcher, eds., E. J. Brill 1990).

33. Justinian's codification of the right was comprehensive, and covered many situations. But the general right was described this way:

> If someone kills anyone else who is trying to go for him with a sword, he will not be deemed to have killed unlawfully; and if for fear of death someone kills a thief, there is no doubt he should not be liable.... But if, although he could have arrested him, he preferred to kill him, the better opinion is that he should be deemed to have acted unlawfully.

1 JUSTINIAN, THE DIGEST OF ROMAN LAW XVIII (Penguin 1979).

34. Islamic jurists, from whatever particular school, have always recognized that other Muslims, at least, have the right to use force to defend their life, liberty, and property. David Kopel, *The Human Right of Self-Defense*, 22 B.Y.U. J. PUB. L. 43, 119 & n. 394 (2007), citing KHALED ABOU EL FADL, REBELLION & VIOLENCE IN ISLAMIC LAW 334–335 (2001).

35. Although until the late 1300s self-defense was viewed not as a justification defense but rather as an excuse pardonable by royal prerogative. THEODORE F. T. PLUCKNETT, A CONCISE HISTORY OF THE COMMON LAW 445–446 (5th ed., LittleBrown 1956). The distinction between justification and excuse is discussed in Chapter 5.

36. "Deprivation of life shall not be regarded as inflicted in contravention of this article when it results from the use of force which is no more than absolutely necessary: (a) in defense of any person from unlawful violence." THE EUROPEAN CONVENTION ON HUMAN RIGHTS art. I sec. 1, available at http://www.hri.org/docs/ECHR50.html. Interestingly, the United Nations Declaration of Human Rights contains no explicit right of self-defense, although it does recognize the "right to life, liberty and security of person." THE UNITED

NATIONS' UNIVERSAL DECLARATION OF HUMAN RIGHTS art. 3, available at http://www.un.org/en/documents/udhr/index.shtml.

37. BRUCE A. HAINES, KARATE'S HISTORY AND TRADITIONS 25 (Charles E. Tuttle Co., rev. ed. 1995).

38. JOSHUA DRESSLER, UNDERSTANDING CRIMINAL LAW 275 (4th ed., LexisNexis 2006). Plato also describes the right as a right to defend "father, mother, brother, wife *or other relations.*" Note 29 supra.

39. In my jurisdiction, for example, the self-defense jury instruction explicitly combines self-defense with defense of others. COLO. JURY INSTR. (CRIM.) 2.8–1 Self-Defense and Defense of Others.

40. The Model Penal Code has retained the alter ego rule. MODEL PENAL CODE § 3.05(1). This additional requirement seems largely redundant, if the self-defense inquiry is truly objective. If a reasonable third-party would have intervened, it is hard to conjure up more than a few unlikely scenarios in which a reasonable victim in the same circumstance would not have been justified to act in self-defense.

41. See Dressler, supra note 38, at 571. There was a fourth element often articulated – that the provocation caused the homicide – but of course causation is embedded in the notion of true provocation. In fact, because the provocation has to be sufficient to cause a reasonable person *under the same circumstances* to kill, the cooling-off requirement is also arguably redundant.

42. Even though modern provocation statutes are on their face gender neutral, there is a growing critique, especially a feminist critique, of the provocation defense. These critics quite rightly note that men are more likely to be the killers and women to be the killed, at least in the infidelity version of provocation. Victoria Nourse, for example, has argued that provocation should not be applied to infidelity because infidelity is not illegal, and that it is therefore not appropriate for the law to recognize that passions can be inflamed by the legal act of infidelity. Victoria Nourse, *Passion's Progress: Modern Law Reform and the Provocation Defense,* 106 YALE L.J. 1331 (1997). Whatever one's view on this policy question – and Joshua Dressler, for one, has made some powerful arguments against the continuing utility of provocation – it seems to me that Professor Nourse's analysis of the nature of justifying passion is rather too narrow. There are a myriad of legal but plausibly provoking acts, just as there is a universe of illegal acts that are not provoking. Most of these critiques, feminist and nonfeminist alike, boil down to the argument that in our shiny new modern world, we just should not tolerate the brutish passions of yesteryear. But those passions are here whether we like it or not, because they are inside us whether we like it or not. With appropriate constraints, I for one would much prefer having a jury of twelve, rather than a law professor of one, deciding whether a given passion was reasonable or unreasonable, and whether it should or should not reduce the wrongdoer's blameworthiness.

43. The other categories of provocation recognized by English common law were mutual combat, commission of a serious crime against a close relative and illegal arrest. Id. at 572–573.

44. For a comprehensive and thought-provoking tour of the role of mercy in law, and the tensions that role creates, see MERCIFUL JUDGMENTS AND CONTEMPORARY SOCIETY: LEGAL PROBLEMS, LEGAL POSSIBILITIES (A. Sarat, ed., Cambridge 2011).

45. FRANS DE WAAL, GOOD NATURED 194 (Harvard 1997).

46. See, e.,g., Nancy J. King et al., *When Process Affects Punishment: Differences in Sentences after Guilty Plea, Bench Trial and Jury Trial,* 105 COLUM. L. REV. 959 (2005).

47. The law in most jurisdictions wisely gives trial judges a chance to reconsider criminal sentences. In my state, we have 126 days after the imposition of the sentence to reconsider it.

48. John L. Kane, "Judicial Diagnosis: Robe-itis," 34 LITIGATION 1 (Spring 2008).

49. Alan Moses, "The Mask and the Judge," Margaret Howard Lecture (May 15, 2006), transcript available at http://www.judiciary.gov.uk/media/speeches/2006/speech-moses-lj-15052006#fb15.

50. Oscar Wilde, *The Critic as Artist,* in INTENTIONS (Metheun 1891).

5   THIRD-PARTY PUNISHMENT: RETRIBUTION

God will punish the wicked. And before He does, we will.

John Green

THE PUNISHING ANIMAL

Ask anthropologists to list the things that make us most human – those special triggers of the human spark – and among the usual fare of language, consciousness, and of course the big social brains that make language and consciousness possible, will be an unlikely candidate: third-party punishment. We seem to be the only animal on Earth with a strong urge to punish wrongdoers when their wrongs cause harm to others but not to us.

Let's go back to that bus stop (or cattle crossing or town square) from the previous chapter, and instead of us getting pushed and knocked over by the wrongdoer, let's imagine that he pushes another innocent bystander. Through the miracle of empathy, remarkably similar feelings of fight or flight well up inside us, although admittedly not as sharp as when we are the victim. We get that same gnarl in our stomach, that same anxiousness about intervening, that same flash from our amygdalas telling us *we* are at risk, that same little dash of disgust from our insulas telling us this kind of aggression is intolerable. Just like when we are the victim, those instincts compete against a myriad of other inputs to produce a behavior. We might walk away, we might intervene, or we might pretend we don't see anything. But an unavoidable part of our decision is the urge we instantly feel to punish the wrongdoer, even though we are not at risk of being injured by him.

Some of these feelings are driven by mirror neurons. We feel pushed when we see others pushed, so part of our third-party punishment instincts are really just mirrored second-party punishment instincts. They are less intense than our second-party punishment instincts for the same reason all mirrored responses are less intense than the original: only a fraction of the neurons that fire when we experience a stimulus fire when we merely observe others experiencing it. But mirror neurons are not the entire explanation. After all, our primate cousins have mirror neurons, and they also have some kinds of empathy, but they do not exhibit widespread third-party punishment behaviors.

We evolved third-party punishment instincts more powerful than mirrored second-party punishment instincts because of the intensity of our groups and the power of our devious, cheating brains. Let's imagine a social animal similar to us, but with a brain programmed only for second-party punishment. They can retaliate and be vengeful, so they know if they cheat other group members those cheated victims will retaliate. Let's even imagine they have empathy, so that they have mild second-party reactions when they see others wronged. They don't need anything more because their level of required cooperation is fairly low. They live in trees, which means they are not only protected from most predators but also have a reliable supply of food. Group living gives them a net survival advantage, but not a giant one. Retaliation and a little bit of empathy were all they needed to glue together their loosely held groups.

But now imagine the kind of drastic environmental changes that happened to our predecessor primates. Their arboreal lands disappeared and they found themselves on the open savannahs, hunted and hunting. Now their survival required greatly increased levels of cooperation, and greater cooperation meant increased opportunities for defection. The Social Problem was ratcheted way up. They had to hunt together and defend together (not just from big cats but also from each other), and their lives depended on it. They needed a much more powerful social network now, instead of the weak one that worked in the trees.

What new traits might assist in the construction of such a network? Language would be one key. They could now talk to each other to plan their hunts and defenses. Consciousness would be another. Being aware of their innermost needs and desires would allow them to imagine that other members had those same needs and desires, and that knowledge helped them communicate with each other and be appropriately cautious of each other. Internalizing Rules 1 and 2 with conscience would be another great way to reduce the temptation to cheat, without any external institutional costs. Reinforcing those moral intuitions with guilt would also help.

But these instincts were not enough. Cooperation was now at a premium, meaning it would take only a few defecting members to eliminate the survival advantage of the new network. Not only that, but our more sophisticated brains, now armed with language, made our defections even more dangerous. Second-party punishment, even mirrored into a kind of weak third-party opprobrium, was just not enough. A stronger stand-alone third-party punishment urge was needed. Such an urge glued us together in ways that simple second-party punishment could not. It multiplied deterrence, both by increasing punishment's reach and increasing its deterrent force. A sneaky member trying to get away with a defection that might be undetectable to the victim – for example, stealing a bit of food when the victim is not around – must now deal with the entire group of watchful policing members. A single retaliating victim no longer needed to worry about the costs of re-retaliation, because now the wrongdoer faced punishment by a large number of members, perhaps even the whole group.

Now our new animal has three layers of protection against defections. Each member's conscience is weighted against defecting. If that's not enough, each also knows that if he cheats another member he risks retaliation by that member. If those two deterrents are not enough, he knows there is a big risk that other members will punish him. One can imagine that under the conditions of our emergence this type of triple-layered solution to The Social Problem might have been just right: just deterrent enough to make the individual long-term benefits of living in stable groups outweigh the individual costs of cooperating; but just porous enough to keep this balance delicate – so that, for example, if group norms or dominant members got too overbearing individuals could leave the group.

In this account, it might not be an exaggeration to claim that we didn't really become civilized until we became willing to punish each other for generalized wrongs to each other. That willingness allowed us to rely with more confidence on the promises we gave to each other (Rule 2), which in turn allowed us to make delayed promises, which gave us trade, divisions of labor, and economies of scale. Not having our groups unravel by too much killing or stealing (Rule 1) was also a key. By cementing the idea that an injury to one member was an injury to all its members, third-party punishment was able to weakly mimic behaviorally what the social insects could do genetically. Our intense groups remained intact even as they grew in size.

There are admittedly some difficulties with this account of the evolutionary advantages of third-party punishment. First, there is the detection problem. Retaliation needs no reporting system. The injured member does the retaliating. For third-party punishment to be effective, especially if it is to be extended beyond the family, the third-party punisher somehow needs to become aware of the defection. Language solved most of this problem. As we saw in Chapter 2, in our small groups the most important defections were probably there for at least someone to see. Armed with language, that someone could then tell everyone else. This might be one reason third-party punishment seems so rare in other species. Without language, its advantages are limited to defections a sufficiently large number of other members happen to witness.

Another problem with the proposition that we evolved an instinct for third-party punishment is that if every single group member had an instinct to punish every single wrong he was told about, as opposed to those he witnessed himself, there would have been a substantial risk that the group would have dissolved into an anarchy of busybodies. Fights even over who should be the punisher would also have contributed to this social breakdown.

In addition to being limited, at least at the beginning, to wrongs we actually witnessed, this problem of too much punishment by too many punishers might have been solved in two other ways. First, as we have already seen, our general third-party punishment urge is by its very nature muted and restrained, at least compared to our instinct to retaliate. Our groups may have had many potential punishers for every third-party wrong, but not every third-party wrong was serious enough to inflame our third-party punishment instincts. Remember our Rule 3: only *serious* violations of Rules 1 or 2 must be punished. Second, this busybody problem was constrained by having the group as a whole, as it often did with many important tasks, delegate third-party punishment to a smaller number of members.

Finally, and maybe most troubling of all, there is a serious public goods problem inherent in the idea that third-party punishment, even if delegated, could have evolved. It is difficult to see how a mutated tendency to punish people who don't hurt us directly could have been advantageous enough to take hold. Unlike retaliation – which gives the punisher a direct benefit in deterring defections aimed at him – third-party punishment provides only a diffuse benefit to the entire group. It seems impossible, at least at first blush, that a third-party punisher would ever have a fitness advantage over non-punishers, when in exchange for a potential and indirect benefit – increased group solidarity – he must pay the very direct, and often exorbitant, costs of punishment. We would have all been better off if a sufficient number of us were willing to act as third-party punishers, but until that critical number was reached any particular third-party punisher will be significantly worse off.

But this is really just a special case of the idea of kin selection, discussed in Chapter 1.[1] Punishing wrongdoers may come at a cost to my genes, but deterring other wrongdoers not only helps my genes it helps the genes of all my relatives. Behaviors that are damaging to an individual's survival (such as risking retaliation by the punished wrongdoer) may still be a net advantage to the individual's genes if the behavior benefits enough of those genes being carried by relatives. In groups with many related individuals, it is not at all hard to see how the short-term costs of third-party punishment might have been outweighed by the long-term benefits of group living conveyed on the punisher's and his relatives' genes. Third-party punishment also has the double whammy not just of benefiting all of our genes by keeping our groups stable, but also of reducing the risks faced by the punisher. The very threat of third-party punishment would have reduced punishment costs. Wrongdoers and their families would think twice about retaliating against being punished if they faced the whole group rather than just the wronged victim and his family. Spreading the costs of punishment in this fashion not only lowered its costs, it simultaneously increased its deterrent benefits. Lower-cost punishments could be imposed more often, and that very fact decreased the need for such punishments by further deterring cheats. This triple whammy aspect of socialized punishment may well have made the benefits so outweigh the costs that third-party punishment became adaptive.

Delegation also helps. If third-party punishment instincts evolved simultaneously with instincts to delegate punishment, we would have been able to enjoy all the socialized benefits of punishment without being exposed individually to their costs. The costs could be shuttled off to designated individuals – dominants, for example – who could withstand them.[2]

Some biologists also believe that emergent humans may have undergone natural selection at the group, rather than individual, level, and that third-party punishment in these circumstances would have given some groups a significant fitness advantage. The idea of group selection is that certain traits may have given a group such a big fitness advantage over other groups that the traits would have been favored by natural selection, even if they would not have otherwise been favored as between individuals in any particular group. Although group selection remains a controversial subject amongst biologists, even just a tiny bit of group-based fitness from third-party punishment could have been enough to overcome the public goods problem within a group.

Some have also argued that human third-party punishment became highly adaptive only when we developed clubs and thrown missiles, so that we could inflict punishment at a distance with a reduced risk of being injured by the individual being punished.[3] Another explanation has to do with the particulars of dominance hierarchies. In species such as chimpanzees and bonobos, in whom widespread third-party punishment by anyone other than the dominant member has not been seen, there is typically a sharp difference between the few dominant members and the rest of the troop. In other species, such as macaques and, it seems, humans, the dominance hierarchy is weaker and more evenly distributed. Primatologists have theorized that when, as in humans, the difference between dominant and nondominant members is not so great as in other primate species, and therefore the position of the dominants less secure, it was more important for the dominant members to delegate third-party punishment to nondominant members.[4]

Third-party punishment may also be more common in humans simply because human children are exposed to parental punishers for a much longer period of time than our primate cousins. In this account, third-party punishment may just be the way an intensely social and dependent species learns to express second-party punishment.

Finally, the public goods critique really proves too much when it comes to third-party punishment. After all, social living itself – without any third-party punishment at all – suffers from the very same public goods problem. Cheaters are always theoretically better off cheating, until a sufficient number of cooperators are able to create the advantages of group living. Those cooperation genes would never have spread if any single cooperator was always at a disadvantage in a world of cheaters. Yet we know that it did spread. The world is full of social species, primitive and complex, proving that at least in this more generalized context the public goods problem was something evolution was able to solve.

In fact, many evolutionary theorists not only believe that third-party punishment *could* have been adaptive in our emergent environment, they believe we could never have evolved in our closely-knit social groups without it.[5]

Quite apart from these theoretical arguments about whether third-party punishment in humans could have evolved, or indeed whether we could have evolved without it, there is considerable evidence that it did in fact evolve. Like first- and second-party punishment, third-party punishment is a human universal.[6] Every civilization that has left a record has left a record of third-party punishment, both real and mythological. As with conscience and revenge, show me any society anywhere on the planet at any time, and I will show you a society that recognizes that the group as a whole must sometimes punish some wrongdoers. This special group blame might well be reserved for just a few special wrongs, including killing the tribal leader. And the nature of these special wrongs might well change dramatically from one society to another. But third-party punishment – the idea that some kinds of wrongs are just too important to leave punishment to the victims – is as universal as cooperation, defection, conscience, and revenge.

Our myths are preoccupied with third-party punishment. Gods in all cultures spend an inordinate amount of time punishing humans and each other for wrongs committed not just against them but also against other gods and other humans. The Greeks devoted an entire form of deity – the Furies – to the problem of third-party punishment. These subterranean goddesses regularly intervened in Greek life to avenge the wronged, most commonly the victims of intra-family murder. Norse gods also regularly punished humans, heroes, and other gods for wrongs committed against others. And so it goes in all cultures.

Hindu mythology is somewhat unique in this regard because it expressly recognizes what all our other mythologies only imply: we simply would not be human without third-party punishment. In the oldest Hindu versions of creation, Brahma sacrificed himself so that the four classes of humans could be created: Brahmin from his mouth and the three lower classes from his arms, thighs, and feet. In later versions Brahma's dismemberment produced a more complicated species – containing mixtures of both good and evil across all classes.[7] With evil thus distributed among all of us, third-party punishment was necessary to prevent evil from crowding out good – a remarkably modern insight into what we would now call evolutionarily stable strategies:

> This is how punishment arose to protect the moral law, for punishment is the eternal soul of dharma. Brahma performed a sacrifice in order to create, and as happiness prevailed, punishment vanished. A confusion arose among men: there was nothing that was to be done or not to be done, nothing to be eaten or not to be eaten. Creatures harmed one another and grabbed from one another like dogs snatching at meat; the strong killed the weak, and there were no moral bounds. Then Brahma said to Siva, "You should have pity on the good people and abolish this confusion." Then Siva created punishment, which was his own self.[8]

In Brahma's misguided effort to maximize happiness, we no longer had any social norms. Our groups dissolved, and we all became self-interest machines – psychopaths. So Brahma suggested that Siva create third-party punishment – a willingness in humans to punish defectors even when the punisher is not the victim of the defection. Third-party punishment – Siva's gift – gave us the missing deterrence we needed to regain our social natures.

This third-party punishment instinct is what criminologists call retribution. Unfortunately, that word has acquired some political baggage over the years, and to many it is a pejorative description of a kind of inappropriately vengeful punishment. But in fact it is Siva's gift of civilization. Without the urge to punish others, we could not have survived in our small groups, let alone in our tribes or towns. Our myths and religions are full of retribution because our brains are full of retribution.

When experimental economists modify the classic economic games to contain a third-party punishment component, they see over and over again that we are willing to punish cheaters even though they do not personally harm us. We are even willing to pay for the privilege of doing so, although we are not willing to pay as much as when we are punishing players who have directly injured us. Our retribution instincts are strong, but not as strong as our retaliation instincts.

That third-party punishment has deep roots in natural selection is also evident from the fact that a wide variety of animal species exhibit precursors to it. Although classic third-party punishment seems absent in nonhuman primates, there are some tantalizing signs that its building blocks are there. In the early 1990s, in the Mahale mountains of Tanzania, Japanese primatologists observed a young adult chimp being attacked by eight nondominant members of his own group. They have suggested that he was attacked because he failed to conform to various norms, including attacking females without provocation and failing to defer to more senior males.[9] Similarly, in 1996 Frans de Waal and his colleagues at the Arnhem Zoo in the Netherlands observed members of a captive group of chimps attack two female members who failed to come into their cages when called, delaying the evening meal for everyone else.[10]

Admittedly, these field examples are isolated, and they may also just be examples of second-party punishment, especially the case of the attacks on the tardy females. After all, everyone's meal was being delayed, including the attackers'. However, a kind of third-party punishment by nonhuman primates has been repeatedly confirmed experimentally, suggesting that its general absence in the field may have more to do with the inherent difficulties of observing troops of primates in the wild than that the behavior is rare.

For example, researchers have discovered that groups of captive rhesus macaques enforce a kind of norm about informing the group when an individual finds food. In the wild, macaques give off a characteristic scream when they find food. When experimenters surreptitiously gave food to individual macaques in captivity, they noticed that the individuals sometimes announced the food but other times did not (presumably, they also cheat like this in the wild). When the group discovered that an individual had obtained food and had failed to announce it, the individual was frequently attacked by higher ranking members.[11] Many experiments have uncovered these kinds of norm-enforcing behaviors in captivity – what researchers have come to call "policing" behavior. Policing of one sort or another has been observed not only in all the great apes (chimpanzees, bonobos, gorillas, and orangutans), but also in several species of monkeys, including golden monkeys, hamadryas, baboons, and macaques.[12]

The same way that some nonhuman primates have the rudimentary building blocks for moral judgment, they also seem to have the rudimentary building blocks for third-party punishment, and in fact many of the building blocks are the same: complex brains with the ability to recognize social defection, mirror neurons to drive empathy, and memories sufficient to keep the defections in mind. Sure, not telling the group about a discovery of food injures all members of the group, so in some sense this rudimentary third-party punishment may again just be second-party punishment in disguise. But that's the whole point – that many primates can now recognize that a generalized harm to the group is an indirect harm to themselves. One of the keys to transitioning from second- to third-party punishment is broadening the whole idea of who is being harmed. You harm me when you harm my family, my group, my tribe, my town, my nation, my species. These experiments show that several nonhuman species have evolved a primitive notion of the harm-to-one-is-harm-to-all principle that is at the heart of true third-party punishment.[13]

Some new neuroscience evidence has strengthened the case that third-party punishment is an evolved human trait. Researchers at Vanderbilt have demonstrated that the very same brain areas associated with blame and second-party punishment are also associated with third-party punishment.[14] This study, though the first of its kind, strongly suggests that the two systems are evolutionarily related. It also goes a long way to confirm our Chapter 2 account of blame, responsibility, and punishment.[15]

The researchers asked subjects to read various crime scenarios in a scanner, and to indicate how severely they would punish the hypothetical criminal, on a scale of 0 to 9. As expected, subjects punished intentional acts substantially more severely than identical acts committed by someone the experimenters call "diminished." These diminished capacity examples included things such as being forced to commit the wrong with threats against one's family (the law calls this duress), or being insane. As we have seen, because we blame based primarily on our assessment of intentionality, we blame wrongs committed by mentally healthy people more than wrongs committed by irrational people. Subjects still sometimes punished irrational wrongdoers a little, because there was a range of how "diminished" these diminished wrongdoers really were. We also probably punish them a little just to reflect that we do not trust that they are not faking. Finally, there is the residual effect that, because we punish based on harm but blame based on intent, some punishment will leak through even of the most diminished wrongdoer, if he causes sufficient harm.

The researchers also asked the subjects after the scanning how aroused they felt when they punished various scenarios. Subjects blamed and punished in rough correlation to how aroused they reported they felt, but only if the wrongdoer was responsible, that is, was not under duress or insane. When the wrongdoer had diminished responsibility, subjects were still aroused, though not as aroused as when the wrongdoer was fully responsible. Most interestingly, punishment levels, although lower when the wrongdoer was diminished, were not as low as the low arousal results might predict. Subjects are somehow cognitively able to transcend their low levels of blame and impose more punishment on diminished wrongdoers than their emotional states seem to justify.

All of these results are consistent with the model we discussed in the last two chapters: our second-party punishment instincts get initially inflamed (and we get aroused) by the harm; but when we are third-party punishers our blame is driven by different circuits in the same regions, tuned to our assessment of the wrongdoer's intent; once we have blamed we punish on the basis of harm, but the level of that punishment is usually greatly reduced in the third-party context.

MOVING FROM SECOND- TO THIRD-PARTY PUNISHMENT

The blood revenge is one example of how treating our own families as ourselves automatically turns second-party punishment into third-party punishment. The dead victim of an intra-group homicide isn't around to retaliate against his killer, so his surviving family members must. But there are many other ways revenge against our wrongdoers developed into group retaliation against wrongs done to others.

Animals that spend a relatively long time being reared by parents are taught, as an inherent part of the socialization of child-rearing, to extend second-party punishment to third-party punishment. When a female gorilla swats her misbehaving infant for poking her in the eye, she is engaging in second-party punishment. But if she does exactly the same thing when the infant pokes a sibling in the eye, it is third-party punishment. It is not hard to imagine how evolution might have recruited these intra-family punishment urges and directed them toward non-kin. The same kin selection forces that drive us to sacrifice ourselves for our children drive us to punish those who injure our children. As our groups grew into clans, and clans into tribes, our family-based instinct to retaliate grew right along with them. Now, any injury to any member of the clan or tribe is an injury to self, and second-party punishment grows into third-party punishment.

This transition was probably even more important to humans than to our closest primate relatives, and much easier for us to achieve, because of our long childhoods. Human children are dependent on their parents for a longer time than any other primate – a fifth of our entire life span is spent in dependency. We spend more than a dozen years, not just many months, making sure our children don't poke each other's eyes out. Our unmatched intelligence and language were also critical to the generalization of second-party punishment into third-party punishment. Gorillas swat their young when they misbehave, but at some point we have to explain to our young why we are swatting them, and the moment we do that the rule tends to become generalized.

"Don't poke your brother in the eye" is a much more complicated rule to convey, and to follow, than "Don't poke anyone in the eye." Once we use language to generalize our rules, we have painted ourselves into the corner of enforcing the generalized rule through third-party punishment.

We therefore spend years punishing our young for behaviors that hurt nonfamily members. As our families aggregated into larger and more complicated groups, our generalized norms became aimed at members less and less related to us, and geographically more distant. Third-party punishment institutions – capable of punishing strangers over long distances – grew out of these embedded generalized third-party urges.

One the most effective ways deeply social animals can punish wrongdoers is simply to exclude them from the group, either physically or emotionally. Physical exclusion, in our emergent ancestors' time, meant certain death, unless the excluded wrongdoer could find another group to admit him, or took his own extended family with him. Something less drastic than physical exclusion would have come in handy for less serious defections – the social banishment we call ostracism.

OSTRACISM: "THE COLD SHOULDER IS JUST A STEP TOWARD EXECUTION"[16]

When my wife's maternal grandfather Rudy was just fourteen years old, his parents shunned him for more than a year. His offense was that he had passed letters between his older sister and a man of whom their father disapproved, the disapproval rooted in the fact that the man was neither German nor Lutheran. When the two lovers eventually eloped, and Rudy's complicity discovered, Rudy was "placed on the shunned list," as he put it. His siblings and their spouses stopped talking to him altogether. His father Rolfe stopped using his name and never spoke to him about anything other than to communicate about his chores. His mother reluctantly went along, and became cold and distant. Here's how he recalled the manner in which the shunning ended, after more than a year:

One summer morning Dad, Bert [an older brother] and I were in the yard working on a hayrack that needed repairs, when our neighbor . . . drove in the yard and said, "Rolfe, I've got some good news you can be proud of. In fact, the school district is proud, too. Rudy had the highest grade in the eighth grade examinations in Clay County [Nebraska]." Dad kind of grunted, and said "You'd better tell his mother, she'll probably be glad to hear it." [W]hen I came in the house, my mother put her arms around me, and told me how proud she was through her tears. About a week or so later, Bert and I got into a scuffle during the evening, and Dad grabbed me by the arm and pushed me up the stairs and said, "You get to bed." And then my mother spoke up, and these were her words: "You've driven one child away [the eloping daughter] and if you drive a second one away I'm going along." The next morning when I came downstairs, Dad said "Good morning," and Mother said, "Do you want a cup of tea before you go out to do chores?" My shunning period was over and conditions as far as I was concerned gradually improved. But I was never close to my Dad. The wounds healed but the scars remained.[17]

When he wrote this story down for us some seventy-two years later, when he was eighty-five, it was clear the scars were still there. He begins the story by announcing, "These memories that I am about to record are not pleasant ones, and over the years I've tried to forget them, but they still remain vivid."

There is nothing more terrible that social animals can do to one another than shun them, cut them out of the social network, precisely because our sociality is such an important feature of our evolved natures. Ostracism, by which I mean any kind of socially-exclusionary behavior when it is employed to punish, spans a wide continuum. In its most extreme forms, it can include banishment from the group and even execution. In its mildest forms, it can include a mother's disapproving glare at a misbehaving child. But it is all of a piece, as the wonderful quote from Jane Lancaster that forms the title of this section conveys, and that piece tells us important things about the way in which second-party punishment may have been transformed by evolution and by our punishing institutions into third-party punishment.

Anthropologists have found evidence of ostracism in virtually all societies across all technological, geographical, and temporal domains.

The Cheyenne banished for one to five years anyone who killed a fellow tribesman; abortion was also a banishable crime among the Cheyenne.[18] Defecting Samoans had their property confiscated and, for more serious crimes, they and their families were expelled from the village; Samoan adulterers were banished to neighboring islands.[19] The Pathan Hill tribes of eastern Afghanistan and western Pakistan to this day still ostracize by exile, though, interestingly, the exiled members' family maintains ownership of the family lands.[20]

Long before the time of Solon in 700 BC, Greeks practiced a form of ostracism they called *atimia*, in which the wrongdoer was not expressly banished but his property was confiscated and he was denied the right in the future to possess any goods, which usually required him to flee. *Atimia* was used only for the most heinous crimes under Greek law – including treason and sacrilege.[21]

A different, highly ritualized practice, called the *ostraka* – from which we get our word "ostracize" – also began at about this time, principally in Athens, and reached its height in the fourth century. Every year, citizens would write down the name of a fellow citizen they believed was particularly overbearing or otherwise dangerous to social stability. No formal crime needed to have been committed, only the crime of unpopularity, which in Athens during this time usually meant the crime of hubris. The names were written down on *ostraka*, which means shards of pottery. The votes were tabulated and the "winner" was banished from the city-state for one year, though, like the Pathan Hill exiles, his family could retain his property.[22]

Under Roman law, banishment was authorized only for serious crimes against the state, including treason and, before and after the republic, regicide. It was not, like the Greek *ostraka*, an exercise in unbounded democracy. The banishment decision was made by the Senate, or in imperial times by the emperor or his designees. The outcast criminals were banished from their city, town, province, or even from the whole empire, depending on the seriousness of the crime. For the most serious of crimes, the criminal was banished from all Roman protection, and all other citizens were free to kill him on sight without any consequences. The Romans called this most serious decree of banishment *caput gerit lupinum* – literally, "to wear the head of the wolf," meaning to be outcast and hunted down like a wolf. The name of this Roman decree of banishment became anglicized in English law as the decree of the "wolsved," which was the earliest form of the English order of banishment, or what the English later called "transportation."[23]

In the Middle Ages, as the organized Church became more and more entangled with the state, ostracism was expressed in both ecclesiastical and civil law. People could be excommunicated from the Church or banished from the entire empire, temporarily or permanently and in any combination. Serpentine refinements in degrees of excommunication began to develop, and some have persisted. *Excommunicato minor* disabled the miscreant only from communion. *Excommunicato major* disabled him from all contact with others, religious and civil. In between, any particular set of church and civil rights could be suspended for particular kinds of misbehavior, in a process called "the personal interdict." As late as 1983, the Church formally differentiated between the *excommunicati tolerati* (those who were excluded from the mass and the sacraments) and the *excommunicati vitandi* (those who were suspended from civil relations).[24]

Ecclesiastical and civil ostracism survived the Reformation, and indeed flourished after it, especially in their Lutheran and Calvinist forms. In John Calvin's own Geneva, the most severe form of excommunication combined the ecclesiastical *excommunicato major* with a complete barring of social relations and expulsion from the city-state.[25] Remnants of this severe form of Protestant ostracism found their way to the New World with the Pilgrims, and persist in modern times in the shunning, or "meidung," practiced by the Old World Amish, and apparently also by my wife's great-grandfather.[26]

Ostracism is not just a human universal. Its roots are quite apparent in many of our living primate relatives. Several of the basic features of human ostracism exist in nascent form in nonhuman primates, particularly the great apes. Chimp and human children alike shun playmates, chimp and human parents alike glare at misbehaving children, and juvenile chimps and humans alike spend an inordinate amount of time forming, breaking, and reforming teenage social alliances. When a young male chimpanzee challenges the dominant male, both may solicit support from females, and the group is often thrown into a short period of turmoil. Even juveniles, who normally would know their place, harass the pretender, "ostracizing" him for his boldness.[27]

The ubiquity of ostracism suggests that primate brains are indeed primed to punish wrongs even when the punisher is not the victim of the wrong. Ostracism by its very nature requires the whole to punish a norm-violating member, and that necessarily means that many members must endure the costs and trouble of enforcing the exile, even though they were never directly injured by the violation. Think of my wife's grandfather and his mother. She may not have had a problem with her daughter marrying a non-German non-Lutheran, and she certainly did not impose the shunning as punishment for Rudy's complicity. But she endured for more than a year the pain of being emotionally separated from her youngest son.

The law in its most general form, at least as it's aimed at punishing wrongdoers, is an abstract kind of ostracism. When states were small and weak, and most Rule 1 and 2 violations were punished privately, an important part of the toolbox of private punishment was ostracism – first from family, then from group, tribe, city-state, and empire. But as the state grew in size and complexity, and especially in the extent to which wrongs against one member were now considered wrongs against all members, the state began to take over more and more of the responsibility for the punishment of what would otherwise have been considered private wrongs. Private second-party punishment became public third-party punishment. Eventually, the state in its modern form has occupied the field of punishment to the exclusion of private enforcement, and in the course of that occupation ostracism has reemerged in the form of prison.

As the size and complexity of our social organizations grew, traditional social ostracism became impossible. A drunk might be shunned in his hometown but not in towns miles away. Complex trading and distribution networks could not risk having key components fail simply because one of their members was being ostracized. So today we ostracize criminals physically, by forcing them to live in their own separate prison societies, rather than shunning them socially while permitting them to remain in our physical midst.

PUNISHMENT OVER TIME: FROM BANISHMENT AND BACK AGAIN

Very little is actually known about the punishment practices of pre-historical societies. Anthropologists and scholars of primitive law have had to make educated guesses using the two usual sources: the practices of existing nomadic foragers; and what natural selection suggests our emergent groups might actually have been like. But in both cases, we need to be careful not to mix up in-group punishment practices with out-group punishment practices. We forged two sets of blame and punishment instincts – one nuanced and restrained by the challenges of group living, and the other largely unrestrained and in fact exaggerated by the threat of the outsider.

In our emergent groups 100,000 years ago, insider punishment was significantly more restrained than outsider punishment. Our groups were probably no larger than 100 members, and most of us were related. When we caught another group member stealing, we no more thought of lopping off his hand than we would have lopped off the hand of our own defecting sister. Punishment of insiders in these very early times was probably as much an exercise in gentle learning as anything else. And in fact, harsh corporal punishment is a rarity in known primitive societies. In most North American Indian tribes, for example, the harshest corporal punishment was beating, and it was reserved for very serious adult offenses.[28]

Another challenge in understanding early punishment practices is that those practices often overlapped with other customs that look like punishment but were not. Rites of passage, for example, often involved testing young boys with the same pain-inflicting practices occasionally used to punish the most serious of wrongs. Attempts to cure disease also sometimes used the same practices. There is great variation across existing primitive societies in the extent to which punishment overlaps with these other social practices. For many Australian aboriginal tribes the overlap is complete – they use the same flagellation techniques whether they are welcoming a young boy into adulthood, trying to cure a disease, stimulating sexual appetite, or punishing a miscreant.[29]

Despite the small and tight-knit nature of our ancestral groups, extraordinarily serious wrongs occasionally happened, and had to be punished in ways that went far beyond the gentle corrections we used in our families. The serious crimes for which these special punishments were reserved probably included things such as regicide, treason, and incest – exactly the kinds of wrongs around which grew strong cultural taboos, and therefore exactly the kinds of wrongs that could not be handled by an intra-family swat or lecture. From what we know from existing nomadic foragers, punishments for these extraordinarily serious crimes were likewise extraordinarily serious. Death was probably common for many of them, as it is in many existing primitive societies. Existing primitive societies carry out their death penalties in a countless variety of ways, including stoning, impalement, hanging, and drowning, and there is no reason to suspect our more distant ancestors were any less creative.

Banishment was probably also popular for capital-type offenses during our emergence, as it is in existing primitive societies. It had the benefit of being the practical equivalent of a death sentence, without all the messy attributes of an actual death sentence. There was risk in banishment, in the sense that the banished member might survive, join a new group, and seek revenge. An even greater risk was that his entire family might leave with him. But they might not, and by sparing him the group increased the chances that his family would remain contributing members of the group.

By contrast, and as strange as it may sound to our modern ears, even the most serious of private, non-taboo wrongs, even up to and including homicide (of any non-leader), were commonly punished only by the assessment of fines. From Mesopotamia to the ancient Chinese, early societies enacted complex systems of fines for serious private wrongs. One of the most famous of these was the *wergeld* of the primitive Germans. *Wergeld* means "man-money," and it was a detailed system by which a murdered man's worth was converted into a value, based on his ownership of lands and goods (and, later, his feudal rank). The murderer was punished by being ordered to pay that determined sum to the dead man's survivors. Fines for murder may seem lenient by modern standards, but remember that in many early societies, where we were often on the brink of starvation, paying such fines could be the equivalent of a death penalty.[30]

Fines also provided a more precise way to insure proportionality. Over-punishment risked damaging cycles of violence, especially in eras when the state was weak or nonexistent. It was therefore imperative that all concerned – the punished, the punishers, and everyone watching – have confidence that the punishment fit the crime. This became especially important as the number of public wrongs grew and private ones shrank. Imposing fines also resonated with the way economic wrongs must have been handled in our close-knit family groups, and indeed compensation probably first emerged in that context. If cousin Johnny stole food from cousin Teddy, older family members would force Johnny to repay Teddy, either with food or, later, with the monetary equivalent of the food. These compensatory systems may have had their roots in economic wrongs, but as the *wergeld* shows, compensation became just as paramount for crimes of physical violence.[31]

By ordering that the sum be paid to the victim, early proto-states were also taking the first steps toward converting private wrongs into public ones. The state was not yet punishing private wrongs directly, but it was enforcing the private compensation system. At some point, the failure of the wrongdoer to pay the fine became a public wrong, punishable as all public wrongs were punishable – by the severest sanctions, including death or banishment.

These two very different systems of punishment – banishment and death for a few taboo crimes deemed to be crimes against the whole group, and a system of fines even for the most serious, but non-taboo, offenses – lived comfortably side by side one another for thousands of years.

An entirely separate system of unrestrained vengeance applied to wrongs committed by outsiders. These were not exactly wrongs; they were acts of war. They required punitive responses, not reparative ones. None of the restraining circuits we evolved to blame and punish each other got triggered by such outside wrongs. This was us against them, with no holds barred. We no more thought of "punishing" outsiders than we think of D-Day as a form punishment.

As our groups got bigger, and as more private wrongs turned into public wrongs, these three systems were soon on a collision course.

Brains built to be lenient and forgiving with insiders faced the prospect of blaming and punishing members they did not know and did not trust. The group itself, familiar only with the most serious of punishments for the taboo crimes, was now being called upon to punish non-taboo crimes. The result of these pressures was that punishment for the new crimes started out at the old taboo baseline – banishment or death. Fines no longer felt serious enough to deal with these strangers. Our compensatory urges, however, remained strong. So instead of the ancient fine we would have to pay a group member whom we privately wronged, the state began punishing in kind.

This was the beginning of the concept of an eye-for-an-eye. Adulterers were now castrated, the hands of thieves now amputated. The Romans dubbed it the *lex talionis*, meaning the "law of retaliation," but it actually began as an alternative to monetary compensation, and applied even when the wrong was private. Across many societies a victim injured by another had the option of demanding the standard fine or inflicting an equal injury against his wrongdoer. This principle came to be wide-ranging in the ancient world, from Hammurabi's Code to the Laws of Moses. Ancient critics, including some early Jewish philosophers, attacked the new practice on the grounds that two people cannot suffer exactly the same injury, and Jewish law reverted to fines as the sole remedy for private wrongs. By the fifth century AD, even the Romans abandoned the talionis and replaced it with a system of mandatory fines. But it remained a rich part of other legal traditions.

Codes like Hammurabi's in ancient Babylon, written around 1750 BC, not only socialized great swaths of private wrongdoing, they also prescribed detailed punishments, which included some eye-for-eye corporal punishments.[32] For the first time, punishment practices came to be written down, and almost all we know about ancient punishment comes from these first written codes. So, for example, we know that Babylonians in Hammurabi's time were punished not only according to a fairly rigid set of fixed punishments for defined crimes, but also that there were different levels of punishment depending on the class to which the criminal and victim belonged. The punishments ran the usual gamut from death and banishment for the most serious of public crimes, to some limited corporal punishments for less serious public crimes, to fines for private crimes, even the most serious.[33]

These two unrelenting and reinforcing trends – our groups getting bigger and our criminal laws reaching further into what used to be matters of private revenge – eventually drove the creation of punishing institutions. Single decision makers still ruled the day, whether they were ancient Greek magistrates or Japanese feudal lords, but over time punishment became governmentalized in much the same way that other civic chores accreted to an increasingly complex state, such as the building of roads or the raising of armies. By the time of the Greek city states and the early Roman republic, an expanding list of crimes came to depend on state institutions for their enforcement, although the list of those crimes deserving of state punishment was still remarkably short by modern standards.

In the West, the influence of the Church accelerated this trend, with more and more religious offenses becoming state offenses. Canon law also reinvigorated what was, until then, the rather limited ancient tradition of corporal punishments. By the Middle Ages, the punishing church-state had gone from banishing and killing only the worst offenders and fining the rest, to inventing a seemingly limitless list of ghastly corporal punishments for those public wrongs not deemed worthy of execution. Flagellation and mutilations became the punishments of choice, not just in Europe but in the emerging feudal states in Asia as well.[34] Even the New World civilizations got into the act: the Aztecs, for example, punished some wrongdoers by driving long cactus needles into various sensitive parts of their bodies. Forms of corporal punishment were limited only by the limits of sadistic imagination. The fun even spilled over into the death penalty, where simple forms of capital punishment started giving way to procedures such as boiling alive, burning at the stake, drawing and quartering, garroting, and pressing.

The terrible violence we once committed only against opposing groups was now being committed in the name of the state against our fellow citizens, whom our laws told us were part of our group but whom our brains continued to brand as outsiders. These Dark Ages of punishment continued through the Renaissance and for two hundred years after it. These new punishments were now being aimed at theological wrongdoers as well as social wrongdoers, and who could be more of an outsider than a witch or heretic? Neither the

Reformation nor the Enlightenment did much to slow our blood lust for mutilating punishments and excruciatingly painful death sentences. Indeed, corporal punishment was not officially banned in England until 1948.[35] Still, by the end of 1600s most societies had limited their capital punishment methods to hanging and (for the high born) beheading, and their less serious punishments to banishment and flogging.[36]

Throughout all of this history, virtually all societies simultaneously recognized various forms of reputational punishment, common for less serious crimes but also quite often imposed after a debilitating but nonfatal corporal punishment. Being forced to wear certain clothing or marks indicating the wearer was a convicted wrongdoer was a popular form of reputational punishment. Simply being paraded around a village following conviction was also common. The stocks and the pillory – similar devices to secure a wrongdoer in the public square where he could be identified and insulted – have roots going back more than 1,000 years in Europe, and even further in China.[37] These reputational punishments often overlapped with corporal punishment. Prisoners in the stocks were sometimes pelted not just with rotten food, but also with stones, and they even occasionally died from their wounds. Amputations and branding were additional ways to inflict both corporal and reputational punishment.

By the time Americans inherited their criminal justice and punishment systems from the English, there were only two serious punishments for most felonies: banishment (which the English called transportation) and death. Corporal punishment had all but disappeared. Transportation began as a combination of banishment and indentured servitude. Felons were transported to the colonies to work their sentences off as servants to private colonists, America being the most popular destination. At the height of this activity in the mid-1770s, English courts were transporting 2,000 felons to America each year. Historians estimate that during the entire colonial period England transported as many as 100,000 across the empire.

With American independence, England lost its largest transportation destination, but its supply of felons in need of a place to go did not diminish. It solved the problem in two ways. First, convicts were simply placed on transport ships but never transported. These so-called hulks, after whom the notorious practice of "hulking" is named, sat idle in British ports for months, sometimes even years. As the felons died and criticisms of the barbaric practice intensified, Parliament hastily adopted a new transportation law, which permitted felons to be transported to the new colonies in Australia.[38] The first transports arrived in 1787. Because there were so few colonists, Australian transportation was not coupled with any private servitude. Instead, for the first time in English history, transported felons were indentured to the English government itself, which built and operated the penal colonies.

The English experiment with Australian transportation lasted sixty years, with the last large group of transports delivered in 1857. In those sixty years, roughly 135,000 felons were transported. The experiment ended for many reasons, including humanitarian pressure and, less nobly, the Australian gold rush of 1851. The emergence of the Irish prison system also contributed to the demise of transportation.

Prisons are a surprisingly recent invention. Before their prominence, our ancestors punished quickly and decisively. Criminals were deprived of their physical freedom only for short periods of time while awaiting trial or punishment. So-called debtors prisons were places where inmates worked to pay off their debts. Even transported prisoners lived relatively free, albeit indentured, lives, and even in Australia they had a good deal of physical freedom. Not until the end of the 1700s was the notion conceived that punishment could consist solely of the deprivation of physical freedom.

American Quakers built the first true prisons in the 1790s, in Pennsylvania.[39] Determined to provide an enlightened alternative to death and transportation, the Quakers intended their prisons to be places where criminals were to rehabilitate themselves, not through therapeutic programs like today but through their own penitence. The word "penitentiary" means a place of penitence. Of course, prisons have long ceased to be places of penitential rehabilitation. Today, in a world where we no longer banish our worst offenders beyond the geographic reach of our state's powers, we now banish them to prisons, where they are beyond our social networks every bit as much as if they were in Botany Bay.

THE ROOTS OF RESPONSIBILITY, EXCUSE, AND JUSTIFICATION

When you get bumped from behind and spill your coffee on your brand new dress, and then turn to begin some reputational punishment, all of your urges to do so melt away when you see that the bump was caused by a door blowing in the wind. Our brains don't blame inanimate objects because inanimate objects cannot act with intentionality. To be sure, those blame instincts well up inside us right after the bump, because our brains presume the bump was of social origins and was intentional. But as soon as we take a second look, our blame disappears.

That same sort of instantaneous melting away of blame happens if we turn our heads and see, instead of a door blowing in the wind, a cow or a drunk or someone wriggling in a straightjacket. Cows, drunks, and really crazy people are also not acting intentionally in the same way healthy, unimpaired people do. Sure, unlike the blowing door, they might be able to act in ways guided by their mental desires – to "intend" to bump up against us. Even the cow might "intend" to bump us to scratch an itch or get rid of some flies. The drunk and the lunatic might have a deeper intention to cause us harm, but we recognize those intentions probably arise out of a brain that is producing them as a consequence of some mental deficiencies, not to further the owner's rational desires. Our brains don't blame such brains.

The law has long recognized this kind of blamelessness in the doctrines of excuse and justification. Doctrines of excuse deal with the problem of the wrongdoer whose brain did not act intentionally in the same way ours do. Insanity is one important example of an excuse defense. Doctrines of justification, by contrast, deal with the problem of ordinary brains having their moral judgment acutely disabled by some extraordinary circumstances that would cause most of us to commit the same wrong. Self-defense and duress are two common kinds of justification defenses.

Historically, these two exceptions to criminal responsibility were treated very differently. At early English common law, for example, justification was a complete defense to all felonies; a justified felon was acquitted and faced no punishment or any other consequences. The father who is forced to rob a bank by kidnappers who threaten the life of his child has chosen to do what most of us would do. His wrong in robbing the bank is not just a choice of evils forced on him by the real wrongdoers, it is a choice of evils most of us would elect. The law therefore views him as a mere instrumentality of the kidnappers' wrong, and no more holds him responsible than it would hold responsible an inanimate instrumentality of harm, say, a gun.

The doctrine of excuse, by contrast, was not quite as forgiving. The common law held an excused felon responsible, and in theory he faced the same punishment as if he were not excused – death and forfeiture of all of his property for most felonies. He could escape death (though not forfeiture) only with a pardon from the crown. That is, the difficult decision of whether the wrongdoer really was, say, insane, was made post-conviction by the ruler. In the early years, at least, a pardon was hardly a sure thing, so no doubt many defendants were executed who were, by modern standards, insane.

These two categories – excuse and justification – became quite blurred over time, as the pardon of excused felons became more and more routine, and as a royal order called the writ of restitution became recognized as a way for an excused felon who was pardoned to regain his forfeited property.[40] The insane defendant was seldom punished because his post-conviction pardon was routinely granted, and he could even get his property back. Being "excused" in this manner started looking more and more like justification, in which the criminal process never even fired up. In modern Western systems, this blending is largely complete. Justified and excused actors are generally treated the same. Most courts, legislatures, and legal commentators no longer recognize any important differences between these two exceptions to blameworthiness, to the point that some even use the two terms interchangeably.

Occasionally, however, the historical difference rears its head, as in the case of recent American reforms to the insanity defense. The whole trend toward renaming insanity as "guilty but insane," and in a few states even abolishing insanity as a defense and making it pertinent only at sentencing, is in many ways an echo of the original distinction between excuse and justification. So, too, is the universal modern rule that insane defendants must be hospitalized until they are no longer a danger to themselves or others.[41]

The law has struggled mightily with these notions of excuse and justification: how to define them meaningfully without the exceptions swallowing the rule; how to allocate the burdens of proof; and how to integrate the insights of psychiatry and other sciences into these inquiries. In the end, the problem is all about how to distinguish one kind of "intent" – the kind usually sufficient under the law to constitute a crime – from the kind of intentionality required for moral blameworthiness. These are devilishly complicated issues, on which hundreds of treatises and books have been written, and many different sensible positions staked out. But our evolutionary take on responsibility resonates with one particular position: that excuse and justification are grounded on the idea that the wrongdoers' brains, although healthy enough to form intentions and act on them, are simply not rational enough to be blamed. Blame is a proxy for deterrence, and therefore only brains that are sufficiently rational to be deterred can be blamed.

We get no special deterrent benefits from punishing brains that are so diseased they cannot rationally convert their desires into actions. Such brains cannot be deterred. We likewise get no special deterrent benefit from punishing justified crimes. Most fathers will rob the bank at the kidnappers' direction. They will not pause to contemplate that robbing banks is wrong and that, in the absence of justification defenses, they might be punished. They do whatever they must do to save their child. In fact, as we've already seen, there is some evidence that our brains perform these justification assessments inside networks used to assess harm.[42] The father coerced into robbing the bank to save his child does not even perceive his acts as harmful, because they are not harmful to him on a net basis. The rest of us likewise see justified crimes as net benefits, and therefore do not fire up our blame, let alone punishment, circuitry.

True, punishing such activity may give us a small general deterrence benefit by deterring people who fake excuse and justification. But this marginal benefit is quite marginal, for several reasons. First, justification, at least, tends to be hard to fake because it depends on proving the justifying circumstances. Duress is virtually impossible to fake, and although self-defense can be easier to fake, even there the circumstances have to be right to make the defense colorable. Jurors just don't believe that the four guys in the car felt their lives threatened when they emptied fifty rounds into the back of a rival gang member walking on the street.

Excuse is much easier to fake, but perhaps for that very reason we seem almost impermeably resistant to it. Contrary to popular belief, insanity-type defenses are rarely asserted, and even more rarely successful. Our resistance to excuse defenses is part and parcel of our powerful blaming urges, and the theory of mind that underlies those urges. We overwhelmingly believe that all of us are rational creatures, because we assume everyone else's brains are like ours. It is hard to imagine a brain that thinks it must kill children to save them from Hell, but we have no trouble imagining a brain that will falsely make that claim to avoid the electric chair.

And yet, once we become convinced of real insanity, as hard as that might be, we do not blame. Why not? After all, truly irrational people must have been so rare in our emergent groups that natural selection would have been unlikely to arm us with instincts to detect them and then shut off our blame of them. How many John Hinckleys are there?[43] But in fact our groups were infested with an entire class of irrational members to whom our ordinary blaming and punishment instincts needed to be drastically altered – children.

Even if children's brains were armed with the basics of Rules 1 and 2, as I have argued here, those moral intuitions gain social traction only through experience.[44] Children learn the contextual boundaries of these moral intuitions over time. We simply do not hold children as blameworthy as adults because we know that children's moral intuitions are at best rudimentary until they have the chance to apply those intuitions to the real world and thus to learn real responsibility through the process of trial and error, with the errors triggering some mild parental punishment.

Indeed, at common law children under the age of seven were not deemed to be punishable moral agents, at least when it came to third-party punishment for crimes. Parents, of course, punish their children all the time as part of the learning and honing process, and most parents have remarkably sensitive, and largely automatic, systems for not over-punishing children. We instinctively know that children's brains are highly plastic, that we need to be just firm enough to change their behaviors, and that in fact almost all of their behaviors are easily changed with consistent correction. Children are a kind of responsibility sculpture in waiting, slowly being molded through experience until, at least according to the law, they are magically deemed responsible.

The non-responsibility of children is not just a matter of a lack of experience. The kinds of moral judgment we saw lacking in psychopaths – inhibition control, affective memory, moral reasoning – require frontal lobe function that simply is not there in young children or even many adolescents.[45] The brain develops generally from back to front, in to out. Some of the critical prefrontal parts that we require for translating our moral intuitions into good judgment are the very last ones to develop. These areas are typically not fully developed until the early- to mid-twenties.[46]

The development of the brain, and especially the cortex, is not simply a matter of building neural connections, although that's certainly part of it. What happens in development (and for that matter throughout our whole lives) is that some neural connections are pared away as our brains soak up experience and as that experience reinforces some connections and makes others unnecessary. We learn. We learn to instantiate some of our bad experiences viscerally, so that next time we don't make the same mistake. Recall the miracle of how our insulas, originally designed to warn us off poisonous foods, can be trained through experience to signal disgust at a variety of past bad experiences.[47]

Brains with insufficient life experience have not had the chance to model the world into a few heuristics, and must instead try to reason their way to the right result, not unlike how psychopaths, who lack any moral intuitions, must reason their way through moral dilemmas. When teenagers are placed in a scanner and asked things such as whether it is a good idea to swim with sharks, they show substantially more frontal activation than adults, most of whom have learned over many years that swimming with sharks belongs in the "don't do" category without having to think much at all about it. That is, teenagers can reason, but their worldview is still too constricted to allow that reason to reliably result in rational outcomes.[48]

Of course, brains develop at rates that differ across individuals, just as some seventeen year olds have had more brain-tuning experiences than others. As a result, as all parents know, some teenagers are more responsible than others. Likewise, some adults are less responsible than others. Until neuroscience can tell us which brains are sufficiently responsible on an individual level, and indeed what "sufficiently responsible" is, the law must continue to do what humans have always done – make gross classifications based on categories rather than on individuals.

Thus, we draw lines between children and adults, between sane and insane, between sober and drunk. Some lines are deeply arbitrary, as with the United States Supreme Court's ruling that killers may not be executed if they were less than eighteen years old at the time of the killing.[49] These lines are rough attempts to make individual judgments using rather blunt tools. The law's definition of insanity is the most controversial of these, and the story of insanity is an instructive example of how all legal systems have struggled with these conflicting urges to punish wrongdoing, but not to punish irrationality.

Traditionally, the law has used what we modernly call a "cognitive" approach to insanity.[50] That means it asks whether, at the time of the crime, the defendant was able to appreciate the wrongfulness of his actions. We might say that this cognitive approach is an inquiry into whether a particular defendant's brain was sufficiently loaded with our evolved moral software to know about Rules 1 and 2 – that it is wrong to steal and to break promises.[51]

Most defendants who successfully claim insanity suffer not from a loss of rationality in the narrow sense of not being able to think logically from given moral premises, but rather from the same kinds of distorting worldviews that make some healthy teenagers less responsible than adults. John Hinckley was capable of making all the logical decisions he needed to make in order to put him in the position of being able to shoot President Reagan. But his logic was operating within a seriously deluded worldview, in which he was obsessed with actress Jodie Foster and believed he could impress her if he assassinated Reagan. No evolved sense of blame would blame such a deluded wrongdoer, because his delusions, if real, seriously interfered with his rationality and therefore with his ability to be deterred.

Even if our sense of excuse based on irrationality is not evolutionarily grounded, it still makes good policy sense, provided we can reasonably limit it and reasonably detect fakers. If we assume a wrongdoer like John Hinckley is not faking his delusions, then we would all be better off not punishing him, because neither he nor anyone else with such dysfunctional delusions will be deterred by punishment. True, we are giving up some benefits in deterring fakers. In the end, whether those benefits outweigh the costs of punishing the truly insane depends very much on one's sense of whether there are more truly insane people than there are successful fakers, and whether we have the psychiatric and medical tools to distinguish the two.

Having spent more than twenty years in a system in which defendants have every reason to fake all kinds of excusing and even justifying conditions, I have seen them do plenty of both. I will never forget a defendant who was faced with a series of fraud charges all arising out of claims that she serially bilked several elderly people out of their life savings by pretending to befriend them. During her first appearance in my courtroom, she was stuttering so profoundly that she could not get even one word out. Her public defender advised me he could not communicate with her at all. I referred her to the state hospital for a competency evaluation. Competency is a legal inquiry into a defendant's *current* state of mind, and whether that state of mind permits the criminal case to go forward. In most jurisdictions, including mine, competency is a very low threshold – the question is whether the defendant's mind is so diseased that he cannot understand the charges against him or cannot assist his lawyer in his own defense.

The psychiatrists at the state hospital are a notoriously cautious lot. They tend to be involuntary and very reluctant participants in the criminal justice system. Most are young residents who must run the forensic gauntlet as part of their training, and who remain deeply uncomfortable dressing up what are essentially legal opinions – is this defendant competent, is that defendant insane – in the sheep's clothing of medical opinions. So I was shocked to get the competency report on this fraud defendant. It not only reported that she was faking her stuttering – nurse and other hospital personnel noted that the defendant often forgot to keep up the charade and regularly slipped into normal speech – but also that defendant stole money from several other patients. It ended with the very un-psychiatrist-like recommendation that this defendant should be sent to prison so she does not defraud other innocent people.

We can all be fooled about insanity as well. My most memorable object lesson in this regard was a Vietnamese man who shot and killed his wife in front of his two children, while she was on the telephone. He claimed that he was suffering from post-traumatic stress disorder (PTSD) caused by being confined for several years in a North Vietnamese tiger cage, and that his PTSD was so severe it sometimes rendered him virtually catatonic. He claimed he would go in and out of these dissociative states, and that he must have been in one when he killed his wife. He also claimed to speak little or no English. I not only sent him down to the state hospital for a sanity evaluation, I also ordered the state hospital to provide him with Vietnamese interpreters. When their report came back that he was sane, and I saw that they were able to reach that result without the aid of any interpreters, I was livid. I issued a citation to hold the state hospital in contempt.

At the contempt hearing the state presented a video of an interview with the defendant conducted by one of their staff psychiatrists. But the camera was rolling before either the defendant or the psychiatrist came into the room. The defendant came in first, accompanied by a nurse. He appears to be in one of his dissociative states. But as soon as the nurse leaves, and before the psychiatrist enters, you can see him change instantly. He sits up, looks around, and even starts tapping his foot. The moment he hears the psychiatrist opening the door, he slouches back down, becomes perfectly still, and does not respond to any of the psychiatrist's questions. The nursing staff and other witnesses also testified that the defendant understood English, and even occasionally spoke it.

If all that were not enough, it turned out that the prosecution had evidence that the defendant was deeply jealous, and thought his wife was having an affair. There was even some evidence (from the female friend the wife was talking to and, sadly, from the children too) that the defendant thought his wife was talking to her lover when he shot her. And yet this fellow fooled me for many months.

In the end, whether the difficulty in separating the truly insane from the fakers (and, much more commonly, in my judgment, from the mentally ill whose mental illness had nothing to do with the crime) is just too difficult to justify retaining the insanity defense is a policy question on which reasonable legislators might differ. For whatever it's worth, I don't think it is too hard to detect the fakers. Even my own two examples are cases in which we were all deceived for awhile but eventually saw the light. We ask judges and jurors to perform equally stunning feats of mind reading every day, when we ask them what a sane defendant's state of mind was at the time of the crime.

More importantly, I think that an evolutionarily informed view of blame and responsibility supports the conclusion that deterability is the key to responsibility, that every once in a long while a criminal defendant has a brain capable of intentionally causing harm but so irrational as to be undeterable, and that our responsibility systems must take that possibility into account. Like all responses to defection, our response to the possibility of insanity must be vigilant about fakery. The defense therefore needs to be defined narrowly, the burdens need to be allocated with an eye toward fakery, and jurors need to continue their skepticism about forensic psychiatry. But in the end, any system that cares about the moral foundations of blame needs to recognize the small crack of space between intentional actors and responsible ones.[52]

Notes to Chapter 5

1. Chapter 1, p. 29.
2. I will discuss delegation in Chapter 7.
3. Paul M. Bingham, *Human uniqueness: a general theory*, Q. REV. BIOL., **74(2)**, 133–169 (1999).
4. J. Flack et al., *Social structure, robustness, and policing cost in a cognitively sophisticated species*, AM. NATUR., **165(5)**, E126–E139 (May 2005).
5. J. Buckholtz & R. Marois, *The roots of modern justice: cognitive and neural foundations of social norms and their enforcement*, NATURE NEUROSCI., **15(5)**, 655–661 (2012); J. Bendor & P. Swistak, *The evolution of norms*, AM. J. SOC., **106**, 1493–1545 (2001). Much of the experimental and theoretical work on third-party punishment, and on the broader phenomenon of strong reciprocity, has been done by Sam Bowles and Herb Gintis, who've recently published a survey of their insights in A COOPERATIVE SPECIES: HUMAN RECIPROCITY AND ITS EVOLUTION (Princeton 2011).
6. DONALD E. BROWN, HUMAN UNIVERSALS 138 (Temple 1991).
7. WENDY DONIGER O'FLAHERTY, THE ORIGINS OF EVIL IN HINDU MYTHOLOGY 139 (Univ. Cal. Press 1976, reprint 1988).
8. MBH 12.122.14–29, cited in WENDY DONIGER O'FLAHERTY, THE ORIGINS OF EVIL IN HINDU MYTHOLOGY 223 (Univ. of Cal. 1976).

9. T. Nishida et al., *A within-group gang attack on a young adult male chimpanzee: ostracism of an ill-mannered member?* PRIMATES, **36(2)**, 207–211 (1995).

10. FRANS DE WAAL, CHIMPANZEE POLITICS: POWER AND SEX AMONG APES (Johns Hopkins 1989). See also C. von Rohr et al., *Impartial third-party interventions in captive chimpanzees: a reflection of community concern.* PLoS ONE **7(3)** (2012). But see K. Riedl et al., *No third-party punishment in chimpanzees*, PNAS, **109(37)**, 14824–14829 (2012).

11. M. Hauser & P. Marler, *food-associated calls in rhesus macaques* (Macaca mulatta), BEHAV. ECOL., **4(3)**, 194–205 (1993). Jessica Flack and her colleagues have also seen delegated third-party punishment in the pigtailed macaque (*Macaca nemestrina*). J. Flack et al., *Policing stabilizes construction of social niches in primates*, NATURE, **493**, 426–429 (January 26, 2006).

12. See the recent summary in van Rohr et al., supra note 10.

13. Other examples of precursors to third-party punishment abound. Female elephant seals that discover someone else's pup is trying to nurse from them not only shoo the intruder away, they often bite them severely, even to the point of death. J. Reiter et al., *Northern elephant seal development: the transition from weaning to nutritional independence*, BEHAV. ECOL. & SOCIO-BIOLOLGY, **3(4)**, 337–367 (1978). Adult male mule deer regularly attack young males trying to sneak sexual interludes with females being guarded by the adult males. T. H. Clutton-Brock et al., *The logical stag: adaptive aspects of fighting in red deer* (Cervus elaphus L.*)*, ANIMAL BEHAV. **27(1)**, 211–225 (1979). For a general survey of the kinds of behaviors akin to third-party punishment found in a wide variety of species, see T. H. Clutton-Brock & G. A. Parker, *Punishment in animal societies*, NATURE, **373**, 209–216 (1995).

14. Namely, the amygdala, ventromedial prefrontal cortex, posterior cingulate, and dorsolateral prefrontal cortex.

15. J. Buckholtz et al., *The neural correlates of third-party punishment*, NEURON, **60(5)**, 930–940 (2008).

16. This wonderful quotation comes from Jane B. Lancaster, *Primate Social Behavior and Ostracism*, in M. Gruter & R. Masters (eds.), OSTRACISM: A SOCIAL AND BIOLOGICAL PHENOMENON **68** (Elsevier 1986). Much of this section, particularly on the history of ostracism, was previously published in M. Hoffman & T. Goldsmith, *The Biological Roots of Punishment*, 1 OHIO ST. J. CRIM. L. **626** (2004).

17. This quotation, and the larger story from which it was taken, comes from "Sophie's Story," which is a part of the handwritten memoirs of Rudolph Kahmen, now in the possession of my wife, Kate Knickrehm.

18. E. ADAMSON HOEBEL, THE LAW OF PRIMITIVE MAN 155, 157 (Harvard 1954).

19. Id. at 320–321.
20. Niloufer Qasim Mahdi, *Pukhtunwali: Ostracism and Honor among the Pathan Hill Tribes*, in OSTRACISM: A SOCIAL AND BIOLOGICAL PHENOMENON, supra note 16, at 147, 153.
21. Reinhold Zippelius, *Exclusion and Shunning as Legal and Social Sanctions*, in OSTRACISM: A SOCIAL AND BIOLOGICAL PHENOMENON, supra note 16, at 11, 13.
22. David C. Mirhady, *The Ritual Background of Athenian Ostracism*, 11 ANCIENT HIST. BULL. **13** (1997). The ostracism vote could take place only after a preliminary vote, in which a majority of citizens had to agree that such an ostracism vote should take place for that year.
23. FREDERICK POLLACK & FREDERIC MAITLAND, 2 HISTORY OF THE ENGLISH LAW BEFORE THE TIME OF EDWARD I 449 (2d ed. 1888).
24. Zippelius, supra note 21, at 15.
25. Id. at 16.
26. Margaret Gruter, *Ostracism on Trial: The Limits of Individual Rights*, in OSTRACISM: A SOCIAL AND BIOLOGICAL PHENOMENON, supra note 16, at 123.
27. See, e.g., F. DE WAAL, CHIMPANZEE POLITICS, supra note 10.
28. George A. Pettit, *Primitive Education in North America*, 53 CAL. PUBL. IN AM. ANTHRO. **161** (1946).
29. R. Wilson, *A Study of Attitudes Towards Corporal Punishment as an Educational Procedure from the Earliest Times to the Present*, 1999 unpublished master's thesis, available at www.socsci.kun.nI/ped/whp/histeduc/wilson/index.html
30. The Germans inherited the *wergeld* directly from the Romans, who had a detailed system of fines for private wrongs. Like most compensatory systems, the *wergeld* also covered many crimes short of homicide. In its most comprehensive forms, it was a kind of ancient workers' compensation system, in which assaults causing specific injuries triggered specific fines. For example, the Frisian codes in the early Middle Ages called for a fine of two monetary units for the loss of an eyebrow, six to eight for a finger (depending on which one), thirteen for a thumb, twenty for a nose, and almost the full *wergeld* for a hand. HARRY E. BARNES, THE STORY OF PUNISHMENT 50 (2d ed. 1972), quoting EPHRAIM EMERTON, INTRODUCTION TO THE MIDDLE AGES (375–814) 87–90 (Ginn 1891).
31. Rule 2 wrongs – breaking a promise – probably remained a matter of private enforcement. Indeed, breach of contract in modern law is still almost always a civil matter, not a criminal one.
32. Hammurabi's is the most famous of the fertile crescent codes, but it was not the first. That distinction belongs to The Code of Ur-Nammu, a Sumerian code dating to around 2100 BC. MARTHA T. ROTH, ET AL., LAW COLLECTIONS FROM MESOPOTAMIA AND ASIA MINOR 13 (Soc. of Biblical Lit.,

2d ed. 1997). Of course, there may have been many other older codes of law that have not survived.

33. The Egyptians, whose advanced civilization began long before Hammurabi and lasted long after him, left no comprehensive record of their punishment practices, and in fact left no general code of laws. This might simply be because the records did not survive the great fire at Alexandria, though some scholars have suggested instead that the absolute power of the Pharaoh made codes of law superfluous in that civilization – the law was what the Pharaoh said it was. Albert M. Rosenblatt, *The Law's Evolution: Long Night's Journey into Day*, 24 CARDOZO L. REV. **2119**, 2127–2128 (2003).

34. The *bastinado* – the practice of mutilating the bottom of wrongdoers' feet – was one of the more vicious corporal punishments popularized in China. Like many other forms of torture it found its way to the Ottomans and then to the West.

35. This 1948 ban reached only initial criminal punishments, not punishments for misbehavior while in prison. Criminal Justice Act of 1948, § 54. It was not until 1967 that corporal punishment was banned outright in English prisons. Criminal Justice Act of 1967, § 65.

36. Even today of course there are exceptions. Especially in Muslim countries, death can be by stoning, and many medieval corporal punishments, like amputations, still abound.

37. The words pillory and stocks are sometimes used interchangeably. But in fact pillories were originally used for more serious crimes, and were more elaborate in that they always included a hole for the head and hands. Stocks typically restrained only the arms or legs. Prisoners' heads were sometimes secured to the stocks by nailing their ears to the wooden panels. By the mid-1800s most European countries had abolished both methods, in no small part because of the rise of the penitentiary. England abolished the pillory in 1837, but has never formally abolished the stocks. Delaware was the last U.S. state to officially recognize either punishment, abolishing the stocks in 1905.

38. This final phase of English transportation included not just Australia but also much smaller English colonies in Tasmania and Norfolk Island. It was in Norfolk Island, a speck 1,000 miles off the eastern coast of Australia, that the English first began the practice of commuting banishment sentences for good behavior. That moderating practice made its way to Irish prisons then to American ones.

39. The first penitentiary was probably Philadelphia's Walnut Street Jail. NORVAL MORRIS, THE FUTURE OF IMPRISONMENT 4–5 (Chicago 1977). A few historians claim that the original penitentiary was the so-called People Pen constructed by Massachusetts Pilgrims in Boston in 1632. See, e.g., PHILIP D. JORDAN, FRONTIER LAW AND ORDER: TEN ESSAYS 140 (Nebraska 1970). Even if that were true, it is clear that Philadelphia's Walnut Street Jail, and not Boston's People Pen, was the prototype for the early American penitentiary.

Morris, supra, at 4–5 (noting that the Quakers' "vision and initiative gave us our hulking penal institutions").

40. JOSHUA DRESSLER, UNDERSTANDING CRIMINAL LAW §17.01 (4th ed., LexisNexis 2006).

41. Under civil commitment statutes now so prevalent, even defendants who are acquitted outright, not on a plea of insanity, face the prospect of being civilly committed if the court finds they suffer from a mental disease or defect that makes them a danger to themselves or others. Convicted defendants may be committed after they complete their criminal sentences. The United States Supreme Court has ruled that such statutes do not violate double jeopardy because the purpose of civil commitment is not punitive. Kansas v. Hendricks, 521 U.S. 346 (1997).

42. Chapter 2, note 28.

43. John Hinckley was the young man who tried to assassinate President Ronald Reagan in 1981, and was found not guilty by reason of insanity. The kinds of mental disorders that so disable one's rationality as to amount to a legal excuse – things like severe psychoses – are quite rare. The frequency of all psychosis (including schizophrenia, schizo-affective disorder, delusional disorder, and major depression with psychotic features, but excluding substance- and disease-induced psychoses and bipolar disorders) is believed to be less than 1% of the general population. See J. Pirala et al., *Lifetime prevalence of psychotic and bipolar-I disorders in a general population*, 64 ARCH. GEN. PSYCHIATRY **19** (2007).

44. As we saw in Chapter 2, even infants are armed with certain surprising moral instincts – they can distinguish, and they prefer, depictions of helping behaviors as opposed to hurting behaviors.

45. But as we saw in Chapter 3, it appears that psychopaths lack the empathetic machinery located in lower, paralimbic, regions of the cortex. Their higher regions seem fully functional, and indeed there seem to be no IQ differences between psychopaths and non-psychopaths. M Cima et al., *Psychopaths know right from wrong but don't care*, SOC. COGN. & AFFECTIVE NEUROSCI., **5(1)**, 59–67 (2010).

46. B. J. Casey et al., *The adolescent brain*, ANN. N.Y. ACAD. SCIENCES, **1124**, 111–126 (2008).

47. Chapter 3, note 9.

48. A. Baird & J. Fuselgang, *The emergence of consequential thought: evidence from neuroscience*, in *Law and the Brain*, PHIL. TRANS. R. SOC. LOND. B, **359**, 1797–1804 (S. Zeki & O. Goodenough, eds. 2004).

49. Roper v. Simmons, 543 U.S. 551 (2005).

50. The cognitive approach, which long predates the famous M'Naughten Case, which gave it its name, asks whether a defendant suffers from a mental disease or defect that renders him unable to appreciate the difference between right and wrong.

51. For a while, especially after the notoriety of the Hinckley case, several American states experimented with so-called control or volitional definitions of insanity, which generally asked whether a defendant was suffering from a mental disease or defect that substantially interfered with his ability to control his actions to comport with the law.

52. I have therefore joined the chorus calling for restraint in the temptation to abolish or seriously limit the insanity defense. Morris B. Hoffman & Stephen J. Morse, *The Insanity Defense Goes Back on Trial*, NEW YORK TIMES, July 30, 2006; Stephen J. Morse & Morris B. Hoffman, *The Uneasy Entente between Insanity and Mens Rea: Beyond* Clark v. Arizona, 97 J. CRIM. L. & CRIMINOLOGY (Northwestern) **1071** (2007).

6   FORGIVENESS AND ITS SIGNALS

I wondered if that was how forgiveness budded; not with the fanfare of epiphany, but with pain gathering its things, packing up, and slipping away unannounced in the middle of the night.

Khaled Hosseini

THE FORGIVING ANIMAL

Forgiving wrongs is as central to our humanity as punishing them. In fact, forgiveness and punishment are really just two sides of the same evolutionary coin. Punishment evolved only because it evolved in a restrained way, and the urge to forgive was an important restraining force.[1]

The most moving courtroom experiences I've ever had have come during sentencing hearings in homicide cases, when family members of murder victims told their loved ones' killers that they forgave them. Although this is by no means a common occurrence, it happens more often than you might think. Of the roughly three dozen homicide cases I've presided over, I can remember four where at least one member of the victim's family expressed forgiveness. Nothing victims say at a sentencing hearing has more impact, not just on the audience, the lawyers, and the judges, but especially on the defendants. It can be shocking to watch a murderer sit emotionless as his victim's survivors try to express their profound loss. But on those occasions when a survivor said, "I forgive you," in all four cases the murderers broke down and wept. What a strange and complicated species we are when words of forgiveness can touch us but words of the grievous loss we caused cannot.

This is one hint about the power of forgiveness. Another is its prominence across every aspect of human culture. All religions teach us about forgiveness. In fact, the deepest roots of forgiveness might lay, rather surprisingly, in the universal ancient practice of sacrifice. Sacrifice may have been a special kind of signal for forgiveness. Walter Burkert, a preeminent scholar on ancient religious rituals, has suggested that animal ritual sacrifices have their roots in hunters' guilt. The idea is that hunters, feeling remorseful for killing the gods' creatures, attempted to assuage their guilt by offering some of the dead animals back to the gods, in the hopes that by so honoring them the gods would forgive the killings.[2]

Whether or not Burkert was right, it is a short trip from sacrificing for forgiveness to sacrificing for protection. Even when we are asking all-powerful gods (or fellow group members) to forgive our past sins, part of what we are really asking is that they refrain from punishing us, or that at the very least they punish us less. Sacrifice in this sense is always a request for future protection – whether protection from punishment for the just-committed sin or a kind of prepaid get-out-of-jail-free card for future sins. In primitive societies, where dictator gods sometimes caused bad things to happen for no reason at all, sacrifice was also a way to try to bring some restraining order to the chaos of nature. Maybe the Nile won't flood this year if we make enough sacrifices.

Whether for past sins, future ones, or just protection from the vagaries of fate, a sacrifice is not a sacrifice unless we give up something important to us. So, for example, in ancient Greece plough ox were so important for the cultivation of wheat, and therefore for the survival of the city-state, that it was a crime to kill an ox, even one's own. But during an Athenian festival called *Dipolieia*, plough oxen were ritually sacrificed. Over time, the *Diploieia* transformed from a small and intermittent festival to a large and frequent practice designed for protection of the entire city-state. Greeks regularly sacrificed a hundred oxen, called the *hecatomb*, to achieve the maximum amount of divine protection for the maximum amount of citizens. The Romans were especially partial to the spectacle of the *hecatomb*, and regularly celebrated great military victories with these mass animal sacrifices.

When we look back at these protectionist sacrifices, including human sacrifices practiced by many ancient cultures, they tend to lose their sheen of forgiveness. We may think of frightened people doing anything they can to protect themselves from their unpredictable gods. But if Burkert was right, at the core of these seemingly brutal, selfish, and irrational rituals lays the heart of a deep and ancient urge to ask for divine forgiveness. And even if he was wrong, and sacrifice began as an act of protection and not forgiveness, it soon became an important stand-alone signal for forgiveness in most religions.

By the time the three great Abrahamic religions took hold, forgiveness was front and center, and sacrifice became largely symbolic. Even the fire-breathing punisher of the Old Testament can't help but forgive the Jews, breach after predictable breach. Forgiveness is also a vital theme in Islam; one of the ninety-nine names of Allah is Al-Gafir, which means "The All-Forgiver." The New Testament is of course awash in forgiveness, because its central theme is redemption. It uses the main Greek word for forgiveness, *eleao*, an astonishing seventy-eight times, and a related word, *aphiemi* (which means releasing or discharging a debt), another sixty-four times.[3] It also uses another very interesting Greek word, *splanchnizomai*, to connote empathy and compassion in a forgiveness context, a word that comes from a root meaning "intestines."[4] We pour our guts out forgiving one another. Forgiving, it turns out, is just as gut-wrenching as punishing. Ask any trial judge.

The many different words we use to express different kinds of forgiveness also reflect how rich and deep the concept is. "Mercy" seems to connote forgiveness exhibited at the time we are punishing, so it often is a kind of partial forgiveness that results in reduced punishment. It also seems reserved for third-party punishment. Judges show mercy; victims simply forgive. "Leniency" seems to convey a more automatic, pejorative kind of mercy, also typically in the third-party context. "Compassion," by contrast, suggests a richer kind of broad empathy that can arise in many circumstances outside the blame and punishment contexts.

"Absolution," "redemption," and "salvation" seem reserved for divine forgiveness, but they also reflect a special aspect of forgiveness that was critical for its evolution. When we forgive we not only save the wrongdoer from our scorn, we save ourselves from being scornful.

Alan Paton, the renowned South African writer, put it this way: "When a deep injury is done us, we never fully recover until we forgive."[5] But of course our deeply ambivalent strategic brains are also locked in this eternal struggle with other equally ambivalent and strategic brains. Forgiveness can itself take on the shape of revenge. Oscar Wilde reportedly once said, "Always forgive your enemies; nothing annoys them so much."[6]

Punishment and forgiveness, just like cheating and cooperating, are built into our brains in delicate balance. The evolutionary puzzle of forgiveness is the flip side of the evolutionary puzzle of punishment. Too much forgiveness and not enough punishment would have unraveled our groups in anarchy; too much punishment and not enough forgiveness would have unraveled them in rebellion.

But there are many kinds of forgiveness besides this kind that interrupts our blame to prevent or lessen punishment. A wife might forgive the dalliances of her husband, or vice versa. Friends often forgive friends' different kinds of unfriendly behaviors. And although the purest kind of forgiveness might prevent our urge to blame from maturing into an urge to punish, our forgiveness is not always so pure, as Oscar Wilde realized. And of course because so much of our everyday punishment is reputational, forgiveness can be an ambiguous and fleeting thing. We have all had arguments so intense that a certain period of punishing "silent treatment" was required before we could really forgive the harsh words exchanged. We might even "forgive" only after a wrongdoer has endured all his punishment, and we have mulled about it for years. Finally, our forgiveness might be nothing more than a willingness to accept bad behavior because the consequences of rejecting it are too painful – the spouse who "forgives" infidelity probably does not really forgive.

Out of this cacophony of forgiveness we can define two useful ends of a continuum. At one end, there's the kind of forgiveness where the harm is simply too minimal even to trigger our blaming instincts. When we are gently bumped on the subway we don't blame or punish anyone. This may feel like a kind of forgiveness in its broadest sense, but it's a faux forgiveness. We cannot forgive what we don't blame.

At the other end of the continuum, we might say loosely that we "forgive" someone after we punish them, and that seems to ring true in a couple different senses. First, our blaming instincts often seem to evaporate the moment we punish. In the second-party context, the anger we feel build up inside us as we try to resist the temptation to retaliate often disappears the moment we begin to retaliate. Think of those moments you tried your best not to scream at your misbehaving child, and how you felt immediately after screaming. I remember years ago when our new German Shepherd puppy grabbed one of my gloves as I was rushing off to work, already late for a hearing. I cajoled him, yelled at him, and chased him around the yard, all to no avail. I even grabbed one of his favorite tennis balls to lure him to me, but he would not drop the glove. I was getting angrier and angrier, and I finally threw the tennis ball at him as hard as I could, never thinking for a moment that I'd hit him as he was dashing this way and that so far away. But I not only hit him, I hit him smack in the middle of his left eye. He howled a terrible howl of pain and dropped my glove immediately. In an instant, once my "punishment" of him was inflicted, I stopped blaming him and started blaming me.

In a third-party context, we regularly say things like "he's done his time" when talking about how we should feel about ex-convicts, meaning that if third-party punishment is a kind of payment we extract from wrongdoers, then once we have extracted it they should be permitted back in the social fold. We "forgive" their wrong because they have earned our forgiveness by suffering our punishment. Forgiveness in this sense is a wiping away of the original stain of blame. We forgive the debt you owed to us because you have in fact paid the debt. One of the most challenging problems of modern penology is that we often pay lip service to this kind of post-punishment forgiveness, but in fact never stop blaming and punishing ex-convicts, which in turn makes their repatriation even more difficult. We will discuss this problem later in this chapter.

The passage of time alone can effect a kind of forgiveness. That is especially true in the second-party context. My inflamed instinct to retaliate might simply burn out before I get a chance to retaliate. If I had simply given up trying to get my glove back, gone to work, and come home later that night, I doubt I would have had much anger left (or much of a glove left). There is a special variety of this kind of temporal forgiveness, when during the long delay between blame and punishment a wrongdoer does things to signal to us that he has changed his cheating ways. We have all read stories (and I have had cases) where a defendant goes on the lam for decades, becomes an upstanding citizen, and lives an honorable life, only to be discovered and to face punishment for his past wrongs. Most of us have deeply ambivalent feelings about such cases, for good evolutionary reasons.

Natural selection put a premium on punishing only the most serious of wrongs. This is our Rule 3: punish only *serious* violations of Rules 1 and 2. "Serious" in this sense is part of the deterrence calculation for which both blame and forgiveness are proxies. Just as we punish in proportion to harm, we forgive in inverse proportion to harm. Our brains were built to forgive small wrongs and to struggle with forgiving great ones.

But it's not just the amount of the harm that drives our urge to forgive; who the criminal is also matters. It might have made evolutionary sense to forgive even the most serious crime if we had sufficient assurances that this was a one-time event and that the wrongdoer was quite unlikely to pose any significant risk to us in the future. Even then, we probably would not want to forgive entirely (that is, not punish at all), lest we send the message that every group member gets to commit one free serious wrong. But forgiveness based on the circumstances of the wrong and the character of the wrongdoer, including the signals he sends us about his character, might lead us to punish less.

In addition to this pre-punishment function of restraining the amount and frequency of our punishments, forgiveness had the crucial post-punishment function of integrating wrongdoers back into the fold when we were sufficiently confident we could safely do so. If every punished member left the group in either shame or disgust, we would soon run out of members. So it was critical that our punishment instincts, especially our third-party punishment instincts, came with both a built-in governor and a repair kit.

Once we blame, once those fires of finger-pointing well up inside us when we see a wrong, our blaming brains are primed to turn the fires down automatically if we get any signals that the wrong was accidental or the harm not as great as we first perceived. We've all felt those moments. You are sitting in your car at a red light, and are rear-ended by an inattentive driver. Your car is crushed, and you were at some risk of injury, so this is definitely not a "no-harm-no-foul" situation. Your blame instincts are off the meter, especially because this is a second-party situation rather than a third-party one. Your amygdala is reporting a "fight" possibility, your insula is making you disgusted at the insensitivity of this other driver, adrenalin is pumping into your bloodstream, your fists and jaws are clenching, and your temporoparietal junction is priming you to scream, "You idiot, be more careful." You are about to turn your blame into physical, or at the very least reputational, punishment. But as you approach the other car, you see the driver is a young mother, and that she's hit her head on the steering wheel and is bleeding. Her children are crying. In a subconscious instant, your blaming rage turns not only into forgiveness but maybe even into compassion.

Forgiveness was an important kind of damper on our ancestors' blaming instincts. But the damper had to be subtle, without putting out all the fires of blame. It also had to be smart. If blame is a rough proxy for optimizing deterrence, then forgiveness is its opposite – a rough proxy for when we should not punish because its costs outweigh its deterrent benefits. The same two factors that determine blame – intent and harm – determine forgiveness. We have blinked to a blaming conclusion about intent and harm, but now our forgiveness circuits give us a chance for a second blink using those same two proxies.

We are sometimes wrong about the amount of harm a wrong-doer causes. I remember when I was eleven years old – in fact it was my eleventh birthday – and I was running out of school to go home for lunch. I ran over what I thought were just some sprinkler-soaked segments of the sidewalk, but they turned out to be newly repaired segments of wet concrete. I didn't even notice the workers, standing off to the side, as I ran past. After my feet squished into the wet cement one of the workers grabbed me by the arm and, by the look in his eyes, decided he would kill me then and there. But before he could kill me, or even yell at me, a second worker grabbed a trowel and repaired the superficial damage in less than ten seconds. I saw the anger drop out of the killer's face in an instant. The harm I had caused turned out not to be as bad as it first looked (or it might just have been relief at not having to do the repair job himself, or the fact that the school principal was standing nearby). In any event, the workers forgave me, even if the principal did not.

We misperceive intent even more often than we misperceive harm. To judge from his murderous look, it seemed the concrete worker who grabbed me thought I ran through the wet cement intentionally. We are extraordinarily good at judging the minds that harm us or our groups, but we are not perfect, and unlike harm – which we can usually see – intent is something we must imagine. One pretty reliable way to instantaneously reevaluate our initial impression of intent is to hear what the wrongdoer says right after inflicting the harm. A "Take that," will not change anyone's blame instinct. But an "Oh, I am so sorry, I didn't even see you there," will quite automatically cause us to begin to forgive, even if we don't want to. This kind of forgiveness is not a conscious, long-drawn-out balancing act. It happens the instant we perceive the conditions triggering it.

Forgiveness also operates post-punishment. When our blame turns into punishment, the very act of punishment puts out our retributive fires. Forgiveness in this sense is a kind of emotional return to the baseline of grudging trust, or almost to that baseline, before the wrong occurred. This is what allowed us to welcome punished members back into the fold, and to preserve our groups despite our unique instinct to punish third-party wrongdoers.

Whether before or after punishment, forgiveness is an act of social signaling, and what we are signaling are our feelings surrounding blame and guilt. What the punisher is signaling is the loss of his retaliatory or retributive urges. Wrongdoers are naturally skeptical that they are really being let back into the fold, and so they need reliable signals of genuine forgiveness. If they don't get them, they may not feel welcomed back and may be less likely to be successfully reintegrated. There is no better signal that a decision is genuine than to have it accompanied by emotion. A spouse robotically mouthing the words "I forgive you" has much less impact in defusing the risk of an escalating situation than when those words are accompanied by tears.

By conveying forgiveness emotionally, the victim is not just telling the wrongdoer that he's *decided* not to punish, he is announcing that he no longer *wants* to punish. This is what makes the act of forgiveness so profoundly transformative. It needs to be, especially in the second-party context, in order to overcome our powerful urges to punish. The Christian theologian Lewis Smedes once wrote that when we forgive "we set a prisoner free and discover that the prisoner we set free was us."[7] We are prisoners of our retaliatory and retributive urges, until we free ourselves from those urges by forgiving.

The transformative power of forgiveness, at least from the forgiver's point of view, depends in large measure on its social expression. Everyone in the group is watching when we blame, forgive, or punish. When I decide, in the safe confines of my chambers or living room, that I will show mercy to a particular defendant, that abstract decision feels very different than when, in open court, I actually announce that merciful decision to the defendant and his victim. Back in the office or at home I remain angry, and indeed sometimes *more* angry for even considering being merciful. But in open court, the moment I express my forgiveness the anger seems to wash away.

That automatic cleansing aspect of forgiveness is what makes it work. If our ancestors forgave only by mouthing the words of forgiveness, without *feeling* them, they would have remained angry at the wrongdoer, the risk of punishment would remain high, and the wrongdoer might continue his wrongs, not just because he never felt welcomed back but more critically because he kept being punished, whether physically or emotionally. Only by pulling out the emotional rug of retaliation and retribution could forgiveness accomplish its adaptive function of effectively restraining those urges and welcoming the miscreant back into the fold.

Of course, forgiveness can be just as transformative of the wrongdoer, who needs to have his own guilt washed away in the same fashion as his victim's urge to punish. That is, genuine forgiveness restrains not just second- and third-party punishment, but also first-party punishment. Indeed, forgiveness is most effective as a drag on over-punishment and as a tool of social repair if it works at all three levels of punishment. A forgiven wrongdoer who continues to be racked with guilt because his punishment never comes is hardly likely to remain a useful member of the group.

This symmetric draining of the emotions that surround blaming and being blamed helped increase the chances that the wrongdoer could successfully be reintegrated into the group. Other group members were no longer angry with him, and he was no longer angry with himself. In groups so precariously balanced at the edge of survival, where every able-bodied member was critical to survival, those willing to forgive and be forgiven effectively would have had a big survival advantage.

Forgiveness is gut-wrenching in exactly the same way punishment is gut-wrenching. We have these evolved urges that help us skirt the impossible waters of deterrence, but we also have these giant brains that think they can navigate those waters. So I have a strong and quite automatic urge to blame and punish the child-abuser I saw in court yesterday – not as strong, admittedly, as if she had abused my child instead of hers, but still pretty darn strong. But then I read the reports about her upbringing, and my empathy triggers strong and equally automatic feelings of forgiveness. How we integrate these two sets of feelings into a decision – and whether what we do really is a "decision" at all rather than some automatic accommodation of these automatic urges – remains largely locked inside the bigger mystery of decision-making in general. But it is no longer subject to much debate that our urge to forgive is an embedded part of our evolved urge to punish.

In fact, virtually all of the evidence of the evolutionary roots of blame and punishment, discussed in prior chapters, apply with equal force to forgiveness. Forgiveness, like blame and punishment, are human universals. There is no recorded civilization whose records do not contain some discussion of the puzzle of forgiveness. Forgiveness, like blame and at least like second-party punishment, is common throughout the animal kingdom. No social animals, short of the genetically identical ones, can survive without forgiveness, in the broad sense of not punishing every social defection. Indeed, the lack of widespread third-party punishment among nonhumans is a kind of rudimentary faux forgiveness. Chimp A simply does not blame Chimp B when Chimp B steals from Chimp C. Our species' unique third-party urge to punish all wrongs, whether inflicted against us or others, made forgiveness all the more important to us.

There is more to forgiveness in the animal kingdom than the general unwillingness to punish third-party wrongs. Dozens of animal species, social and asocial alike, from birds to wolves to monkeys, exhibit what biologists call "conciliatory gestures" – behaviors following conflict or threats of conflict that signal a willingness to stand down and reconcile.[8] The gestures themselves vary widely across species but they all share the central feature that one party to an escalating conflict is signaling his willingness to stop. Nonhuman primates commonly signal conciliation by grooming, baring their teeth in a certain way, or smacking their lips. Chimpanzees have even been known to kiss to make up. Some birds engage in a special kind of beak-touching to signal reconciliation.[9] Even fish make signals to reconcile, by touching fins.[10]

The frequency of reconciliation varies both across and within species. Not surprisingly, the likelihood of reconciling increases as the importance of the relationship increases. When researchers trained pairs of macaques to bond with each other, by feeding them together, the bonded macaques were more likely to reconcile following non-feeding disputes than other pairs.[11] Male chimpanzees reconcile (and fight) with each other much more than females do with each other or males do with females, simply because in chimpanzees male-to-male relationships are the strongest and most socially significant. Macaques, by contrast, value matrilineal relationships more than all others, and those relationships are therefore more frequently the subject of reconciliation.

Conciliatory gestures, though much more limited than the kinds of full forgiveness we see in sentient creatures, are nevertheless an important kind of proto-forgiveness. Tit for tat in any context risks escalation, and whether it is a pair of chimps fighting over a female or a judge about to sentence a bank robber the idea is the same: the party whose turn it is to re-inflict violence on the other elects not to do so.

All the experimental economic literature showing our willingness to punish, even if it costs us, also shows our willingness to forgive.[12] That willingness, like trust in general, is grudging but it is palpable. So, for example, as we have already discussed, we sometimes choose not to punish in these economic games, even when we are the ones who have been victimized. That's especially true in games involving repeat interactions. Just as in the game of life, it is sometimes advantageous to punish wrongdoers and sometimes advantageous to forgive them, all depending on the pair's history of cooperation and defection, as well as the costs and benefits built into the game.

In fact, these experiments show that in many ways forgiveness is a special kind of trust: "I will refrain from punishing your last transgression because I trust you will not do it again." Like most varieties of social trust, however, forgiveness has a short and non-forgiving memory. In repeat games, forgiveness begets trust – that is, the very act of forgiving does in fact tend to reform the transgressor. Trust also begets forgiveness – a long period of trusting behavior makes it more likely that one act of cheating will be forgiven. But when a forgiven transgressor transgresses again, his punisher is very unlikely to forgive him again, especially when there's little time between the transgressions.[13]

When we are faced with the decision of whether to punish or forgive in these economic games, we are able, quite unconsciously, to keep a remarkably accurate running score of our history of cooperation and cheating, with us and by us, not at all unlike the way those vampire bats keep a running score of reciprocity. The enormous popularity of three strikes laws among ordinary citizens is probably due, at least in part, to our deep urge to forgive a few violations but not more than a few. Fool me once, shame on you; fool me twice, shame on me.

If animals are sophisticated enough, their trust, or lack of it, can be communicated by gestures or even words, rather than just by refraining from punishing. When chimps kiss to reconcile, they are signaling two things at once: that they are prepared to stop fighting, and that they trust they will be reciprocated. Their act of trust is expressed by getting so close to their adversary that they could be injured terribly by him. They are not exactly saying they give up; they are saying they are prepared to stop the row, that they believe their adversary will reciprocate in the stand-down, and that they are willing to expose themselves to great danger to signal both their desire to stop and their trust in reciprocation. Humans have language to communicate these trusting signals, which make the signals both more complex and sometimes less reliable.

APOLOGY

My friend Erin O'Hara, who has written extensively about the role of apology in the law, tells a story to which everyone who has ever had a significant other can relate.[14] Her husband did something dumb and

thoughtless before he left for work, and she was stuck with cleaning up
the consequences before she could start her workday. She spent all day
fuming about it, and planning the angry words she would launch when
she saw him. But when she got home, before she could say anything he
looked at her and said something like, "I am *so* sorry for what I did. It
was incredibly thoughtless, and it will not happen again." She wanted
to continue to be angry, but she felt her anger melt away, which itself
made her angry in a different way, this time at herself for being unable
to sustain her anger at her husband.

There is quite a bit of research about the psychology and neuroscience of apology confirming these kinds of anecdotes. You might
think that our feelings of forgiveness in response to words of apology
come easier for small wrongs than big ones, but that does not seem to
be true. Our initial emotional reaction to apology seems to be involuntary and largely indiscriminate.[15] Like Erin O'Hara, most of us under
most circumstances just can't help but feel our anger drain away in the
face of an apology, almost no matter how intentional or harmful the
wrong has been.

That's probably because our brains evolved a strong urge to forgive
in the face of any apparently sincere apology, especially from a family
member or other in-group member whose sincerity we might be more
prone to assume. We seem to deal with the apologizing cheat the same
way we deal with the accident faker – we trust them unless there is
some obvious reason not to.

Trial judges see and feel this tension between real and fake apologies
every day. Even if defendants have committed the most heinous of
crimes, including murder, when they *seem* to sincerely apologize the
anger directed at them from every direction – judges, prosecutors, even
victims – melts away. We might be able to override that melting away,
oftentimes by trying to convince ourselves that we are still angry or,
more often, that the apology was insincere. But it is still an override, it
takes time, and even after the override the apology may have a lingering
effect in reducing the amount of punishment we would otherwise have
imposed. Wise defense lawyers, and all children, know the power of
apology, even the power of insincere ones.

There was a hilarious scene in the old 1960s sitcom *Leave It to Beaver*
that made this point about the value even of an insincere apology. The

father was lecturing the children about how disappointed he was not just with their misbehavior, but even more with the fact that they did not come clean about it when it first happened. "I would have gone much easier on you if you'd just fessed up," says the father, to which one of the kids says, "Heck, Dad, had we known that we *would* have fessed up."

Of course, feeling our anger drain away does not mean that all of it will go away, or even if it does that we will not still punish. We can, and often do, override our immediate feelings of apology-induced forgiveness. We can relight the fires of blame and punishment once they are doused by an apology, and here, unlike with the automatic emotional effects of apology, our ability to do so seems to depend very much on the nature of the wrong being blamed. That's because our evolved willingness to forgive seems to depend in the end on the amount we blame, despite that initial burst of presumptive forgiveness caused by an apology. The more we blame the harder it is to forgive, which makes sense because blame and forgiveness are reciprocal kinds of proxies for those impossible deterrence calculations.

Because our blame is driven largely by our assessment of the wrong-doer's intent (harm being secondary), apology is most effective when it signals we were mistaken in our assessment of the wrongdoer's intent. When someone tells us they are sorry because their harmful act was an accident, it means much more to us than when they say they are sorry to have caused so much harm from a palpably intentional act. That's one of the reasons why the scene in the movie *Animal House* strikes us as so funny, when Blutto, the character played by John Belushi, grabs the guitar from the folksinger on the stairs, hits him over the head with it, and then immediately says, "Oh, sorry."

In my world, when someone says they are sorry for driving drunk and killing another person, they are of course telling me they never intended to cause harm to anyone. Those apologies are profoundly powerful. But when a rapist says he is sorry, he is saying something much more complex and less resonating – he is sorry he could not control himself, he is sorry he got caught, he is sorry he hurt the victim – all much less likely to trigger lasting feelings of forgiveness. We might still respond to those words by feeling our anger drain away, but it is not very hard to rekindle the fires of blame in those circumstances.

Apology is an example of what economists and social psychologists call cheap talk – a signal whose very reliability is diminished by how easy it is to send. The result is that apology's emotional effect, though powerful, can also be quite transient. Our processes to override such cheap talk don't take too terribly long to kick in, and they can often overcome the loss of anger without much difficulty.

Apology also seems to lose almost all of its emotional salience after the first time it is used. This is the apology version of the serial wrong-doer. In a criminal context, I suspect that once we detect, or think we detect, a fake apology – whether because of its tone or because this was the third time this defendant apologized for his criminal acts – we will be more angry and sentence more harshly than had the defendant not apologized at all. One of the institutional difficulties in detecting the multiple apologizer is that criminals commit crimes all over, and typically get sentenced by many different judges, even in the same jurisdiction. Defendants seem to sense that they shouldn't say things like "I am really sorry, and I promise you will never see me again" twice to the same judge. But even they occasionally get forgetful about which judge sentenced them when. I know from my own experience that there is seldom anything that inflames my retributive fires more than when I remember a serial apologizer. Most of us have presentence reports that tell us about a defendant's prior record, but we do not usually have access to the transcripts of the prior sentencing hearings to see if the defendant is a serial apologizer. Really good prosecutors keep notes on their files when defendants say things like "you will never see me, again, judge." Judges should probably do the same.

We may think some apologies are real when they are fake, but we may also think some are fake that are real. This is especially likely with people who may not be as articulate or self-reflective as the average person. I worry about whether an apology that seems inane and forced may be sincere but inarticulate. In the end, we are either moved or unmoved by a particular apology.

There is also real danger in conflating all the first-time apologies we hear every day into one giant serial apology. I sometimes feel myself drifting toward the following attitude: "Every day I hear the same thing from that podium. You're sorry. You made a mistake. And you ask for mercy." But of course these are usually different defendants with different apologies, and all of us on the trial bench must be constantly vigilant about remembering the myriad of individual differences between crimes and between criminals, including differences in the meanings of their apologies. It isn't always easy, at least for me.

Is there anything criminal systems could do to improve how we deal with apology? Other than somehow flagging prior apologies, I can't think of anything sensible. We could say to ourselves, as individual judges, that we will pay no attention to the apology, on the theory that we simply cannot know when one is real or not, and that in any event it should not matter. I know judges who say they take this position, and in fact it makes some sense if one tends to be a retributivist – one who pays more attention to punishing and less attention to rehabilitation. But saying we will not pay attention to apology does not make it so, precisely because our feelings in response to apologies have such deep evolutionary origins. Moreover, because the best way to "ignore" an apology may be to convince ourselves it is insincere, any successful policy of ignoring apology may have the perverse effect of treating people who sincerely apologize more harshly than those who don't apologize at all.

Despite these difficulties, the power of apology is finding traction in many different legal contexts. In the criminal law, at least for low-level crimes, there's been a significant movement over the past several decades to recognize the potential healing value of apology, under the general rubric of "restorative justice."[16] Although there are endless varieties of restorative justice courts, in both England and America, they all share one central feature: procedures for bringing the victim and wrongdoer together in ways that will allow the victim to explain to the wrongdoer the impact the crime has had on the victim, with the idea that this communication will be the beginning of sincere apology and real forgiveness.[17] These efforts seem to me to be important and worthwhile; a system grounded on blame and punishment cannot just ignore apology and forgiveness. Of course the criminal law is also all about self-interested strategic actors, so there are real debates about the ultimate value of a system that in effect forces criminals to apologize and at least strongly encourages victims to forgive.[18]

The law's infatuation with apology has not been limited to the criminal law. Apology is now being written about, and institutionalized, in everything from mediation strategies in divorce cases, to manufacturers developing apology strategies when they must recall products, to the expressions of sorrow by negligent physicians. In this last regard, there is some empirical evidence that doctors who personally apologize to patients suffering bad outcomes – whether from negligence or not – are significantly less likely to be sued for malpractice than those who don't apologize.[19] These data have even spurned efforts in many states to make such apologies inadmissible in the malpractice case, and in fact my state, Colorado, was the first state to pass such legislation.[20]

Paradoxically, by making malpractice apologies cheaper, such statutes may make them less effective. Much of the scholarly criticism of the trend toward encouraging apology by immunizing its legal effects is based on the idea that apology is then rendered too cheap to be reliable because it can be easily faked. These critics suggest that apology alone should never be enough to justify any significant legal consequences, such as making it inadmissible. This criticism recognizes that whether real or fake, the brains of malpractice victims will tend to forgive if a doctor apologizes, and that the law should not encourage such cheap but effective apologies.[21] In the old days, when a doctor was risking liability by apologizing, saying sorry really meant something and therefore was a reliable signal that triggered forgiveness. But now that malpractice apologies don't subject the doctor to any increased risks, my hunch is that in the long run they will become less and less effective in reducing litigation, although I am unaware of any data on this question. Of course, a doctor's "apology" can come in many flavors, from the least likely "I am sorry I was negligent" to the less damning "I am sorry the outcome was bad." The surprising lesson of the power of medical apology is that the latter seems just as effective as the former in reducing litigation. Patients don't really want doctors to fall on their swords; they just want them to act human.

ATONEMENT

One way an apologizing wrongdoer might get more forgiveness bang for his apology buck is to add in some self-imposed cost. If a defendant were willing to couple his apology with an act that inflicts a cost on him – that makes his apology less cheap – then our brains might pay more attention to protestations of remorse and we might be more likely to forgive. There are two evolutionary reasons such signals might resonate with us, and result in forgiveness in the form of less punishment.

First, less punishment might be warranted for the simple reason that the wrongdoer has already punished himself. If a wrong justified thirty lashes, we might be inclined to impose only twenty if the wrongdoer has already given himself ten.

Second, because blame, forgiveness and punishment are all evolutionary shortcuts for deterrence, we should be more likely to believe an atoning wrongdoer than a mere apologizing one. A defendant who renounced his property, imposed his own self-flagellating penance, or even just cried in front of some other tough guys, might be sending reliable signals that we do not have to worry about him reoffending once we let him back into the group.

If you are the sentencing judge, and two otherwise identical defendants appear before you, your third-party punishment instincts will quite automatically forgive an atoning defendant more than just an apologizing one. I can't tell you how many times defendants have appeared before me and mouthed the following words or their equivalent: "Judge I apologize for my actions and am ready to take responsibility for them." But then when I sentence them to jail or prison they are angry because they expected their naked words of apology to result in a light sentence. Most of those defendants are not really sorry at all, and are not really ready to take responsibility. They are just ready to say the words.

Contrast them to defendants, and I've seen many over the years, who voluntarily give up something important – such as their freedom – as a signal for true repentance. Defendants with drug problems, for example, might voluntarily enroll themselves in inpatient drug treatment programs. A few defendants have been so horrified at their crimes that they have had emotional breakdowns and as a result lost their jobs and families. Which set of defendants would you treat less harshly – the apologizers or the atoners?

Our word "atonement" comes from the Middle English phrase *at oon*, which means "being at one." Someone who punishes himself before anyone does it for him becomes "at one" with his victim by self-inflicting some harm symbolic of the harm he inflicted on the victim.[22] But the self-punishment need not always be corporal. Precisely because our brains are so acutely sensitive to reputation, an apology alone, in the right circumstances, can be a profound form of social atonement. This is forgiveness's mirror image of reputational punishment.

Erin O'Hara recounts the story of the apology by the captain of the U.S.S. Greenville, the American submarine that accidentally sank a Japanese fishing trawler in 2001. Despite the fact that he was facing a court marshal, and against the advice of his lawyer, the submarine's captain met with family members of the dead Japanese fishermen, bowed deeply as his tears struck the floor, and said he was very sorry. One father of a dead fisherman reported that "his anger suddenly dissipated."[23] In Japanese culture, the captain's expressions of sorrow were viewed as a crucial loss of face, and were therefore treated as a deeply reliable signal for forgiveness. Such behavior may have been substantially less effective, say, in Minsk or Los Angeles.

Despite these kinds of compelling anecdotes, our troublesome social brains often get in the way of effective atonement. In a palpably strategic setting like a courtroom (or our ancestors' small groups), every wrongdoer will have an incentive to offer atonement if its cost were exceeded by the resulting benefit in forgiven punishment. Is that real atonement or fake atonement? Catholics recognize the notion of "perfect contrition," which requires a kind of suspension of disbelief that the contrition will have any benefits. The Arab word for atonement is *kafara*, which literally means "to hide," suggesting the view that one who thinks he can pay for forgiveness is just hiding, if not compounding, his sins.[24] Similar ambiguity, no doubt linguistically related, resides in the Hebrew word for atonement, *kafat*, which, depending on context, can mean either to cover or to forgive.

The checkered meaning of the word reflects that when it comes to atonement our blaming brains come perilously close to a depressingly cynical paradox: all atonement is either a strategic fake (if it costs less than its expected payoff in forgiveness) or wholly irrational (if it costs more than its expected payoff in forgiveness).

But there still seems to be room for atonement as an evolutionarily effective strategy. It may well have been a way to keep punishment private, between the wrongdoer and his victim, without resort to the group. If an apology just doesn't seem to be doing the job, we can start punishing ourselves and keep punishing ourselves until the victim seems content. This is exactly what happens when we say, as part of an apology, that we "feel bad" about having caused harm. By "feeling bad" we are announcing that we are psychically punishing ourselves, in the hopes that our apology will be seen as an honest signal and result in forgiveness. If we get signs that "feeling bad" is just not enough, we can ramp up our self-punishment until it is enough. Atonement thus becomes a vehicle to negotiate forgiveness directly with the victim or his family, and thus avoid having the group get involved at all in any punishment. That would have been a valuable strategy in a social animal requiring punishment but not too much punishment.

THE PROBLEM OF REPATRIATION

As we saw in the last chapter, for all but the last instants of the human story we imposed largely instantaneous punishment and then expected everyone to go on with their lives with as little disruption as possible. We executed or banished the worst among us, and merely fined the rest. When corporal punishment came into vogue, we imposed it, then comforted and attended to the wounds of a whipping or amputation. We released criminals from the stocks once their humiliating punishment was complete. The ways in which we punished most wrongdoers contained their own seeds of forgiveness.

Still, repatriation was difficult. Because blame and punishment are just proxies for deterrence, we sometimes got the punishment amounts wrong. If we punished less than we should have, we might be letting people back into the group who had not been sufficiently deterred, and who would therefore continue their cheating and maybe even killing ways. Under-punishment might also embolden others to cheat. On the other hand, over-punishment not only risked the usual costs, it might turn good reintegration risks into bad ones. A wrongdoer who feels he was over-punished might be resentful and angry, only increasing the risks he will reoffend. Even when our amounts of punishment perfectly mirrored their deterrent purposes – we might say such punishment was "just" – people are different and therefore react differently to being punished. Just as everyone is not deterred by the same amount of punishment, not everyone can recover from the same amount of punishment. By punishing wrongdoers, we always risked that the punishment itself might turn onetime miscreants into permanent pariahs.

Our own attitudes about whether a punished member is a pariah or can be brought back into the fold are not only crude guesses, but the guesses themselves can sometimes be affected by our act of punishment. Blaming then punishing wrongdoers is a way of recognizing wrongdoers, and recognizing them labels them as members likely to cheat. Forgiving them labels them as members likely to reform. But our labels are not perfect. Our blame-prone brains might become blind to genuine redemption, and our forgiveness-prone brains blind to real wolves in the fold.

Natural selection solved much of this problem, as we have already seen, by investing our brains with powerful urges to stop punishing once we punish. Those forgiving emotions allowed the rest of the group to return almost to baseline in their treatment of the wrongdoer. But "almost" is the key to the repatriation problem. We are creatures who remember the cheats among us, and whose grudging trust can be a fleeting thing. We may not want to continue to punish wrongdoers after they suffer their punishment, but we will suspect them of the next unsolved crime.

Perhaps even more deeply, delegated third-party punishment comes with its own built-in tendency for blame to linger long after punishment has been inflicted. Because someone else is doing the punishing, we who blame continue to blame because we never get the personal satisfaction of punishing. This is one reason public punishment was so important. When all group members got to witness the punishment, they got to share in the social satisfaction of punishment, even when they were not the ones doing the actual punishment. That social recognition of the punishment helped dampen the blame instincts of non-punishers.

The problem of repatriation is just as intractable from the wrongdoer's point of view. He knows he will never regain the group's complete trust. Depending on the magnitude of that reticence, he may have a more difficult time succeeding in the group, or think he will, which may in turn only increase his temptation to cheat again.

But the evolutionary picture was not entirely bleak. The good news was that because we are all tempted to cheat, today's punisher will be next week's wrongdoer. The principle of "there but for the grace of God go I" restrained over-punishment and also encouraged reintegration after punishment. We can't have held too much of a grudge against cheaters when all of us are, by our very natures, tempted to cheat in the right circumstance.

However, modern punishments, including severe corporal punishment, the invention of the penitentiary in the late 1700s, and the rise of the rehabilitative ideal in the early 1900s, have made reintegration much more difficult, from both the punisher's and the punished's perspectives. Wrongdoers damaged by severe corporal punishments, such as amputation, were physically and permanently labeled as wrongdoers. The labeling aspects of their physical punishment hindered their reintegration every bit as much as the sheer physical disabilities they caused. Long prison sentences are the psychological version of amputation; spending twenty years in that environment makes it almost impossible for most ex-convicts to succeed on the outside, not only because of the damage it does to their abilities to live with the rest of us, but also because the rest of us can spot an ex-con a mile away. And just in case we can't spot them, many of them engage in ritual tattooing, which no doubt is an important social signal within prison environments, but which on the outside acts as a modern version of branding. Would you give a job to a felon I once sentenced who had the word "HOPELESS" tattooed in two-inch letters across his forehead?

Well-intentioned rehabilitationists have just made things worse. Now felons are labeled as having the social disease of criminality, a disease that seems by all accounts hopelessly incurable. Once we label them incorrigible that label sticks, whether or not they manage to survive prison with their moral intuitions intact. We no longer see wrongdoing as a behavioral risk to which we are all subject, but instead as a deep and incurable disease. Would you give a job to a felon suffering from the incurable disease of criminality?

Our prisons are also largely hidden from the rest of us, which makes it even harder for us to forgive. When I sentence a defendant to prison,

Percentage of Prisoners Reconvicted			
	1, 2, and 3 Years after Release		
Country	1 Year	2 Years	3 Years
England & Wales	N/A	58.2	N/A
Iceland	N/A	N/A	37.0
Netherlands	43.4	55.5	62.0
N. Ireland	N/A	45.0	N/A
Scotland	46.0	60.0	67.0
Switzerland	12.0	26.0	34.0
United States	21.5	36.4	46.9

Figure 6.1. Comparative recidivism rates, Europe/United States. B. Wartna & L. Nijssen, *National Reconviction Rates*, 5 CRIMINILOGY IN EUROPE no. 3, 3, 14, tbl. 2 (December 2006).

the victim's family watches him disappear behind a hidden door in the side of the courtroom. Unlike when the whole town witnessed punishment in the stocks, and in fact even participated in the social aspects of that punishment, we feel no connections to our modern punishments, and therefore get no satisfaction from it. "He killed my sister and the only punishment he will suffer is to be taken behind that hidden door?" Victims, and in fact all citizens, will tend to continue to blame wrongdoers they never see punished.

In today's world, the punished and the punishers hold up mirrors to each other that begin a destructive reflective cycle that has long gone out of control. Virtually all of our modern institutions seem designed to make it difficult if not impossible for felons to reintegrate. In many states, felons cannot vote or serve on juries. More importantly, they are legally disqualified from several occupations, and culturally disqualified from most others. Companies across industries routinely ask job applicants if they have a criminal record, and vet their answers with criminal background checks. Felons who cannot find work are more likely to return to crime. Recidivism is appallingly high across all Western countries for which we have data. A sample of that data, comparing U.S. rates with European rates, appears in Figure 6.1.[25] These seven countries have wildly different legal systems, incarceration practices, and incarceration rates, all of which no doubt impact recidivism. For example, if the Netherlands imprisons only the most violent offenders, while the United States is imprisoning large numbers of nonviolent drug offenders (and, indeed, the U.S. rate of incarceration is seven times greater than the rate in the Netherlands), then it may well be that prisoners in the Netherlands are by definition more likely to reoffend. And of course there are vast differences in geography, density, racial and ethnic heterogeneity, and overall culture across all of these countries. The important point, however, is that in societies as different as these seven countries recidivism rates are all appallingly high.

To understand just how appalling, compare them to general incarceration rates. That is, how much *more* likely are you to find yourself in prison if you've already been there? Even in a society as (supposedly) criminologically enlightened as the Netherlands, the answer is that being in prison astronomically increases the chances you will be back. If you are an average citizen of the Netherlands, the chances that you are presently incarcerated are about one in 1,176, or 0.085 percent. But if you are being released from a prison in the Netherlands, your chances of going back there just in the first year jump to 43.4%, an increase of 500-fold. This relative recidivism number in the United States is not nearly as bad, mainly because we start out with such a high incarceration rate. But it is still high. One in 167 Americans is in prison, or 0.60 percent; but if you are already in an American prison your chances of being back one year after release are 21.5 percent, a 35-fold increase. Similarly increased risks have been reported in virtually all countries around the world. Prison begets prison. Modern punishment, far from deterring future wrongs, seems to guaranty it.

There are many explanations. Some people are just inherently more prone to crime, and once released those bad people return to their regularly high rates of criminal activity. That certainly is the case with psychopaths, whose rates of recidivism, as we have already seen, dwarf even these already depressing rates. Even so, psychopaths make up only 20–25 percent of prison populations, and even if that number were close to 100 percent their high recidivism rates could not alone explain why being in prison increases by 500 percent a Dutchman's chances of being back there in one year.

Another popular explanation is that prisons become a kind of criminal finishing school, where not-so-bad people turn into very bad people. There is no doubt much truth in this explanation, but, again, it is hard to believe it is powerful enough to explain such massively increased risks. Besides, when one looks at recidivism only for people on probation, most of whom have not served a day in prison for their offense, one sees similar explosions in the risk of recidivism compared to the general incarceration risk.[26]

The better, and more troubling, explanation has to do with the way modern penology interferes with our ability to forgive. We have no emotional stake in hidden punishment, and therefore continue to blame. We label all criminals as diseased, and that label profoundly changes the way we see them, and they see themselves, when they get out. Our natural, if grudging, willingness to accept wrongdoers back into the fold is now being hugely compromised by the label "felon." "Almost" trusting them back to baseline has now become "almost never" trusting them with anything. They are no longer like us, all stained with original sin, but instead have a disease; and none of us has much confidence that the priests of penology know how to cure the disease, not with these kinds of recidivism numbers. So the labeling reinforces itself, and this vicious attitudinal cycle blooms into institutions that seem almost designed to insure that convicted felons will keep going back to prison.

Probation can often be a more tender version of this same trap. For example, in gang cases in my jurisdiction prosecutors regularly ask for so-called area restrictions as a condition of probation. These prohibit defendants from being in certain designated areas of the city, with the idea that these are the gang-ridden areas and that keeping out of those areas will help gang defendants from committing more crimes. I think this is all nonsense, and when I sentence a gang defendant to probation I refuse to enter area restrictions. In the first place, most of these defendants deserve prison, not probation. Second, they *live* in these areas, and forcing them out of these areas forces them away from what little family support they might have. But most importantly, these restrictions are a kind of self-defeating labeling. We are telling these defendants we expect them to reoffend, and sure enough most of them do, with or without area restrictions.

So what's a modern criminal justice system to do? To the extent the sheer length of sentences is interfering with repatriation, the problem might correct itself if we just returned to our retributive roots by imposing more sentences of incarceration but of shorter duration. Small crimes deserve small punishments, regardless of our sociological guesses about their causes and likely future effects. Drug laws are a big driver of our long sentences, and they also contribute greatly to the labeling problem. It might be a stretch to label an armed robber as being diseased, but we don't seem to have any problem with that label if the armed robber is also a heroin addict.[27]

Our very reluctance to impose short sentences the first time around paradoxically contributes to this stigmatization of felons, especially ex-convicts. One of the dirty little secrets of most criminal systems is that the vast majority of defendants are not sent to prison for what they did, but rather for their failure to comply with probation. Sure, there are some really violent offenders who are sentenced to prison from the get go, and also some nonviolent drug offenders who get sent there because of statutes that require mandatory minimum prison sentences. But the vast majority of prisoners in the United States, at least in state systems, are nonviolent offenders who were initially given probation, often many times over. As one of my former colleagues used to put it, most defendants really have to work their way into prison. We give them chance after chance, which they consistently blow. Finally, we have no choice but to send them to prison.

The public, however, believes prison is reserved for the most violent offenders, perhaps because of Hollywood caricatures of prisons and the people who populate them. As a result, the label "ex-con" is a kind of branding that conjures in the minds of most people visions of rapists and murderers. We would probably all be better off if we abolished probation and sentenced all convicted criminal offenders to shorter jail and/or prison sentences, which should then over time lose some of their stigmatizing character.

Realistically, though, with prison populations continuing to sky-rocket, expecting to turn the repatriation problem around merely by turning sentencing practices around seems unrealistic. Many people have instead promoted specific programs designed to reintegrate convicts. There are even specialized reintegration courts, often called "reentry courts," whose whole function is to increase the likelihood convicted criminals can become functioning members of society.[28] To my mind, and quite in contrast to drug courts and other so-called treatment courts, these reintegration courts seem to be a very good thing, not only because they show convicts that they can make it back into the fold, but more importantly because they show the rest of us that not all convicts are diseased monsters. Whether they work, in the sense of reducing recidivism, is probably still unknown at this early stage.

In the end, maybe our attitudes about wrongdoers can be turned around, although it will take time. After all, we didn't always view prisons as failed moral hospitals. They started out as places for reflection and self-healing. It took a while, but most criminologists and legal philosophers managed to get around to rejecting rehabilitation as the primary purpose of the criminal law.[29] Now, if only the rest of us would get on board, including judges, maybe we can recapture our evolved urges that most wrongdoers not only deserve punishment, but also deserve to be forgiven when they've completed their punishment.

Notes to Chapter 6

1. For a comprehensive and compelling treatment of the evolutionary roots of forgiveness, see MICHAEL E. MCCULLOUGH, BEYOND REVENGE: THE EVOLUTION OF THE FORGIVENESS INSTINCT (Jossie-Bass 2008).
2. WALTER BURKETT, HOMO NECANS: THE ANTHROPOLOGY OF ANCIENT GREEK SACRIFICIAL AND RITUAL AND MYTH (U. Cal. 1993).
3. FORGIVENESS: THEORY, RESEARCH AND PRACTICE 20 (M. McCullough et al., eds., Guildford 2000).
4. Id.
5. ALAN PATON, TOO LATE THE PHALAROPE 278 (Simon & Shuster 1953).
6. ANDRÉ GIDE, OSCAR WILDE: REMINISCENCES 251 (B. Frechtman, tr., Phil. Lib. 2012) (electronic edition).
7. LEWIS B. SMEDES, THE ART OF FORGIVING 178 (Ballentine 4th ed. 1997).
8. See, e.g., F. AURELI & F. DE WAAL, NATURAL CONFLICT RESOLUTION (Berkeley 2000); G. Cordoni & E. Palagi, *Reconciliation in wolves* (Canis lupus): *new evidence for a comparative perspective.* ETHOLOGY, **114(3)**, 298–308 (2008); M. Cords & F. Aureli, *Patterns of reconciliation among juvenile long-tailed macaques,* in JUVENILE PRIMATES: LIFE HISTORY, DEVELOPMENT, AND BEHAVIOR 271–284 (M. E. Pereira & L. A. Fairbanks, eds., Oxford 1993).
9. A. Seed et al., *Postconflict third-party affiliation in rooks,* CURRENT BIOL., **17(2)**, 152–158 (2007).
10. R. Bshary et al., *Cleaner fish* Labroides Dimidiatus *manipulate client reef fish by providing tactile stimulation,* PROC. ROY. SOC., **268**, 1495–1501 (2001).
11. M. Cords & S. Thurnheer, *Reconciling with valuable partners by long-tailed macaques,* ETHOLOGY, **93(4)**, 315–325 (1993).

12. See generally, S. Marsh and P. Briggs, *Examining Trust, Forgiveness and Regret as Computational Concepts*, in COMPUTING WITH SOCIAL TRUST 9 (J. Karat, ed., Springer 2009).

13. The law is full of these kinds of "fool-me-once" propositions. Three strikes laws are one form. Another is the so-called two prior felony rule, under which, in many jurisdictions, defendants with two prior felony convictions are no longer eligible for probation without the prosecution's consent.

14. Erin O'Hara, Group-Conflict Resolution: Sources of Resistance to Reconciliation, 72 L. & CONTEMP. PROB. I (2009); Erin O'Hara, *Apology and Thick Trust: What Spouse Abusers and Negligent Doctors May Have in Common*, 49 CHI.-KENT L. REV. 1055 (2004); Erin O'Hara & Douglas Yarn, *On Apology and Consilience*, 77 WASH. L. REV. 121 (2002).

15. A. Hayashi et al., *Neural correlates of forgiveness for moral transgressions involving deception*, BRAIN RES., **1332**, 90–99 (May 2010).

16. Two of the most powerful academic calls for the criminal justice system to start paying attention to apology are S. Bibas & R. Bierschbach, *Integrating Remorse and Apology into Criminal Procedure*, 114 YALE L.J. 85 (2004); and N. Smith, *The Penitent and the Penitentiary: Questions Regarding Apologies in Criminal Law*, 27 CRIM. J. ETHICS 2 (2010).

17. The restorative justice movement seems particularly popular in England. See J. Shaplan et al., *Restorative Justice in Practice: The Second Report from the Evaluation of Three Schemes*, Centre for Criminological Research, University of Sheffield (July 2006), available at www.shef.ac.uk/polopoly_fs/1.783!/file/RestorativeJustice2ndReport.pdf.

18. For a comprehensive, updated and balanced summary of the restorative justice debate, see GERRY JOHNSTONE, RESTORATIVE JUSTICE: IDEAS, VALUES, DEBATES (Routledge 2nd ed., 2011).

19. See, e.g., Jennifer K. Robbennolt, *Apologies and Legal Settlement: An Empirical Examination*, 102 MICH. L. REV. **460**, 510–511 (2003); MICHAEL S. WOODS, HEALING WORDS: THE POWER OF APOLOGY IN MEDICINE (Doctors in Touch, 2004).

20. COLO. REV. STAT. ANN. § 13-25-135(1), which was adopted in April 2003, provides that in any medical malpractice action a health care provider's apology to a patient is inadmissible as evidence of liability, with apology laboriously defined, as only legislatures can, as "any and all statements, affirmations, gestures, or conduct expressing apology, fault, sympathy, commiseration, condolence, compassion, or a general sense of benevolence." Similar statutes quickly followed in Oregon and Oklahoma.

21. See, e.g., Lee Taft, *An Apology within a Moral Dialectic: A Reply to Professor Robbennolt*, 103 MICH. L. REV. **1010** (March 2005); WILLIAM IAN MILLER, FAKING IT (Cambridge 2005). Taft and Miller take a slightly different approach to the problem of cheap apology – Taft viewing the act of apology as an act of reparation and Miller as an act of humiliation – but in

the end both are signals for forgiveness. And both Miller and Taft recognize, correctly, I think, that in some strategic settings our brains require, and our public policy should require, something more than apology.

22. See generally *Doctrine of Atonement*, THE CATHOLIC ENCYCLOPEDIA, at http://www.newadvent.org/cathen/02055a.htm.

23. O'Hara & Yarn, supra note 14, at 1124.

24. Abdessalam Najjar, *Atonement in Islam*, JERUSALEM POST (September 24, 2009). And yet, the Qur'an has fifteen different words for sin, each denoting a different kind of wrong and requiring a different kind of atonement. Id.

25. The base years on which the three-year recidivism periods are grounded are different for each country, and range from 1988 for Switzerland to 2001 for England, Wales, and Ireland.

26. P. Langan & M. Cunniff, *Recidivism of Felons on Probation*, U.D. Dep't of Justice, Office of Justice Programs (1992), available at http://bjs.ojp.usdoj.gov/index.cfm?ty=pbdetail&iid=1409 (62% of all probationers had violated their probation within three years, and 46% were resentenced to prison or jail).

27. In fact, treatment courts in general are a terrible problem when it comes to repatriation. The treatment is not nearly effective enough to make up for the massive increase in cases caused by the phenomenon called "net-widening" – police trolling for patients instead of making arrests in provable cases. In the bargain, these defendants not only get labeled as having diseases, they eventually get sent to prison in higher numbers than before. See generally Morris B. Hoffman, *The Drug Court Scandal*, 78 N.C.L. REV. 1437 (2000). Don't get me wrong. The drug problem is a pervasive problem in most societies, and we need to address it on many fronts, including treatment. But treating defendants inside the criminal justice system gives us a wholly unwarranted and dangerous license to mix up punishment with treatment, exacerbating the problem that modern punishment labels rather than punishes. See also Morris B. Hoffman, *Problem-Solving Courts and the Psycho-Legal Error*, 160 U. PA. L. REV. PENNumbra 129 (2011), available at http://www.pennumbra.com/essays/12 - 2011/Hoffman.pdf.

28. See, e.g., Eric J. Miller, *The Therapeutic Effects of Managerial Reentry Courts*, 20 FED. SENT. REP. 127 (Dec. 2007).

29. Francis Allen, THE DECLINE OF THE REHABILITATIVE IDEAL: PENAL POLICY AND SOCIAL PURPOSE (Yale 1981).

7 DELEGATING PUNISHMENT

I was married by a judge. I should have asked for a jury.

Groucho Marx

CONSENSUS DECISIONS: BEES, MONKEYS, JUDGES, AND JURORS

Widespread third-party punishment may be rare or even nonexistent in nonhumans, but it turns out that the problem of third-party punishment is just a special case of the much more general problem of collective action, a problem that faces every group of social animals. Some decisions, by their very nature, will apply to the entire group as long as it remains an entire group, and will therefore require some mechanism for deciding what the group as a whole will do. Examples include where insects build their hives, where flocks of birds go to forage, and where troupes of chimpanzees stop to sleep for the night. Somehow, these decisions need to get made for the entire group. Nothing removes the benefits of group living faster or more fundamentally than getting left behind.

Dominance hierarchies themselves are one solution to this problem of the need for collective action. Dominant members can, and often do, make many of these activity, timing, and travel decisions themselves, and all the other members follow. This may even be one of the main evolutionary advantages of dominance. But it turns out that dominance – or "despotism," as biologists call it in the context of group decision-making – is not natural selection's only solution to the problem of collective action. It's not even the most common solution. Non-despotic decision-making – either by the whole group or a part of it – has been discovered across a wide variety of social animals, as diverse as bees, swans, buffalo, capuchin monkeys, gorillas, and baboons.[1]

In late spring or early summer, when colonies of honeybees (*Apis mellifera*) reach a certain size, they divide. The queen goes off with roughly two-thirds of the hive to a new location, leaving her daughter as the new queen to preside over the remaining third. As you might imagine, selecting the location of the new hive is a critical task, with enormous survival implications. It has long been known that scouts search out new hive locations, and that they return and dance in a way that not only describes where the proposed new location is, but also conveys, by the length of the dance, the scout's judgment about its suitability. But of course many scouts are scouting many locations, and each returns with its own report. How is a consensus reached, and by whom? It turns out that the queen does not make this decision, nor does the entire hive. Instead, the dancing scouts communicate with each other, they start visiting the sites strongly recommended by other scouts, the scouts themselves reach a consensus, and then they lead the rest of the moving bees in a swarm to the new location.[2]

What a wonderful way to solve the collective action problem! The queen could not possibly afford to risk doing her own scouting, even if she were able to do so. Besides, scouting for new locations is precisely the kind of task that is best done by many scouts canvassing a wide area. Entomologists still know very little about the process by which the scouts themselves reach a consensus. However, a recent paper, which used computer modeling to tackle the problem, suggests some interesting possibilities.

Researchers surmised that some scouts might be very good hunters for and evaluators of new locations, but not so good at articulating their findings to the scout group, and hardheaded, so to speak, about the competing suggestions of others. Conversely, some scouts might not be good locators but are good communicators, and also might tend to be more open to the suggestions of others. The researchers showed that too many of either of these extreme types makes for disastrous consensus decisions. Too many "Strong but Silent" types dramatically slow down the migration decision, sometimes even stopping it dead in its tracks, leaving the swarm confused and vulnerable. But too many of the "Touchy Feelies" lead to rash and disastrous relocation decisions, as they fall into the group-think trap and simply go along with whatever a few of the Strong but Silent types suggest. As the researchers put it, the challenge of quickly finding the optimal site depends on "the interplay of bees' interdependence in communicating the whereabouts of the best site and their independence in confirming this information."[3]

That is, the best relocation decisions may be reached by involving more than one decision-maker and more than one kind of decision-maker. Bees may well avoid the group-think problem by populating the "jury" with a sufficient number of independent thinkers not too willing to follow the other guy without checking it out for themselves. They avoid the reciprocal problem of deadlock by including a sufficient number of cooperators who value consensus over independence. This example also shows that some awfully complicated notions – initiative, leadership, prudence, communication skills – may not be the exclusive bailiwick of so-called higher creatures. What drives these behaviors is the social nature of the social insects, not their brainpower.

Even in social species with great brainpower and strong dominance hierarchies, where one might guess that all decisions would be despotic, scientists are finding many examples of consensus decision-making. For example, primatologists studying the morning departure routines of chacma baboons (*Papio ursinus*) have discovered that the departure decision is the product of a rather complicated consensus between dominant and nondominant members.[4] There had been suggestions that the dominant males might share such group-wide decisions with one or two dominant females, but these primatologists saw much broader and more complex patterns of decision-making. The departure decisions they observed were made by dominant and nondominant adults of both genders, with adult males being somewhat more influential than adult females, the dominant male being most influential, but the decision was clearly the product of a weighted consensus rather than despotism by dominants.[5]

The idea that, at least in some circumstances, many individuals might make better decisions for the group than a single individual or a handful of dominant individuals seems sensible. The more deciders, the more information. The more information, the better the decision, subject, of course, to the countervailing goal of avoiding deadlock and undue delay. But the wisdom of groups may lie even deeper than an increase in information. The numbers themselves can boost a group's accuracy quite apart from information gathering.

This idea was expressed as a kind of mathematical political theorem in 1785 by the French philosopher and mathematician Nicolas di Caritat, better known as the Marquis de Condorcet. His so-called jury theorem is a pretty elementary consequence of the arithmetic of probability. It states that if a number of individuals each have the same probability of reaching a correct decision (and assuming the decision is binary, that is, there is one correct decision and one incorrect decision), then the overall probability of a correct decision increases as the number of individuals increases.[6] At the limit, juries of infinite size are infallible. Condorcet used this result to make all sorts of broader arguments about political theory and democracy. His target, of course, was not the European trial system but France's entire ancien régime.

But Condorcet's jury theorem makes so many assumptions that it ends up being largely useless in the real world. It assumes the decisions of the "jurors" are independent; that is, the jurors do not deliberate with each other, they just vote. This assumes away not only the deliberative benefits of the jury, but also its two primary and reciprocal dangers of group-think and deadlock. The theorem also assumes non-unanimity, which has been the exception over the history of the jury. Condorcet also assumes *all* jurors are blessed with the same probability of making a correct decision. Most important, he assumes that that probability (P) is more than 0.5; that is, that all individual jurors are more likely than not to get the correct result. If P is less than 0.5 (that is, if individuals are more likely to get it wrong than right), then the best jury is a jury of one, and a jury with an infinite number of members always gets it wrong. Condorcet's theorem turns out to be nothing more than an algebraic artifact that group size compounds both the wrongness and rightness of non-deliberative individual judgment.

Condorcet's formulation was too simple for another important reason. No creatures, even judges and jurors, have an infinite amount of time to reach decisions. As we saw with the honeybee's decision to move hives, some group decisions involve a trade-off between accuracy and speed. So a better formulation of the trial task is that it must optimize the accuracy of its decision given the constraints of time. This might very well explain why history is, with a couple famous exceptions we will discuss later in this chapter, devoid of very large juries.

Still, if individual group members are reasonably good deciders (they need only be slightly better than chance), and if the group of deciders has a sufficient mix of leaders and followers so as to avoid the twin problems of deadlock and group-think, it seems plausible that on average better decisions will come from a subset of group members than from the group leader alone. This might explain, in part, why consensus behaviors appear in so many different kinds of social animals.

With social animals such as primates, whose group members are not all siblings, who come equipped with brains that allow strategic selfishness, and who generally follow weak dominance hierarchies, there is another important advantage to delegating collective action to more than just the dominant member, one that goes beyond both mere information gathering and Condorcet's theorem. Allowing others besides the dominant member to make important decisions may not only make the decisions more accurate, it may defuse in-group tensions. A smart alpha will delegate some important decisions to others precisely because if he gets an important decision wrong he will risk his reputation, his standing, and maybe even his life. A dominant ancestor's risks may even have increased over evolutionary time, as our small groups got bigger and more young males eyed the top spot.

Third-party punishment is a collective action that is especially ripe for delegation, either to a subgroup or to a dominant member. In fact, in a sense it comes pre-delegated, because by definition it is punishment by someone other than the victim. When A punishes B for a wrong B committed against C, A has in effect taken on himself the right to retaliate in C's name, and C has in effect delegated that task to A. As we've already discussed, once humans evolved the third-party punishment instinct, some kind of centralized punishment system became absolutely essential in large groups. With everyone's blame and punishment everyone else's business, our small groups would have become punishment circuses.

It wasn't just a process problem. If our second-party urges to retaliate were simply converted whole cloth into third-party urges, our small groups would have punished too much. If every group member joined, say, in the beating punishment of a food thief with the same zeal as if the thief had stolen their food, no thieves could have survived. Punishment amounts would also have been unpredictable. Who beats the wrongdoer, and for how long? The 6 members who happened to see a theft, the 50 family members who were victims of the theft, or the whole 500 who were told about it? Natural selection solved these very dicey problems of transitioning from retaliation to retribution in three ways.

First, it muted our blaming urges in the third-party context. As we have seen, we simply do not feel as outraged when see someone robbed as when we ourselves are robbed. Dampening down blame helped with the risk of over-punishment. We might all join in on the beating, but none of us is punching as hard as if we were the wrongdoer's victim.

This still leaves the problem of everyone punishing everyone else, inflicting less punishment to be sure, but still as part of an uncoordinated mess. So as a second force to restrain third-party punishment, as we have seen, evolution built our brains not even to blame small slights. Our groups might degenerate into punishment anarchy for big violations, but at least we will stay calm about small ones.

Finally, as to the big violations, our brains shuttled off the urge to punish to someone else. This made all kinds of sense. We could keep our blame fires hot enough to *do something* about third-party wrongs, without that something being inflicting the punishment ourselves. We could then enjoy all the deterrent benefits of socialized blame without the over-punishment risks of socialized punishment.

There are no known human societies that did not centralize in some fashion the third-party punishment urges of their members.[7] Once the group as a whole acquired the right to punish its own members – a form of collective action not so different from a group of chimps making the departure decision – the group almost had to re-delegate back to some individual or group of individuals the actual task of punishment. Punishment, like departure, wasn't something that the group as a whole could decide simultaneously. And that became even more apparent as our groups got bigger and the relationships within them more complex. We've been delegating our third-party punishment – whether to grandfathers in the family, leaders of the clan, chiefs of the tribe, elders of the village, sheriffs of the manor, or, for really important disputes, juries – for as long as we've been punishing.

It is a common view, especially among some economists and legal historians, that members of primitive societies were more "retributive" than members of highly developed ones; that they engaged in more "vigilantism."[8] But these views miss the essential point that even vigilantism is delegated third-party punishment. When larger states were unstable or even nonexistent, we still delegated our third-party punishment urges to some central representative of the group.[9] Whether we delegate our third-party punishment to a magistrate in a functioning state, or to a posse in a nonfunctioning one, does not change the fact that we are delegating.

To be sure, for much of our unwritten history we probably delegated most third-party punishments to dominant members, as nonhumans often delegate other collective action decisions to dominants. Later in this chapter we will see the traces of this tendency in our own written history, where trials were almost always conducted by the tribal leader and not by juries. In fact, this kind of "delegation" was not so much delegation from the group to the dominant member as it was simply the behavioral practice of the dominant taking on the task of punishment along with all his other rights and responsibilities.

Our drive to make someone else responsible for third-party punishment no doubt meant that that someone else was almost always the dominant member. It would have made sense for the dominant member to be responsible for the vast majority of third-party punishments. After all, his very dominance meant that he, more than any other member, was most likely to be able to withstand the considerable costs of punishment. The punished wrongdoer and his family and supporters were less likely to retaliate against the dominant member than against any other member. That is the very definition of dominance.

But there may have been some kinds of defections, and some kinds of defectors, that would have been impossible even for the most dominant member to punish. Close calls, in the sense of whether the wrong was serious enough to warrant punishment, or even in the sense of uncertainty about whether the accused was factually guilty, might be decisions a smart dominant member might leave for others. Even the mildest punishment inflicted when it shouldn't be may have risked mutiny. Mutiny is nicely avoided, or at least substantially reduced, however, if the punishment is inflicted by a broader subgroup than just the dominant member.

Another kind of punishment ripe for delegation from the dominant to a subgroup would have been punishment for very serious offenses. Inflicting punishment was a risky enterprise, even for dominants. As the stakes went up with the degree of harm, so did the punishment risks. Killing or banishing another member would have been a deadly prospect, even for the most dominant and secure leader. By delegating that task to many other members the dominant member not only placed himself out of harm's way, he reduced the chances the banished or condemned member and/or his family would retaliate. They would have to think twice about retaliating against a punisher when that punisher was many members rather than a single member.

Finally, delegation would have been sensible when the wrongdoer, no matter how serious the crime or convincing the evidence, was powerful, or associated with a powerful family or coalition. Delegation removed the sharpest political aspects of punishment, and relocated the task to a group of members with no direct interest in the punishment decision. "Don't blame me," the dominant member could plausibly say to an angry and powerful member who was just punished, "it wasn't my decision it was theirs." As with serious crimes, a disgruntled wrongdoer and his family would also be less likely to retaliate against many punishers than against one.

Third-party punishment might also have been conducive to delegation because delegated punishment might have been more likely to be, or at least seem, just. Unlike other kinds of collective action, such as relocating a hive, blame and punishment cannot be evaluated in hindsight, precisely because they are emotional shortcuts to impossible calculations about deterrence. Having more members involved in those decisions reduced the risk that a single decision-maker might make a wholly inappropriate decision because he was simply not attuned to the needs of the group. Just as important, a punishment decision by many would tend to be viewed by the punished as more legitimate.

Just like bees and chimps, however, the benefits of delegating collective action disappear if there are too many decision-makers. They risk group-think if too many of them are collaborative, and deadlock if too many of them are free-thinkers. These twin pressures put limits on the numbers and kinds of members to whom the punishment decision was delegated. A myriad of circumstances might drive the decision first whether a dominant member might delegate at all, and then to whom and to how many. Those circumstances are all the things embedded in the same two large considerations that drive any collective decision in a social milieu: the significance of the decision (that is, the benefits of a correct decision compared to the costs of a wrong one) and the speed with which the decision needs to be made.

Some small wrongs might have been dealt with simply by a dominant member's disapproving swat, but others (intragroup murder, for example) would have been severe enough to make the punishment decision critical to the group's survival. If the decision on these serious crimes didn't have to be immediate (for example, the offender was not deemed a present threat to the group), the dominant member might be wise to delegate the punishment decision to many. If swift action was needed, but the benefits of delegation still palpable, then the dominant member might delegate punishment to just a few members. It might also have been wise to include more collaborative members in the punishment decision if a quick decision were needed – more females, for example, as we saw in the case of the departure decisions of baboons. If it was likely to be a closer, difficult decision that was not particularly time sensitive, more independent thinkers and fewer collaborative ones would have been appropriate.

Punishment by the dominant member also made less sense as our groups got bigger. In the first place, our dominance hierarchies, such as they were, got even weaker as our groups grew in size. The dominance a leader may have enjoyed in his small tightly-knit group of 100 mostly-related individuals was substantially diluted when the tribe now consisted of ten different such groups, each with its own dominant member. In addition, wrongs between these subgroups presented the challenge of deciding which of the many dominant members should do the punishing. In fact, the oldest roots of the jury might lie in the simple fact that once our groups agglomerated into larger groups, we now had multiple dominant members instead of just one. These earliest juries may simply have been a collection of those multiple dominant members.

More complicated groups also increased the political risk of an unpopular punishment decision (or, for that matter, any other kind of despotic collective action). The ever-present tension between "real" group members – that is, the close family ties of our original small groups – and the artificial families being created by our political associations must have been daunting in those early years of tribal formation. Imagine that you are a dominant member of a group that just recently joined forces with another group, and you discover that one of your original members killed one of the newcomers. If you take on the punishment duties, the newcomers will not trust you to be harsh enough. Your own members will worry that you will be too harsh just to avoid the appearance of being too lenient. Your counterpart in the new group faces all the same problems. All of this increased the pressures for the group to delegate certain kinds of third-party punishments to a subset of the whole group instead of just to one dominant member or faction.

If this sounds suspiciously like the proposition that juries and democracy are somehow related, it is no coincidence. There is a large body of legal, historical, and, now, evolutionary, literature recognizing the connections between the two.[10] We will see in the next section that although institutional juries long predated the emergence of anything like formal democracy, Greek democracies made important contributions to the jury's development. After all, legal systems and political systems are both answers, along different dimensions and scales, to the same central questions that plague social animals: what are the rules and how do we enforce them?

There is mixed evidence of delegated punishment in existing nomadic forager societies. As we have already seen, when our groups were very small most punishment, even for serious offenses, was done privately, inside families. Our early groups really were just extended families. So, for example, anthropologists report that when an Mbuti hunter was caught stealing meat from the group, the other band members as a whole joined in to ridicule, insult, and laugh at him.[11] The undelegated third-party punishment in this example is really just a kind of collective second-party punishment because the harm was suffered by the whole small group.

But when the harm goes beyond the immediate family or group, primitive societies have been known to delegate third-party punishment, often to the members most injured. For example, a young Mardu man who had incestuous sex with several women was punished not by the chief or the whole group, or even by the women's nearest male relatives, but by the males in his band who were the most likely husbands for the dishonored women.[12] This is an example of another important point when it came to the human transition from second- to third-party punishment: often early states allowed victims to inflict the punishment, but victims had no right to do so until getting the green light from the state. Victims retaliating without state permission are engaging in second-party punishment; victims engaging in retaliation with state permission are engaged in a primitive form of delegated third-party punishment.

Of course, these evolved third-party punishment urges bloomed into a cornucopia of different punishing institutions, as our groups grew larger and more complex, and as each society faced its own unique cultural challenges. Still, we can see traces of the original evolutionary trajectory of these evolved urges by looking at their expression in some very early societies.

TRIAL AS PUNISHMENT

The jury, in this very generalized sense of a subgroup of members to whom the dominant member (or state) has delegated the job of blaming then punishing, is a human universal. Myths from every culture involve the delegation of third-party blame and punishment to jurors. Our mythological juries were convened not to decide factual guilt – which was a given – but to assess blame and impose punishment. When the gods put Orestes on trial for killing his mother, the six-god six-human jury deciding his fate was not deciding whether he was guilty in the factual sense. Everyone knew, and he admitted, that he killed his mother. Instead, the jury that Athena convened was charged with deciding whether Orestes was guilty in the moral sense – that is, how blameworthy his actions were and the extent to which he should be punished for those blameworthy actions.[13]

The whole of the Norse universe was ruled by a kind of jury – twelve gods, with Odin as the foreman. Mundane matters involving earthly blame and punishment were left to a different jury of twelve demigods appointed by Odin. But the big questions – such as whether and how to punish a hero or even a god himself – were decided by the jury of gods presided over by Odin.[14]

These myths reflected, and were reflected by, actual historical practices. Every ancient society that has left any substantial record has left at least some record about these kinds of special blaming and punishing juries. From Druid England to the Holy Roman Empire and Saracen Jerusalem long before the Crusades, juries were used in some form or another for some disputes or another.[15] Muslim juries, called the *lafif*, were drawn from neighborhoods in the hope that some jurors actually witnessed the crime, and they were bound to tell the truth about what they had seen.[16] There were real Norse juries, too, but because the Vikings did not have a strong written tradition we know very little about them, other than what we can infer from the jury traditions of the Viking successors on the European continent – groups including the Franks and Jutes. These groups, and especially the Franks, may well have combined their own Norse traditions with the Muslim *lafif* to form the basics of a sophisticated and detailed jury procedure that they eventually passed to England through William the Conqueror.

Juries are not unique to the West. Buddhist texts describe ancient Indian trials, both civil and criminal, as being presided over not by the village leader or even by the village monk, but rather by "men of learning and pure descent, who are aged, clever in reasoning, and careful in fulfilling their duties."[17] There is also a rich monastic tradition within Buddhism of having theological disputes ruled on by juries of monks, including the famous "settlement of the ten questions" in 377 BC.[18] Even in ancient China, where Confucian influences favored trial by the enlightened elite, there is some evidence that nonelites were consulted and even sometimes participated in those decisions. Even if important Chinese trials were conducted by village elites, they were often conducted by a *group* of elites, and not just by the village elder or priest.[19]

There were, however, two significant limitations when it came to most ancient juries. First, they were rarely used, even in the democracies of classical Greece and pre-imperial Rome. They have always been cumbersome and expensive, and so until their explosion in the early thirteenth century in England they were almost always reserved only for the most important disputes – our version of when and where to move the hive.

Second, almost all ancient juries were presentment juries, meaning generally that they blamed but did not punish. After deciding an accused should be blamed, they "presented" the person to the ruler or a designee for actual punishment. The role of the presentment jury varied across ancient societies and over time. Some took on full blaming roles, but others acted merely as blame screening devices, leaving both the final blame and punishment decision to the ruler. These kinds of limited presentment juries are the ancestors of our modern grand juries, which decide whether there is sufficient evidence against an accused to go to trial.

Greek and Roman juries were important exceptions to this general rule that ancient juries were presentment juries that did not decide punishment. Ancient and then classical Greek juries – called *dikasteria* in Athenian law – decided both blameworthiness and punishment, though, again, they were reserved only for the most important of disputes. They appear as early as 700 BC, but their beginnings are quite hazy. It seems from the records of the most famous court in Athens – called the *Eliaia* – that jury involvement began as a way for Athenian citizens to appeal the judgments of local magistrates. The *dikasteria* heard the appeals *de novo*, meaning that they were not required to give the magistrate's decision any weight, and heard the case as if they were the first decision-makers hearing it. By the end of the fifth century, disgruntled citizens were appealing magistrates' decisions so frequently that local magistrates stopped rendering important decisions entirely and sent the parties directly to the *Eliaia*, where the decisions were rendered by the *dikasteria*. There was no appeal from the verdicts of the *dikasteria*, probably because of their origins as appellate courts.

The members of the *dikasteria* were selected by lot from the rolls of citizens. An ingenious kind of stone bingo-ball machine, called the *kleroterion*, was used to randomize the selections.[20] Jurors had to be male, over thirty, and owe no debts. There was no recorded mechanism for the litigants to participate in jury selection. Those selected by the *kleroterion* served. The *dikasteria* were huge, ranging from 200 to 1,500 members, depending on the era, the city-state, and the controversy.[21]

There was, of course, no unanimity requirement for bodies so large. They must have acted more like focus groups than modern juries.

The way in which judges "presided" over a trial in the *Eliaia* says much about the distrust Athenians had of single-judge decisions in important cases. The presiding magistrates did not preside at all. Their only role seems to have been to announce the outcome of the trial to the citizens waiting outside the court.[22] Modern judges should be humbled to know that, at least in the cradle of western democracy, we started out more like town criers than philosopher kings.

The Romans copied the institution of the *dikasteria*, adapting them to senatorial trials and renaming them "*judices*." Senatorial trials by *judices* were limited to very serious allegations – political cases, disputes between senators (or, later, between imperial officers), particularly scandalous crimes, and other important cases to the state. Individual prefects or other officials resolved ordinary, day-to-day disputes.[23] The members of the *judices* were drawn exclusively from the senatorial class, although there was a brief time during the republic where members of other classes also served.[24] Each year, the Senate would designate which of its members would serve as prospective jurors in all senatorial trials for that year. From this pool, eighty-one senators would be drawn by lot for any particular trial. Each litigant could remove fifteen prospective jurors, leaving a jury of fifty-one (although these numbers varied a bit over time).[25] Still much larger than we are used to, but a far cry from the near plebiscites that were the *dikasteria*.

Despite their common evolutionary root in our urge to delegate third-party punishment, ancient juries were more different than they were alike. Jury systems changed over time to reflect the political realities of a particular society, and our central urge to punish manifested itself in quite different ways as the punishing societies grew and changed. With apologies to non-Western jury systems, and even to the jury systems on the continent that continued for a while in their own special tradition, I will focus in the next sections on the history of the common law jury in England, because for the most part these other jury systems did not survive. Interestingly, the jury system seems to be making a comeback in some of these other legal traditions. Some Europeans, most notably the Italians, are flirting with American-style

civil juries, and the Japanese have in the past several years began exper-
imenting with mixed juries in criminal and civil cases. But it was the
English common law, perhaps with the early assistance of the Muslim *lafifs*, that preserved the jury for modern use. To understand how
this happened, we first need to understand the non-judge non-jury
traditions with which the early English jury was competing.

NON-JUDGE NON-JURY TRADITIONS

Decision-making by methods other than the dominant member simply
making the decision himself, or delegating it to a subset of the whole
group, has a tradition just as long as the judge/jury tradition. These
alternative decision-making methods varied tremendously across cultures, but generally fell into three categories: trial by battle, trial by
ordeal, and trial by compurgation.

There is evidence of trial by battle, sometimes also called trial by
combat, in many ancient societies, from Jews to pre-Roman Germans
and Goths. It was a method particularly favored by the Vikings, and
they spread it across northern Europe. It was especially popular for
disputes between members of the ruling class. It tended to flourish in
times and places where states were generally weak, and where in any
event the state simply did not get involved in most private disputes,
as we have already seen. Trial by battle began as nothing more than
a kind of formalized second-party punishment, designed to break the
cycle of retaliation and re-retaliation.

The victim and the alleged wrongdoer would themselves fight, and
in early systems the outcome would usually be its own punishment, or
vindication. As the state became more and more involved in private
wrongs, it began to construct more and more rules governing the
battle. Some accusations required a battle to the death, others only
submission. Different charges and different systems determined the
kinds of weapons, if any, and whether the combat would be mounted
or hand-to-hand. As feudal systems spread across Europe, combatants
began to be able to hire champions to conduct their battles in their
place. The losing side, or his estate, was generally required to pay
for the winning side's champion, a rule that may be the origin of the

so-called English Rule, a modern rule under which the losing side in litigation must pay the other side's attorney fees.

Because of the influence of the fight-loving Normans, trial by battle was for many centuries the dispute resolution mechanism of choice throughout England for disputes between members of the ruling classes. But it never captured the imagination of the local Anglo-Saxons, in no small part because they were no longer in charge and resented anything associated with the Norman invaders. Trial by battle also lost its original Viking cachet as soon as one could hire others to do the fighting. Like most of the Viking seed sprinkled over the top of Europe, the Normans quickly settled down and ceased to be a nomadic band of seafaring pirates. The sharpest edges of the Norse tradition began to be sanded off by the forces of modernity, and trial by battle was one of the first of the sharp edges to go. The strongest modernizing force was the Church. Church officials just didn't care much for pagan traditions invented by guys wearing horns. Within a generation of the Conquest, trial by battle was virtually extinct, although it was, rather remarkably, not officially banned in England until 1819.[26]

For serious offenses, trial by battle was replaced by the already existing practice of trial by ordeal. The ordeal, also sometimes called the judgment of God, is just as old and widespread as trial by judge, jury, or battle, long predating the Catholic Church. Most ancient societies believed that gods actively intervened in the affairs of humans, and that with the right attention getting prompts the gods might be called on to decide some earthly disputes. But it was another problem entirely to try to discern their verdicts. In the myths, the gods told us their verdicts in words. In the real world, gods had to speak indirectly, either through priestly intermediaries or by actions.

The idea behind the ordeals was to let the judgments of the gods reveal themselves in action. The accused would be put to some test, and the gods would announce their verdict by causing the accused to fail or pass the test. The kind of test required, and the evidence of whether the accused passed or failed, varied across societies, and often depended on the seriousness of the accusation. Priests conducted the ordeals, a fact, by the way, that may explain the lingering tradition of judges wearing robes. The ordeals were performed according to strict and often excruciatingly detailed religious rules.

There were as many ancient ordeals as there were ancient gods and societies. The ones that survived into the Middle Ages, and became prevalent both in England and on the continent to resolve accusations of serious offenses, can be broken into three main types: hot iron, hot water, and cold water. Contrary to popular belief, these most serious of the medieval ordeals were not always the automatically losing propositions one thinks of when one thinks of their relatives, the heresy and witch trials that began the Inquisition. The trials of the Inquisition were famous for their built-in infallibility – surviving the ordeal was a sign of guilt, so the accused either survived the ordeal and was then put to death or died from the ordeal itself, presumably because God willed it for some other, uncharged, reason. By contrast, people could, and occasionally did, survive the medieval trial ordeals, many of which treated survival as a divine sign of innocence, not guilt.

In the ordeal of cold water, the accused was bound and thrown into a body of water. If he survived (admittedly a long shot), it was seen as an intervention by God, and he was acquitted and released. If he died then he was guilty, and we were neatly able to combine blame and punishment in one procedure.

The ordeals of hot iron and hot water were more akin to the trials of the Inquisition, and were for that very reason used only for the most serious of crimes. The accused was required to carry a piece of hot iron (or in some versions walk across hot materials) or stick his arm in boiling water, and was deemed innocent if God intervened and prevented any burning. If the defendant was burned, and survived the burning, then he was deemed guilty and put to death. The hot ordeals occasionally resulted in a kind of conviction for lesser offenses when defendants were burned but just not as badly as expected. The consequences of these mixed verdicts were sometimes the subject of detailed ecclesiastical regulations and sometimes left to the discretion of the presiding priest, all depending on the community and its customs.

There were less serious ordeals for less serious crimes. In the ordeal of the consecrated morsel, for example, the accused was required to eat a wafer after taking an oath proclaiming his innocence and asking God to punish him if he were lying. If the accused choked to death, he was guilty; if he survived he was innocent. Just in case you think this ordeal was always a walk in the park, the Earl of Kent reportedly died in 1194 during the ordeal of the consecrated morsel, undoubtedly extending for many years the public's faith in this particular ordeal.[27]

There were also a few ordeals for disputes we would today label as civil disputes, including disputed claims over property. My favorite, called the ordeal of the cross, worked this way. The two litigants would take an oath that their position in the dispute was the correct one. They would then hold their hands out to their sides in the manner of a crucifixion, in later versions sometime holding bibles. The first to drop his arms lost.[28]

The third prevalent medieval form of non-judge non-jury dispute resolution was called compurgation, which means "oath-helping," and which was sometimes also called the wager of law. Compurgation is probably not as old or widespread as judge, jury, trial by battle, or the ordeals, but it was practiced by a few ancient peoples, most notably the Babylonians and Jews.[29] Across medieval Europe it was used for both civil disputes and minor criminal cases. In the criminal version, the accused first took an oath, swearing his innocence. He then called a sufficient number and quality of people, called oath helpers or compurgators, who then vouched under oath for his trustworthiness and general truthfulness. The oath helpers did not themselves vouch that the defendant was innocent; they just vouched that he was the kind of person who would not take an oath in vain. If the oaths were all properly taken, and given by a sufficient number of people of sufficient social rank (all depending on the seriousness of the crime and the social rank of the defendant and victim), the defendant was declared innocent, with no messy inquiry into the actual facts.[30]

The civil version worked a little differently. The plaintiff took the initial oath and called his compurgators, and if those oaths and compurgators were sufficient (again, based on complex class-based rules), then the burden shifted to the defendant to take his oath and call his compurgators. If the defendant's oath and compurgators were sufficient, then the defendant won, again without any time-consuming inquiry into the facts.[31]

Compurgation may sound awfully strange to modern ears, but it made perfect sense in societies where the oath was taken very seriously. In medieval Europe, nothing was more serious than the oath. In Robert Bolt's play, *A Man for All Seasons*, Thomas More explains to his daughter Meg why he has chosen to die rather than take a false oath of allegiance to King Henry VIII:

> What is an oath, then, but the words we say to God?
>
> When a man takes an oath, Meg, he is holding himself in his own hands. Like water. (*He cups his hands.*) And if he opens his fingers then – he needn't hope to find himself again.[32]

Violating an oath was a big deal. It was a mortal sin, punishable by eternal damnation.

Given these widely held beliefs, it made perfect sense to test allegations by testing the litigants' willingness to trade a temporary terrestrial victory in court for the everlasting fires of Hell, especially when the dispute itself was not a matter of life and death. Even so, as the Middle Ages ended, the English in particular developed an increasingly practical, and skeptical, view of the sanctity of the oath and therefore of the utility of compurgation. By 1300, compurgation in English systems was no longer available for cases involving allegations of official misconduct, suits on debts secured by real property, or perjury – the first two being deemed simply too tempting and the latter, of course, involving someone who had already allegedly demonstrated a willingness to violate the oath.[33]

THE GOLDEN AGE OF THE ENGLISH JURY

With battle and compurgation out of the picture, only the ordeal and the jury were left for serious disputes, and the ordeal was far more common than the jury trial. In fact, it seems that juries, in both England and on the continent, were limited to deciding disputes over real property ownership. The very first English juries (not counting any Druid proto-juries) were the so-called assizes commissioned by William the Conqueror to figure out which Normans now owned the lands they stole from the Anglo-Saxons.[34] These assizes persisted after the Conquest, and would eventually become the civil, then criminal, juries of English common law. But they were a disorganized, ad hoc mishmash in terms of the scope of their authority, their frequency of meeting, and the methods of their selection.

Henry II changed much of that in 1166, when he announced a law called the Assize of Clarendon. The Assize of Clarendon created a uniform, regular system of assizes across the country, although they continued to be limited to civil disputes, mostly, but no longer exclusively, about real estate. The Assize of Clarendon also officially banned trial by battle for most felonies, and officially limited compurgation to minor disputes, further cementing the ordeal as the primary English method to decide serious criminal cases. All of that changed in an instant in 1215.

You might think from that famous year that what changed everything for the English jury was the signing of the Magna Carta. Most of us have been taught that among the rights enshrined by that great writ was the right to be tried by a jury. But in fact the Magna Carta did not guarantee the right to a criminal jury trial, although its original meaning has certainly expanded over time in a sort of revisionist history of the sanctity of the criminal jury.[35] No, what happened in 1215 that would forever change trial by jury was that Pope Innocent III banned the ordeal, and the jury was suddenly the only method left for serious criminal cases.[36]

There were two main reasons for the ban. Many influential Church scholars by this time had come to the conclusion that God was really just too important to be concerned with whether a particular serf in a particular village did or did not steal a horse. God was becoming more the detached watchmaker and less the involved parent. The second, more practical, reason for the ban was that the ordeal was starting to come into disrepute. There were increasing numbers of reports that some priests were being bribed to favor certain outcomes by the manner in which they administered and interpreted the ordeals. As those reports increased in numbers and intensity, Innocent was forced to act. He did so decisively, by banning the ordeal altogether.

The ban found its way into English law in 1219. With ordeals gone, jury trials were the only method left for serious offenses. Thus began what historians have called the golden age of the English jury, a fifty-year period from 1220 to 1270 during which the frequency of jury trials skyrocketed and many of its modern features began to take shape.

There was still an awkward barrier, however. Criminal jury trials, as distinguished from the civil assizes, were still limited presentment trials. Jurors were still inquisitors rather than neutral judges. They investigated potential crimes and were still a strange combination of preliminary hearing judge and witness, as they traditionally passed their findings on to feudal lords or other rulers who would then conduct a guilt trial and impose punishment. Odd as it may seem to those of us who today think that jurors must be impartial, it was a plus in presentment juries of this era for a juror to know the parties and the witnesses. Better still if a juror was himself a witness to the alleged crime. Because English presentment juries at this time were investigatory, not decision-making, having presentment jurors who had witnessed a crime was no more problematical to the medieval mind than having a modern-day police officer arrest someone he observes committing a crime.

Over time, as part of the long struggle between King and Parliament, pressure began to mount for juries to be involved in both the presentment and guilt phases, and thus began a slow process of the transformation of the English presentment jury into the English trial jury.[37] The process was slow because it posed so many challenges. There was the question of whether both kinds of juries, however they might be constituted, should still be convened. Although not as large as the *dikasteria*, presentment juries were still quite large in the 1200s and 1300s – they typically consisted of twenty-four to eighty-four members, all of whom had to be knights. It would have been quite unwieldy, and expensive, to have such large presentment juries sit twice, once as grand juries and once as trial juries. This raised the question of whether the trial jury should be a smaller subset of the presentment jury, or whether it should contain new jurors who had not heard the presentment case. The subset model presented the problem of what to do about witness-jurors, who were acceptable – indeed even preferred – at the presentment stage but who arguably now had a conflict if they were also to sit as jurors during the trial phase.

In England at least, these questions were not answered top-down, but rather groped at bottom-up. Despite the reforms of Henry II, the medieval English court "system" was no system at all. There were still all kinds of different, overlapping, and disconnected courts. There were innumerable and lingering "manorial courts," which were remnants of the feudal lord's obligation to hold court for his tenants. There were "franchise courts," created by the King for the benefit of large landowners, so that disputes in far-flung lands could be handled at a single court.[38] And despite the ban on the ordeal, there were still the ecclesiastical courts. There was no clear allocation of jurisdiction between any of these courts, and the outcome of a particular dispute often depended on the vagaries of which court the litigants got to first, which court first agreed to hear the case, and sometimes which court was first able to execute its judgment.

The reforms of Edward I in the late 1200s went a long way toward centralizing and systematizing this crazy quilt of courts. He created three kinds of court systems, whose essential categories remain to this day: the Court of Common Pleas, which handled private civil disputes between litigants; the King's Bench, which handled criminal cases; and the Exchequer, which handled disputes over taxes, revenues, and land ownership. Even after Edward I's reforms, however, the English court system remained a decentralized hodgepodge, with the three kinds of courts often fighting with each other and issuing conflicting rulings.

It was in this atmosphere that the English courts had to deal with Innocent III's ban of the ordeal, and they dealt with it in a typically heterogeneous and undirected manner. A thousand different responses bloomed, leaving the judge-made common law to sort them out. In very general terms, however, at the beginning of this period, if a presentment jury found probable cause then it typically split into a smaller subset to hear the trial. As a result, trial jurors slowly transformed from investigators and witnesses to impartial fact finders. It eventually become clear in most courts that the trial jurors would need to be different people than the presentment jurors, precisely because the trial jurors needed to be impartial. Eventually these two systems separated – the King keeping the presentment jury for his most important and politically sensitive investigations, and ordinary but serious criminal offenses tried to stand-alone trial juries. Indeed, the stand-alone trial juries became an important political limitation on the King's presentment juries. This transformation from presentment jury to trial jury took almost 300 years, and was not complete until the beginning of the 1500s.

By the seventeenth and eighteenth centuries – periods that are particularly important because of their influence on the American colonies – the English criminal jury had many of its modern features. The break from the presentment juries was now complete, and in fact the word "jury" now presumptively meant trial juries, and the King's presentment juries were called "grand juries." Trial jurors were expected to be impartial, and prospective trial jurors could be excused if they were connected to any aspect of the case or if for any other reason they simply could not be impartial. The break between civil and criminal law was also sharpened, the state having recognized that many heretofore "private" wrongs were in fact wrongs against the common good. The number of criminal trials exploded as the number of answerable crimes exploded. Parliamentary reformers were busy reinterpreting the Magna Carta to guarantee the right to a criminal jury, at least in serious cases, so this explosion of criminal trials also saw an explosion of criminal juries.

But many modern features were yet to come. The English criminal defendant still had no right to be represented by a lawyer except in treason cases, and even that right was not created until 1675. He had no right to testify in his own defense. Appeals were also restricted. The only appeal of criminal verdicts from the King's Bench was to Parliament.

Punishment methods, even as late as the 1700s, were also unusual by modern standards. There were no prisons, leaving four kinds of criminal punishments: 1) fines for the least serious of offenses; 2) corporal punishment (whipping, and some stigmatizing punishments including the stocks) for the more serious; 3) transportation (banishment) for even more serious offenses; and 4) death. Most crimes were punishable by death. This reflected not so much an extraordinary harshness as it did the mere fact that only the most serious of crimes were even recognized as crimes. Less serious wrongs were still mostly a matter of private revenge. As more and more of these private wrongs became criminalized, they, too, were automatically made capital offenses, at least in theory.[39] But in actual practice death was rarely used for this growing category of new crimes. Juries played a critical role in these cases keeping English defendants off the gallows.

The division of sentencing labor between judge and jury is a complicated historical gnarl. The orthodox view, promoted most recently by opponents of the American federal sentencing guidelines, is that

English juries decided guilt or innocence, English judges imposed punishment, and never the twain did meet. But the real story is much more complicated. First, within the patchwork of the English system, there are many examples of courts in which jurors decided punishment, including a few manorial courts as late as the 1700s.[40] These are isolated examples to be sure, but they are far from rare. Second, the "power" that English judges enjoyed in sentencing was largely illusory. Sentences were typically fixed by Parliament for particular crimes, and, with prisons still not invented and therefore no prison terms to be imposed, there was really very little for English sentencing judges to do.[41] Certain crimes required fines, others corporal punishment, others transportation, and others death.

The real sentencing power therefore resided with jurors, who could in effect decide the sentence by deciding whether to convict the defendant of the charged crime or of a less serious one. They could reduce a death sentence to transportation, transportation to corporal punishment, or corporal punishment to a fine, simply by convicting defendants of crimes less serious than originally charged. And they did so regularly and enthusiastically, primarily because they recognized that the death sentence remained the required punishment for far too many newly-created and relatively minor crimes. This practice of convicting a capital defendant of a less serious crime, especially to avoid the death penalty, became so common in the 1700s that William Blackstone dubbed it "pious perjury."[42] These jurors had violated their oaths to decide the case according to the law, but they did so for the pious reason of avoiding an unjustly harsh punishment.

Early American juries were also very much punishing institutions. Colonial records are scant, and scholars disagree about whether colonial juries routinely imposed sentences.[43] This disagreement, however, is really just a matter of timing. By the early 1800s, juries imposed sentences in about half the states. Because prisons had been invented by then and had rapidly spread as a recognized form of punishment, these juries had to make judgments not only about the type of punishment to be imposed but also, in the case of a prison sentence, its length. Even in states that did not require juries to sentence, a handful permitted them to make sentencing recommendations. Thus, for the entire nineteenth century, American sentencing schemes with no input from juries were the exception, not the rule. And even in those few states that allowed no formal jury input, American jurors, like their English ancestors, continued to impact sentencing by making decisions about the degree of crime on which they were willing to convict.

MODERN JURORS AS PUNISHERS

As penitentiaries spread, and as their original redemptive purpose slowly transformed into a rehabilitative one, states began to turn punishment decisions over to judicial professionals. Criminals were diseased patients who needed prison hospitalization. Only trained experts – judges, wardens, social workers, psychologists, and psychiatrists – could treat these diseased patients. This trend accelerated as alternatives to imprisonment began to take root, including probation (supervised release in lieu of prison), community corrections (halfway houses), and parole (early supervised release from prison). A new set of expertise came to bear, practiced by probation officers, community corrections and parole boards, and others whose job was to decide whether our diseased criminals were cured. These progressive forces dramatically reduced the extent to which juries were formally involved in sentencing. By 1960 – at the height of the rehabilitative movement – only thirteen American states involved jurors directly in sentencing. Today, there are only five holdouts.[44]

And yet jurors continue to exert their moral force in essentially the same way they did in Blackstone's England, at least in the most serious criminal cases, by deciding between charged crimes and less serious ones. Often, the difference between the two depends on the jury's decisions about a defendant's mental state. As we've seen, Anglo-American law has come to recognize four traditional states of mind – purposeful, knowing, reckless, and negligent.[45] In almost every criminal case, the jury must decide not only whether the defendant committed the criminal act but also whether he did so with the required state of mind. This latter assessment becomes an opportunity for a kind of pious perjury, because it is a rare serious case where the jury is not instructed on both the charged crime and a lesser crime, the difference often being a difference only in the levels of a defendant's state of mind.[46]

So, for example, in my au pair case discussed in the Introduction, the defendant was charged with first-degree murder, but at both sides' request I also instructed the jury on second-degree murder. First-degree murder requires a purposeful killing after deliberation. Second-degree murder requires only a knowing killing. When the jury was deliberating the case, they were in effect deciding how much to blame the defendant for his conduct. They were doing the same thing jurors did in seventeenth-century England, or in the *dikasteria* of ancient Greece or in the Pleistocene, when they decided what must be done when one of us seriously defected.

In capital cases, modern American juries no longer have to resort to pious perjury, because every state that recognizes the death penalty requires that it be imposed by jurors, not by judges.[47] This so-called death exception to the trend away from jury sentencing tells us much about the role of the jury as a blaming and punishing institution. As Justice Stevens famously wrote in a dissent in a capital punishment case:

> [I]n the final analysis, capital punishment rests on not a legal but an ethical judgment – as assessment of what we have called [in another case] the "moral guilt" of the defendant. And if the decision that capital punishment is the appropriate sanction in extreme cases is justified because it expresses the community's moral sensibility – its demand that a given affront to humanity requires retribution – it follows, I believe, that a representative cross section of the community must be given the responsibility for making that decision.[48]

But this moral role is hardly limited to capital cases. Justice Stevens' quote rings just as true if we take out the word "capital" from "capital punishment." All sentencing is an act of third-party punishment, and all third-party punishment is an act of moral blaming. Modern law has tried very hard to remove any explicit connection between blame and punishment, the division between blaming jury and sentencing judge being just one example. But the moral jury keeps oozing across this divide, whether in the form of the death-exception or by pious perjury.

Jurors know full well, just as they did in Blackstone's England, that they are making punishment decisions. They know it explicitly in capital cases, but even in noncapital cases they know second-degree murder is less blameworthy and therefore less harshly punished than first-degree murder, simple robbery less than aggravated robbery. They may not know any of the details of that difference, and indeed in most states neither the lawyers nor the judge may inform jurors about the punishment consequences of their decision prior to the verdict. But, as we know from Paul Robinson's work, ordinary people are extraordinarily good at judging relative blameworthiness. There is therefore little doubt that jurors know, for example, that simple robbery is less blameworthy, and will therefore be punished less severely, than aggravated robbery.[49]

In my experience, most jurors are not familiar with the nuances of a life sentence. Many still seem to believe that life is not life, just like twenty years is not really twenty years because of early release on parole. In a few states that is still true even of a "life" sentence. In my state and most others, however, a life sentence, which is the mandatory noncapital sentence for first-degree murder, means life without parole. When a defendant is convicted of first-degree murder in a noncapital case in my courtroom, it means he will die in prison.

I typically impose a life sentence immediately after the jury returns its verdict, with them still present, not just because there is no reason to delay but also because I think the system owes some honesty and respect to the jurors in allowing them to see firsthand the consequences of their decision. And as I talk to jurors after such sentences, there is almost always one juror who asks whether life means life, sometimes even admitting that this was a topic of their deliberations. When I tell them life really means life, and that the defendant will die in prison, it is a rare case where at least one them does not break down into tears. On the other hand, murder juries are almost always in tears anyway, no matter the verdict.

The jury's moral role is not limited to criminal cases. Great chunks of tort and contract depend on normative judgments just like the judgments jurors have to make in criminal cases. All tort cases boil down to the jury's judgment about whether defendants were as careful as they should have been under the circumstances. In malpractice cases, the law hides behind the fiction of the "standard of care," the ethereal rules by which all reasonable professionals are expected to abide. But jurors in these cases quickly realize this "standard" is not standard at all, when the plaintiff's expert testifies about one standard of care and the defense expert about another, or, more commonly, when the experts disagree about whether the defendant met or did not meet an agreed-to standard of care. All these cases end up with the jury having to make a moral judgment about whether this was an excusable or inexcusable accident – a sufficiently serious violation of our Rule 1 (don't steal the defendant's health) to justify punishing by way of a monetary award.

Even ordinary contract cases can teem with these kinds of moral judgments, both explicit and implicit. For example, many contracts give one side the right to decide an issue, but expressly impose on that side the obligation not to decide it unreasonably. Leases are one such kind of contract – they often require tenants to obtain their landlords' permission before they can sublet their space, but require that the landlords not unreasonably withhold that permission. Whether in any given case a landlord has been reasonable or unreasonable – whether he has violated Rule 2 (don't break promises) and must pay money damages – is a normative judgment for the jury, if such a case goes to a jury trial.

We are blaming and punishing animals, and no matter the particular form that our blaming and punishing institutions may take, the acts of blaming and punishing, and the emotional shortcuts we use to accomplish those acts, remain a central part of our natures and therefore a central part of our legal institutions, whatever their form. The law itself is in many respects an expression of those instincts, both in terms of what we blame (violations of Rules 1 and 2) and how we decide whether and how much to punish (Rule 3).

Law, like the family, is also a quintessentially cultural institution. Families and legal institutions pass enormous amounts of information across generations much more effectively, and much more quickly, than evolution ever could. But that fact should not obscure the evolutionary foundations of blame and punishment on which all our legal edifices are built. Whether those evolutionary foundations any longer have anything important to teach us about the complicated cultural edifices of the law is a question we address in the next three chapters.

Notes to Chapter 7

1. J. M. Black, *Preflight signaling in swans – a mechanism for group cohesions and flock formation*, ETHOLOGY, **79(2)**, 143–157 (1988); H. H. T. PRINS,

ECOLOGY AND BEHAVIOR OF THE AFRICAN BUFFALO (Chapman & Hall, 1996); J. B. Leca et al., *Distributed leadership in semifree-ranging white-faced capuchin monkeys*, ANIM. BEHAV. **66(6)**, 1045–1052 (2003); K. J. Stewart & A. H. Harcourt, *Gorilla vocalizations during rest periods: signals of impending departure?*, BEHAV. **130**, 29–40 (1994). The bee example is discussed in the text in the immediately following paragraphs, and the baboon studies are discussed later in this section. The evolution of consensus in social animals has become quite a hot topic in evolutionary theory. See, e.g., W. I. Sellers et. al., *An agent-based model of group decision-making in baboons*, PHIL. TRANS. R. SOC. B, **362**, 1699–1710 (April 11, 2007); L. Conradt & T. J. Roper, *Democracy in animals: the evolution of shared group decisions*, PHIL. TRANS. R. SOC. B, **274**, 2317–2326 (July 20, 2006).

2. For a comprehensive treatment of consensus decision-making in honeybees, see THOMAS D. SEELEY, A HONEYBEE DEMOCRACY (Princeton 2010).

3. C. List et al., *Independence and interdependence in collective decision-making: an agent-based model of nest-site choice by honeybees*, PHIL. TRANS. R. SOC. B, **364**, 755–762 (2009).

4. S. Stueckle & D. Zinner, *To follow or not to follow: decision-making and leadership during the morning departure in chacma baboons*, ANIMAL BEH. **75**, 1995–2004 (June 2008).

5. Troops of baboons "decide" when and where to go simply by watching individuals suggest a time and direction, then either following or not following. When a critical mass of sufficiently influential members (in dominance or sheer numbers) begins to go, the whole troop follows. This allowed Stueckle and Zinner, in the paper cited in note 4 supra, to measure with some precision exactly the numbers and rankings it took to reach this critical mass.

6. Condorcet's proof used what we would today call induction, or iterative logic. Assume a jury of N members, all with a probability P of being correct, and with M of them voting correctly. (Let's also assume N is odd, so we don't have ties, but the same proof works if N is even and we break ties with a coin flip.) Now let's see what happens when we add two new jurors (two in order to preserve the odd number). Some thought will convince you (and here was Condorcet's real insight) that there are only two possible cases in which the new jurors will change the result: 1) if M was just one vote shy of being the majority, and both new voters vote correctly; or 2) M was just equal to a bare majority ($M = (N + 1)/2$), and both new voters vote incorrectly. The probability of a change from right to wrong is the product of three probabilities: the probability that the last and prior deciding vote was right times the probability of the first added one being wrong times the probability of the second added one being also wrong, or $p(1 - p)^2$. The probability of a change from wrong to right, using the same analysis, is $(1 - p)p^2$. Because we are assuming $p > 0.5$, the first of these numbers is always greater than

the second, meaning adding jurors always increases the chance of a correct majority verdict.

7. Kenworthy Bilzhas, *The Puzzle of Delegated Punishment*, 87 B.U. L. REV. 1059, 1096 (2007).

8. See, e.g., V. Fon & F. Parisi, *Revenge and Retaliation*, in THE LAW AND ECONOMICS OF IRRATIONAL BEHAVIOR 141 (F. Parisi & V. Smith, eds., 2005).

9. As Kenworthy Bilzhas has put it, "the important difference [in the punishment institutions of primitive societies] may not be in relative levels of retributive sentiment in such societies, but simply in their relative unwillingness to delegate punishment to the State due to a widespread lack of identification with the emerging government." Note 7, supra at 1059.

10. See, e.g., JOHN GASTIL ET AL., THE JURY AND DEMOCRACY: HOW JURY DELIBERATION PROMOTES CIVIC ENGAGEMENT AND POLITICAL PARTICIPATION (Oxford 2010); JAMES J. GOBERT, JUSTICE, DEMOCRACY AND THE JURY (Ashgate/Dartmouth 1997); Conradt & Roper, supra note 1; Seeley, supra note 2.

11. COLIN M. TURNBULL, THE FOREST PEOPLE (Touchstone 1987). The Mbuti, also known as BaMbuti or Bamuti, are pygmy nomadic foragers who live in the Ituri rainforest in the eastern Congo.

12. ROBERT TONKINSON, THE MARDU ABORINGINES: LIVING THE DREAM IN AUSTRALIA'S DESERT (2d ed., Harcourt Brace 1997). The Mardu are aboriginal hunter–gatherers who live in Australia's Western Desert.

13. The jury hung, six to six. Apollo represented Orestes, no small conflict of interest because it was Apollo who originally infected Orestes with the irresistible urge to kill his mother.

14. PETER MUNCH, NORSE MYTHOLOGY: LEGENDS OF GODS AND HEROES 5–6 (Kessinger reprint 2008, 1954).

15. LLOYD MOORE, THE JURY: TOOL OF KINGS PALLADIUM OF LIBERTY 1–20 (Liberty 2d ed. 1988).

16. J. Makdisi, *The Kindred Concepts of Seisin and Hawz in English and Islamic Law*, in THE LAW APPLIED: CONTEXTUALIZING THE ISLAMIC SHARI'A 35 (P. Bearman et al., eds., I. B. Tauris 2008).

17. Âpastamba II, 11, 29 ¶ 5, quoted in ROMESH CHUNDER DUTT, 2 A HISTORY OF CIVILIZATION IN ANCIENT INDIA 44 (Thacker Spink 1899).

18. Id. at 283 and 296. The "settlement of the ten questions" was an effort, undertaken at a council of monks held in the Indian city of Vaisali in 377 BC, to settle ten famous metaphysical questions that had arisen in the hundred years since Buddha's death.

19. BERRY FONG–CHUNG HSU, THE COMMON LAW: IN CHINESE CONTEXT 46 (Hong Kong Univ. Press 1992).

20. The word *kleroterion* comes from the Greek root *kleros*, which means "lot" or "chance." It was a large stone slab, usually several feet high and wide, with

rows and rows of slots cut into the front. All citizens were issued identity cards, and reporting prospective jurors handed their cards to the officials in charge, who placed them into the slots. Running vertically along one edge of the slab was a bronze tube, fed by funnels along the top. The officials would pour white and black balls into the funnels, in amounts that reflected both how many citizens reported for jury duty and how many jurors were needed that day. The funnels were connected to a crank device that mixed up all the balls and then sent them into the side tube. A black ball next to a row meant that every citizen in that row was excused. A white ball meant that everyone served. See generally, S. Dow, *Aristotle, the Kleroteria, and the Courts*, in ATHENIAN DEMOCRACY 62 (P. J. Rhodes, ed., Oxford 2004).

21. JOHN PROFFATT, A TREATISE ON TRIAL BY JURY § 6 (Rothman 1986).

22. DOUGLAS MACDOWELL, THE LAW IN CLASSICAL ATHENS 29–33 (Cornell 1978). References to this practice appear in various passages of *The Iliad* and *The Odyssey*.

23. PETER GARNSEY, SOCIAL STATUS AND LEGAL PRIVILEGE IN THE ROMAN EMPIRE 19–25 (Oxford 1970).

24. For about fifty years, from 122 BC to 70 BC Moore, supra note 15, at 3.

25. Id. The practice of permitting litigants to summarily excuse senators from the *judices* sounds very much like the modern practice of peremptory challenges. In fact, seventeenth-century legal scholars surmised that the roots of the peremptory challenge were Roman, and more generally that the Western jury was inherited directly from the Roman *judices* during the Roman occupation of England. These beliefs that the English jury owed its existence to democratic traditions going back to Greece and Rome fit nicely with antiroyalist sentiments at the time. But it is now generally believed that English juries owe their beginnings to the Franks, and that there were no antecedents to the modern English jury before William brought them over during the Conquest. HEINRICH BRUNNER, THE ORIGINS OF JURIES (Berlin 1872); JOHN P. DAWSON, A HISTORY OF LAY JUDGES (Harvard 1960).

26. EDWARD J. WHITE, LEGAL ANTIQUITIES: A COLLECTION OF ESSAYS UPON ANCIENT LAWS AND CUSTOMS 118 (F. H. Thomas 1913) (trial by battle all but disappeared by the end of the reign of Edward III); Moore, supra note 15, at 123 (trial by battle officially banned in England in 1819).

27. Proffatt, supra note 21, at 16; WILLIAM FORSYTH, HISTORY OF TRIAL BY JURY 68 (B. Franklin 2d ed. 1971).

28. ROBERT VON MOSCHZISKER, TRIAL BY JURY, at App. 2, p. 388 (Bisel 2d ed. 1930). This ordeal may sound familiar to readers who have experienced the game of chicken that is the modern American civil litigation system, and in particular the costs of pretrial discovery, which often exceed the entire amount in controversy.

29. EDWARD J. WHITE, LEGAL ANTIQUITIES: A COLLECTION OF ESSAYS UPON ANCIENT LAWS AND CUSTOMS 197 (F. H. Thomas 1913).

30. von Moschzisker, supra note 28, at 34–37.

31. WILLIAM BLACKSTONE, 3 COMMENTARIES ON THE LAWS OF ENGLAND *343 (W. L. Dean 1846); von Moschzisker, supra note 28, at 34–36.

32. Robert Bolt, *A Man for All Seasons*, Act II. A script is available online at http://www.cooper.edu/humanities/classes/coreclasses/hss2/library/man_for_all_seasons.html#act_two. Thomas More lived at the end of this period when the oath was taken so seriously, but he was a famous throwback to times when oaths meant something. For a less complimentary take on More, see HILLARY MANTEL, WOLF HALL (Picador 2010), a captivating fictional exploration of the relationship between Thomas Cromwell and Henry VIII.

33. von Moschzisker, supra note 28, at 37–38. Our modern ideas about character evidence, embodied in Federal Rules of Evidence 404 and 608, have their origins in compurgation.

34. The word "assize" comes from the Old French word "assisses," which meant seatings or sessions of a court.

35. Cap 39 of the Magna Carta prohibited the Crown from imprisoning any free man "unless by the lawful judgment of his peers." J. C. Holt, *Magna Carta*(Cambridge 1965). But most scholars agree that this reference was to the arrest authority, and was not originally intended to grant, and did not in fact grant, the right to a criminal jury after that arrest. As Professor Holt has put it:

    [Parliament later] interpreted the phrase "lawful judgment of his peers" to include trial by peers and therefore to include trial by jury, a process which existed only in embryo in 1215 [in the form of the *civil* assizes].

    Id. at 9 & n. 3. See also JOHN DAWSON, A HISTORY OF LAY JUDGES 289–290 (Harvard 1960); THEODORE F. T. PLUCKNETT, A CONCISE HISTORY OF THE COMMON LAW 24 (5th ed., Little Brown 1956). One jury historian has argued that the right to jury resides in Cap 36, which provides that "henceforth nothing shall be given or taken for the writ of inquisition of life or limb." The argument is that the word "inquisition" is a reference to the jury trials of the Franks, which they called "inquisitos." See, e.g., Moore, supra note 15, at 49. But this argument, as well as the argument under Cap 39, are both belied by the fact that, despite these alleged guarantees, the English criminal jury trial remained almost unknown for the first quarter of the 1200s.

36. The ban was part of the Fourth Lateran Council in 1215. Innocent III's most important political legacy was his reassertion of the Vatican's power in vetting the Holy Roman Emperor. He gets his famous bad reputation mostly for two things: he was the Pope who launched the corrupt Fourth

Crusade; and, as a pal of Bad King John, he declared the Magna Carta void on the grounds that it was extracted from John under duress. Both of these bad reputations are probably only partially deserved. The Fourth Crusade was quite successful as a military matter, at least by the standards of the other Crusades. It managed to take back Constantinople and all of the Greek Empire. There was unprecedented corruption to be sure, but a large part of that was the result of the Venetians taking charge; most of the looted gold ended up in Venice. As for Innocent III's conclusion that the Magna Carta was extracted from John under duress, that conclusion may have been correct as a legal matter.

37. One of the biggest drivers of this transformation, and of the various protective procedures that came along with it, was that members of Parliament were being targeted by the King on trumped up criminal charges.

38. Cambridge and Oxford were among the first franchise courts.

39. In his *Tale of Two Cities*, Dickens famously repeated this hyperbole about the prevalence of the English death penalty in the 1700s:

> [P]utting to death was a recipe much in vogue with all trades and professions. . . . Death is Nature's remedy for all things, and why not Legislation's? Accordingly, the forger was put to Death; the utterer of a bad note was put to Death; the unlawful opener of a letter was put to Death; the purloiner of forty shillings and sixpence was put to Death; the holder of a horse as Tellson's door, who made off with it, was put to Death; the coiner of a bad shilling was put to Death; the sounders of three–fourths of the notes in the whole gamut of Crime were put to Death.

CHARLES DICKENS, A TALE OF TWO CITIES 62 (Signet 1960). As mentioned in the text, however, death was seldom imposed for these kinds of crimes, in large part because English juries convicted defendants of crimes less serious than the crimes charged.

40. Frank O. Bowman, *Fear of Law: Thoughts on* Fear of Judging *and the State of the Federal Sentencing Guidelines*, 44 ST. LOUIS U. L.J. 299, 310–311 (2000).

41. 3 Blackstone, supra note 31, at *396; John Langbein, *The English Criminal Trial and the Eve of the French Revolution*, in THE TRIAL JURY IN ENGLAND, FRANCE, GERMANY 1700–1900, at 36–37 (A. Schioppa, ed., Duncker & Humblot 1987).

42. 4 Blackstone, supra note 31, at *238–239.

43. Compare Adriaan Lanni, *Jury Sentencing in Noncapital Cases: An Idea Whose Time Has Come (Again)*, 108 YALE L.J. 1775, 1790 (1999) ("Jury sentencing in noncapital cases was a colonial innovation") with Nancy King & Susan Klein, *Essential Elements*, 54 VAND. L. REV. 1467, 1506 (2001) ("American juries at the time of the adoption of the Bill of Rights played a minor role in sentencing").

44. The five states are Arkansas, Missouri, Oklahoma, Texas, and Virginia. Oklahoma abandoned jury sentencing in 1997, but readopted it in 1999.

45. Chapter 2, Gradations of Intent.

46. In fact, in most states both the prosecution and defense have a right to demand that the jury be instructed on all lesser offenses, at least if the lesser offense is what the law calls a "lesser included offense." This means, in most states, that the elements of the lesser offense are necessarily included in the elements of the greater offense; that is, that as a matter of definition, one who commits the greater offense also commits the lesser offense. An example would be simple robbery and aggravated robbery. Aggravated robbery *is* simple robbery with the additional element that it was committed with a deadly weapon. Thus, every aggravated robber has also committed simple robbery. In a case charging aggravated robbery, in most states both sides would therefore have the right to ask the judge to instruct the jury on simple robbery, giving them the option, if they conclude the prosecution has not proved that a deadly weapon was used, of convicting the defendant only of simple robbery. A crime that differs from another crime only in that it requires a lower level of mens rea is, under this doctrine, also a lesser-included crime, on which both sides would therefore ordinarily have the right to have the jury instructed.

47. Before the United States Supreme Court's decision in Ring v. Arizona, 536 U.S. 584 (2002), only five states permitted judges to decide life or death in capital cases. When the Court in *Ring* declared unconstitutional Arizona's scheme of giving the life/death decision to a panel of three judges, every single state with the exception of Nebraska returned to the practice of having jurors, not judges, decide life or death. Nebraska's statute requires jurors to decide aggravating and mitigating factors, but then allows a three-judge panel to balance those factors in making the ultimate sentencing decision. NEB. REV. STAT. § 29–2520 (2002).

48. Spaziano v. Florida, 468 U.S. 447, 481 (1984) (Stevens, J., concurring in part and dissenting in part).

49. See the discussion in Chapter 3 of Paul Robinson's work on the concordance of relative blameworthiness.

8   LEGAL DISSONANCES

People crushed by laws have no hope but to evade power. If the laws are their enemies, they will be enemies of the law.

                                                     Edmund Burke

THE NATURALISTIC FALLACY: MIND THE GAP

As any trial lawyer or trial judge will tell you, there are a handful of cases where the law requires jurors to follow rules that seem especially hard for them to follow. These are not cases about difficult factual determinations, such as whether the sex was consensual in a "he-said/she-said" rape case, or even whether a defendant had a certain required state of mind. Instead, there are some legal rules that jurors have trouble with because they just don't seem to believe in them. Blackstone's "pious perjury" is an example. Jurors in sixteenth- and seventeenth-century England simply did not believe that citizens should be put to death for certain relatively minor crimes, and therefore regularly acquitted them of the charged crime and convicted them of a less serious crime that did not carry the death penalty.

    Modern legal scholars call this general kind of jury rebellion against the law "nullification." Drug cases are a big part of modern nullification. It is not at all uncommon, though it is still the exception and not the rule, for jurors in my courtroom to acquit defendants charged with possession of very small amounts of drugs. This is true even when, and maybe especially when, the evidence of guilt is overwhelming. A few years ago I presided over an open-and-shut possession case where the defendant was caught up in a much larger undercover operation. Police were trying to get from a middleman to his supplier, using

undercover officers armed with hidden microphones. This particular
defendant was unlucky enough to get captured on tape buying a tiny
amount of heroin from the middleman, and when he would not accept
the very favorable plea bargain the prosecution offered him, the case
went to trial. I talked to the jury after they acquitted the defendant, and
although they were sheepish about not following the law, they were
quite incensed at what they thought was a waste of police and judicial
resources to capture a single heroin addict.

Nullification in its broadest sense can be anything from the kind of
pious rejection of the law we saw in Blackstone's England or (arguably)
in my drug possession case, to considerably less pious reasons for refusing to follow the law. Even though outright nullification is rare – when all
twelve jurors decide to violate their oaths – it is much more common to
have juries hang because a single juror decides to violate his oath. I once
presided over a rape case in which the African-American defendant was
caught on security cameras entering the women's bathroom where the
rape happened. In addition to being identified by the victim, the defendant's own mother identified him from the video. In fact, the defendant
had a distinctive spot of white hair on the back of his otherwise entirely
black head of hair, and the video clearly showed that spot. But the first
trial ended with a hung jury when one African-American juror simply
refused to vote to convict, telling the other jurors she did not care what
the evidence was, she was not going to send another young black man
to prison. The defendant was convicted in a second trial.[1]

When I use the phrase "legal dissonance" in this chapter, I mean
to describe a narrow segment of nullification involving legal rules that
seem to conflict with our evolved intuitions, especially our evolved
notions of blameworthiness, and that for that reason either end in
nullification or, perhaps worse still, a more general loss of respect
for the law. For example, imagine that John and Judy decide to rob a
bank. They both go in, but only John is armed. If John gets killed in a
shoot-out with the guards, under the most robust form of what we call
the felony-murder rule, Judy can be charged and convicted of first-
degree murder.[2] The law blames her as if she had planned and then
intentionally caused John's death. Although we can all agree that bank
robberies and shoot-outs are bad things that the law should discourage,
I doubt that any reader truly feels that in this circumstance Judy

deserves to be blamed and punished just as severely as a gangster who assassinates a rival.[3] Judy, after all, did not *intend* for John to die, and as we have seen intent is the bellwether of our evolved instinct to blame.[4]

We can divide the most dissonant of these legal blaming rules – the ones that seem to give jurors the most difficulty – into two main categories, based on the two main drivers of blame: 1) no-intent rules (such as the felony-murder rule), which blame and punish wrongdoers even though they did not intend to cause the harm; and 2) no-harm rules, which blame and punish harmful intentions even when they cause no harm. In both cases, when we ask jurors and judges to act in ways that fundamentally conflict with blame and punishment instincts evolution spent 100,000 years building into our brains, we should not be surprised when they resist.

We can respond to this resistance in two ways. First, if we want to keep the legal rule then we had better think of ways to help our jurors get past their dissonant intuitions. Legal rules do no one any good if our juries and judges are not capable of applying and enforcing them. Second, if a particular dissonance is so strong that it seems nothing will help, then we might want to consider abandoning the dissonant legal rule in favor of the evolved moral intuition. In the real legal world, most of these kinds of utterly unenforceable laws have been ferreted out long ago, either by the common law, legislation, or the exercise of prosecutorial discretion. Legal rules that are *impossible* to follow are not the problem. The problem is legal rules that we can follow but that are so difficult to follow that they exact a cost in the form of a decrease in respect for the law.

Felony-murder is the poster child for this problem. In every felony-murder case I have ever tried, virtually every prospective juror expressed surprise about the doctrine. "Yes, Judy should be blamed and punished more than just for bank robbery, but she did not intend John's death and should not be blamed as if she did. In fact, she was John's partner!" In every one of those cases, the jury that eventually got seated sent out a note during deliberations again asking about the felony-murder instruction. Jurors simply do not *believe* in the felony-murder rule. Even judges don't. There was a rather infamous felony-murder case in my jurisdiction a few years ago that nicely illustrates this point that even judges lose respect for the law when laws are deeply unjust.

In November of 1997, a nineteen-year-old woman named Lisl Auman left her abusive boyfriend, and was staying overnight at a girlfriend's apartment. The girlfriend was having her own boyfriend problems, and she asked a couple friends of hers, including a skinhead named Matthaeus Jaehnig, to act as muscle when the two women went to retrieve their belongings from their respective exes. Auman's ex was not at home, so one of the other men cut the lock off the apartment door, as Jaehnig stayed outside as lookout. Auman went in and took her belongings, plus several things belonging to her ex. Another resident of the apartment complex became suspicious, wrote down Jaehnig's license number, and called police. A high-speed chase ensued, during which Auman told Jaehnig several times that she was afraid and he should stop the car. Instead, Jaehnig drove to the girlfriend's apartment, and even shot at police a few times along the way. Before police managed to catch up to them, Jaehnig and the others split up. Police arrested Auman, handcuffed her, and placed her in the back of a police car. They even drove the squad car a little further away in the parking lot to get away from the scene. Other officers pursued Jaehnig. By the time the five-minute foot chase was over, Jaehnig had shot and killed one of the officers, and then turned the gun on himself. At the moment of the officer's and Jaehnig's deaths, Auman was cuffed and sitting in the back of the police car hundreds of feet away.[5]

Under Colorado's version of the felony-murder rule, Auman was charged with and convicted of first-degree murder, and sentenced to the mandatory life in prison without parole. Colorado has a very strict version of the felony-murder rule, which not only applies to the death of an accomplice, but has also been interpreted to apply when the accomplice dies long after the defendant is in custody, as long as the accomplice's criminal episode is continuing to play out. There were outcries about the *Auman* case before, during, and after the trial, from ordinary citizens, criminal defense lawyers, and journalists alike.[6] Our intermediate appellate court, the Colorado Court of Appeals, affirmed Auman's conviction in 2002.[7]

But the Colorado Supreme Court reversed the conviction, ostensibly not for any reason having to do with the felony-murder rule (indeed, it affirmed application of the rule), but rather because it detected an error in a jury instruction on the underlying burglary charge.[8] It remanded the case to the trial court for a new trial. On remand, the two sides negotiated a plea bargain under which Auman pleaded guilty to burglary and accessory to murder, and the felony-murder charge was dismissed. She was sentenced to twenty years in a halfway house, with eight years credit for the prison time she had already served by that time. Part of the plea bargain was that Auman had to spend an six additional months in residential custody at the halfway house. She was released from the halfway house in April of 2006, although she will be under probation supervision for the balance of her twenty-year sentence.[9]

I have great respect for our state Supreme Court, not just as an institution but also because of the individual justices who sit on that court, most of whom I have known for many years. And in fact had I been a member of the Colorado Supreme Court I may well have supported the decision in the *Auman* case. But it seems clear to me, as it did to the dissenting justices, that the error the majority detected in the burglary instruction had nothing to do with the outcome of the case, and therefore did not justify reversal.[10] This conviction was not reversed because of that tiny error, but because the presence of that tiny error gave the Court an excuse to undue a profoundly unjust result. The craziness of the felony-murder rule in the *Auman* case not only forced a jury, trial judge, and intermediate appellate court to reach an unjust result, it then forced a state's highest court to torture some other legal principle to avoid that unjust result.

But wait. Who's to say that the felony-murder rule is "crazy" just because it is sometimes hard to follow? Many laws are hard to follow. Some evolutionarily dissonant legal rules may even be intentionally designed to try to combat moral intuitions that legislatures have rejected on policy grounds. The felony-murder rule may well need to be a rule precisely because the law has made a policy judgment that people like Lisl Auman should be held as guilty as if she had planned to murder the officer, recognizing that without such a rule it would be hard for judges and jurors to blame her to that degree. How do we distinguish between rules that "conflict" with our moral intuitions and rules that "cure" them, without simply picking between rules we like and rules we don't like? Two other examples outside the felony-murder realm may further illustrate the problem.

In England as well as in all American states, a jury generally may not be told about a criminal defendant's prior felony convictions.[11] Based on my discussions over the years with hundreds of jurors after trials, not to mention my own human intuitions, I suspect that this rule against the admissibility of a defendant's prior convictions violates a deep and strongly-held sense that the best predictor of future behavior (and the best measure of whether charged behavior is true) is past behavior. It is not hard to imagine that natural selection would have favored such a strategy, when our main predator was each other. In fact, there is an extensive social science literature recognizing that there is no information more important to a strategic actor than the other strategic actor's past behavior, which this literature calls "priors."[12] He's probably trustworthy if he was trustworthy before, and he's probably dangerous if he was dangerous before. The skeptical nature of our cooperation and our trust are examples of this more general proposition that, to one degree or another, we were built to learn from the past. And yet few would argue that the legal rule against the admissibility of prior convictions should be abandoned because it "conflicts" with our natural predilection to want to know about, and act on, priors.

Instead, we tolerate and even demand this particular dissonance because this rule is itself a recognition of the unacceptable dangers lurking in the evolved intuition. Relying heavily on priors may have made perfect evolutionary sense in deciding whether that large male coming over the hill was friend or foe, but modern law has made a policy judgment that our intuition about priors is simply too strong for the purposes of the criminal law. In a weak criminal case – a case in which the ordinary principles of burden of proof and proof beyond a reasonable doubt should result in an acquittal – the sheer power of the intuition about priors may, or so goes this argument, overpower the jurors and increase the chances that innocent prior felons will be convicted. It's the "usual suspects" problem all over again. We may not all agree with this policy assessment, but we can probably all agree that in making it the law is attempting to deal head-on with the impact of our strong intuition about priors. Maybe this is not the kind of dissonance that needs fixing.

Other legal principles, however, seem to conflict with our intuitions in an entirely different, less satisfying, way. The harshness of American sentencing practices seems like one example. Contrary to what appears to be popular opinion, the levels of punishment that ordinary Americans think are appropriate in many kinds of cases are significantly lower than the levels that American law currently imposes in those cases. The reason is the existence of particular sentence-enhancing doctrines within the law, including strict liability, three strikes, mandatory minima, the prosecution of juveniles as adults, complicity, the felony-murder rule, and the narrowing of, or in a few states the abolition of, the insanity defense.[13]

This gap between what ordinary people think is an appropriate sentence and what the law requires through these doctrines has been convincingly demonstrated by studies that ask subjects to impose punishments in hypothetical cases, and then compare the results to the actual sentences required by these legal doctrines. Researchers using this method have shown that strict liability crimes are the most dissonant (that is, the difference between how the law punishes them and how ordinary people would punish them is the greatest), followed by three strikes laws, drug sentences for possession, felony-murder, narrowing insanity, and life without parole for first-degree murder.[14]

These experiments could be criticized as unrealistic. Believe me, there is nothing more daunting than having to sentence a real rapist with a real family in a real courtroom in front of a real victim and her family. But the artificiality of these studies is actually their strength. Asking test subjects with no ax to grind, unburdened by the emotions of revenge or the weight of real decision-making, to tell us how they would punish hypothetical wrongdoers gives us a powerful tool to gauge just deserts. It is, to my mind, all the more amazing that experimental subjects, who could take this cost-free opportunity to be tough on crime, are in fact substantially less harsh than the laws themselves.

These punishment dissonances, unlike the rule against admitting a defendant's prior convictions, should trouble all of us, at several different levels. What does it say about the effectiveness of our political systems that elected officials believe the best way to stay elected is to vote to increase the penalties for crime, when present sentences already exceed what ordinary citizens think are appropriate? What does it say about those ordinary citizens as voters, who, in the privacy of a behavioral study or jury room, will be less harsh than what they seem to demand of our elected representatives in the privacy of the voting booth? And, perhaps most importantly, what will this kind of chronic and gnawing gap do to the enduring legitimacy of the law?

This troubling political phenomenon may have its own evolutionary explanation. As we've seen, there is increasing evidence of a neurological difference between how we blame and how we punish, between our powerful second-party urge to retaliate and our more measured third-party urge for retribution.[15] Maybe when ordinary citizens clamor for higher punishment in the abstract they are expressing their second-party sense of blameworthiness, their revenge, because they imagine themselves as the victim of the crime. But when those same citizens are asked to impose third-party punishments, say, as jurors in capital cases or even subjects in hypothetical experiments, their zeal gets muted, perhaps because now their more restrained third-party punishment circuits are getting engaged. As every prosecutor turned judge knows, it is one thing to ask for a harsh sentence and quite another to impose one.

When citizens' unmuted and generalized zeal for blame gets transferred to politicians, politicians convert it into new crimes and into increased punishments for old ones. Every time a heinous crime is committed and news of it spreads in the media, ordinary citizens quite rightly express their outrage, an outrage that is an expression of *blame* but which then gets converted by the legislative process into an expression of *punishment*. The one-way punishment ratchet gets turned up a notch.

But now we are back to our original difficulty. How can we distinguish, on any kind of principled basis, the difference between dissonances such as the rule against the admission of a defendant's prior felony convictions, which I have characterized as a conscious effort by the law to overcome a dangerous evolutionary intuition, and unnaturally long sentences, which I have characterized as the danger? Maybe the real danger is that "natural" sentences are too short, and that the law in its wisdom recognizes that without draconian doctrines like mandatory minima and three strikes laws the sentences that judges impose will be inadequate. Maybe I am just picking and choosing between intuitions and legal doctrines I like and those I don't like.

This is a particular version of a problem well-known to moral philosophers, called "the naturalistic fallacy." It all started in 1740 with the Scottish philosopher David Hume. In one tiny passage in a big treatise, Hume observed that there is often a gap between what is and what ought to be, and that just because something happens regularly in nature doesn't necessarily mean it's right.[16] Rapes and murders happen all the time, but their regularity doesn't make them acceptable. In modern philosophical parlance, moral truths (the "ought") cannot be derived solely from nonmoral ones (the "is"). The naturalistic fallacy is also sometimes called the "is-ought problem" or "Hume's Gap."

When Darwin argued that animal traits, including behaviors, evolved because they provided their owners with a fitness advantage, Hume's Gap became the Grand Canyon. In fact, the phrase "naturalistic fallacy" is not Hume's; it was coined in the 1940s by the English philosopher G. E. Moore, who expressly applied it to evolution by posing this single question: "This conduct is more evolutionarily successful, but is it good?"[17] The moral inquiry, in this way of thinking, needs somehow to get outside the evolutionary observations. To know that killing your sexual rivals is wrong requires us to look to some other source of right and wrong than natural selection, because killing your sexual rivals can be spectacularly adaptive.

How, then, could all the observations in the prior chapters of this book – about how natural selection built our brains to blame and punish (not to mention having built-in moral preferences for not stealing and not breaching) – possibly inform us about how the law *should* blame and punish in today's world? The answer is that Hume's Gap is not really quite as big as some people think, as Hume himself recognized.

THE FALLACY OF THE NATURALISTIC FALLACY[18]

Hume was actually complaining about the way in which moral and political philosophers moved from the "is" to the "ought" without as much as a pause. But he never suggested the trip couldn't be made. He was just insisting that moral thinkers acknowledge the distance, and, as he put it, that "a reason should be given" for claiming that observed behaviors are either right or wrong, beyond the observation that they happen.[19] Hume, like every other serious philosopher before the postmodern era, very much believed that the worlds of nature and morals were connected.[20] As we've seen, he tried to begin a theory of connection by suggesting that it was through the phenomena of empathy and socialization that our own selfish desires to avoid pain cause us to hesitate to inflict pain on others. It was that Golden Rule of hesitation that Hume surmised to be the root of morality.[21]

As we have also seen in all the preceding chapters, modern evolutionary theory has now supplied a more rigorous connection between the "is" and the "ought." We not only evolved spines and opposable thumbs, we also evolved some moral intuitions. I have focused on three of them: don't steal (property, life, health, or the freedom from pain); don't break promises; and punish people who do steal or break promises. These are not just human behaviors that we can all agree are widespread. The reason they are widespread is that evolution has armed us with emotions that make us feel their moral bite. We sense that it is wrong to steal and breach, and we all have an urge to blame and punish serious stealing and breaching, because we evolved in circumstances in which too much stealing and breaching, and not enough punishment, would have unraveled our small groups. Morality itself is an evolved trait.

That doesn't entirely get us out of Hume's Gap. Many a moral judgment must be exercised in the vast areas between these three very general moral rules, areas where we will have to look beyond natural selection for guidance. Is it wrong to give an insincere compliment to a friend who desperately needs it, to neglect an animal, to lust after your neighbor's wife, or to not give to charity? If so, what if anything should we as a society do about such wrongs? These are moral questions that require answers that evolution alone cannot supply.[22] The same is true with political questions. Our moral instincts cannot tell us where the line between collectivism and individuality should be drawn, only that the line we do draw will always be subject to deeply evolved tensions flowing out of The Social Problem.

Our three evolved moral rules are not just incomplete, they often conflict with each other. Whether and how we should punish people who rob liquor stores to feed their starving children, or who do or do not pull that lever to divert the runaway trolley, are all questions that need some outside guidance for answers. Whether we think that guidance must come from some divine source, from wise leaders, from majoritarian fiat, from a constitution, or from anywhere else, we should all be able to agree it cannot come from evolutionary analysis alone.

The law is just as incomplete. Should this bank robber be given probation or prison, was this physician negligent, should this violation of the securities acts be a felony or a misdemeanor or not even a crime at all? These kinds of refined questions about legal details cannot be answered by our three very general rules. Our overarching moral intuitions are just too big, too general, to shed much light on legal details that require a slew of gritty policy judgments.

But that doesn't mean our evolutionary insights don't matter. In the first place, just keeping our evolved intuitions in mind might make our policy judgments better. Knowing that everyone will have trouble following a rule because it sharply conflicts with a deeply-held intuition may help us sharpen the rule. We might want to tweak it, or couple it with some other rules, or do any number of other things to help our decision-makers get over their evolved resistance to it.[23] For example, if legislatures know that judges simply won't blame and punish a given crime as harshly as the legislatures want, they might couple the crime with mandatory minimum penalties.[24] Likewise, judges who know jurors will resist blaming when the law requires them to blame might have to take extra time explaining why we blame this particular crime, and might also want to emphasize the instructions that remind the jurors they must follow the law regardless of their personal opinions about it.

Conversely, knowing that a legal rule is powerfully driven by a moral intuition might help us focus the rule and avoid its overapplication. For example, if we want to loosen jurors' deeply- and tightly-held presumptions of individual responsibility, so they are at least open to the possibility of an insanity defense, we may have to spend extra time explaining the insanity defense to them, and exactly why it is that the law does not blame insane actors.

We can even use one moral intuition to help overcome the influence of another. We saw this with the problem of soldiers not firing their guns.[25] Military trainers were able to increase firing rates dramatically not just by using simulated human targets in training, but also by making those targets look like out-groups. They were able to overcome soldiers' innate in-group resistance to killing by using their equally innate distain for out-groups. We have, of course, seen this demonization of the enemy throughout history, both in military and political contexts. This phenomenon also exists in many legal contexts. For example, it is easier for us to blame and especially punish people if we convince ourselves they are different from us. Judges are much more willing to send young men to decades of prison if we label them "gangbangers." I am not suggesting that's necessarily wrong, and indeed gangs are real, are dangerous, and in fact consist of individuals who have self-labeled themselves as dangerous outsiders. But demonizing in this fashion risks overkill. Not every alienated teenager with baggy pants is a gangster.

These in-group/out-group tensions pervade all sentencing hearings. When I hear about the terrible things some of my defendants have done, I am often overcome by two simultaneous and seemingly incongruent feelings: 1) these people are not humans; and 2) there but for the grace of God go I. The latter feeling no doubt has origins in our profoundly social natures, and the former in the out-group exception to those natures.

Finally, and admittedly most controversially, there may be some limited circumstances in which a legal rule is so dissonant with a moral intuition, so difficult for judges and jurors to follow, and so damaging to respect for the rule of law when we force ourselves to follow it, that we might want to consider limiting it or even abandoning it. Now we are falling back into the abyss of Hume's Gap, so let me suggest a five-step approach to distinguish legal dissonances that may unacceptably distort our moral intuitions from those that seem curative of an unacceptable intuition.

CLOSING THE GAP[26]

First, we need to be as sure as we can that the moral intuition that conflicts with the legal rule is in fact a real moral intuition. This isn't always easy, because our guesses about evolutionary psychology, though educated, remain guesses. Still, if a behavior has a palpable evolutionary value in theory, if it seems universal across human societies, past and present, and if the same behavior or an antecedent is exhibited by our primate relatives, then we should feel pretty good about our guess that the behavior may have some evolutionary roots.

In our example about the rule against the admissibility of prior convictions, there really should be little doubt that our intuition to place great weight on priors is evolutionarily rooted. Not only do humans and nonhuman primates rely on priors, but in some ways the very definition of life is the ability to adjust to the entire environment of "priors." Whether it is a single-celled bacterium reacting to a change in pH, a corn plant turning its leaves to the sun, or Konrad Lorenz's dog reacting to his new housemate, all living things have some ability to change their future behavior on the basis of data about the past. There is very little doubt that the legal rule against admitting a defendant's prior convictions is bumping up against a version of an extraordinarily deep and powerful evolved urge to pay attention to a wrongdoer's past wrongs.

But what about long versus short sentences? Remember, the Robinson concordance studies were about *relative* blameworthiness, not absolute punishment amounts.[27] Other than the proportionality command that the punishment must fit the crime, it seems quite unlikely that there is any tangible, widely shared, natural "core" against which we can reliably measure absolute sentence lengths. Amounts of punishment vary widely between societies. They even vary within societies; in America they vary greatly state to state. They vary in my courthouse, judge to judge.[28]

The discrete legal doctrines that drive these long sentences are themselves fair game for a dissonance critique. They may in their own right unacceptably conflict with some important aspects of our blaming and punishing natures, and in Chapter 10 I will engage in just such a critique of some of these doctrines. But it seems unlikely that there is any general dissonance that demands fixing when it comes to harsh sentencing, because it seems unlikely there is any identifiable evolutionary core when it comes to the absolute severity of punishment. True, we've seen some traces of a very general punishment trajectory over time and across societies.[29] But at any one time, the severity of punishment has varied wildly between societies. If there were any evolutionary roots associated with the severity of punishment, those roots have long been obliterated by the pressures of culture.

To see this we need go no further than this moment in our own times. Compare the general punishment practices, say, in Massachusetts, with those in Saudi Arabia. In one case, theft of minor valuables is a misdemeanor or petty offense, in the other it is still punishable by amputation. The most heinous mass murderer in one jurisdiction faces only imprisonment, while in the other an adulteress faces being stoned to death. Remember, too, that even in the Ultimatum Game – which models costly punishment – primitive societies showed significant differences depending on things such as the nature of their religious norms and the presence of working markets.[30]

So our two test cases come out differently on this first factor of whether the moral intuition is likely real. Our legal rule against the admissibility of prior convictions conflicts with an intuition – our reliance on priors – that is almost certainly evolved. Long sentences, by contrast, probably don't violate any evolved intuitions, even though, as we saw earlier in this chapter, there may well be an evolutionary explanation for *why* punishments have gotten so long (the one-way punishment ratchet driven by a neural dissociation between blame and third-party punishment). By the way, when this first factor fails we can probably stop the inquiry. When there is no evolved intuition against which, in this example, long sentences conflict, then we can retire to the more comfortable, or at least more familiar, confines of public policy to debate whether current sentences really are too long, and if so what we should do about it.

For our second factor, I propose that we examine whether the legal doctrine itself is evolutionarily rooted. If we are dealing with competing evolutionary cores then maybe there is no dissonance at all, just a policy choice about how the clash of two naturally-selected core principles should be resolved in a particular cultural and legal context. To determine whether a legal principle is evolutionarily rooted, we should look at all the same things we looked at to determine if a moral intuition is evolutionary rooted: does the legal principle confer a palpable evolutionary advantage, is it widespread across human societies, and does anything akin to it seem to be taking place in predecessor or other closely related species?

We will run into this phenomenon of legal principles that themselves are evolutionary rooted when we discuss complicity and conspiracy in the next chapter, which arguably have evolutionary origins in our deep suspicion of out-groups. Other examples, to name just a few, might include the doctrine of abandonment in the law of attempt (arguably rooted in forgiveness); the lines the criminal law often draws between levels of theft offenses depending on the amount taken (arguably rooted in our notion of harm as blame's tiebreaker); and the myriad of doctrines in both civil and criminal law that have a de minimis escape clause (arguably rooted in Rule 3's command that only *serious* violations be punished). In fact, it is hard to identify a substantive legal rule of conduct that does *not* seem to have an evolutionary core. As we have seen, our Rule 1 (don't steal) is the foundation of most of the criminal law and the law of negligence; Rule 2 (don't breach) is the foundation of the law of contract. To be sure, these two evolved rules do not occupy the entirety of the law – driving on the right side of the road no doubt has no evolutionary pedigree – but they sure seem to cover most of it. This means, admittedly, that our search for evolutionary answers to legal questions will almost always be fruitless, because the dissonant rule will almost always have its own evolutionary core. But it's the "almost" that is intriguing. There are a few legal rules that do not seem to touch on these core moral intuitions, and that are therefore susceptible to the rest of our five-part test.

Our two test cases are good examples. Neither the prohibition against the admission of a defendant's prior felony convictions nor long sentences seem to have any arguable evolutionary core. I suppose ignoring a wrongdoer's past wrongs is a kind of forgiveness, but we forgive in the same kind of grudging way that we cooperate. We may forgive a past wrong but we never really forget it, especially when it comes to judging new wrongs. As for long sentences, we certainly have a predisposition to blame and punish serious wrongdoers – that's what this book has been all about – but there does not seem to be any evolutionary foundation to the particular way we punish, let alone to the length of prison sentences. In fact, as we have seen, prison is quite a recent development; we punished one another in our emergent groups with fines, perhaps some limited corporal punishment, banishment, and death.

The third factor is how far the dissonant legal rule has in fact strayed from the core evolutionary principle. This will often be a difficult thing to measure. In the case of the rule against the admission of a defendant's prior felonies, there is really no quantitative aspect of this rule. For punishment dissonances, however, we can actually measure the dissonance, at least as between punishments of the same kind, such as the lengths of prison sentences. So, for example, for those legal doctrines that drive sentences beyond the levels of punishment that ordinary people impose, it might be good to know how *much* beyond. We will see this with felony-murder and complicity in the next chapter. Other legal doctrines that drive punishments up can also be quantified in this manner, and in fact they have. As we've already seen, researchers looking at six different sentence-enhancing legal doctrines, and comparing how ordinary subjects would sentence in the absence of the doctrine, have found that strict liability is the most dissonant (that is, that it drives sentences furthest from where ordinary people would punish), followed by three strikes laws, drug sentences for mere possession, felony-murder, and the narrowing of insanity.[31]

Fourth, in some instances we might think of a directional kind of test. If an evolved core principle tends to result in judgments in a certain direction (e.g., more punishment), we would want to know if the dissonant legal rule takes the judgments in a different direction (less punishment). For example, those who propose a rule that would excuse some psychopaths – that is, that would include severe psychopathy as a mental disease or defect that could come within the definition of insanity – are probably proposing a directionally dissonant rule, if we assume we all have intuitions to punish people who have no empathy or moral judgment *more* than people who do have empathy and moral judgment.[32] The rule against the admissibility of a defendant's prior felony convictions is also a kind of directional dissonance. Our evolved urge is to want to know about all prior acts by any strategic actor, and the rule against the admissibility of prior felonies keeps that knowledge away from our jurors. More versus less punishment is not exactly directional in this sense.

Finally, we might ask whether the legal rule is riddled with exceptions, or with jurisdictions rejecting it outright, with the idea that it may be a dissonant core driving those exceptions and rejections. The rule against admitting a defendant's prior felonies is not exactly riddled with exceptions, but it does have one big American exception. If the defendant elects to testify, then his prior felony convictions come in, for the limited purpose of letting the jury consider those prior felonies in deciding whether to believe the defendant's testimony.[33] That is, the American version of this rule abhors the proposition "once a felon always a felon," but has no trouble allowing jurors to conclude "once a felon always a liar."[34]

Many of the doctrines that drive lengthy sentences also have significant exceptions. Serious strict liability crimes are relatively few and far between. Three strikes laws in America have been limited to some extent by United States Supreme Court decisions requiring that the sentence be proportional to the crimes: a three-time shoplifter is thus often protected from what would otherwise be a long (sometimes life) mandatory prison sentence. As we will see in the next chapter, felony-murder has been abolished in England and has almost disappeared in America, at least in its most robust form. Complicity and conspiracy, by contrast, seem alive and kicking.

So how should these five factors work when we are deciding whether to abandon or limit a legal rule because it conflicts too much with an evolved intuition? As mentioned earlier, if the intuition really isn't an evolved intuition then we can stop our evolutionary analysis. We can also stop if the legal rule seems just as firmly rooted in evolution. But if we get past these first two inquiries, then we should try to measure how far from the evolved intuition the legal rule has strayed. Big differences should concern us more than little ones. If the legal rule takes us in an entirely different direction, we should be especially concerned. And if the legal rule is stuffed with exceptions or is already on its way out, that might be a sign that the conflicting moral intuition has already begun to win the battle.

I do not pretend that this framework will revolutionize law. Law in large part is already the product of a relentless process of cultural evolution, including, in the Anglo-American west, the processes of the common law. Through these cultural mechanisms the law has already spent untold years testing our moral intuitions against the changing demands of particular societies. But not all law is common law, especially in modern societies heavy with regulation. Besides, the common law's essential feature is its flexibility, and some evolutionary insights may at the very least lubricate the joints of some of that flexibility in some important ways. Our five-part evolutionary test may even suggest some reforms in a few narrow substantive areas. Before we jump right into Hume's Gap, let's tackle a broader but perhaps less controversial topic: how our brains process information and what that may teach us about the processes of the law.

Notes to Chapter 8

1. People v. Hill, Denver District Court Case No. 06CR4898.
2. In states that recognize the death penalty, Judy could theoretically be put to death, although the United States Supreme Court has held that the death penalty is categorically unconstitutional for mere felony-murder (as a violation of the Eighth Amendment's prohibition against cruel and unusual punishment). Tison v. Arizona, 481 U.S. 137 (1987); Enmund v. Florida, 458 U.S. 782 (1982).
3. In fact, researchers have shown that ordinary people punish Judy for the bank robbery, plus blame her more because of John's death, but only roughly as if she had recklessly caused the death. In one particular study, subjects sentenced Judy to an average of 17.9 years in prison, compared to the life without parole required by most felony-murder statutes. Paul Robinson, Geoffrey & Michael Reisig, *The Disutility of Injustice*, 85 N.Y.U. L. REV. 1940 (2010).
4. I will address the felony-murder dissonance in more depth in Chapter 10.
5. There was evidence that was both favorable and unfavorable to Auman. I've included most of the favorable facts in the rendition in the text – most importantly, that Auman was far away and in police custody at the time of the killing. But there was also evidence that during the car chase she held the steering wheel as Jaehnig leaned out the window to shoot at police, and that when she was first arrested she refused to tell police where Jaehnig had run.
6. Hunter S. Thompson, the self-described gonzo journalist, was among the champions of Ms. Auman's cause.
7. People v. Auman, 67 P.3d 741 (Colo. App. 2002).
8. Auman v. People, 109 P.3d 647 (Colo. 2005).
9. In most states, a halfway house sentence begins with a short custodial sentence (a month or so) in a local jail, followed by a custodial placement in the halfway house. A defendant must spend a designated amount of time in twenty-four-hour custody at the halfway house, as if he or she were still in jail. After some time, the defendant can move to a work release kind of phase, where the defendant is permitted to leave the facility to work. Eventually, through good behavior, a defendant can graduate to a so-called

non-residential phase, in which the defendant no longer spends any time at the halfway house, but still regularly reports to a probation officer. In Colorado, the typical amount of residential time is 120 days, although in Auman's case the parties agreed she would spend six additional months in residential custody.

10. This is because of what is known as the "harmless error" rule, law's version of no-harm-no-foul. Errors are made in every trial, because humans are involved in every trial. If an error clearly ("beyond a reasonable doubt") had no role in the defendant's conviction, then the appeals courts will not overturn the conviction just because of that error. In fact, Auman's trial lawyers did not even raise this jury instruction issue during the trial, meaning that the harmless error test becomes the even more difficult "plain error" test: was the error so obvious and serious that there is a reasonable probability it contributed to the defendant's conviction?

11. The American federal rule is Federal Rule of Evidence 404(b), which has also been adopted in one form or another in all states. The English have the same general rule in § 101 of the Criminal Justice Act 2003 (c. 44), although its exceptions are generally more forgiving than the American version. As discussed later in the text, one giant and unique American exception is that a defendant's prior felony convictions may be disclosed to the jury if the defendant chooses to testify, although the jury is then instructed that they may consider those priors only for the purpose of impeaching the defendant's testimony, and not for propensity.

12. See, e.g., S. Sutton, *Predicting and explaining behaviors and intentions: how well are we doing?*, J. APPL. SOC. PSYCHOL., **28(15)**, 1317–1338 (1998); J. Oulette & W. Wood, *Habit and intention in everyday life: the multiple processes by which past behavior predicts future behavior*, PSYCHOL. BUL., **124(1)**, 54–74 (1998); H. Aarts et al., *Predicting behavior from actions in the past: repeated decision making or a matter of habit?*, J. APPL. SOC. PSYCHOL., **28(15)**, 1355–1374 (1998).

13. Strict liability crimes are crimes that do not require intent – that is, we hold people criminally liable for accidents. Speeding is an example. Even if your speedometer is broken and you *think* you are going just 55 mph, you are guilty of speeding merely by exceeding the limit, whether or not you intended to do so. Strict liability crimes have traditionally been a tiny part of the criminal law, although their numbers have grown as the regulatory state has grown.

Three strikes laws are laws that automatically set high fixed punishments for repeat offenders. With many variations, they typically work this way: if a person is convicted of a sufficiently serious felony, and has within a designated look back period been previously convicted of X numbers of other sufficiently serious felonies, then the judge must sentence him to prison for a set, and very lengthy period, often a multiple of what would otherwise have been the maximum sentence.

Mandatory minima are statutes that require trial courts to impose a minimum prison sentence, depriving us of what would ordinarily be a choice between prison, a halfway house, and probation.

Complicity is a no intent dissonance discussed in the next chapter.

14. Robinson & Reisig, supra note 3. See also Paul Robinson & John Darley, *Intuitions of Justice: Implications for Criminal Law and Justice Policy*, 81 S. CAL. L. REV. 1 (2007).

15. Chapter 2, Blame and Punishment.

16. In every system of morality with which I have hitherto met, I have always remark'd. that that the author proceeds for some time in the ordinary way of reasoning, and established the being of a God, or makes observations concerning human affairs; when of a sudden I am supriz'd to find, that instead of the usual copulations of propositions, *is*, and *is not*, I meet with no proposition that is not connected with an *ought*, or an *ought not*. This change is imperceptible; but it is, however, of the last consequence. For as this *ought* or *ought not*, expresses some new relation or affirmation, 'tis necessary that it should be observ'd and explain'd; and at the same time that a reason should be given, for what seems altogether inconceivable, how this new relation can be a deduction from others, which are entirely different from it.

D. HUME, III A TREATISE OF HUMAN NATURE 469 (1740) (MacMillan 1888).

17. G. E. MOORE, PRINCIPIA ETHICA (Cambridge 1948).

18. I borrow this section title from Francis Fukuyama, who used it as a section title in his book, OUR POST-HUMAN FUTURE: CONSEQUENCES OF THE BIOTECHNOLOGY REVOLUTION (Picador 2002).

19. Hume, note 16 supra, at 469.

20. See A. MacIntrye, *Hume on "Is" and "Ought,"* PHIL. REV., **68(4)**, 451–468 (1959), reprinted in THE IS-OUGHT QUESTION 35–50 (W. Hudson, ed., St. Martins 1969).

21. Chapter 3, page 106.

22. As we saw in Chapter 2, these kinds of "wrongs" are what Paul Robinson would call "non-core" crimes, precisely because they do not involve violations of our core rules against stealing and breaching.

23. This proposition – that understanding the relationship between law and evolved behavioral tendencies will help the law be more effective – is discussed in depth in Owen D. Jones, *Time-Shifted Rationality and the Law of Law's Leverage*, 95 NW. L. REV. 1141 (2001).

24. Reasonable people can argue about the general wisdom of mandatory minima, and they certainly have when it comes to mandatory minima for drug offenses. See JONATHAN P. CAULKINS ET AL., MANDATORY MINIMUM DRUG SENTENCES: THROWING AWAY THE KEY OR THE TAXPAYERS' MONEY? (Rand 1997). Indeed, earlier in this chapter I criticized the one-way American sentencing ratchet, and mandatory minima are a key piece of

hardware in that ratchet. But once legislatures make the decision to criminal-ize certain actions they know ordinary people simply will not blame, at least to levels they wish, they'd be foolish not to consider mandatory minima.

25. Chapter 3, pages 103–106.
26. This five-part analysis first appeared in Morris B. Hoffman, *Evolutionary Jurisprudence: The End of the Naturalistic Fallacy and the Beginning of Natural Reform?*, in LAW AND NEUROSCIENCE 433 (M. Freeman, ed., Oxford 2011).
27. Those concordance studies are discussed in Chapter 2.
28. Remember from Chapter 2 that Robinson argued that judge-to-judge varia-tion was a problem of endpoint – that is, that different judges have different yardsticks on which they place their virtually identical list of crimes ordered by blameworthiness.
29. Chapter 5, Punishment Over Time: From Banishment and Back Again.
30. We discussed Joseph Henrich's work on this topic in Chapter 1. J. Henrich et al., *Markets, religion, community size and the evolution of fairness and pun-ishment*, SCIENCE, 327, 1480–1484 (March 2010). Even before this paper, it was well-known that, although all primitive societies engage in costly pun-ishment, the magnitude of that punishment varies dramatically between soci-eties. See, e.g., J. Henrich, *Costly punishment across human societies*, SCIENCE, **312**, 1767–1770 (June 2006).
31. Robinson & Reisig, supra note 3.
32. For an example of this argument that severe psychopaths may be insane, see Stephen Morse, *Psychopathy and Criminal Responsibility*, 1 NEURO-ETHICS 205 (2008). The intuition to punish psychopaths more than non-psychopaths might also be a simple application of the rule that we pay atten-tion to priors. The very label "psychopath" conveys the notion that this person violates norms, has done so in the past, and is likely to so do in the future.
33. In which case we give the jury a special instruction telling them that they may use any prior felony convictions for the limited purpose of deciding whether to believe the defendant's testimony, but not to conclude that just because the defendant committed prior felonies then he is more likely to have committed this one.
34. The rule against a defendant's prior convictions being admitted is a small part of a broader rule, Rule 404(b), which generally prohibits any witness's prior wrongs from being admitted to show the witness acted consistently with those wrongs. This larger broader version of the rule, unlike the part limited to prior felony convictions, is in fact riddled with exceptions, all of them enumerated in the rule itself.

9   EVALUATING SOME PROCESS DISSONANCES

[L]ike a flash of lightning in the clouds. We live in the flicker.

Joseph Conrad

Our brains make us angry, disgusted, fearful, jealous, or anxious, often in a very short fraction of time and often based on exposure to a narrow set of stimuli. The whole idea of an evolved emotional shortcut is to use limited information to be able to take quickly what was, at least 100,000 years ago, the action most likely to be favorable to our fitness. The architectures of our legal institutions, and of our trial systems in particular, must somehow accommodate the fact that we are creatures who are sometimes prone to act in this emotionally sudden fashion.

BLINKING TO VERDICTS

In my introductory remarks to jurors, I spend lots of time and effort trying to alert them to the problem that a trial is a completely unnatural process, and that their biggest challenge will be to resist the temptation to jump to any conclusions. We simply are not built to wait passively until all facts are in before we start making judgments, let alone to do so in the artificially linear way that trials proceed – with one side submitting all of its evidence before the other side even starts. We make judgments constantly, on the smallest bits of information, and those initial judgments can drastically alter the way in which we receive and process additional information, especially information that conflicts with our initial judgments. The single most daunting problem for all jurors is how to transform themselves from continuous blinking judgment machines into patient receptacles of considered judgment.

Most Anglo-American trial systems already have several well-recognized rules in place, whether by statute, court rule, or culture, to deal with this problem of the blinking verdict. Unfortunately, some of these norms are coming under fire from well-meaning jury reformers. For example, it is a widespread practice for trial judges to advise jurors that they may not discuss the case with each other until all the evidence is in and they actually begin their deliberations. This is a direct effort to slow down the blinking verdict. If jurors are talking to each other as the case is going on, there is an enormous risk – in my view a virtual certainty – that they will be deciding cases in these early discussions. In civil cases, however, several American states now allow, and some even require, the trial judge to tell jurors they may discuss the case in the jury room during recesses, as long as all jurors are present.[1]

This reform quite rightly recognizes the reality that we are instinct-driven and highly social creatures, for whom *not* having pre-deliberation discussions about the case will be quite unnatural and difficult. But it assumes that we cannot transcend these difficulties, and it also assumes that the practice is any more damaging when it is forbidden than when it is permitted. Yet there simply is no reliable empirical evidence to substantiate either of these critical assumptions. True, by telling jurors they cannot discuss the case unless all of them are present, this reform has the arguable benefit of reducing the times when just a few jurors discuss the case. But there's no data showing jurors are any more likely to follow this reform command than they are to follow the original prohibition against talking at all. Yes, some jurors will talk about the case even after we instruct them not to, just as some citizens rob banks even after the law tells them not to. What an odd place – in the citadels of individual responsibility – for the law to surrender to the "instincts" of our citizens.

There are several other widespread practices that are designed to help jurors not decide cases too early. An important one is that we don't give the jury the substantive instructions that define the offenses or claims until the close of evidence. Like the rule against pre-deliberation discussions, this rule is designed to prevent jurors from deciding cases too early. In fact, I try to have these two rules reinforce each other, by reminding jurors at every recess that it will actually be impossible for them to have any meaningful discussions about the case because they still don't know the legal definitions of the charged crimes. This rule is also under attack by some jury reformers, in both civil and criminal cases. Many states now allow the trial judge in civil cases to give preliminary substantive instructions, and even allow the lawyers to make mid-case arguments. A few states have even adopted this reform in criminal cases.

Another common rule – forbidding jurors from talking to their spouses, friends, or other non-jurors about the case during the trial – is also designed, at least in part, to address this problem of deciding cases too soon. The traditional justification for this rule has been that we don't want jurors influenced by other people who are not jurors. But this is really not a significant worry. In my experience jurors take very seriously their oaths to decide their cases, often extraordinarily important cases, based only on the evidence and the instructions of law, and the world in which a juror's mind is, say, changed by a meddling spouse is not the world I live in. Does that sometimes happen? No doubt. But that would happen with or without the no-talking-to-anyone-else rule. A juror's spouse or friend who changes the outcome of a case, or a juror willing to let that happen, will hardly be slowed down by a rule that prohibits talking about the case.

No, the real reason for this rule is that we don't want jurors talking about a case off hours because to talk about a case requires them to pick out bits and pieces of the evidence, and by doing so that evidence might become, even subconsciously, more important than other evidence, increasing the chances that the juror will be deciding the case too soon. To my knowledge, thankfully, there are no existing or proposed reforms to change this rule.

The blinking verdict is not just a problem for jurors. In bench trials, where there is no jury and the parties are asking me to render the judgment, there is always a point in the evidence, sometime early sometimes late, when the lightbulb seems to go on, and it *feels* like I understand the big picture and see what the result should be. I consciously fight that moment, try to unwind my mind to its earlier state of confusion, and sometimes even try to pay extra attention to the evidence suggesting the opposite result. Despite all these efforts, I must confess that when the lightbulb moment comes I rarely change my mind on the fundamentals.

When I was practicing law, I remember a federal judge who took sporadic notes in bench trials. But there was always a point in the trial – to be fair, usually near the end of the evidence – when he suddenly went from taking almost no notes to having his head buried in his notepad, so buried that he often missed objections and had to have his reporter read the question and the objection back to him. We all knew what was happening – he'd reached his decision and was writing out his order. I always worried about whether, if I was already on the short end of his decision, any of my additional evidence would matter at all.

I've spent many years thinking about ways we can help the problem of the blinking jury and judge. It seems to me these lightbulb moments will come, no matter our best efforts. They are part and parcel of the way we make decisions. Perhaps the best we can do is to try to push those moments as far back into the process as possible. The best way to do that is probably just to acknowledge that there is a problem, and to force the jurors, or the judge, to acknowledge it in their own minds. Remind them, and remind ourselves, as often as we can, that the trial is an unnatural process in which we expect the decision-makers to resist their natural tendency to jump to conclusions.

One of the techniques I have discovered that seems to unwind the lightbulb moment, or at least dim it, is to take bench trials under advisement, meaning not ruling from the bench but rather taking days or weeks to write a written order deciding the case. Ironically, most young judges do this as a matter of course, because issuing a coherent oral ruling from the bench shortly after the close of evidence is a difficult task for most of us, one that seems to improve with experience. I issued almost no bench rulings in cases of any complexity during my first three years on the bench. Now, I almost always rule orally from the bench, no matter how complex the case.

But even now I am occasionally forced to take a case under advisement and write an opinion later, either because of the sheer quantity of the evidence, or because I need to research the law, or because I just don't feel strongly about the result. In the latter kinds of cases – when I just don't feel strongly about the result – maybe I've already been able to unwind the lightbulb moment, or never had it. But in the former kinds of cases – where I leave the bench almost certain of the result I will reach, but with a need to review some pieces of evidence or some cases or statutes – I have noticed that it is not unusual that by the time I write the order I have changed my mind about parts of the case, and occasionally even about the outcome. The sheer delay between the lightbulb moment and the moment of decision seems to help. Maybe the formality of doing a written order also helps.[2]

In any event, perhaps one way for trial judges to avoid deciding bench trials too soon is to return to our rookie days, when we took nearly everything under advisement and wrote our orders days or weeks after the close of evidence. One trade-off, of course, is that the passage of time can dim our memories of the evidence. But it can also dim our lightbulb moments. The best course, as tedious and time-consuming as it is, may be to get a transcript of the trial and read that transcript once the lightbulb moment has sufficiently dimmed, so that we can reopen ourselves to the evidence that came when we may have been blinded to it.

I'm not sure how we might implement such ideas with juries. More detailed jury verdicts asking specific question – called special interrogatories – might help, because they force the jury to answer specific questions rather than just sign a conclusory verdict. More radically, forcing jurors to explain their verdicts in writing might have the same effect on jurors that doing a written order has on judges.[3] Maybe it would be a good idea simply to build some time in between closing arguments and deliberations, recessing, for example, after closing arguments no matter when in the day we finish, and having the jury begin their deliberations the next morning. Frustrated jurors raring to go won't like it, and neither will judges worried about their dockets. But maybe such a pause will make for better verdicts.

SIGNAL-TO-NOISE PROBLEMS: STORYTELLING

We are built not only to make snap judgments, but also to send and receive information in socially relevant ways. Our brains are able to take in enormous amounts of information, but not all of it is relevant. So we needed strategies to separate the wheat from the chaff, the evolutionarily important information from the noise.[4] Because we evolved in small groups, it is not hard to imagine that our brains would be built to pay special attention to socially relevant information. Recall the experiments discussed in Chapter 2, where subjects were better able to reason logically when the logical propositions were framed in socially relevant ways.[5] The same is true of our ability even to register information, let alone reason about it. When you notice the attractive passenger across from you on the subway, you are disregarding, at least consciously, a million other bits of information about the world at that moment, including the temperature, the color of shoes being worn by the toddler next to you, and maybe even, for a short while, the conductor's announcements of the stops.

The late biologist Stephen Jay Gould once called humans "the storytelling primate."[6] We are inveterate storytellers, and almost all of our stories are about people, either expressly or symbolically. We simply do not pay as much attention to information when it is not conveyed as part of a unifying social narrative. When we receive asocial information, we make up our own social stories to make sense of it. As we've seen, even infants impose a social narrative on pictures of moving geometric objects, not only paying more attention to movements that seem to be directed by some intentional forces, but also distinguishing between good intentions and bad ones.[7]

A jury trial is one kind of formalized process of sending information. Three senders (two lawyers and one judge) are conveying information to some number of eventually-networked receivers (the jurors). As with any transmission of information, the trial process must convey information under several constraints, including sequencing constraints (we've already talked about how one side goes first) and time constraints (we don't have forever). The senders must satisfy these constraints and still make their signal-to-noise ratio high enough for the information to be discernible. How do the best lawyers do that? By storytelling.

I will never forget the advice an old and wise trial lawyer once gave me when I was just starting out. He said he spends days, sometimes even weeks, trying to summarize his case in a single phrase or sentence, often trying out dozens of candidates on his beleaguered partners and family until he finds the one that seems most resonant. Once he settles on that single phrase or sentence, he builds his whole case around it, starting with jury selection and opening statements. No matter how complicated the issues, how far-ranging the evidence, he knew that the best way to convey the most important evidence to the judge or jury was with the title of a story followed by the story itself.

I've seen many such phrases used effectively over the years. I once presided over the jury trial of an extraordinarily complex commercial case, involving complicated allegations of breach of contract inside a bankruptcy reorganization. In discovery, the plaintiff found an internal memo from the records of the defendant corporation, in which one corporate officer told another that they planned to honor the contract "when pigs fly." The entirety of the plaintiff's case was infused with that metaphor, from jury selection through closing arguments. That one neat phrase simultaneously conveyed the idea that the defendant had breached the contract, and that that breach was quite intentional, even malevolent.

Similarly, in the famous 1980s litigation between Pennzoil and Texaco, Pennzoil's lead trial lawyer, Joe Jamail, used the phrase "a handshake deal" over and over to convey to the jury Pennzoil's central theme: when Getty Oil orally promised to sell out to Pennzoil, that oral promise was enforceable, and Texaco tortiously interfered with that oral contract by offering Getty more money. Handshake deals are what we do with each other every day, and what we've been doing for 100,000 years. We make promises, we expect promises to be kept, and we punish people who break promises. The Pennzoil jury applied our Rules 2 and 3 to punish Texaco to the tune of US$11 billion.[8]

When jurors are not presented with a socially coherent narrative, they will make one up. Just like infants attributing good and bad intentions to moving geometric shapes, jurors (and judges) will attribute good and bad intentions to actors in a trial dispute, whether or not the lawyers present the trial in that fashion. Perhaps even more remarkably, jurors reconstruct the evidence in their post-verdict memories so that it becomes consistent with their verdict. In interviews of jurors after verdicts, researchers discovered that jurors often could not even remember evidence that conflicted with their verdict.[9] We can infer from this rich storytelling literature that jurors do the same thing in deliberations that they do after deliberations – they take the trial evidence and make it into a story, disregarding the facts that don't fit the story, and perhaps overvaluing the facts that do.

I don't at all mean to suggest that our natural yearning for a story is necessarily a process dissonance that needs some "solution." The good news is that the stories jurors weave, with or without the help of gifted storytelling lawyers, seem not to interfere terribly with their truth-finding function. I've presided over almost 400 jury trials, and I can count on the fingers of two hands the verdicts that shocked me. Admittedly, a judge being "shocked" at a verdict may be a poor metric of jury reliability; and there's no telling whether my own yearning for a good, but false, story is any less distorting than the average juror's. Besides, as we have already seen, the "truths" jurors are called upon to discover in most trials are more often moral truths about blameworthiness than factual truths about whodunit. Still, especially in that handful of cases that really are whodunits, our yearning for a story might have truth-distorting impacts.

There is also the problem of a good storyteller matched against a poor one. This doesn't happen often, because, at least in my experience, so few trial lawyers, especially civil trial lawyers, are truly gifted storytellers. But when one of the lawyers in a case is a gifted storyteller, the other usually isn't, and one-sided stories might have an impact on the reliability of the jury's (and judge's) verdict.

The asymmetry of the Anglo-American criminal trial may also give an inherently unfair storytelling advantage to the prosecution, at least when the prosecutor is a gifted storyteller. Most, and usually all, evidence in an Anglo-American criminal case is presented by the prosecution, because the defense has no burden, and a defendant cannot be forced to testify. In my experience, criminal lawyers are generally much better storytellers than civil lawyers, in part because human defection and cruelty are stories easily told, and in part just because criminal lawyers get so much more trial practice. Because of the asymmetry of the criminal trial, however, the storytelling skills of criminal defense lawyers are seldom on display, at least in the sense of weaving the evidence into a coherent social narrative. Instead, they have an essentially negating role. Their job is to argue that the prosecution's evidence was not a coherent narrative, that it had gaps where reasonable doubt might reside. Jurors and judges, just like all people, might not respond to, indeed might not even hear, these kinds of abstract arguments about what a story lacks in the same way they hear and respond to the story itself.

Perhaps the truth, both moral and factual, is better served in systems, like many continental systems, which expect, and in some cases even require, the defendant to take the stand and tell the jurors or judges what happened.[10] Our Anglo-American constitutional commitments to the burden of proof and to the criminal defendant's right to remain silent will never allow us to experiment too wildly with these kinds of changes in the storytelling processes of trial.[11]

UNANIMITY AND THE DILEMMA OF DECISION VERSUS DELIBERATION

One of the great, and enduring, debates about the Anglo-American jury system is whether verdicts should be unanimous. The United States Supreme Court rekindled the American version of the debate in 1972 in a case called *Johnson v. Louisiana*, when it held that the U.S. Constitution does not mandate unanimous verdicts in state criminal cases, upholding Louisiana's system, which permitted convictions based on 9–3 verdicts.[12] A few years earlier the Court had ruled that the Constitution does not mandate twelve-person criminal juries.[13] After these two cases, a few states began to push the envelope both of non-unanimity and numerosity, authorizing smaller and smaller juries with narrower and narrower majority requirements. The Supreme Court responded by drawing the following lines: in criminal cases with twelve jurors, 9–3 verdicts are permitted, 8–4 and below are not; in criminal cases with six or fewer jurors the verdict must be unanimous; and criminal juries may not be smaller than three.[14] There is no federal constitutional floor for either numerosity or consensus for civil cases.[15]

Although many states, including mine, Colorado, have retained both the unanimity and twelve-juror requirements for felony criminal trials, many other states have experimented with non-unanimity at the constitutional boundaries set by the Supreme Court, generating a debate in legal as well as psychological circles about the optimum number of jurors and the utility or disutility of unanimity.[16]

In England and Wales, non-unanimous verdicts of 10–2 in criminal cases have been permitted since 1967, although the act of Parliament adopting this reform also requires jurors to deliberate at least two hours before returning non-unanimous verdicts. The rule in Australia is similar – verdicts of 11–1 and, in some jurisdictions, of 10–2 are permitted, although jurors must deliberate between three and six hours, again depending on the jurisdiction. Scotland and Belgium are among the most forgiving when it comes to non-unanimity, Scotland permitting verdicts of 8–7 in its fifteen-member juries, and Belgium permitting verdicts of 7–5 (tied verdicts are acquittals). In a few countries, the amount of permitted non-unanimity is different for verdicts of not guilty than for verdicts of guilty. In Spain, for example, a guilty verdict requires seven of nine jurors, but a not guilty verdict only five of nine (anything in between is a nondecision, or what we would call a hung jury).

The rules of non-unanimity can be even more complex in the many systems that use juries composed of a mixture of lay people and judges. In France, for example, verdicts must be at least 8–4, without distinguishing between the nine lay jurors and the three judges. But in Austria, the eight lay jurors first deliberate outside of the presence of the three judges, with a simple majority sufficient to establish the lay portion of the verdict. At their request, they can ask the three judges to join them in their deliberations, although the judges cannot vote during this initial phase. Once a majority of lay jurors reaches a verdict, the three judges may override that verdict or require the case to be tried again before a different lay jury. If the second lay jury agrees with the first, the judges cannot override the verdict.[17]

The debate about jury unanimity and size is a microcosm of the much larger debate in political philosophy about the relationship between the demands of deliberation and the need for decision-making. This debate, in turn, is the political version of the collective action tension we've already seen between the scout bees who are so sure of themselves that they are difficult to persuade to change, and those who listen so well to others that they cannot make up their own minds.[18] Whether the decision-maker is a single ruler seeking advice from a small cadre of advisors, or a Greek city-state seeking the input of all of its citizens, there is a point at which deliberations must stop and a decision must be made. Where that point is, and how to get there, is just one part of the more generalized collective action problem. Every group is faced with decisions that will apply to all members, and in making those kinds of decisions it must balance the need for timely action against the benefits that the decisions might be more accurate and/or more palatable to the minority if they are the product of a process with broad input.

All of these considerations apply to the small group world of jurors. Jurors may be deciding just a single case, but they are enforcing laws that apply to the whole group. They are not only blaming and sometimes punishing in the name of the whole group, but the whole group is watching. Indeed, as we have seen, our urges to blame and punish are evolved proxies for deterrence, so we expect and want others to be watching.

Requiring unanimity spreads the decision-making to the entire jury. This not only may have the benefit of increasing public confidence in jury verdicts, it also forces the majority to listen to the minority. If nothing else, unanimity forces everyone, in both the majority and minority, to rethink positions they may have reached too early by blinking before all the evidence was in. Majority jurors who may have ignored evidence inconsistent with their lightbulb narrative will be forced to consider that evidence, as the minority presents it as part of its counter-narrative. The same goes for blinking members of the minority.

On the other hand, there are substantial costs to unanimity. One irrational juror, in either direction, can force a mistrial, which in most circumstances means that the defendant can be retried, re-incurring all the original expenses and delays.[19] Not surprisingly, the greater the number of jurors required for a decision, the greater the risks of hung juries. The hung jury rate in American jurisdictions requiring unanimous verdicts of twelve generally hovers between 3 percent and 6 percent.[20] But in states permitting non-unanimous criminal verdicts of 9–3, their hung jury rates have dropped significantly. Oregon's rate, for example, went from 3.2 percent before non-unanimity to 2.6 percent after.[21] This may not sound like a significant difference, but considering that more than 100,000 felony jury trials are conducted in the United States every year – and this number does not even consider the even larger number of misdemeanor jury trials – even a small decrease in hung jury rates will come with enormous aggregate savings.[22]

Of course, whether those costs are justified depends on one's perspective. Although the data are not all clear, it seems the conviction rate on retrial is considerably less than the rate the first time around.[23] That's a good thing for defendants but a bad thing for prosecutors and victims. There are also some intriguing papers arguing that outcomes on retrials after hung juries may be more reliable than the outcomes the first time round.[24]

The debates about jury size and unanimity have traditionally been driven by assumptions about the reliability of the system, and judgments about which values we are willing to trade off for others. People both within and outside the criminal justice system have wildly different ideas about its reliability. Some think penitentiaries are teeming with innocent people; some think wrongful convictions are vanishingly rare; most have views in between. Once we concede there is a nonzero risk of wrongfully convicting an innocent person, then the next question is what we are willing to do to reduce that risk. Blackstone once said it is better that ten guilty men go free than that one innocent man be convicted, but of course there must be limits to that proposition. What about letting 1,000 guilty men go free, or 1,000,000?[25] We can insure that no innocent person is ever convicted by letting all guilty people go free, that is, by abolishing the criminal justice system entirely. Most sensible people recognize that is a price we will not pay. So the risk of wrongful convictions remains above zero, we do our best to keep it as low as we can, and where particular scholars stand on jury size and unanimity is usually driven by how big those scholars think the wrongful conviction rate really is, whether they accept the arguments that retrials after hung juries are more reliable than first-time trials, and in general how effective they think keeping juries big and requiring unanimity will help reduce the wrongful conviction rate.

Our evolutionarily-informed view of punishment may add a few insights to this traditional debate. First, given that the bulk of criminal trials are about moral guilt and not factual guilt, and given that people are in remarkable agreement about relative blameworthiness, the marginal benefits of requiring unanimity may well be illusory. Jurors are seldom deciding whether a defendant committed the charged act.

They are instead deciding his blameworthiness, and they do that quite well, and quite reliably, whether they are a single judge or a *dikesteria* of 1,500 Greeks.

On the other hand, precisely because blame is an act of social opprobrium, effective blame requires a social aspect to its pronouncements. A single judge is clothed with the trappings of delegated authority; but the smaller the jury the less clear their social authority. We have seen this diminution in the legitimacy of delegated decision-making most dramatically on the civil side. Business's rush to include binding arbitration provisions in virtually all commercial contracts – quite understandably, to avoid the scandalous costs of civil litigation – has come at the steep price of lost social legitimacy. It is one thing for a jury of six ordinary citizens in Texas, after a public trial, to tell Texaco it must pay Pennzoil US$11 billion for breaking its handshake deal, and quite another for an anonymous arbitrator to enforce an oral promise in a sealed decision delivered after an arbitration conducted behind closed doors.

These evolutionary insights into the debate about the decision rules for juries, and whether and when we should value the demands of decision-making over the ideals of deliberation, will not settle the debate. It's been going on for thousands of years. But as with the insights about how our brains process information, appreciating the evolutionary origins of this debate should enrich and inform it. In the next chapter, we get a little more aggressive, suggesting that our evolutionary insights might actually bear on a handful of substantive legal doctrines, and on policy decisions about whether to reform those doctrines.

Notes to Chapter 9

1. Jury reformers in my state, Colorado, have taken a middle ground. Our civil procedure Rule 47(a)(5), effective in June of 2010, provides that trial judges must permit pre-deliberation discussions unless they make case-specific findings of good cause why those discussions should not be permitted.
2. Jurisdictions, and even judges within jurisdictions, vary widely in their practices regarding written versus oral rulings. A few American states require written orders, but many of these do so only after the fact. So, for example, Pennsylvania requires a written order for every case that is appealed, civil or criminal. Pa. Rules of Appellate Procedure 1925(a). This means judges

can either file a transcript of their oral ruling or put together a written order after they've ruled orally. Similarly, in California and Louisiana the trial judge must prepare a written order at the request of either party. Cal. Ann. Codes, Rule 3.1590(d); La. Stat. Ann. Art. 1917. A few states recognize a few narrow circumstances in which a written order is required. Ohio, for example, requires a written order only in criminal cases in which the trial judge is denying a defendant's motion for post-conviction relief (typically claiming he was denied some constitutional right in the manner in which the trial was conducted). Ohio Stat. Ann. § 2953.21. But most states leave the matter entirely up to the individual trial judge, and my informal survey of judges around the country suggests there is a general preference for written orders. By contrast, English trial judges have a long tradition of reading their rulings from the bench, or "ex tempore." My English judge friends tell me that even in the face of this long tradition many of them do written orders in cases that are complex, seem close, seem likely to be appealed, or have lawyers whom the judge suspects have not provided all the pertinent law. The commonwealth countries seem to have succumbed to the prevalent American tradition of requiring written rulings after the fact, and complying either by filing a transcript of the oral ruling or preparing a new written order based on that oral ruling. There are a few countries, including Belgium, that have statutes or in some cases even constitutions that require all bench judgments to be issued in writing. Belgium Const., art. 149. For a wonderful survey of the contrast between the written legal tradition and the oral one (both for lawyers and judges), see Suzanne Ehrenberg, *Embracing the Writing-Centered Legal Process*, 89 Iowa L. Rev. 1159 (2003–2004).

3. The general verdicts typical in English (and American) jury trials may well have been outlawed in the European Union had the Rome Constitution been ratified. It provided that all "judgments shall state the reasons on which they are based." Treaty Establishing a Constitution for Europe, Protocol 3, Title III, art. 36 (Rome, October 29, 2004). It was never ratified.

4. In order to have reliable information pass between two points, the signal containing that information must be distinguishable from the noise inherent in the transmission. The ratio of the signal-to-noise must be high enough to make the signal discernible from the noise. Claude Shannon, the founder of the branch of applied mathematics called information theory, proved that in any arbitrarily noisy channel there is always some way to code a signal with sufficient reliability to make the reception errors arbitrarily small. The way human brains seem to have solved this problem of signal-to-noise is to be specially attuned to social narratives.

5. Chapter 2, note 6.

6. Reid Hastie & Robyn Dawes, Rational Choice in an Uncertain World: The Psychology of Judgment and Decision Making 118 (Sage 2010).

7. Chapter 2, pages 72–73.

8. THOMAS PETZINGER, JR., OIL AND HONOR: THE TEXACO-PENZOIL WARS (Beard 1999).

9. Reid Hastie has been particularly prominent in studying the storytelling aspects of trial, and his research is among a large body that suggests that jurors do indeed weave the evidence into their own social story, often disregarding, and in post-verdict interviews forgetting, evidence that conflicts with their constructed story. See, e.g., Reid Hastie, *A Cognitive Theory of Juror Decision Making: The Story Model*, 13 CARDOZO L. REV. 519 (1991); Nancy Pennington & Reid Hastie, *Reasoning in Explanation-Based Decision Making*, 49 COGNITION 123 (1999). See generally INSIDE THE JUROR: THE PSYCHOLOGY OF JUROR DECISION MAKING (R. Hastie, ed., Cambridge 1993).

10. For a provocative comparative critique of the American criminal trial process, including the right to remain silent, see WILLIAM T. PIZZI, TRIALS WITHOUT TRUTH (N.Y.U. 1999).

11. It might surprise some American readers that the first of these two fundamental rights of criminal procedure – that the state must prove the case beyond a reasonable doubt – is not enumerated in the U.S. Constitution. The burden of proof in a criminal case is not mentioned anywhere in the Constitution or in any of its Amendments – either the placement of that burden on the prosecution or the setting of that burden at the level of "beyond a reasonable doubt." These are creatures of the Supreme Court's interpretation of the Fifth Amendment's Due Process Clause. In re Winship, 397 U.S. 358 (1970). The second fundamental right – the right to remain silent – is of course enumerated in the Fifth Amendment, but it provides only that a criminal defendant may not be "compelled in any criminal case to be a witness against himself." For almost 175 years this was interpreted to mean just what it says – that judges could not compel criminal defendants to testify in their criminal cases by threatening them with contempt. It was not until the Court decided Miranda v. Arizona, 384 U.S. 436 (1966), that the right to remain silent in court was extended to the right to remain silent at the police station. In England and many commonwealth countries, these same rights to remain silent in court and during interrogation are enshrined by statute. But the rule in other countries is very different. In Norway, for example, a criminal defendant is expected to take the stand and respond to the criminal charges before any other witnesses are called. Pizzi, supra note 10, at 104.

12. 406 U.S. 356 (1972). Unanimity is still required for *federal* criminal trials.

13. Williams v. Florida, 399 U.S. 78 (1970) (upholding Florida's six-person juries in felony cases).

14. Johnson v. Louisiana, supra note 12 (9–3 OK, but 8–4 not); Burch v. Louisiana, 441 U.S. 130 (1979) (criminal juries of six and less must be unanimous); Ballew v. Georgia, 435 U.S. 223 (1978) (a felony jury must consist of at least six jurors).

15. Indeed, the federal constitutional right to a jury in civil cases, guaranteed by the Seventh Amendment, is limited, and in any event does not apply to the states.

16. See, e.g., REID HASTIE ET AL., INSIDE THE JURY (Harvard 1983); Shari Seidman Diamond et al., *Revisiting the Unanimity Requirement: The Behavior of the Non-Unanimous Civil Jury*, 100 NW. U. L. REV. 201 (2006); Michael Glasser, *Letting the Supermajority Rule: Nonunanimous Verdicts in Criminal Cases*, 24 FLA. ST. U. L. REV. 659 (1997).

17. For a good summary of the different kinds of juries in Europe, and different voting requirements, see Ethan J. Leib, *A Comparison of Jury Decision Rules in Democratic Countries*, 5 OHIO ST. J. CRIM. L. 629 (2008).

18. Chapter 7, Consensus Decisions: Bees, Monkeys, Judges and Jurors.

19. In both civil and criminal cases, a so-called hung jury, if it remains hung, results in a mistrial. How long a jury must remain undecided before a mistrial is declared is generally left to the discretion of the trial judge. Many of us gauge that decision by comparing the time the jury has deliberated to the amount of time it took to present the evidence. I might declare a mistrial after one day of unfruitful deliberations in a case that took only a half day to try. By contrast, in the rare cases that take weeks or months, most of us assume it will take the jury several days just to slog through the evidence, let alone reach a unanimous verdict. Prosecutors in hung criminal cases can, and often do, elect to retry the case. Double jeopardy is no bar because the accused was not acquitted. Typically, prosecutors interview jurors after such mistrials in order to determine what the numerical split was, and over which issues. Defense lawyers do the same in case they are faced with a retrial and a renewed opportunity to negotiate a plea bargain.

20. HARRY KALVEN & HANS ZEISEL, THE AMERICAN JURY (Boston 1966) (5.5% nationally); Paula L. Hannaford et al., *How Much Justice Hangs in the Balance? A New Look at Hung Jury Rates*, 83 JUDICATURE 59 (Sept.–Oct. 1999) (2%–3% in federal cases, 6% in state courts in several large urban areas). But there are also some outliers, such as California, where some studies have shown the hung jury rate to be as high as 20%. Hannaford, id.; Leo J. Flynn, *Does Justice Fail When the Jury is Deadlocked?*, 61 JUDICATURE 129 (Sept. 1977). Anecdotally, I doubt that in my own time on the bench I have seen more than 2% of my trials end in a hung jury. By the way, the statistical inquiry is a bit more complicated than it seems because a jury can hang on one count, convict on another, and acquit on yet another. Most studies look at the most serious charge and disregard the rest.

21. Office of Public Defense Services, Appellate Division, "On the Frequency of Non-Unanimous Felony Verdicts in Oregon," A Preliminary Report to the Oregon Public Defense Services Commission, May 21, 2009, available at http://www.oregon.gov/OPDS/docs/Reports/PDSCReportNonUnanJuries .pdf.

22. I derive this 100,000 estimate from two sets of numbers: total felony cases filed, and plea bargaining rates. In state courts alone, roughly two million felony cases are filed each year. NATIONAL CENTER FOR STATE COURTS, EXAMINING THE WORK OF STATE COURTS 2003, at 38, available at http://www.ncsconline.org/d_research/csp/2-3_Files/2003_Criminal.pdf. The federal contribution to total felony filings is relatively small, consisting of less than 100,000 per year. BUREAU OF JUSTICE STATISTICS, U.S. DEP'T OF JUSTICE, COMPENDIUM OF FEDERAL JUSTICE STATISTICS 1997, at 16 tbl.1.2, available at http://www.ojp.usdoj/bjs/pub/pdf/cfjs9902.pdf. The plea bargaining rate is roughly 95%, meaning that of these 2.1 million felony cases filed each year roughly 105,000 end up being tried.

23. In large part that's because on retrial a significant portion of the cases are not in fact retried. In one study of 453 state cases ending in hung juries between 1996 and 1998, 32% of them were plea bargained and 22% were dismissed outright. Paula L. Hannaford-Agor et al., "Are Hung Juries a Problem?," National Center for State Courts (September 30, 2002), available at http://ncsc.contentdm.oclc.org/cdm/singleitem/collection/juries/id/27/rec/1.

24. William S. Neilson & Harold Winter, *The Elimination of Hung Juries: Retrials and Nonunanimous Verdicts*, 25 INT'L REV. L. & ECON. 1 (2005).

25. See Eugene Volokh's wonderful essay, *N Guilty Men*, 146 U. PA. L. REV. 173 (1997).

10 INTO THE GAP: EVALUATING SOME SUBSTANTIVE DISSONANCES

The Reformer is always right about what is wrong. He is generally wrong about what is right.

G. K. Chesterton

We've seen that our brains have been organized by natural selection to blame wrongdoers on the basis of two central considerations: the wrongdoer's intent and the amount of harm he causes. Unless we are psychiatrically disabled, or are having parts of our brains deactivated by transcranial magnetic stimulation, we blame intentionally harmful acts most, intentionally harmful but ultimately harmless acts next, and unintentionally harmful acts least. In legal parlance, we blame intentional crimes most, attempted crimes next, and reckless or negligent crimes least. Inside each of these broad categories – when intent is a tie – we blame and then punish graded to harm.

There are, however, some legal doctrines that alter these two drivers of blame and punishment. In this chapter we apply the test we developed in Chapter 8 to four such dissonances: the felony-murder rule, corporate criminal liability, attempt, and conspiracy. This is hardly an exhaustive list of blame-dissonant legal doctrines. There's the whole world of strict liability, where the law holds people criminally responsible for harms regardless of whether they intended the harms or even whether they were as careful as they should have been.[1] There are even civil doctrines that seem to conflict with our blaming instincts.[2] There is also a whole category of legal rules and expectations that conflicts not with our blame instincts but with other evolved predispositions surrounding our decision-making. These include some of the process dissonances we discussed in the last chapter, as well as legal

notions about causation and proof that seem in deep conflict with
instincts we evolved about risks and probability.[3]

Nor is this analysis meant to be a fully-developed call to reform these
four legal doctrines. Instead, the idea is to use the five-part test developed in Chapter 8 to get us thinking about the relationship between
some settled legal doctrines and our evolved notions of blameworthiness. Whether we should strengthen a particular dissonant doctrine or
abandon it is a "should" that in the end our exercise will not definitively
answer. The hope, however, is that thinking about legal issues in this
evolutionary way might better inform legislatures, judges, legal scholars, and even the general public as they consider the policy implications
of these and other legal doctrines.

Our four examples consist of two "no intent" dissonances (the
felony-murder rule and the doctrine of corporate criminal liability)
and two "no harm" dissonances (attempt and conspiracy). Before
we begin with our no intent dissonances, we need to ask a threshold
question: Are our brains even capable of distinguishing between the
kinds of intent that the law cares about?

MENTAL STATE BOUNDARY PROBLEMS

As we've already discussed, the law in all societies has always recognized subcategories of intentionality more refined than just intentional
versus accidental.[4] The Model Penal Code (MPC), and many states,
divide criminal culpability into four main categories – purposeful acts
(desiring the harmful outcome), knowing acts (willing to cause the
harmful outcome as a side effect to some other desire), reckless acts
(being consciously aware of the substantial and unjustifiable risk that
the act will cause harm), and negligent acts (being unaware of the
substantial and unjustifiable risk that the act will cause harm). Harm
being equal, we blame and punish purposeful acts most, knowing acts
next, reckless acts next, and negligent acts least. To use homicide as an
example, a purposeful murder is the most serious grade of homicide,
often called first-degree murder in many states; a knowing murder
is next, often called second-degree murder; a reckless one is next,

often called manslaughter; and many states also criminalize negligent homicide.[5]

Until recently, there has been very little study of whether ordinary people really do blame and punish at these four levels of culpability, or indeed whether ordinary people can even distinguish between these four mental states. However, some very recent work suggests that, with one important exception, we are very good at appreciating all of these mental state boundaries, both recognizing them and blaming them in the way the law requires.[6] We are so good that we don't even need any definitions of the four mental states, although in all jury trials the judge gives the jury definitions of the appropriate mental states as part of the jury instructions.

I was quite pleasantly surprised by the results of this study. Whenever I instruct jurors on mental state definitions, especially in a case where the evidence requires me to give them definitions of different mental states and requires them to decide which, if any, the prosecution has proved, I always get an uneasy feeling in the pit of my stomach that the jurors are not understanding the definitions. Here's Colorado's jury instruction definition of "knowingly":

> A person acts knowingly with respect to conduct or to a circumstance described by a statute defining an offense when he is aware that his conduct is of such nature or that such a circumstance exists. A person acts knowingly with respect to a result of his conduct when he is aware that his conduct is practically certain to cause the result.[7]

Do you understand this? What does it mean to be "aware" of your own conduct, as opposed to being "aware" of a circumstance? What does "practically certain" mean in the second sentence? And what's the difference between the first and second sentences? Why do we say the defendant has to be "aware" of his conduct or a circumstance, but "practically certain" of the result of his conduct? There are sensible answers to all of these questions, but I suspect they don't really help our jurors understand this definition.[8]

Now imagine you are a juror who has to decide whether a defendant acted "purposefully" or only "knowingly." Here's the "purposefully" instruction you will get in my courtroom:

>A person acts [purposefully] when his conscious objective is to
>cause the specific result proscribed by the statute defining the
>offense.[9]

This seems a bit clearer than the definition of knowingly. A person acts "purposefully" when he actually desires to cause harm and then goes out and causes it. But is there really a difference between purposeful and knowing, between desiring to commit the harm and being "practically certain" that the harm will occur? Even if jurors can distinguish these, is there a moral difference? That is, should we really blame purposeful acts more than knowing acts?

After two decades of giving jurors these kinds of definitions, I became convinced of two things. First, jurors do not really understand the differences between any of these mental state definitions, especially at the purposeful and knowing boundary. Second, even if they could distinguish these mental states, they really don't blame purposeful behavior more than knowing behavior. But I was wrong on both counts.

The experiment proving I was wrong came out of a series of conversations I had several years ago with colleagues in the John D. and Catherine T. MacArthur Foundation's Law and Neuroscience Project.[10] When I suggested that jurors just don't understand the definitions of these mental states, my project colleagues on the law side were quite troubled, because they know how important these differences can be in real criminal cases. When I suggested that in any event jurors (and judges) do not believe purposeful behavior is any more blameworthy than knowing behavior, my philosopher colleagues became quite troubled. Philosophers since Aquinas have argued that it is more blameworthy to cause desired harm than to cause it as a side effect of a different desire.

After all of these conversations, we decided to test the following two propositions empirically: do people understand these four mental states enough to distinguish them, and if so, do they blame them in the order the law does?[11]

We conducted an experiment similar to the Robinson experiments on blame, in which we had subjects read various crime scenarios and then tell us how much they would punish our hypothetical criminal, John.[12] However, instead of drafting the scenarios so that John intentionally caused different levels of harm (which is what Robinson did), we drafted the scenarios to show John having the different mental states of purposeful, knowing, reckless, and negligent, as well as causing different levels of harm. We wrote thirty different crime scenarios, and for each one we wrote five different versions: purposeful, knowing, reckless, negligent, and, as a control, blameless. So there were a total of 150 scenarios.[13] To make sure harm was not affecting our results, we varied our thirty stem scenarios over a wide range of harm.

We presented the scenarios to subjects in an almost-random order, making sure no subject saw two different mental state versions of the same stem. For each scenario we asked subjects to tell us, on a scale of 0–9 (0 being no punishment and 9 being the most severe punishment they could imagine) how much they would punish John.[14] In some versions of the experiment we gave them the definitions of the four mental states only at the beginning, in some we let them have continuous access to the definitions, and in some we never showed them the definitions. We made these changes to see if having the definitions mattered, and also to replicate the fact that in some jurisdictions judges just read the jury instructions, including these mental state definitions, before the jurors retire to deliberate, and in other jurisdictions judges read the instructions but also give the jurors copies of the instructions for them to take back with them during deliberations.

We found, quite contrary to my folk wisdom, that with the exception of the boundary between knowing and reckless, ordinary people are extraordinarily good at detecting these traditional mental states, distinguishing them from each other, and appropriately ordering them by blame and punishment, with or without the aid of definitions. Figure 10.1 shows just how robust this ability was.

The axis on the left depicts the subjects' average punishment ratings and the axis on the bottom represents all thirty stem scenarios, from the least harm on the left to the most harm on the right. The dark line on the top represents subjects' average punishment scores for the purposeful version of the scenarios; the grey line in the middle is for negligence and the light grey line on the bottom represents the blameless control.

No real surprises here, other than that the bottom line shows that a few people feel obligated to blame the blameless, especially when harm is high (a tendency all good insurance defense lawyers, who

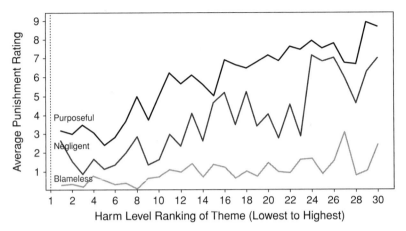

Figure 10.1. We are good at sorting purposeful and negligent harms. From F. Shen et al., *Sorting Guilty Minds*, 86 N.Y.U.L. Rev. 1306, 1338, Fig. 1 (2011).

represent defendants charged with negligence, worry about). This graph is consistent with the idea that we have deeply evolved sensitivities that discriminate between intentional wrongs and accidents. It also shows we are good at distinguishing between avoidable accidents (negligence) and unavoidable ones (blameless). And within a given mental state the punishment we inflict increases as the harm increases, just as our blame theories, and the law, would predict.

However, our subjects were quite poor at distinguishing between knowing and reckless wrongs, as we can see in Figure 10.2, which

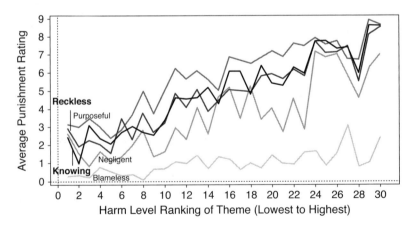

Figure 10.2. Not so good at the K/R boundary. From F. Shen et al., *Sorting Guilty Minds*, 86 N.Y.U.L. Rev. 1306, 1338, Fig. 2 (2011).

overlays the knowing and reckless results onto Figure 10.1. These knowing and reckless curves are hopelessly intertwined; indeed, the average reckless punishment across all scenarios was a bit *more* than the average knowing punishment, even though the law blames knowing wrongs more than reckless ones.[15]

But it's not all bad news. Notice that these intertwining knowing and reckless lines nevertheless fit neatly below purposeful and above negligent, just where our blame theory, and the law, would predict. In other words, if we consider knowing and reckless as a single mental state (K/R), then, contrary to my folk wisdom, ordinary people are quite good at distinguishing purposeful from K/R. So Aquinas and my philosopher colleagues can relax. Subjects were equally good at distinguishing K/R from negligence, so criminal scholars can also forget about my initial worry that none of these categories means anything to real people. Notice also that, like the purposeful and negligent curves, the K/R curve increases in punishment as the harms increase, again just as the law would predict. But what to do about the K/R problem?

The K/R Boundary

It turns out, maybe because the law in its wisdom has always sensed a difficulty at this boundary, that there are not too many crimes that depend on a judge's or jury's ability to discern knowing from reckless behavior.[16] But one huge exception is murder. Under the Model Penal Code, and in many states, there is a big difference between a knowing murder and a reckless one.[17] In Colorado, for example, a knowing murder is called second-degree murder, and carries a mandatory prison sentence of between sixteen years and forty-eight years. A reckless murder, by contrast, is called manslaughter, and carries a nonmandatory sentence of two to six years, meaning that a judge could sentence a defendant convicted of manslaughter to probation. Thus, in the very worst case in my state, the difference between a jury finding a knowing murder and a reckless one is the difference between a forty-eight-year prison sentence and probation. The very *smallest* this difference could ever be is ten years – the difference between the minimum of sixteen years for a knowing murder and the maximum of six years for a reckless murder.

This is not just a theoretical problem. Homicide juries are quite often instructed on lesser forms of murder, including reckless manslaughter.[18] I have tried many second-degree (knowing) murder cases where the jury was also instructed on manslaughter (reckless). Indeed, I have also tried several first-degree murder cases where the jury was also instructed on second-degree murder and manslaughter. I shudder to think that the jurors in those cases had absolutely no basis to distinguish knowing conduct from reckless conduct, and that some defendants are serving long prison sentences and some only very short ones, or none at all, simply because jurors randomly picked between these two states of mind.

Interestingly, in England and Wales, there are currently only two grades of homicide: first-degree murder, which requires a purposeful killing; and manslaughter, which is any non-purposeful killing that is more than mere negligence. The English thus solve this potential problem at the K/R boundary by refusing to recognize any form of what we in America would call second-degree murder. Parliament's Law Commission has at various times considered adopting first and second grades of homicide, but even under these proposals the difference between the two would be whether the purposeful killing was accompanied by deliberation. First-degree murder would be purposeful with deliberation, second-degree murder would be purposeful without deliberation, and manslaughter would remain as it is, without requiring any distinction between knowing and reckless.[19]

We are doing additional studies to look into our results, including one in which we have modified the language in the hypotheticals that signal the mental states. After all, it might very well be that ordinary people can distinguish K from R, but that the language we chose to signal these two states of mind just wasn't good enough. For example, by defining reckless using the pejorative word "disregards," and knowing with the inherently positive word "aware," the words alone might be pushing these two mental states toward each other. Our preliminary results suggest we can improve the separation at the K/R boundary with better signaling language, that is, with better jury instructions defining these two mental states, but that even with the best language we may not be able to solve the conflation between K and R to the degree we need. If these preliminary results hold, what should we do? Several solutions are possible.

First, we could simply abolish the differences between a knowing and a reckless murder. We could adopt the existing English architecture and recognize just two varieties of nonnegligent murder: first-degree murder, which requires a purposeful killing (with or without deliberation); and manslaughter, which could be everything else above a negligent killing. Or we could follow the English proposals of first-degree murder being purposeful with deliberation, second-degree murder being purposeful without deliberation, and manslaughter being knowing or reckless.

If we wanted to retain knowing murder as a grade of homicide between purposeful and reckless, then we might try to redefine knowing and reckless in a more fundamental way, rather than just tinkering with the language. I suspect part of the confusion between the two has to do with the fact that, at least in its Model Penal Code form, we seem to define both knowing and reckless as risk-based states of mind – the only apparent definitional distinction is that a knowing actor realizes the harm is "practically certain" to occur, while the reckless actor knows there is a "substantial risk" that it will occur. But if, as the legal philosophers have argued, a knowing act is really an act about harmful side effects that the actor is willing to cause in order to achieve some other desired result, then we could redefine knowing in that fashion. Such a definition might look something like this:

> A person acts knowingly with respect to a harmful result if he desires a different result, but is willing to cause the harmful one in order to accomplish his desires.

Of course, care will need to be given that in achieving this kind of desire-based separation between knowing and reckless we do not confound purposeful and knowing. We also need to be careful about what I call the "hit man" problem. Could a hit man avoid a first-degree murder conviction by arguing to the jury that he didn't really intend to take his victim's life, and that the killing was just a means to a different desire, to make money? He shouldn't be able to. The difference between the hit man and, say, the pilot who knows he will almost certainly kill civilians when he drops a bomb on the neighborhood factory, is that the hit man's killing is necessarily part of the stream of his desires. Killing his target is the only way, in this particular act, that he can accomplish his real desire of making money. For the pilot, he would be perfectly happy if his act of destroying the factory could be accomplished without killing any civilians. This is the central moral difference between purposeful and knowing wrongs. Any redefinition of knowing that emphasizes the side effect aspects of knowing will be susceptible to this misuse.

Alternatively, if we want to stick with the risk-based model of knowing, we might try to achieve some separation with reckless by using words that more clearly convey a different order of magnitude of risk. The Model Penal Code definition of reckless is:

> A person acts recklessly [with respect to a result] when he consciously disregards a substantial and unjustifiable risk that [his conduct will cause the result].

So we might retain "practically certain" for knowing, but use only "probably" or "likely" for reckless, rather than the "substantial risk" the MPC definition currently requires.[20] Here again, care will have to be taken that by redefining reckless as a lower risk, we do not create confounds with negligence, if that is a category we decide to retain for these crimes. If culpable risks get low enough, jurors might be hard pressed to believe any defendants were "consciously aware" of them.

If we want to keep these two forms of murder but discover we cannot improve the definitions of knowing and reckless as much as we hoped, then at the very least we should consider reducing the gross disparity in punishment between a knowing murder and a reckless one.

The P/K Boundary: The Knobe Effect

Our study shows jurors were quite good at distinguishing purposeful from knowing/reckless, and equally good at blaming purposeful acts more than knowing/reckless ones. But there is still a potential problem at the boundary between purposeful and knowing/reckless. It is called the "Knobe effect," named after the philosopher Joshua Knobe who first detected it experimentally.

Knobe discovered that our ability to detect purposefulness in others seems intractably, and asymmetrically, bound up with harm. When others cause harm, we presume they did so purposefully. No evolutionary problem there. We've already discussed at length how evolution armed our brains with strong presumptions that harms were intentionally caused. But when others do *good*, the presumption of purposefulness seems to evaporate, and we require other proof of good intentions beyond the good results.

In Knobe's experiment, he gave one set of subjects the following hypothetical. A corporation's VP tells the CEO that a new project will increase profits but hurt the environment. The CEO responds, "I don't care about the environment, proceed." The VP proceeds, and the new program does in fact increase profits and hurt the environment. When subjects were asked whether the CEO "intentionally" harmed the environment, 82 percent of them said yes.

But a second set of subjects was given a virtually identical hypothetical, in which the side effect was changed from a harmful one to a beneficial one. The VP tells the CEO that a new profitable program will *help* the environment. The CEO says exactly the same thing, "I don't care about the environment, proceed." The VP proceeds, and the new program does indeed increase profits and help the environment. Now, when subjects are asked if the CEO intentionally *helped* the environment, only 23 percent say yes.[21]

This asymmetry is seldom a problem in the law because people are seldom accused of intending to do good. But there are a small number of cases where a defense might be based on allegations that a harmful outcome was the product of good intentions, and in those cases judges and jurors may be inherently incapable of giving such defense a fair airing. Cases that raise the choice of evils defense – defendant intentionally caused the harm but only to avoid a greater harm – will automatically implicate the Knobe effect.

For example, a few years ago police in Dallas arrested a pastor for burglary, when she was seen taking valuables from the home of one of her parishioners, through a broken window. She claimed she saw two suspicious men lurking near the house, discovered the broken window, and removed the valuables so the burglars would not come back to steal them.[22] I suspect readers' reactions to the pastor's claimed defense were as skeptical as mine. Why did she have to remove the valuables to protect them? Why didn't she just call the police? Why didn't she call her parishioners? Why was she there in the first place? These are all perfectly legitimate questions, but Knobe's results suggest that in some cases like this a defendant actually trying to do good may find it very hard to convince a jury, because our deeply asymmetric impulses may make it hard for us to give such defendants a fair shake.

Even in less exotic kinds of cases, jurors' willingness to infer bad intentions from bad results may create a problem if we ask them to distinguish a defendant's bad intentions from a willingness to cause bad side effects – that is, to distinguish between the culpability categories of purposeful and knowing. This, of course, was exactly the kind of problem Knobe used in his experiment. The hypothetical corporate CEO in the first version of the experiment is arguably guilty only of knowingly causing harm – because it was a mere side effect of his main intention to increase profits. He would have been perfectly happy if the new project increased profits with no damage to the environment. If jurors overpoweringly assume purposefulness in high-harm cases, then perhaps in those cases we also need to rethink the boundary between purposeful and knowing.[23]

TWO NO INTENT DISSONANCES: THE FELONY-MURDER RULE AND CORPORATE CRIMINAL LIABILITY

The Felony-Murder Rule

We saw an example of the felony-murder rule in Chapter 8, when we discussed the Lisl Auman case. In its most general form, this rule treats a defendant who commits a felony during which another person was killed as if the defendant intentionally killed that person after deliberation. There are a myriad of versions of the felony-murder rule, with the strictest applying to any death that occurs during a felony. So, for example, under this strict version, a bank robber would be guilty of first-degree murder if a teller dies of a heart attack suffered during the robbery. He would also be treated as a first-degree murderer if his co-robber were killed by police. The death need not even happen near the defendant, either in time or space, as we saw with the *Auman* case.

Less drastic versions of the rule limit it in various ways. For example, some jurisdictions do not apply it to the death of a co-participant or when the death was accidental, some cut off its application once a defendant is in custody, and some limit it to only the most serious of felonies. Even in its most limited version, however, the felony-murder rule is still a "no intent" dissonance, because it forces jurors and judges to punish a defendant who may have had no intention to kill as if he intentionally and deliberately killed. Let's subject this strange legal rule to our five-part test.

First, does the felony-murder rule conflict with what is likely an evolved intuition? Absolutely. It requires us to blame and punish people as if they had an intent to kill when they had no such intent. As we've seen, intent is one of the two key drivers of our evolved instinct to blame, so the felony-murder rule is deeply dissonant with our deepest notions of blameworthiness. The outrage people expressed when Lisl Auman was sentenced to the mandatory life in prison without the possibility of parole emanated from this deep dissonance. We simply do not have the urge to punish non-killers as if they were killers.

The second factor is whether the legal rule is itself evolutionarily rooted. Here, the answer is a definite no. Nothing about the evolutionary roots of blame discussed in this book supports an argument that we evolved an urge to punish murders without regard to the murderers' intentions. Yes, killing is the ultimate genetic harm, but it is hard to see how punishing accidental killers, let alone non-killers, would have ever had any net adaptive advantage. As with punishing any accidental harm, punishing accidental killers incurs high cost with very little benefit. Given that the punishment for killing was almost always death or banishment, you can bet that the accidental killer and his family would have resisted (to the death) any attempt to punish him. Yet punishing accidents has very little deterrent benefit: it might marginally deter fakers and might also make people more careful, but that's about it. One cannot deter unintentional acts.

Punishing robbers whenever a death occurs in the course of the robbery will certainly deter robbers from bringing guns to robberies. But how will it deter tellers from having heart attacks, or police from shooting at robbers, or, as in the Lisl Auman case, a co-defendant from shooting police then killing himself?

History also suggests there is no evolutionary foundation for the felony-murder rule. As a limited, stand-alone version of strict liability the felony-murder rule has no known ancient or even medieval antecedents.[24] No societies have left any record indicating that they treated ordinary criminals as murderers if for some reason beyond the criminals' control someone died in the course of the crime. Even in modern systems the felony-murder rule seems a peculiar and quite unique invention of late nineteenth-century English common law. It is unknown in any Continental legal systems. Its first articulation appears to have been in a series of English cases decided in the 1880s, but even then these courts often required proof that the defendant was culpable in some fashion. And in those few cases where the instructing judges did not require any culpability, they openly invited jurors to ignore the rule.[25]

The felony-murder rule got imported from England to America by academic accident. A handful of American states adopted it only because some English legal commentators had quite incorrectly reported that the rule was robust and well established in England. In fact, it was never widespread in England, and by the time it was gaining traction in America it was already being criticized roundly by English commentators. It was formally abolished by Parliament in 1957.

This uneven and quite recent history belies any notion that the felony-murder rule might itself be grounded on any deep evolutionary truths. This is not, of course, to say there are not policy arguments in its favor. Death is such a serious and permanent harm that one can imagine perfectly good reasons for rational lawmakers to say that when someone dies during the commission of a felony we will make the felon pay the price for the death. But these policy reasons are not rooted in our blaming natures, which, as we've seen, care more about a wrongdoer's intent than the harm he causes.

The third factor in our analysis is to try to quantify the degree of the dissonance. There have been several recent studies that show that ordinary people punish much less severely than the felony-murder rule requires. For example, in a 2009 study subjects were asked to rank twenty-four different crime scenarios ranging across harms. The blaming scale therefore went from one (for the least blameworthy) to twenty-four (for the most). The twenty-four scenarios included the following four scenarios at the high-harm end: a first-degree intentional and deliberate murder, two felony-murders, and a reckless manslaughter. One of the felony-murders involved a residential burglary in which John and his co-participant are both unarmed, but his co-participant kills the resisting victim with the victim's gun during a struggle. The second felony-murder was a drug dealing scenario in which John brings drugs to a party, and one of the guests uses too much and dies from an overdose.

On the 24-point scale, subjects ranked the intentional deliberate murder at an average of 23.3, the burglary felony-murder at 17.9, the drug felony-murder at 14.7, and the reckless manslaughter at 19.0. That is, ordinary citizens viewed both of these kinds of felony-murderers as being substantially less culpable than the intentional and deliberate killer, and in fact even less culpable than the reckless killer.[26] These studies confirm what probably needs no confirmation: the felony-murder doctrine is much harsher than ordinary people think is warranted.

The fourth factor asks whether the legal rule is directionally dissonant from the evolved trait. The answer for felony-murder is no. We all have the urge to punish felony murderers more than if no death occurred during the commission of their felony. This dissonance is about the *amount* of punishment the felony-murder rule requires.

The final factor is whether the legal rule has become riddled with exceptions or outright rejections. The answer for the felony-murder rule is a resounding yes. Its English inventors abolished it only eighty years after its invention. In America, it has become so riddled with exceptions and limitations that it's hardly recognizable as a coherent doctrine. Two states (Hawaii and Kentucky) do not recognize it at all, and a third (Michigan) has abolished it by judicial decision. Several states expressly reject its central equivalency outright, making a felony-murder some lesser degree of murder. The Model Penal Code effectively abolished it by requiring that the prosecution prove the defendant acted recklessly with regard to the death. Even in the remaining forty-three states that have operating felony-murder rules, all but a handful of them severely limit the reach of the rule, in all the ways we have already discussed, including requiring the felon to be the proximate cause of the death and not applying the rule when it is the felon's accomplice who dies.

Putting these five factors together makes out a pretty compelling case for rethinking the felony-murder rule. It conflicts with our deepest notion that we blame only intentional wrongs, it is not itself deeply-grounded either in our evolution or in our jurisprudence, it grossly over-punishes in the eyes of ordinary citizens, and in its one-hundred thirty years of existence it has already almost winked out either by outright abolition or by exceptions that swallow it.

Corporate Criminal Liability

Another giant modern exception to the principle that we only blame and punish intentional actors is the doctrine of corporate criminal liability. A corporation is not a person, it has no mind and it therefore cannot act with any particular state of mind. Of course, its officers, directors, and employees can, and if they act criminally with the required states of mind they can be prosecuted. In fact, in those circumstances they quite often have also committed the crime of conspiracy, itself a potential dissonance that we take up later in this chapter. But a corporation has no mind and therefore cannot have a guilty mind, as the criminal law generally requires.

Yet under current American federal law and the laws of all American states, corporations can themselves be held criminally responsible for certain criminal acts of their officers, directors, and employees. Corporations cannot be imprisoned, so the criminal sanction imposed on them is a criminal fine, paid ultimately by the shareholders. How odd that if conspirators incorporate, they have created a third "person" who might now be deemed to have intentionally committed the crime they carried out. Of course, if the conspirators are the only shareholders, then it doesn't make much difference. But corporations often have many shareholders who have no idea that corporate officials are committing a crime; some corporations are even publicly held. These circumstances raise the question of whether it makes sense to hold the corporation criminally liable for the acts of its principals, when the only additional real people punished by such a rule are arguably innocent shareholders.

The public policy answer given by most courts and legislatures is that by making shareholders ultimately pay the financial price for the crimes of their officers, directors, and employees, we incentivize shareholders to be watchdogs over those officials. This may make sense in some instances, but it is hard to see how much watchdogging a teacher in Altoona, who acquired her stock through her teacher's union's pension, can reasonably be expected to perform over corporate officers in a publicly-held New York bank.

English law has been much more restrained in holding corporations criminally responsible. It will do so only in three circumstances – where a crime is a strict liability crime, which requires no state of mind; where an act of Parliament specifically imposes corporate criminal liability (and there are very few of those); or where a guilty individual is the corporation's "directing mind and will."[27] This latter category has been interpreted by English courts very narrowly, and it is quite difficult in England for a corporation to be found criminally liable on the basis of the criminal intentions of its officers or directors.[28]

In the United States, there have been some recent rumblings that might turn into a healthy debate on the continuing legitimacy of corporate criminal liability. Much ink was spilled when my friend Jed Rakoff, a trial judge on the federal court in the Southern District of New York, refused to accept a $33 million settlement between the Securities and Exchange Commission (SEC) and Bank of America. In its civil lawsuit against the bank, the SEC claimed that the bank paid huge bonuses to executives of Merrill Lynch right before the bank took Merrill over, without disclosing the bonuses to the bank's shareholders. Thus, the SEC was suing the bank on behalf of the bank's shareholders to remedy a wrong done to the shareholders.

And who would ultimately pay the $33 million? Why, the injured shareholders, of course, because the shareholders are always the ones who ultimately pay any corporate fine. So, these poor bank shareholders first get scammed by their own directors into paying huge bonuses to the executives of another corporation, and then to "cure" the wrong they have to pay another $33 million to the government. In rejecting the settlement, using language that sounds suspiciously like an expression of our evolved moral intuitions, Rakoff concluded that the settlement "does not comport with the most elementary notions of justice and morality, in that it proposes that the shareholders who were the victims of the Bank's alleged misconduct now pay the penalty for that misconduct."[29]

There have been a few other instances of judges expressing frustration with the fact that punishing a corporation only punishes its shareholders. Most of these cases were part of the legal fallout from the great corporate scandals of 2008 and 2009. For example, in a criminal case the SEC brought against Barclays, Judge Emmet Sullivan of the Federal District Court for the District of Columbia chastised federal prosecutors for failing to prosecute the individual corporate officers who actually committed the acts and had the guilty minds:

> You agree there must have been some human being who violated U.S. laws? Can I just share a thought with you? You know what? If other banks saw that the government was being rough and tough with banks and requiring banking officials to stand before federal judges and enter pleas of guilty, that might be a powerful deterrent to this type of conduct.[30]

But is holding corporations responsible for the wrongs of their officials really the kind of evolutionary dissonance that requires closure, that demands we abolish or limit corporate criminal liability? To answer that question, let's subject the law of corporate criminal liability to our five-part test.

The first inquiry is whether we are confident that the evolutionary proposition really is evolutionary. As we have discussed throughout this book, natural selection armed us with powerful blaming and punishing instincts, and we aimed and have always aimed those instincts at real people intending us real harm. There is little doubt that extending criminal liability to a fictitious person conflicts with our evolved notions of individual blameworthiness. A corporation can no more intentionally cause harm than a wheel, or a town.[31] The moral intuitions that drive our blame were forged in an era of intense social living, and are finely tuned to other *people*. People have intentions, people act on those intentions, and people are responsible for those intentional acts. Holding a fictitious entity criminally liable for acts it could not have intended is deeply dissonant with our evolved blame and punishment urges.

The second inquiry is whether the legal rule might advance its own evolutionary core. The answer here is a definite no. There is nothing I can think of that is even arguably adaptive about holding corporations criminally liable. There were no "corporations" in the Pleistocene, other than our own close-knit groups. One might at first blush argue that the notion of corporate criminal responsibility springs from our fear of group crime, just like the doctrine of conspiracy, discussed later in this chapter. But that explanation has it backwards. Our innate fear of group crime might very well explain why some legal doctrines operate to increase the punishment for crimes committed by individuals acting in concert, but those individuals, even when they act through a corporation, are already subject to those enhancing doctrines. Holding an entire corporation liable for the acts of its criminal members has exactly the opposite effect: it punishes members (shareholders) who might have known nothing about the crime and did not participate in it at all. Our evolved Rules 1 (don't steal) and 2 (don't breach) were aimed at individual members of our small groups, not at groups, and certainly not at groups we pretend are people. Likewise, our blaming and punishing instincts (Rule 3) were aimed at the individuals violating the other two rules. We did not engage in the symbolic punishment of punishing the "usual suspects," nor did we blame and punish whole groups. We hold individuals morally responsible for their actions.

That corporate criminal liability is itself not a core evolutionary concept is further evidenced by the fact that corporations and other legal group fictions have long populated the law, but the idea they might be criminally responsible is a very recent invention. For the first 700 years of the common law, criminal guilt was personal, and no corporation, venture, or other association of individuals could be held criminally responsible. As William Blackstone put it, "Punishments . . . are only inflicted for that abuse of that free will, which God has given to a man. . . . A corporation cannot commit treason, or felony, or other crime."[32]

Corporate criminal liability was invented by the U.S. Congress in the early 1900s, when it passed legislation making corporations criminally liable for undercutting government price controls.[33] Since that time, in both federal and state legislation, the notion that corporations could be held criminally liable has expanded into virtually every aspect of the law, although it is most commonly invoked in the regulatory arena. Thus, corporations in almost all American jurisdictions have been found criminally liable for violating environmental laws, securities laws, and banking laws.

The third inquiry is to try to gauge how far from the core the dissonant rule has in fact strayed. There really is no quantitative aspect to this inquiry for corporate criminal liability. The evolved core says corporations can't be morally responsible because they are not moral agents; the dissonance makes them morally responsible. This dissonance is instead the kind of "directional dissonance" that is the subject of the fourth inquiry. Before this legal rule, corporations were not treated by the law (or by our evolved blaming instincts) as moral agents. After it, they were.

Finally, the fifth inquiry is whether the dissonant rule is riddled with exceptions, or with jurisdictions rejecting it outright. Here, the legal landscape is mixed. The Model Penal Code limits corporate criminal liability to those circumstances in which the crime was authorized or "recklessly tolerated" by the board of directors or by a "high managerial agent."[34] And although twelve states have adopted this limitation, Congress, the federal courts, and other states have not. They permit corporations to be held criminally responsible for any criminal act of any employee performing his or her customary duties, if that act benefitted the corporation.[35] The decisions of judges like Jed Rakoff and Emmet Sullivan, in rejecting settlements or plea bargains grounded on blaming nonmoral agents and then punishing blameless individual shareholders, may be the beginning of a reexamination of these broad and dissonant rules. At the moment, however, the rule is fairly entrenched.

Of course, proponents of making corporations criminally responsible have plausible policy reasons for doing so, including arguments about deterrence. But the whole purpose of our evolutionary inquiry is to shift the debate from a mere clash of policies to a clash between policy and human nature. Making corporations criminally responsible comes at the cost of violating one of the deepest moral intuitions people have: that only people, not things or even animals, are moral agents who can justly be blamed. I recognize that unlike some other morally blameless but sentient entities, such as animals and small children, we need not worry about the harm that unwarranted blame might inflict on corporations, precisely because corporations are fictional beings. But we need very much to worry about the harm it inflicts on innocent shareholders.

As we tally our five factors, a good case can be made that corporate criminal liability must yield to our most basic notions of blameworthiness and responsibility, and should either be severely restricted or abolished entirely. Admittedly, there is little hope that legislatures will be the laboratories in which these kinds of reforms will percolate, given the current political climate in which general corporate-bashing seems popular across the political spectrum. Maybe this reform will begin to catch fire in the criminal courts, where judges have great discretion in approving plea bargains, and where we should be especially committed to blaming only the blameworthy.

TWO NO HARM DISSONANCES: ATTEMPT AND CONSPIRACY

Attempt

When a person attempts to inflict harm, he may in some circumstances be held criminally responsible for the attempt, even though the attempt failed and no harm resulted.[36] When John decides to murder Victor, follows him home from work, pulls a gun, and tries to fire it as Victor goes from his car to his house, but the gun jams, John has committed in most jurisdictions the crime of attempted first-degree murder. But what if John didn't get so far along? What if all he did was buy a gun? In all jurisdictions that would not be enough for attempted murder, because of course at that point, without more, we have no idea whether John is on his way to a murder or to a shooting range.

As this example shows, attempt requires us to think carefully about two difficult issues: the nature of "harm" and the point at which mere preparation should become punishable as a crime. Victor was not harmed in the manner John intended, but surely he was harmed, assuming he became aware of the attempt on his life. Imagine your emotional state if you discovered you'd be dead if a gun didn't jam. Even if Victor was not aware of the attempt on his life as it was happening, by the time the law becomes involved he will have learned about it from police, prosecutors, and witnesses. The witnesses themselves would also suffer a kind of emotional harm. Indeed, some legal philosophers justify the criminalization of attempt not as an exception to the harm principle, but as a recognition that "harm" can be a very broad matter of disturbing the ordinary social order.[37]

Judge-made common law phrased the acts required to constitute an attempt in many different and often conflicting ways, from anything "beyond mere preparation," to a "dangerous proximity to completion" to "unambiguously and unequivocally indicat[ing] the intent to commit the completed crime."[38] The Model Penal Code uses the phrase "substantial step," and follows the "indicative of intent" approach.[39] To qualify as an attempt under the MPC, an actor must take steps toward the commission of the target offense substantial enough to indicate that he intended to commit the target offense.

As you might guess, deciding what is and what is not a step sufficiently "substantial" to constitute an attempt is a difficult inquiry, about which the law has had much to say, little of it terribly enlightening. On the one hand, just buying the gun with the unexpressed idea of using it to kidnap and murder Victor – what the common law called "mere preparation" – will not be enough. On the other hand, acts much further from actually pulling out the gun and firing it at Victor might be enough, such as merely laying in wait for him.[40] However phrased, most legal scholars agree that the gist of the substantial step requirement for attempt is that the wrongdoer must take a step that is a kind of moral point of no return.[41] Although this point is often difficult to locate, the broad policy considerations driving its setting seem clear enough. Not criminalizing any attempts will leave some dangerous people on the streets, many of whom will try the crime again and succeed the second time round. But authorizing state intervention too soon comes at the cost of punishing people who may just have been engaged in some sort of active fantasy or, even if they were serious, might come to their moral senses before doing any damage at all.

Attempts to commit a target offense are universally punished less than the target offense itself. In some jurisdictions, attempts are punishable by some stated fraction of the punishment for the target offense, typically one-half. Other jurisdictions, like mine, reach similar if not exactly identical results by classifying attempts to commit felonies as one level below the target offense. For example, in Colorado first-degree murder is a Class 1 felony, carrying a penalty of death or mandatory life in prison. Attempted first-degree murder is a Class 2 felony, carrying a mandatory prison sentence of between sixteen and forty-eight years.

What might an evolutionary perspective tell us about the propriety of the attempt exception to the harm principle? Let's consult the oracle of our five-step approach.

First, as with all of our blaming dissonances, the evolved predisposition that we are considering – our predisposition to blame and punish third-party wrongdoers based on intent and harm – is most likely evolutionarily rooted. Intent without any harm does not trigger our blame instincts the way that intent plus harm does.

But is the law of attempt itself evolutionarily rooted? Here, the picture is pretty fuzzy. Adults, and even children and subjects with their rTPJs knocked out, still blame attempts, they just blame them less than intentional harms. We can certainly construct an evolutionary story in which punishing mere attempts would have been advantageous to our emergent groups. Group members who intentionally tried to hurt other members to satisfy their desires would probably have been just as dangerous to the group as those who did in fact hurt others to satisfy their desires. The touchstone of this danger is the actor's intentionality – he is saved from harming others only by a version of moral luck. Had we known about such failed attempts, there would certainly have been a benefit to punishing them. But would that benefit have been worth the punishment costs? It all depends on how frequently we were able to detect attempts, and how frequently yesterday's attempt became tomorrow's completed crime. If these frequencies were high enough, then there's no reason our blaming and punishing brains would not have been tuned to attempts just as much as they are tuned to completed crimes.

Much depends, however, on how one defines "attempt." Our ancestral groups, like our current ones, were full of unexpressed harmful intentions. We all brood about cheating and even physically harming one another. For some of us the brooding is all we do, for others we do brooding plus a little bit of acting out, for others still the brooding is just the beginning of what will become a completed crime. It seems unlikely that natural selection would have built into our blame instinct a sense of blame for mere brooding, for no other reasons than that everybody broods, and mere brooding is not reliably detectable. We all have defection fantasies, even when we are smiling and cooperating. Fantasies seldom mature into wrongs. On the flip side, plotters are sometimes pretty good at hiding their intentions. Is John just sad because we scolded him for being out of position during this morning's hunt, or is he plotting revenge? Even our best social brains would probably not have been very good at distinguishing these two circumstances.

Requiring some action – some objective sign of the beginnings of an intention to act out – solved each of these problems. It freed us from impossible mind reading, and simultaneously separated the wheat of nascent wrongs from the chaff of just blowing off some internal steam. The law's requirement of a "substantial step" toward the commission of the crime may well reflect an evolved restraint on punishing bad intentions.

But even with this action requirement, blaming attempts might still not have been adaptive. Attempts could have been disruptive in our emergent groups, but on the whole they were probably not nearly as disruptive as a completed crime that inflicted harm on another member – usually fatal harm for it even to be considered a crime. The discovery of an attempt might itself have reduced the chances that a second attempt would be successful. The target victim would surely become more vigilant. More subtly, the attempt might transform the criminal, in a way similar to how inflicting punishment can immediately wash all the blame urges out of the punisher, or how a punisher's forgiveness can transform both the punisher and the punished. In our small close-knit groups, if I threw a spear at you in a fit of anger and it just missed you, the attempt itself might have been cathartic enough to convince me, and more importantly you, that we needed to patch up our differences. That is, attempt might not even have been blameworthy in the second-party context. When we move to third parties, our brains might very well have been built to ignore attempts altogether. If I see you throw a spear at someone else, and it just misses him, are my genes really better off incurring the costs of punishing you?

This gets us to another, perhaps more important, reason why we might not have been built to blame attempts. Second-party punishment could take care of most attempts. If I don't manage to patch things up with the guy I just missed with my spear, he'll retaliate. Other group members need not get involved. The cycle of violence in these circumstances does not get ratcheted up like it does with real harm. Think about the different ways you feel between being the victim of an attempt and the victim of a completed crime. When the guy next to you at the football game punches you in the nose, the retaliation game is on. If he swings and misses, cooler heads – yours, his, and everyone around you – have a chance to defuse the situation.

As for whether other species punish attempt, even in a second-party context, there is no literature on the subject, but my guess is that the answer is no. Attempt is almost entirely a state of mind, and few animals can perceive intentionality in other animals. They lack what we have already described as "theory of mind." When I throw a tennis ball at my dog and it misses him, he probably feels no threat at all. I'm playing fetch. When I shoot a gun at you and it misses, you perceive something not just about the world of physics but also about the intentions that are swirling inside my head. A few nonhuman primates might have primitive theories of mind,[42] but I am unaware of any literature on whether they perceive, let alone blame and punish, attempts.

Finally, the dubious historical pedigree of attempt is some evidence that it might not be evolutionarily grounded. The criminalization of attempt seems to be quite a recent invention. As we have seen, ancient states did not even intervene for most serious crimes. They certainly did not intervene for attempted crimes. In fact, the harm principle – which requires actual harm before the criminal law will act – has a long tradition dating back to Hammurabi, and no doubt in unwritten forms long before. Even at English common law, attempt was not recognized as a stand-alone crime until 1784.[43] Until then, as one legal historian put it, "in those forthright days, a miss was as good as a mile."[44] Even when the common law finally got round to criminalizing attempt, all attempts – even to commit felonies – were themselves just misdemeanors.[45] This recent legal pedigree suggests that the fact that all of us seem to blame attempts might well be a modern cultural artifact. It would be fascinating to see how existing primitive societies deal with attempts; I am unaware of any literature about this.

So the answer to our second inquiry – is blaming attempt itself evolutionary grounded – is a definite "not sure," although it most likely is not.

The third inquiry is to try to quantify the dissonance between the legal rule and the conflicting evolved urge. People do in fact blame attempt less than the completed crime, but they also blame it considerably more than an unintentional harm. Remember the Grace poison experiments from Chapter 2. Unimpaired subjects blamed and punished Grace most for intentionally poisoning her friend, next for trying to poison her but failing, and least for accidentally poisoning her. The way we all blame Grace corresponds nicely to the way most jurisdictions punish attempts – less than the completed crime (how much less varies considerably between jurisdictions), but substantially more than reckless or negligent acts (much more in almost all jurisdictions).

The fourth factor is the directional test: does our legal rule make blameworthy what our evolved predisposition does not, or vice versa? If in fact our ancestors had no predisposition to blame and punish attempts, then the law of attempt would indeed be one of these directional dissonances. But if, armed with theory of mind and an intense interest in the intentions of others, they really did blame and punish some attempts, then the law of attempt would not be directionally dissonant with our evolved blame and punishment instincts.

Finally, the last factor asks whether the legal rule is the subject of many exceptions or has even been abandoned in many legal systems. Here the answer is an unequivocal no. The law of attempt is alive and well in every judicial system I know about, and seems to be a universally recognized exception to the harm principle. Everywhere there is a defined crime there is also the crime of attempting to commit that defined crime.[46]

How does our five-part test come out on attempt? Things are mixed, mixed enough that I would never hazard to argue that we should abandon or limit attempt because it allegedly conflicts with our evolved blaming instincts. Attempt itself might have some evolutionary roots. Even if it doesn't, it's hard to see how attempt conflicts in any deep way with our blaming instincts. We blame based on an interaction between intent and harm, with intent being the more important factor. The doctrine of attempt blames based on intent with no harm, as long as there is some act sufficiently suggestive of such intent. How much conflict is there, really, between these two rules?

There are behavioral studies that show our punishment instincts do not get as strongly engaged when we perceive a wrongful intent unaccompanied by any harm, but they still seem to get engaged.[47] Modern humans, whether by natural selection or culture, are quite morally comfortable blaming attempt. Just ask any parent whether we should blame and punish a pedophile whose child kidnapping gets foiled.

Yet many legal scholars, especially legal philosophers, seem pretty confused all around when it comes to attempt. We judges are not much better, with our confusing definitions of what it takes to constitute a "substantial step" toward the commission of the target crime. The confusion may have its origins in the fact that our blame and punishment circuits are not integrated. As with the general case of moral luck, we feel deeply conflicted whenever our blame instincts tell us one thing ("blame that terrible intention") and our punishment instincts another ("no harm no foul").

Fortunately, jurors don't seem quite as confused. I can't remember a single attempt case I have presided over where the jury's verdict seemed to be the product of confusion over issues like "substantial step." This may be because stand-alone attempt cases are, at least in my experience, quite rare. Cases in which attempt is charged almost always include other charges as well, often crimes alleged to have been committed along the way toward the attempted crime. In our hypothetical, if John lays in wait for Victor he probably has already committed the crimes of stalking and perhaps even criminal trespass, depending on where he chooses to wait. In my au pair case mentioned in the Introduction, if the girl had survived, then the defendant would still have committed burglary (entering the bedroom through the window), first-degree assault, and attempted first-degree murder.

In the rare stand-alone attempt case, if our policy judgment is that attempts should still be prosecuted and punished – and there is no indication of any reforming zeal to abolish attempt – and if we harbor any serious concern that jurors might not be naturally attuned to blame attempt in these kinds of cases, then perhaps judges in their instructions, and certainly prosecutors in their presentation, could help jurors get over any resistance by focusing on harm. There *is* harm in these cases, it just takes a slightly expanded perspective to see it. I can imagine jury instructions that might explain that expanded perspective to jurors in stand-alone attempt cases, perhaps something like this:

> Members of the jury, you may be wondering why our laws make it a crime to attempt to _____. First, as I have already instructed you, laws are passed by the General Assembly, and you as jurors have taken an oath to uphold those laws, whether you agree with them or not. But it may help you to know the reasons behind the law of attempt. In olden days in England, attempt was not a crime. If someone fired a gun at another person and missed, the law took

the view "no harm no foul." But we have come to realize that in our modern, complex, and interrelated world such behaviors can in fact cause great harm. They can psychologically harm the intended victim and his or her family. They can harm the fabric of society, as we all then have to worry about whether there will be another attempt, and whether this one will succeed.

I doubt I would ever give such an instruction over what would surely be the objections of defense lawyers, and I also doubt our Supreme Court would approve such an instruction. So perhaps the better way to convey this information is through the lawyers. Prosecutors in stand-alone attempt cases need to realize, as most good ones do, that they may be swimming upstream against a powerful intuition not to punish because there has been no harm. They need to pound away, as early as jury selection, about how there really is this broader kind of harm in attempts. The challenge for defense lawyers is more subtle. They are probably better off staying away from the lack of harm, and relying on the juror's suspected intuitions not to punish when there is no harm, especially when the jury will be getting traditional jury instructions, which do not mention harm as an element of attempt.

There is a more radical approach. We could expressly add to the definition of attempt the requirement that the victim suffer harm, but then define harm broadly enough to include the pure emotional harm the victim suffers when he first learns of the attempt.[48] This would have the benefit of addressing any no-harm dissonance head-on, by converting attempt into a harm-based crime, and would force judges, jurors, and lawyers to treat attempt just like any other harm-based crime.[49] On the other hand, proving this more distended form of harm beyond a reasonable doubt might present unacceptably high barriers to the prosecution. Must prosecutors charging attempts prove that the victims actually learned of the attempts, or that their friends and relatives suffered actual emotional harm when they learned of them? Do we really need psychologists testifying that the victim and his friends and relatives were emotionally injured when they learned a bullet missed the victim by an inch?

In the end, it seems to me that attempt is a difficult doctrine mostly because it is difficult to apply, not because it conflicts in any serious way with our blame instincts. It is hard for jurors to decide how far toward the commission of the completed crime a defendant must go before he's taken a "substantial step," particularly in the rare case where a defendant is only charged with attempt. That difficulty would probably exist whether or not our ancestors evolved an instinct to blame attempts.

Conspiracy

At common law, the crime of conspiracy was completed the moment two or more people reached an agreement to commit a crime, whether or not they took any steps toward its commission.[50] Although the Model Penal Code and most states have added the requirement that the conspirators take some "overt act" in furtherance of the conspiracy, that requirement is miles short of the "substantial step" required for attempt.[51] Any act at all, no matter how trivial, and no matter whether legal or illegal, is an "overt act" for conspiracy purposes if it furthers, however slightly, the object of the conspiracy. If John and Charlie agree to kidnap Victor, and John buys some duct tape to be used for it, John and Victor have completed the crime of conspiracy.

Conspiracy is quite a different legal and evolutionary animal than attempt. First, with conspiracy we don't have to guess about unexpressed intentions to cause harm. The conspirators have expressed their intentions to each other. Yes, some "conspiracies" might just be a sort of loud group brooding. But we are not left, as we are with attempt, to wonder about the nature of a wholly internal fantasy. For that same reason, conspiracy's "overt act" is really the second act, the first being the act of mutual agreement.

Most significantly, defections by two or more members were substantially more dangerous to our emergent groups than single defections. Like many of our primate cousins, we constantly formed and reformed alliances. Those alliances could threaten dominant members and could even result in a permanent dissolution of the group. Just as living in groups boosted our fitness, defecting in groups boosted the threat of the defection. At the very least, we needed to pay attention to these shifting alliances as we navigated our way through The Social Problem. It would therefore not be surprising at all if natural selection armed us with a special sensitivity to agreements between two or more

members to defect. And indeed, there is lots of social science literature, both psychological and economic, demonstrating that we do in
fact perceive a special kind of danger in group criminality.[52]

The special nature of this danger was recognized by the early common law of conspiracy, under which our fear of group crime ran so
deep that there was no general requirement of an overt act. The mere
agreement between two or more people to commit a crime was a
crime.[53]

There has always been a palpable political aspect to the law of conspiracy. It bloomed in the common law as a tool by which English
kings could fight real and perceived attempts at rebellion.[54] Its first
English formulation and application happened in the Star Cham-
ber in 1611.[55] Political considerations remain a big part of the contemporary controversy over the utility of conspiracy, as legal scholars debate whether our deeply-seated fears of group criminal action
any longer justify the sweeping manner in which the law of conspiracy is sometimes used by modern prosecutors. Some critics of
conspiracy have argued that we should now be *less* fearful of group
crime than individual crime, because the modern technology that con-
nects conspirators also increases the risks that the conspiracy will be
discovered.[56]

To put this in the terms of our five-part analysis, criminalizing
conspiracy itself seems to have obvious evolutionary roots. That means
we never get past our second factor, and that any debates over the law
of conspiracy and our evolved blaming intuitions must be fought on
an equal evolutionary playing field.

Two small but important points remain as we leave this discussion of
conspiracy. The first is the problem of uncompleted conspiracies. Conspirators are often convicted and punished for completing the target
crime, then punished additionally for the conspiracy. No evolutionary
dissonance there. These conspiring wrongdoers may be blamed and
punished because they caused actual harm. And they may be blamed
and punished even more severely because their harm was accomplished through their conspiring group, behavior that deserves special
approbation.[57] But what about uncompleted conspiracies? These are
a kind of attempt, and therefore suffer from all the same conceptual
problems. When the conspiracy is uncompleted, when the only crime is

the agreement and an overt act short of actually completing the crime, and even short of being a "substantial step" toward its commission, it is harder to see how our heightened fear of group crime justifies heightened punishment for group attempted crime.

Perhaps the better explanation is that when we punish conspirators who did not complete the target crime what we are really doing is punishing attempt, but because of the fear of group crime we are willing to relax what would ordinarily be the substantial step requirement for attempt into the much less-demanding overt act requirement for conspiracy. If John alone decides to kidnap and kill Victor, buying duct tape will not be a sufficient substantial step to make John guilty of attempted murder. But when John and Charlie agree to kill Victor, we are willing to attach more significance to buying the duct tape. Here again, buying the duct tape was really the second step toward killing Victor; the first was the agreement between John and Charlie.

The second problem relates to the Knobe effect we discussed at the P/K boundary. At common law, conspirators needed to "intend" the object of their conspiracy, and this included both the purposeful and knowing states of mind. That is, if two people conspired to achieve one end with knowledge that it was also practically certain to result in a second, harmful, end, then that agreement was sufficient for conspiracy purposes. The classic example is two people who agree to sell goods or services they are practically certain will be used for illegal purposes – let's say answering machines for prostitutes. They know the machines will be used illegally, but that is not their main purpose. They just want to make money, and they'd be perfectly happy if the suspected prostitutes turned out to be legitimate massage therapists. At common law, the sellers of these machines would be guilty of conspiracy, even though they only acted knowingly.

Although many jurisdictions have retained this common law rule, the Model Penal Code and the conspiracy laws of several states require a "purposeful" conspiracy. Under those stricter laws, our answering machine business partners would not be guilty of conspiracy, because they only "knowingly" agreed to sell the machines for an illegal purpose. And here's where our Knobe blindness may be working an injustice. Because we all have a powerful tendency to infer purposefulness from bad results, jurors may conclude our answering machine conspirators' purpose was to provide their machines to prostitutes, when that was merely a side effect. Interestingly, this danger has even been codified in some states by case law that holds that jurors may be instructed that they may infer purposefulness from knowledge.

LESSONS FROM THE GAP

We can see from these applications that the value of our evolutionary approach will likely be spotty. Most legal doctrines will not be affected at all by our evolutionary scrutiny, either because they themselves have evolutionary roots or because they simply do not conflict in any significant way with our evolved moral intuitions. Many of those that seem most dissonant have, over time, had their roughest edges smoothed off, precisely because legislatures, judges, and jurors could not accept them. But there are a few legal doctrines, some admittedly still alive only in a few jurisdictions, that so deeply conflict with our evolved blaming and punishment instincts that they deserve reexamination. In these few situations we will have three basic choices: 1) bite the bullet and forge ahead, hoping our jurors will follow the legal rule even though all their urges tell them to ignore it, thus risking nullification; 2) try to do something to increase the chances our jurors will follow the rule, for example, by using more explanatory jury instructions, including those that meet the dissonance head-on and try to explain to the jury why the law insists on such an "unnatural" rule; or 3) abandon or severely limit the doctrine.

The first choice might be dangerous in some circumstances. Forcing jurors to conclusions that do not resonate with their moral intuitions, not to mention disclosing this disconnect to other citizens by way of the media in high profile cases like *Auman*, could quickly cause all of us to lose respect for the rule of law. Whether we toss the rule or try to save it will depend not only on the results of our five-part test, but also on a myriad of policy judgments surrounding the rule. Our five-part test will never determine the outcome, but it could help in informing it. Just acknowledging the dissonant elephant in the living room may in a few limited circumstances go a long way toward repairing the dissonance.

Notes to Chapter 10

1. I also exclude from this chapter the two examples we briefly discussed in Chapter 8: the rule against admitting a defendant's prior felony convictions and the general problem of over-punishment.

2. The doctrine of employment at will – under which employers may fire employees for no reason – may be one of these. I see jurors in employment cases struggle mightily to grasp this principle, which seems to conflict not only with our notions of blame but more particularly with our Rule 2 – promises must be kept. Ordinary people seem to hold to powerful assumptions of an implied promise of continued employment as long as the employee doesn't screw up. The idea they can be fired even if they don't screw up feels like a blameworthy violation of Rule 2. See Morris B. Hoffman, *Ten Legal Dissonances*, 62 MERCER L. REV. 989 (2011).

3. These dissonant instincts include the fact that, like most living things, we are hyperbolic discounters. We grossly overvalue present benefits compared to future benefits, and likewise grossly underestimate current risks compared to future risks. Another probabilistic dissonance is our blind spot for Bayesian reasoning – the kind of reasoning that requires us to be cognizant of changes in probabilities from a base rate, and to update current probabilities based on those changes. These probabilistic dissonances can wreak havoc in a wide swath of the law, from products liability cases (does that drug really cause that disease?) to cross-racial identification in criminal cases. See Hoffman, supra note 2.

4. Chapter 2, Blaming Cheaters, Gradations of Intent.

5. First-degree murder also typically requires that the defendant killed "after deliberation." If the jury finds he did not, then the crime in many jurisdictions is considered second-degree murder. There are many other complications and overlaps between levels of crime based on mental state, including that a reckless homicide might be treated less harshly if the defendant acted in the heat of passion.

6. Francis X. Shen et al., *Sorting Guilty Minds*, 86 N.Y.U. L. REV. 1306 (2011).

7. COLO. JURY INSTRUCTIONS (CRIM.) 6:01 (West 1983).

8. The answers to these questions are:

   1) The first sentence is focused on what we call "circumstance" elements. The law often cares about whether a defendant knew a certain fact before or as he was taking certain action. For example, did he know the girl was underage before he had sex with her, or that the suitcase was full of heroin before he took it across the border? We throw in conduct here because a defendant also needs to be aware of what he is doing, in the grossest sense of not sleepwalking, for example.

   2). "Practically certain" in the second sentence is meant to capture the notion that the defendant knows there is a very high risk that the side effect harm will happen. We can't say the defendant will be "certain" of the harm, or is "aware" of it, because we are talking about a future event: what is the likelihood that this act, in which the defendant desires result A, will also cause harmful result B? We want to punish people who take sufficiently high risks of causing collateral damage. How high is high – how "practically certain" is enough – is a normative question we leave to jurors.

3). We have a different sentence for knowing about a circumstance because of this idea that "knowing" something has two different legal meanings. We can "know" whether the girl is underage, and we can "know" that our acts are practically certain to cause a harmful side effect. This definition therefore requires a defendant to be "aware" of a past or current circumstance, and "practically certain" that the conduct will cause a future result. Of course, even "awareness" is never really binary. We can have suspicions that a fact is true without being certain of it, and even our certainties are seldom certain. The criminal law has developed a rather complicated doctrine called "willful blindness" to address this problem. The idea is that if we have sufficient suspicions that a fact is true, and an opportunity to discover whether it is or not but elect not to take that opportunity, then the law presumes we knew the fact. When, as happened several years ago in my courtroom, the defendant claims he did not know that the unlocked suitcase his drug-dealer friend gave him contained 15 pounds of heroin, and that he never looked inside the suitcase, the law treats it as if he did look and did know. We are conducting a follow-up study to our *Sorting Guilty Minds* study, note 6 supra, to examine whether jurors can distinguish, and appropriately blame, knowing, willful blindness and reckless mental states when it comes to facts or circumstances, as opposed to results of conduct.

9. Note 7 supra. The word "purposefully" is bracketed in this quotation because Colorado, like a handful of other states, uses the word "intentionally" rather than the word "purposefully."

10. The John D. and Catherine T. MacArthur Foundation's Law and Neuroscience Project was a four-year effort beginning in 2007 to begin to build the discipline of law and neuroscience. It consisted of approximately forty members – roughly fifteen legal scholars and fifteen neuroscientists, plus a few philosophers and judges. I was lucky enough to be one of the four judge-members. Michael Gazzaniga, the father of cognitive neuroscience, led this initial effort. A successor effort, also funded by the MacArthur Foundation, and dubbed The Research Network on Law and Neuroscience, is currently underway. It is being directed by Owen Jones, and I have again been lucky to be one of two judge-participants. This current effort has a website at www.lawneuro.org.

11. In addition to me, the participants were Francis Shen, one of the fellows in the Law and Neuroscience Project and now a law professor at Minnesota, and four project members: Owen Jones, a professor of both law and biology at Vanderbilt, who would later become the director of the second phase of the project; Joshua Greene, a neuroscientist at Harvard; and René Marois, a neuroscientist at Vanderbilt. We needed the neuroscientists so we could design the study with an eye toward eventually doing a version of it inside a brain scanner, to see if there are neural signatures of blame that differ across these perceived mental states of the wrongdoer. As of the publication date of this book, that scanning phase of the experiment has not been completed.

12. The Robinson blame experiments were discussed in Chapter 2.

13. Each scenario consisted of three sentences – an initial one for context, a second one signaling John's state of mind, and a third one setting the harm. So to create the five alternative states of mind, we varied only the second sentence. We used signaling language to signal the appropriate mental state, and pretested the validity of that signaling language with several criminal law professors around the country. Here's an example of five scenarios from a single stem involving a middle level of harm (remember, no subjects were shown scenarios from the same stem):

> Purposeful: John is doing carpentry on his house, which abuts a public mountain bike trail. Angry at the mountain bikers for making too much noise when biking past his house, one day while carrying a large armload of planks, John desires to injure some bikers and drops some of the planks on to the bike trail. Two bikers passing by at that moment hit the planks, crash as a result, and are seriously injured.

> Knowing: John is doing carpentry on his house, which abuts a public mountain bike trail. While carrying wood planks, John drops some onto the trail and doesn't pick them up because he wants to start the carpentry work, even though he is practically certain that in doing so bikers will hit the planks and be injured. Two bikers passing by at that moment hit the planks, crash as a result, and are seriously injured.

> Reckless: John is doing carpentry on his house, which abuts a public mountain bike trail. While carrying wood planks, John drops some onto the trail and doesn't pick them up because he wants to start the carpentry, even though he is aware that there is a substantial risk that bikers will hit the planks and be injured. Two bikers passing by at that moment hit the planks, crash as a result, and are seriously injured.

> Negligent: John is doing carpentry on his house, which abuts a public mountain bike trail. One day while John is carrying wood planks from his shed to his workshop in order to begin building a new set of steps for his house, he drops some of the wood planks onto the bike trail

without noticing. Two bikers passing by at that moment hit the planks, crash as a result, and are seriously injured.

Blameless: John is doing carpentry on his house, which abuts a public mountain bike trail. One day while John is carefully carrying wood planks from his shed to the backyard where he is building a wood porch, a sudden strong gust of wind causes John to inadvertently drop several planks, despite his best efforts not to. Two bikers passing by at that moment hit the planks, crash as a result, and are seriously injured.

Shen et al., supra note 6, at Tbl. 1.

14. We ran the experiments online, using the internet research service Qualtrics. To approximate jury qualifications in most American jurisdictions, we screened subjects by self-report for U.S. citizenship, being at least eighteen years old, and not having any prior felony convictions. We had a total of 934 subjects across all the experiments, with reasonably representative demographic distributions (53% female, 88% Caucasian; age and income distributions comparable to U.S. average; incomes slightly higher than U.S. average).

15. This difference, however, was not statistically significant.

16. Apart from murder, the only MPC crimes that require an ability to distinguish K from R are arson (MPC § 220.1), false imprisonment (§ 212.3), and sexual assault (§ 213.4).

17. Under the Model Penal Code, murder is defined as either a purposeful or knowing killing. The less serious crime of manslaughter is defined as a reckless killing. MPC § 210.3(a).

18. In general, if a charged crime by its definition includes a lesser crime, then both the defendant and prosecution has the right to insist that the jury be instructed on the lesser crime. Strategically, it is almost always in one side or the other's best interest to ask for such an instruction. In a weak case, the prosecution will often insist on the lesser charge just to make sure the defendant does not walk free; in a strong case, the defendant often insists on the lesser charge so that it gives the jury a less serious alternative on which to compromise. As a result, especially in very serious cases, it is very rare that both sides will "go bare" and ask that the jury be instructed only on the original charge.

19. T. Whitehead & L. Roberts, *Murderers 'to Escape' Automatic Life Sentences*, THE TELEGRAPH, July 12, 2010.

20. In fact, in one of the experiments we are currently conducting we lower the risk language of recklessness in just these sorts of ways.

21. Joshua Knobe, *Intentional action and side-effects in ordinary language*, ANALYSIS **63**, 190–194 (2003).

22. *Pastor Says she was Helping, Not Stealing*, DENVER POST, December 28, 2010.

23. Although in our *Sorting Guilty Minds* experiment, subjects were very good at distinguishing P from K, regardless of the level of harm.

24. There are only a few isolated and temporary historical examples of strict liability rules for homicide. Under Roman law, there was a period of time when slave owners were strictly liable for all the acts of their slaves, including homicide. But because slaves were considered property, this rule was more like the rules for strict tort liability imposed on owners of animals for damage caused by the animals. It also applied to all the acts of slaves, and was not limited to homicide, as is the felony-murder rule. Under an ancient Norman doctrine called frankpledge, all members of a village could be liable for the crimes of a single member if they failed to turn the criminal over. But the punishment of frankpledge was hardly a rule of strict liability, because villagers could avoid it by turning in the criminal. Frankpledge punished villagers not for the criminal's crime but for not cooperating with officials. The harshness of the doctrine lay in its use of the criminal's crime as the metric to punish the uncooperative villagers, not in any strict liability feature. Finally, there was a short time in England when homicide was a strict liability crime, but this was more a temporary jurisdictional accident than a broad rule of strict liability. When the royal courts took jurisdiction of all homicides in the middle of the twelfth century, accidental killings were theoretically fully prosecutable as if they were intentional. In practice, however, defendants in such cases were eligible for, and routinely received, royal pardons. In any event, this practice stopped by the end of the thirteenth century. F. POLLACK & F. MAITLAND, 2 THE HISTORY OF ENGLISH LAW (2d ed., Cambridge 1898).

25. G. Binder, *The Origins of American Felony Murder Rules*, 57 STAN. L. REV. 59 (2004).

26. Paul H. Robinson, Geoffrey P. Goodwin, & Michael D. Reisig, *The Disutitlity of Injustice*, 85 N.Y.U. L. REV. 1940 (2010).

27. See, e.g., Bolton Eng'g Co. v. Graham, 1 Q.B. 159 (Eng. 1957).

28. Jonathan Cotton, *United Kingdom: A New, More American World?*, INT'L FIN. L. REV. 2009 GUIDE TO LITIGATION, Apr. 1, 2009, *available at* http://www.iflr.com/Article/2176832/Channel/193438/United-Kingdom-A-new-more-American-world.html (imputing criminal liability to English corporations is "notoriously difficult").

29. Securities and Exchange Comm'n v. Bank of America, Case No. 09 Civ. 6829 (JSR), Memorandum Order, p. 4 (S.D.N.Y., September 14, 2009), copy available at link in newspaper article, *Judge Rejects Settlement over Merrill Bonuses*, NEW YORK TIMES (September 14, 2009).

30. *U.S. Judges Sound Off on Bank Settlements*, NEW YORK TIMES (August 23, 2010).

31. One legal scholar has suggested that one way to look at the idea that corporations can be criminally liable is to compare the practice to the ancient

practices of occasionally punishing animals and inanimate objects ("deo-dand," as mentioned in Chapter 2, note 29) and punishing all members of a town when it failed to turn over a criminal ("frankpledge," as mentioned in note 27 of this chapter). Albert W. Alschuler, *Two Ways to Think about the Punishment of Corporations*, 46 AM. CRIM. L. REV. 1359 (2009).

32. 4 WILLIAM BLACKSTONE, COMMENTARIES *300; 1 WILLIAM BLACK-STONE, COMMENTARIES *27.

33. That invention was upheld by the United States Supreme Court in 1909 in a case called Central & Hudson River RR. Co. v. United States, 212 U.S. 481 (1909). One commentator has described the ruling in this case as "a giant step backwards," and described the opinion itself as the Court "mutter[ing] something about 'public policy' and the power of the corporation in 'modern times.'" Alschuler, supra note 31, at 1363.

34. MPC § 2.07(1)(c).

35. Alschuler, supra note 31, at 1365 & nn. 35–37. In most states and in the federal courts, a corporation may be held criminally liable for the acts of its employees even if the corporation expressly directed the employee not to commit the act, and even if, as in the Bank of America case, the corporation was the victim of the act. Id.

36. See generally Model Penal Code § 5.01; JOSHUA DRESSLER, UNDERSTAND-ING CRIMINAL LAW 440–448 (4th ed., LexisNexis 2006).

37. See, e.g., Andrew Ashworth, *Criminal Attempts and the Role of Resulting Harm under the Code, and in the Common Law*, 19 RUTGERS L.J. 725, 735 (1988).

38. Robert Batey, *Minority Report and the Law of Attempt*, 1 OHIO ST. J. CRIM. L. 689, 695 (2004).

39. MPC § 501(2).

40. Section 5.01(2) of the MPC also contains a laundry list of acts that *might* be substantial steps, including laying in wait, enticing the victim to go to the place of the intended crime, reconnoitering the place of the intended crime, and fabricating materials to be used in the crime at or near the place of the crime. Note that even in these enumerated circumstances, it will still be up to the jury to decide whether the defendant reached the moral point of no return.

41. Herbert Packer once described this as

> the point beyond which external constraints may be imposed but before the individual is free – not free of whatever compulsions determinists tells us he labors under but free of the very specific social compulsions of the law.

HERBERT PACKER, THE LIMITS OF THE CRIMINAL SANCTION 75 (Stanford 1968). For a compelling and creative analysis of this difficult problem of reaching the moral point of no return, see GIDEON YAFFE, ATTEMPTS (Oxford 2013).

42. J. Call & M. Tomasello, *Does the chimpanzee have a theory of mind? 30 years later*, TRENDS COGN. SCI., **12(5)**, 187–192 (2008).

43. In the English case of Rex v. Scofield, Caldecott 397 (1784).

44. JEROME HALL, GENERAL PRINCIPLES OF THE CRIMINAL LAW 560 (2nd ed., Bobbs-Merrill 1960).

45. Dressler, supra note 36, at § 27.02, p. 406.

46. There are only two modern doctrinal exceptions to attempt – called "abandonment" and "impossibility" – but even these are very narrow. The doctrine of abandonment asks the question of whether, having crossed the line of taking a substantial step toward the commission of a crime, a defendant can avoid being convicted of attempt by stepping back over that line, by abandoning the attempt. The MPC recognizes abandonment, as do many but far from all states, as long as the defendant can show the abandonment was complete and voluntary. Dressler, supra note 36, at §§ 27.08 and 27.09[2]. The doctrine of impossibility asks the question of whether a defendant who thinks he committed a crime can be held guilty of attempt when the crime isn't really a crime, either because of some mistaken fact or some mistaken belief in the law. The classic example of factual impossibility is a defendant who shoots a person he thinks is sleeping, but who in fact is already dead. Is this attempted murder? The classic example of legal impossibility is the fence who buys property he thinks is stolen but turns out not to be stolen. At common law legal impossibility was a defense to attempt, but factual impossibility was not. Most states have now abolished even legal impossibility as a defense to attempt. Dressler, supra note 36, at §§ 27.07 and 27.09[1].

47. Paul H. Robinson & John M. Darley, *Objectivist versus Subjectivist Views of Criminality: A Study in the Role of Social Science in Criminal Law Theory*, 18 OXFORD J. LEGAL STUDIES 409, 430 (1998).

48. In fact, this is the common law approach for the civil tort of assault – which is defined as an attempted battery that causes the victim emotional harm.

49. It would also have the effect, which I think might be good, of eliminating the greater part of an entire class of controversial attempts – those that used to be subject to the common law defense of impossibility. See note 46 supra. If we required proof of at least emotional harm, then these kinds of legally impossible attempts would go back to no longer being crimes.

50. Robinson & Darley, supra note 47, at 490.

51. The Model Penal Code requires an overt act for conspiracies to commit any misdemeanor or third-degree felony. It does not require an overt act for conspiracies to commit first- or second-degree felonies. MPC § 5.03(5).

52. See the studies collected in Neil Kumar Kaytal, *Conspiracy Theory*, 112 YALE L.J. 1307, 1315–1328 (2003).

53. Dressler, supra note 36, at § 20.01[A].

54. The first formal English grand juries were convened by Henry II in large part to sniff out plots to overthrow him. They were also a more generalized

attempt, and a successful one, to seize power from the Church's ecclesias-
tical courts and from feudal lords' baronial courts. See generally MARVIN
E. FRANKEL & GARY P. NAFTALIS, THE GRAND JURY: AN INSTITUTION
ON TRIAL (Hill & Wang, 1977); Helene E. Schwartz, *Demythologizing the
Historic Role of the Grand Jury*, 10 AM. CRIM. L. REV. 701 (1972).

55. Dressler, supra note 36, at § 29.01[A].
56. See, e.g., Abraham S. Goldstein, *Conspiracy to Defraud the United States*, 68
YALE L.J. 405 (1959).
57. This is because of the legal doctrine called "merger." If two crimes merge,
then a defendant can be punished only for one of them. Unlike attempt, and
some other no-harm crimes that merge with the target offense, conspiracy
does not merge with the target offense. Callanan v. United States, 364 U.S.
587, 593–594 (1961). A conspirator may therefore be sentenced once for
completing the underlying crime and again for conspiring to commit it.

11 BRAINS PUNISHING BRAINS

You shall [punish] your crooked neighbor
With your crooked heart

With apologies to W. H. Auden

THE PUNISHMENT ETHOS

We have been punishing each other for 100,000 years. We do it because
we are intensely social creatures, more tightly interconnected by far
than any other genetically heterogeneous species on the planet. We
do it because through those connections evolution has bequeathed us
rules for group living, grounded on the importance of property and
promises, and has armed us with exquisite sensitivities to when other
group members violate those rules.

But of course we are both the cheaters and the cheated, the punishers and the punished. Our unmatched predisposition to cooperate
with one another is just one side of natural selection's schizophrenic
coin. Yes, we cooperate, but we also cheat, because in the end it is
our individual survival, and the survival of our genes, that evolution cares about, not the survival of our groups. So our brains come
equipped with deeply incoherent urges – the urge to cooperate and
the urge to cheat, the urge to punish cheaters and the urge to forgive
them.

These conflicting urges were forged in the unrelenting evolutionary
fires of costs and benefits. How much do my genes and I gain in the long
run by cooperating – in alliances, trust, reciprocity, mutual defense,
economies of scale, and all the other synergies of group living – and
how much do my genes and I lose in the short run in the lost benefits

of cheating? When do I gauge that the risks of being detected and the costs of being punished are so low that they justify cheating? How much do my genes and I gain when I endure the costs of punishing a cheater, especially a cheater who hasn't cheated me directly?

These cost/benefit calculations were impossible for our ancestors to make with sufficient accuracy to justify the costs of the calculations themselves. A Pleistocene relative mulling over the costs and benefits of retaliating against a fellow group member who just stole his wife and all his food would never have survived long enough to have sufficient offspring to pass such an unhelpful tendency to us. So instead of these case-by-case calculations, natural selection built into our brains three different levels of instincts that together sufficiently dampened the Mr. Hyde in us so that the Dr. Jekyll could flourish in our interconnected groups.

First, we have brains that actually make us feel the pain others experience. Our great cognitive powers allow us to convert that real time empathy into future empathy. We can imagine that we will feel pain when we consider inflicting pain on others. Because most of us have brains that want to avoid pain, most of us avoid causing others pain. When, despite all of those feelings, we go ahead and inflict pain on others anyway, perhaps driven by some other overwhelming force such as hunger or jealousy, we get a dose of post-wrong pain. These systems, which we call conscience and guilt, create a first line of defense against the lure of defection.

Molded by these empathetic forces driving us to avoid pain, our brains were built with a preference for cooperating, especially along two evolutionarily important lines: not stealing (the property or the health of others) and keeping promises. Our brains are tilted toward not stealing (our Rule 1) and not breaking promises (Rule 2). Whenever we consider violating either of these rules, and as long as we are not psychopaths, we feel an inner voice – conscience – telling us we will feel bad if we proceed. And when the temptation is too strong we hear another voice, right after we've stolen or breached – guilt – making us feel bad just like our conscience predicted.

However, because the temptation to cheat will so often just be too great, and the corresponding bites of conscience and guilt just too weak to change our cheating hearts, we evolved a second line of defense to take advantage of the very social connections our defections put at risk. We evolved a deep-seated urge to retaliate, to lash out, when we are the objects of the defections of others. If our own consciences will not stop us from smacking a competitor, maybe the knowledge that he will smack us back will.

Finally, in a species as social as we, and especially in one so dependent for so long on our mothers, we quickly learn that the punishers among us don't just care about retaliating when we do *them* wrong, they also seem to care about when we do wrong to others, first to their relatives then to other group members, kin and non-kin alike. It is again that strange and mysterious force of empathy that causes us to care when others are hurt, and to care so much that we blame wrongdoers, and sometimes even punish them, even when their wrongs are not committed against us.

Now, our prospective wrongdoer has a lot to think about. He must not only overcome his own conscience and worry about future feelings of guilt and how his victim might retaliate, now he must consider the real possibility that other group members will punish him. Chances that he will defect have been greatly reduced by this kind of socialization of revenge. Now a wrong to one is a wrong to all. Now even a psychopath may have to think twice before preying on a helpless victim.

Because the costs of third-party punishment were significant, immediate, and often very personal (including physical retaliation by the wrongdoer and his family), but the benefits only indirect and impersonal (deterring future cheating), there was tremendous pressure to restrain our third-party punishment urges. Natural selection equipped our brains with four restraining devices. First, we don't blame small wrongs. Second, we seem to have separate blame and punishment circuits when it comes to third parties, in part to give us a moment to reflect on whether we should forgive; that is, whether we should stop our third-party blame from growing into third-party punishment. Third, when our third-party blame does mature into punishment, our consciences and fear of retaliation restrain us from hurting others by way of punishment, just like they should have restrained the wrongdoer from committing the wrong in the first place. Finally, our punishment instincts seem to come pre-delegated; we blame the remote wrongdoer, but want someone else to punish him.

Groups full of third-party blamers who want someone else to inflict punishment had two choices: let the dominant member punish, just like he makes many collective action decisions, or spread that task out to a small subset of the group. These were probably not mutually exclusive. The dominant member likely retained most of the third-party punishment authority, but for certain special kinds of cases – where the cost of punishment might be especially high – he might have had a significant interest in delegating that authority to others. If the wrongdoer was powerful or came from a powerful family, or if the allegations were tenuous or otherwise carried significant political risks, a dominant member might be wise to turn the blame and punishment decision over to a small but representative group of nondominant members. His willingness to do so may well have been increased by his own urge to delegate third-party punishment.

We have seen the traces of this bio-legal history play out across human civilizations. Although jury trials were rare until thirteenth-century England, every civilization recognized their importance for very serious cases, from the mythical Norse juries who heard charges against gods and heroes, to the very real citizen juries of Greece and Rome, to the theological juries of early Buddhism. By whatever mechanism, evolution or not, the delegation of third-party punishment almost certainly became universal shortly after we emerged. As our small groups grew into larger tribes, neither group-wide punishment nor punishment by a single dominant member was as workable as it used to be. Twenty members inflicting punishment is one thing, as we saw with the Mbuti, but expecting all 500 members of a tribe to punish is quite another. In this environment, third-party punishments almost had to be delegated. As groups got bigger, they also became more dispersed, which made third-party punishment by dominants more difficult. Indeed, the far-flung nature of these early societies may have contributed to the relative weakness of human dominance hierarchies.

In any event, we settled into a common pattern across time and across societies: most wrongs, even murders, were resolved informally, between the wrongdoer and his family and the victim and his family. For wrongs sufficiently serious to be recognized as wrongs against all the members of a group (such as treason or killing the tribal leader), the dominant member likely handled punishment in most cases. But for a small fraction of this small fraction, where the crime was serious but the political risks of punishment high, punishment decisions were made by a subgroup of nondominant members – juries.

What do these perspectives teach us about blaming, punishing, and forgiving each other today, and about our current blaming, punishing, and forgiving institutions? This is a complicated and controversial subject. Pronouncements about our "natures" always run into the problems of Hume's Gap, free will, and our ability to transcend our natures, both individually and institutionally. But an evolutionary perspective might at the very least change the way we look at some legal problems. The traditional, standard social science model views law as an institution created by particular cultures precisely so that we are not injuring each other in endless cycles of defection and retaliation. I hope readers can now see that this model grossly oversimplifies both human nature and the relationships between our natures and our institutions.

We are not the selfish, defecting creatures posited by this traditional explanation. Nor are our governing and legal institutions cultural afterthoughts designed to keep us from defecting. We have always been presumptive cooperators and occasional defectors. We have always been social animals, and have always had and cared about the rules of group living, and what to do about members who violate those rules. We have always been governing and legal animals. Law and morality are not cultural constructs we stumbled on to save us from our natures. They are part of our natures.

As our groups got bigger and more complex, both the rules and the ways in which we were able to communicate them to each other had to change. Our embedded notions of right and wrong, and of retaliation and retribution, like our primitive reaction to poisonous foods, began to take on cultural shapes that quickly diverged group to group, society to society. However, just as our insulas have miraculously been reprogrammed to apply their emergent machinery to the whipped cream that made us sick ten years ago, so too are our deepest moral intuitions about what is right and wrong, and how we should punish wrongdoers, still operating, albeit on new and shiny stimuli we could never have dreamed about 100,000 years ago.

This, in the end, is the miracle and challenge of the plasticity of our brains. Somehow, our brains are able to apply instinctual solutions developed long ago to modern challenges that on their face may seem to have little to do with the original problem, but which in their deepest sense are within the generalization of that problem. Our brains are generalizing machines. The challenge of evolutionary psychology, and of neurolaw in particular, is to develop some strategies that can give us confidence that our "just so" stories are "probably are" stories, that there really are current aspects of the law that are abstractions of deeply held moral intuitions, and that some laws may seem to be aimed just at today's whipped cream but are actually embedded reactions to yesterday's poisonous foods.

What good will that do? It might, as discussed in the last three chapters, inform our decisions about whether, and how, to deal with some legal dissonances. There may be an even bigger prize, however. Our evolutionary perspective might impose some order on the criminal law's famously disparate punishment theories, out of which we may develop a kind of post-evolutionary view of punishment.

A NEW (AND VERY OLD) WAY TO LOOK AT PUNISHMENT

Why do we punish people? Just to punish them, to deter them and others, to cure them of their criminal tendencies, simply to get them away from us for a little while, or all of the above? With apologies to the many criminal law theorists who have spent their lives articulating and analyzing theories of punishment, the very clipped explanations in the preceding sentence are meant to describe the four classic punishment theories: retribution, deterrence, rehabilitation, and incapacitation.[1] Legal philosophers frequently lump deterrence, rehabilitation, and incapacitation together, in a super-category they call "utilitarian" (also "consequentialist"), leaving retribution (also "just deserts") in its own super-category.[2]

For retributivists, punishment is a kind of moral exchange that inheres in the social contract. The wrongdoer, having lost his social standing by defecting, must now suffer his punishment as the price for returning to the social fold. The nineteenth-century German philosopher Georg Hegel wrote this still apt description of the central retributivist creed, which also contained a couple shots at the competing deterrence and rehabilitation theories:

> [P]unishment is regarded as containing the criminal's right and hence by being punished he is honored as a rational being. He does not receive this due honor unless the concept and measure of his punishment are derived from his own act. Still less does he receive it it if he is treated as a harmful animal who has to be made harmless, or with a view to deterring or reforming him.[3]

This kind of a priori explanation of punishment did not sit well with some Enlightenment theorists, who demanded a more rational and analytic approach to punishment. Retributivism started to fall from favor in the eighteenth century, with the ascendency of Jeremy Bentham and his school of utilitarianism. In the utilitarian view, the state had no right to punish (or do anything else, for that matter) unless it could demonstrate that the punishment (or other action) resulted in a greater good. And that greater good was most often described as deterrence, particularly special deterrence – that is, punishment's utility in deterring the criminal from committing future crimes. Bentham once wrote that if the state could be sure that a criminal would never recidivate then the state would have no moral right to punish him.[4]

Economic theorists got into the mix by expanding the utilitarian focus beyond special deterrence to general deterrence. Punishment might or might not deter the wrongdoer, but it may well deter others, and that could be a significant common good that needs to be taken into account in any utilitarian calculation. Oliver Wendell Holmes, Jr., one of the early American utilitarians, once wrote that all law should be stripped of its moral content, and viewed simply as a prediction of what the state will do in response to a citizen's actions.[5] Richard Posner, a federal court of appeals judge and prominent law and economics scholar, has argued that, aside from the problem of judgment-proof criminals, all criminal sanctions could be replaced with a system of fines.[6] Utilitarians such as Bentham, Holmes, and Posner want to take out of sentencing all the icky, vengeful feelings they think are old-fashioned and useless remnants of retribution, and replace them with a rational system based on costs and benefits.

It was a small step from the original utilitarian focus on special deterrence to rehabilitation. If punishment is just only if it deters the person being punished, then perhaps the state has an obligation to cure the wrongdoer of his criminal proclivities. Rehabilitationists believe the state has no right to punish criminals unless it is prepared to, and can, rehabilitate them. This notion of the state's obligation to cure its criminally diseased citizens gained lots of traction as part of the Progressive movement in the early 1900s.

In no small part because it turned out that it wasn't quite as easy to fix criminals as the Progressives had thought, rehabilitation fell out of favor by the 1960s. Incapacitation took over as the preeminent post-modern punishment theory. Incapacitationism is a kind of utilitarian marriage of convenience between retribution and rehabilitation. Incapacitationists, like their retributive cousins, believe the right to punish inheres in the social contract, but especially in society's right to protect itself and to keep criminals away from the law-abiding, at least for a while. If, during their time away from us, we happen to be able to reduce the chances that they will recidivate, then that's just rehabilitative icing on the deterrence cake.

For those pragmatists out there who think this is all much philosophical ado about nothing, you should know that all American jurisdictions, state and federal, operate under sentencing statutes that begin by articulating the goals of sentencing, often repeating these four theories, and commanding judges to impose their sentences on the basis of these theories. For example, the federal sentencing statute provides that federal trial judges "shall consider . . . the need for the sentenced imposed –

(A) to reflect the seriousness of the offense, to promote respect for the law, and to provide for just punishment for the offense;
(B) to afford adequate deterrence to criminal conduct;
(C) to protect the public from further crimes of the defendant; and
(D) to provide the defendant with needed educational or vocational training, medical care, or other correctional treatment in the most effective manner.[7]

These four directives are simplified versions of our four punishment theories: retribution, deterrence, incapacitation, and rehabilitation.

State sentencing statutes also typically refer to one or more of these four general sentencing theories, though how they order them varies greatly. For example, Florida judges are informed that "[t]he primary purpose of sentencing is to punish the offender," that is, retribution, and that rehabilitation is a "desired goal" but is "subordinate" to retribution.[8] In my state, we are first directed to consider retribution ("[t]o punish a convicted offender by assuring the imposition of the sentence he deserves in relation to the seriousness of his offense"), then deterrence, then rehabilitation.[9]

The waxing and waning of these punishment theories has had real-world impacts on the amount and kinds of punishment legislatures set and judges impose. It is no coincidence that punishment amounts increased in twentieth-century America in almost perfect lockstep with the ascension of rehabilitation. If criminals are sociologically diseased, then we need to keep them in prison for as long as it takes for us to cure that disease.

American punishment amounts really skyrocketed in the past few decades of the twentieth century with the ascension of incapacitation. Untethered from any fixed notion that the punishment should fit the crime, modern incapacitationists send folks to prison not just for what they did, but also for what they won't be able to do to the rest of us while they're imprisoned. Especially when it came to drug dealers, incapacitationist legislatures began to pass mandatory minimum sentences, and incapacitationist judges began to impose long prison sentences even in nonmandatory cases, all aimed at getting drug dealers and other bad guys out of our cities for as long as possible. As almost anyone who has paid any attention at all now knows, the fruit of all of this utilitarianism is an American criminal justice system that now imprisons a greater percentage of its citizens than any system on earth.

So punishment theories certainly matter in the big picture, primarily as legislatures set punishment ranges in response to the theory du jure. But how do these grand theories get translated into individual sentences in individual cases? If judges have discretion under the applicable sentencing statute, when do we decide to give a defendant probation, send him to a halfway house, or send him to prison, and for how long, and how should our views about these four punishment theories inform those decisions? We trial judges like to think of ourselves as the world's most practical people, with our feet on the ground and our heads well out of the clouds. Most of us pretend we don't cotton to grand theories; we *say*, at least, that these theories don't matter. But when the rubber meets the road, how we go about imposing sentences is always informed by our rough views of the justifications for and purposes of punishment, even if we've never really thought much about those views, and never fully integrated them.

When I was a young and bright-eyed new judge, one of my grizzled and now-retired colleagues, who admittedly may have been a tad jaded, explained our sentencing options this way: "Probation is nothing; half-way houses are nothing plus a later escape charge when the defendant walks away from the half-way house; and prison is nothing but at least it keeps them away from us for a while." These laments sound like incapacitation. But what struck me about his description was that his yardsticks were really retributive, rehabilitative, and deterrent ones. When he said these alternatives were "nothing," he was complaining not just that probation was insufficiently retributive, but also that probation, halfway houses and prison did not rehabilitate and did not deter. He wished we could do more than the "nothing" of probation when it came to the intrinsic value of punishment. But if he couldn't get that, then he'd settle for deterrence and rehabilitation. Because he believed those also don't work, he settled for incapacitation. Incapacitation, for him and for many subscribers to this theory, was the winner by default.

Judges are trained to follow rules, and when our legislatures direct us to pay attention to all four of these punishment theories, most of us really try to do so. But there are two big problems in grounding our punishment decisions on these four theories: 1) we suspect from our own experiences, and as my former colleague suspected, that some of these punishment theories don't work; and 2) perhaps worse still, if they do work they are incomplete and hopelessly inconsistent with one another.

Almost no trial judges, or anyone else in the criminal justice system for that matter, believe general deterrence works. That's because we keep punishing people, and yet we keep seeing an endless supply of wrongdoers in our courtrooms. It doesn't *feel* like our punishment is doing any good in reducing crime. But in fact our experiences inside the system are far too narrow to reach any conclusions about general deterrence, because of course we are only seeing the people who have not been deterred. We are not, by definition, seeing all the people who were deterred.

Insiders' views of special deterrence suffer from a similar myopic distrust. "I keep punishing (or prosecuting or defending) Mr. Jones, and he keeps coming back year after year." These frequent flyers may not be being deterred, but of course we tend not to notice the criminals we never see again.

My lightbulb moment about this deterrence myopia came several years ago when I was debating an economist and a criminal law professor about whether the death penalty deters. Like almost all trial judges, I was certain the death penalty did not deter because in my judgment not one of the homicide cases I've presided over was deterrable. The economist turned to me and said, "But you only see the cases where the homicide was not deterred!" I looked for support from the criminal law professor, but he just smiled and said, "I'm pretty sure there are one or two people I've come across in my life I may have killed if I thought I could have gotten away with it."

In fact, study after study has shown that punishment deters, both generally and specially.[10] There are great debates about the *extent* to which it deters, most of which center on the problem of the sensitivity of deterrence. That is, punishment certainly deters compared to no punishment, but what will increasing the punishment for aggravated robbery by five years do to the rates of aggravated robbery?[11] Or in the death penalty debate, does the death penalty deter compared to life in prison? It turns out the answers to these questions are affected by many variables, including the type of crime, sex, age, and other demographics of the prospective criminal, the community in which he or she lives, and the type of the proposed punishment.

Rehabilitation feels even more ineffective than deterrence. Most of us have a strong sense that the traditional kinds of punishments we impose in most modern Western systems – incarceration, supervision, fines – are not "curing" criminals of their propensity to commit crimes. And in fact, unlike some of the daunting empirical challenges inherent in measuring the effectiveness of deterrence on people who are considering crime, the data on recidivism (that is, the effectiveness of rehabilitation or even just special deterrence) is pretty grim, as we have already seen.[12] There are still a few hopeful academics who believe that if we just spent more money on rehabilitation, or developed new kinds of rehabilitative programs, we could reduce recidivism enough to justify our punishment, at least in part. But most insiders, including my grizzled former colleague, have a powerful sense, supported by the actual data, that prisons not only do not reform criminals, they may make them worse. In addition to the psychological damage prisons may be doing to some prisoners, prisons are self-fulfilling recidivism machines, for all the reasons we discussed in Chapter 6 when we discussed the problem of repatriation.

These utilitarian failures, both real and perceived, are what drove criminologists in the 1960s and 1970s to the theory of incapacitation. Even if the threat of punishment deters no one, and the punishment itself does not either deter or otherwise rehabilitate the wrongdoer, keeping him away from us prevents him from committing other crimes against us, which has its own not insignificant social benefits. Hard to argue with this theory, but it is just as hard to see how it informs our everyday sentencing judgments in any principled way. And if it is legislators who are the primary targets of the incapacitation theorists, then the utility of incapacitation is probably still up for grabs. Although American crime rates fell dramatically during the 1990s, it remains a point of great controversy whether and to what extent that fall is attributable to the harsher sentences associated with incapacitation.[13] Even if the fall in crime was caused by harsher sentences, was that a benefit worth the cost of massive incarceration rates?

Not only do each of these four punishment theories suffer from all these move expressed practical doubts, each is incomplete, in the sense that none of them fully explains our actual punishment practices. If we only punish to exact retribution, then on what basis do we assess just deserts? Why do we punish murder more than shoplifting? As the philosophers might put it, what are the moral antecedents to retribution? More practically, why do retributivists engage in the widespread practice of probation – a kind of King's X in which we keep wrongdoers under future supervision but often impose no current punishment?

Probation is also one the many examples of how our actual punishment practices reflect our deep schizophrenia about punishment theories. Judges often combine the King's X of probation with a small dose of punishment. In my state, judges can impose a short jail

sentence as a condition of probation – up to sixty days for misdemeanors and up to ninety days for felonies. These retributivist jail
sentences are not just substantially shorter than if we sentenced someone directly to incarceration without probation (the minimum sentence
for a misdemeanor is six months, twelve months for a felony), but in
the case of a felony the defendant avoids prison and serves his sentence instead in a county jail.[14] But not every probationary sentence
we impose gets combined with a short jail sentence. When we give
probation to a forger with no prior felonies, without imposing any jail
time, in what way is that sentence retributive?[15] In what way is it even
punishment?

Deterrence is also incomplete. If we punish only to deter, then why
do we often punish serious wrongdoers, killers for example, whom
we are confident will never commit any serious crimes again? I once
presided over a murder case in which the defendant was by all accounts
a wonderful young man. He had no criminal record, was home from
college, and got into a silly argument with the victim over a girl. The
victim, by contrast, was a drug dealing gang member with a string of
prior serious felonies, including weapons violations. The two agreed to
meet later for a fistfight, but one of the defendant's friends, knowing the
victim was a notorious gangster, gave the defendant a loaded handgun
"just in case." The defendant had never even held a gun before, and
as he approached the meeting place for the fight, at least according
to him, he saw in the great distance what he thought was the victim
pulling a gun. The defendant pulled his gun and fired, and in a one-
in-a million shot, given the distance they were from each other, he
hit the victim right in the forehead. I had no doubt this defendant
was no more likely to commit any future serious crimes than you or
I, and probably a bit less likely given this experience. But after the
jury convicted him of second degree murder I was required by our
statute, quite appropriately I think, to sentence him to a prison term of
between sixteen and forty-eight years.[16] That sentence was not about
deterrence.

Similarly, if the only goal of punishment is to rehabilitate, then why
do we punish the already rehabilitated killer, or, as in my million-to-
one case, the killer who is really not in need of any rehabilitation?
Jeremy Bentham would send my duelist on his way with a warning,

like a forgiven traffic ticket, if he could be sure he posed no significant risk to the rest of us. What would you think of such a sentence if you were the dead man's relative? What would you think of it if you were a drug-dealing gangster facing your own charges of shooting someone to death?

If we only punish to incapacitate, then why don't we give life sentences to incorrigible shoplifters? Property crimes such as shoplifting and forgery have much greater recidivism rates than many serious crimes, including homicide. Even the most ardent incapacitationist must admit that, holding recidivism rates constant, we need to incapacitate those who commit serious crimes for a longer time than those who commit minor ones. That is, incapacitationists, just like everybody else, are concerned about the costs of crime, and those costs differ across crimes and across criminals. Why would a rational incapacitationist spend the money to incarcerate my duelist, if he was sure there would be no benefit in special deterrence? And if he answers, as he should, that the reason has to do with *general* deterrence – with deterring other young men from bringing guns to fistfights – then he is really a proponent of deterrence, not a true incapacitationist.

The four theories of punishment aren't just incomplete, they seem hopelessly in conflict with each other. Pure retributivists don't care whether punishment deters or keeps criminals away from us; they care only about fitting the punishment to the crime. In theory, retributivists would punish Mother Teresa and Pol Pot identically for an identical crime. Utilitarians don't care whether a sentence is proportionate to the crime, they care only whether our punishments deter, cure, or keep criminals away. If they could, they might sentence Pol Pot to prison for a traffic ticket and give Mother Teresa probation for a murder.

If our pragmatists out there think this is also just a theoretical problem that never comes up in court, think again. Trial judges are constantly faced with the tension between punishing the crime and punishing the criminal. Would you give probation to someone convicted of stealing three dollars out of the slots in a parking lot pay device? Of course. But what if this was his seventh conviction for this very offense? Conversely, wouldn't you be tempted to give the maximum sentence to a drunk driver who killed someone? But what if this drunk driver was drinking because he had just phoned his out-of-state parents from home to tell them he was gay, they hung up on him, he began to drink to ease the pain, and then decided, after he was already drunk, to drive to his boyfriend's house to tell him what happened? Both of these hypotheticals are not hypotheticals; they are real cases in which I had to impose sentences. Every trial judge is faced with the problem of good people doing terribly harmful things, and bad people doing largely harmless things. How we approach these kinds of cases depends a lot on whether we tend to be utilitarians or retributivists.

There is a wonderful thought experiment that starkly shows the conflict between traditional punishment theories.[17] Imagine the following punishment system. Murderers are executed during the halftime show of the Super Bowl, by using a vaporizing ray that is said to cause unimaginable pain for a few seconds before death. But what really happens to them, unbeknownst to almost everyone, is that the death ray is actually a transporter beam, and they are transported, unhurt, to idyllic South Pacific Islands, where they live out the rest of their lives in luxury. This system should be fine with true utilitarians. After all, we are getting the maximum amount of general deterrence by showing these painful executions to millions of people around the world, and society is completely protected by having the bad guys removed. But retributivists (and, really, all normal people, because we are all really retributivists at heart) hate this system. It is not fair. The murderers are not receiving their just deserts.

These gaps between practice and theory, and between the theories themselves, not only show that the four traditional theories of punishment are incomplete, inconsistent, and under-theorized, they also show that judges are just picking and choosing from all the theories to cobble together largely unexamined justifications for what we do. It's not terribly satisfying.

I tend to think of myself as a retributivist. I regularly disappoint prosecutors when I give a short sentence to a career criminal for a minor crime, and justify it by talking about the retributivist command that we punish the crime and not the criminal. At other times, however, I disappoint defense lawyers by saying things such as "at some point the sheer number of prior felonies overshadows the minor nature of this crime," and sentence a career criminal to prison for a minor offense.

Likewise, I sometimes give a long sentence to a good person who did a terrible thing; but then sometimes I am persuaded to show mercy even in a very serious case. The theories are not helping. They end up feeling more like menu choices at a Chinese restaurant.

It is not surprising that our traditional punishment theories sit in such fundamental and unsatisfying conflict with one another, given that they spring from our own conflicting and unsatisfying urges about right and wrong, cooperating and cheating, punishing and forgiving. But the evolutionary perspectives developed in this book might go a long way toward explaining the deficiencies of each theory, and even knitting them together in a more satisfying way.

The criticism that retribution has no antecedent moral justification is what this whole book has been about. Our core moral values evolved, and one of them is to punish. There really is no tension between retribution and deterrence once one accepts that our retributive urges are evolved emotional shortcuts for the deterrence calculations that natural selection cared about. We tend to blame and punish serious crimes more than minor ones because on average deterring serious crimes was more beneficial to our groups than deterring minor ones. We tend to blame and punish intentional crimes more than unintentional ones for the same evolutionary reason. In other words, retribution *is* deterrence, seen through the lens of natural selection.

Rehabilitation and incapacitation are a modern recognition of two dimensions of deterrence – changing a wrongdoer so he won't commit future wrongs and punishing him in a way that carries its own benefits in preventing him from hurting us while he's locked up. But of course these are just two very limited aspects of the overall deterrence calculation, and they aren't really any easier to calculate than any other aspect of deterrence. Sure, a jailed shoplifter won't be shoplifting while he's in jail, but do the costs of keeping him in jail really outweigh those benefits? And when he gets out of jail, will he be more or less likely to shoplift again, or commit any other crimes?

Even the palpable benefits of rehabilitation, if we really had any idea how to rehabilitate, are not as palpable as they might seem. Will the rehabilitated addict really stop robbing liquor stores? Not all robbers, after all, are addicts. How long can we expect this miracle of sociological cure to stick? Is a rehabilitated felon at baseline for reoffending, below it, or above it? And perhaps most fundamental of all, what manner of cure is appropriate for the pedophile or the killer?

If we ever get to the point when our brains, perhaps aided by computers, massive empirical studies, and advances in psychiatry and neuroscience, can actually make the daunting special and general cost-benefit analyses for which retribution is an evolutionary proxy, then maybe we could try to ignore our feelings of blame, punishment, and forgiveness, and use our calculations instead. In fact, there is an interesting movement afoot in the past few years that calls itself "evidence-based sentencing."[18] It is from all accounts an admirable effort to make these deterrent calculations possible. But it is also, in my judgment, grossly overoptimistic. Despite our increasing capacity to collect and analyze enormous amounts of sentencing data, our ability to predict individual future behaviors remains appallingly poor. Even more troubling, this movement seems to have returned to narrow issues of special deterrence, and to Bentham's faulty premise. Even if we could predict with 100 percent accuracy that my young duelist would never commit another crime, would it be just to release him with no punishment? What general deterrence message would such a sentence send to everyone else considering taking a gun to a fistfight?

Until we are able not only to crunch the numbers on special deterrence but also to crunch them on general deterrence, our evolved retributive feelings will continue to be the best proxies we have for "evidence-based" sentencing, and for integrating the deterrent values that all of these other punishment theories, in their own way, represent. Looked at in this way, retribution is the theory that best approximates just punishment, although that presumption can then get modified a bit at the margins by specific considerations of special deterrence, represented by rehabilitation and incapacitation. I think this is what most trial judges do when we punish, whether we acknowledge it or not. We get a gut, retributive, feeling about the sentence, and then move in one direction or another off that gut feeling based on information about the criminal that affects our views about special deterrence – the likelihood he will reoffend and the crimes he is likely to commit.

If judges are already doing this, then how can an evolutionary perspective matter? My guess is that rediscovering our punishing natures, and putting these other punishment theories in their proper, marginal, contexts, could in fact have some significant day-to-day impacts on how we treat criminals. First, I imagine that if judges got on board with this evolutionary perspective we would sentence more people to jail and prison but for shorter periods of time. Legislatures might do the same, by shortening sentences but making more crimes carry some mandatory minimum. We might, both judicially and legislatively, rethink the kinds of cases for which criminals should be probation eligible; maybe we should even abolish probation entirely. These changes could all come from recognizing the retributive core of our punishment urges, and therefore focusing on punishing the crime and not the criminal. We will be less likely to have the factors that bear only on special deterrence swallow the retributive rule. We will still take into account a criminal's history – his family, his childhood abuse, his addictions, his prior convictions – but those things will take their proper place in the background of the retributive rule. We should still consider them, but only at the margins.

Overall our sentences would likely become shorter. The Progressive push for rehabilitation had the perverse effect of making sentences longer. Rehabilitation is a time-consuming prospect, and in the rehabilitative ideal the state-as-therapist can take as much time as necessary to cure diseased criminals. The other utilitarian theories also tend to increase the length of sentences. When we focus on a criminal's woeful criminal history, instead of on the crime that brought him to us, our sentences tend to be longer than the crime itself might justify. Pol Pot speeding, for example.

Because far fewer serious crimes are committed than minor ones, and because there are many low-level repeat offenders, evolutionarily-informed judges will probably be sending people to fewer total days in custody even though they may be imposing more custodial sentences. Retributivist legislatures should also care more about the crime than the criminal, and jettison three-strike statutes and other laws that put the entire focus on a criminal's past rather than on the crime he has currently committed. All of this could go a long way toward solving America's mass incarceration problem, given that it is inordinately long sentences that are the primary culprit.

At the back end, as argued in Chapter 6, an evolutionary perspective might help us become more serious about reintegrating convicted offenders back into our communities. These efforts might be catalyzed just by acknowledging that we are all born tempted to cheat, that criminals, at least if they are not psychopaths, do not suffer from some criminological disease, that there but for the grace of God go all of us, that punishment is enormously costly both in real dollars and in the loss of human capital, and that the whole point of this kind of neo-retributivist vision of punishment is to allow wrongdoers back into the moral fold once they've paid the price of their transgressions.

In the final analysis, the most enduring impact of an evolutionary perspective about punishment may be to reground us in our natures as punishing animals, to give us a kind of moral, intellectual, and emotional permission to return to our retributive roots. The twelve jurors who convicted my Czech defendant of first-degree murder were doing what all of us have been doing for 100,000 years. They were not making explicit and impossible utilitarian calculations about the costs and benefits of punishing him, or pretending to do so under the cover of "evidence-based sentencing." Nor were they saying he was socially diseased and in need of prison treatment or quarantine. They were making a moral judgment, an evolved moral judgment, about the nature of his defection from the group and the punishment necessary for him to regain his moral standing. A legal system that explicitly recognizes the evolved moral nature of blame, punishment, and forgiveness will be a better, more just, legal system, quite apart from whether those evolutionary insights result in any legal reforms at all.

Notes to Chapter 11

1. For a thought-provoking survey of how punishment theories have waxed and waned in American jurisprudence, see A. Alschuler, *The Changing Purposes of Criminal Punishment: A Retrospective on the Past Century and Some Thoughts about the Next*, 70 U. CHI. L. REV. 1 (2003).
2. For a survey of recent developments regarding the distinction between utilitarian and retributive views of punishment, see M. Davis, *Punishment theory's golden half century: a survey of developments from (about) 1957 to 2007*, J. ETHICS, **13(1)**, 73–100 (2009).

3. GEORG HEGEL, PHILOSOPHY OF RIGHT 71 (T. M. Knox, trans., Oxford 1942) (1821).

4. JEREMY BENTHAM, *The Rationale of Punishment* in 1 THE WORKS OF JEREMY BENTHAM 396 (C. J. Bowring ed., Russell & Russell 1962) (1838–1843).

5. Oliver Wendell Holmes, Jr., *The Path of the Law*, 10 HARV. L. REV. 457, 462 (1897).

6. Richard A. Posner, *An Economic Theory of the Criminal* Law, 85 COLUM. L. REV. 1193, 1203–1205 (1985). This suggestion should sound familiar. We saw in Chapter 5 that many ancient societies punished even the most serious of crimes with fines, at a time when defendants were not just "judgment proof" but payment of a hefty fine could be life threatening.

7. 18 U.S.C. § 3553(a).

8. FLA. STAT. ANN. § 921.002(1)(b).

9. COLO. STAT. ANN. § 18–1–102(1)(a).

10. See, e.g., CHARLES R. TITTLE, SANCTIONS AND SOCIAL DEVIANCE: THE QUESTION OF DETERRENCE (Praeger 1980); ANDREW VON HIRSCH, ET AL., CRIMINAL DETERRENCE AND SENTENCE SEVERITY: AN ANALYSIS OF RECENT RESEARCH (Cambridge 1999); Daniel S. Nagin, *Criminal Deterrence Research at the Outset of the Twenty-First Century*, 23 U. CHI. L. REV. 1 (1998).

11. One of the seminal works calling for a more nuanced look at deterrence was FRANK E. ZIMRING & GORDON J. HAWKINS, DETERRENCE: THE LEGAL THREAT IN CRIME CONTROL (U. Chi. Press 1973). A more recent treatment is WHY PUNISH? HOW MUCH? A READER ON PUNISHMENT (M. Tondry, ed., Oxford 2010).

12. Chapter 6, Fig. 6.1.

13. For a delightful, and controversial, analysis of what did and did not contribute to this massive fall in criminality, see Steven D. Levitt, *Understanding Why Crime Fell in the 1990s*, 18 J. ECON. PERSP. 163 (2004).

14. The terms "probation" and "parole" can be confusing. Probation means supervision after a criminal conviction, in lieu of a custodial sentence (though sometimes also coupled with a short custodial jail sentence). Parole, by contrast, is the supervision of convicted felons after their release from prison.

15. One answer is that suffering a felony conviction is itself retributive, without the need for any jail or prison time. There is substantial truth to the notion that a felony conviction can often be its own kind of reputational punishment, as discussed in detail in Chapter 6 as the problem of repatriation.

16. This case was People v. Knight, 167 P.3d 147 (Colo. App. 2006). I originally sentenced Mr. Knight to thirty-three years in prison, and after his conviction was affirmed on appeal I reduced it to twenty years. The trial was featured as part of an ABC documentary series originally called "Inside the Jury," and

in its last season called "State v. . . . " It aired August 24, 2004. See the link at http://abcnews.go.com/WNT/story?id=131859&page=1.

17. I stole this from Al Alschuler, who stole it from David Friedman. Alschuler, supra note 1, at 15–16 and n. 87.

18. See, e.g., Roger K. Warren, *Evidence-Based Sentencing: The Application of Principles of Evidence-Based Practice to State Sentencing Practice and Policy*, 43 U.S.F. L. REV. 585 (2009); Robert Weisberg, *Reality-Challenged Philosophies of Punishment*, 95 MARQ. L. REV. 1203 (2012).

INDEX